Imprints

Imprints

The Pokagon Band of Potawatomi Indians and the City of Chicago

John N. Low

Michigan State University Press | *East Lansing*

♾ The paper used in this publication meets the minimum requirements of ANSI/NISO Z39.48-1992 (R 1997) (Permanence of Paper).

Michigan State University Press
East Lansing, Michigan 48823-5245

Printed and bound in the United States of America.

21 20 19 18 17 16 1 2 3 4 5 6 7 8 9 10

Library of Congress Control Number: 2015942736
ISBN: 978-1-61186-188-4 (pbk.)
ISBN: 978-1-60917-475-0 (ebook: PDF)
ISBN: 978-1-62895-246-9 (ebook: ePub)
ISBN: 978-1-62896-246-8 (ebook: Kindle)

Book design by Charlie Sharp, Sharp Des!gns, Lansing, Michigan
Cover design by Erin Kirk New

Michigan State University Press is a member of the Green Press Initiative and is committed to developing and encouraging ecologically responsible publishing practices. For more information about the Green Press Initiative and the use of recycled paper in book publishing, please visit *www.greenpressinitiative.org*.

Visit Michigan State University Press at *www.msupress.org*

To the memory of my mother, Wilma V. Low,
and my father, Joseph N. Low.

Wonderful parents who only wanted me
to be happy and to lead a meaningful life.

This is for you.

Contents

Preface

This is the story of the Pokagon Band of Potawatomi Indians and their relationships with the residents of the city of Chicago. I am an enrolled citizen of the Pokagon Band and grew up in southwest Michigan, where members of the Band are concentrated. I was raised some eighty miles from the city, listening to Chicago radio and watching television broadcasts from across the lake; one of my primary print-news outlets was the *Chicago Tribune*, which I loved reading on many Sunday afternoons. My parents often took me to the museums in Chicago as a child and I remain a diehard Chicago football, baseball, basketball, and hockey fan. I received some of my graduate education in Chicago and worked there as well. I am inexorably connected to both my tribal community and Chicago, and those connections are what motivated me to tell this story.

The nineteenth-century writer Simon Pokagon, son of the patriarch of the tribe that bears their name, noted that the location of what we now call Chicago, at the intersection of waterways that went from the Atlantic Ocean to the Great Lakes and down to the Mississippi River and the Gulf of Mexico, gave it "an importance to our fathers without a rival."[1] Along with being the hub of transportation for the interior of the continent, Pokagon also pointed out that Chicago was important to the Potawatomi before contact with Europeans because it was situated along the twice-yearly migration route of the buffalo heading to summer and winter feeding grounds. Pokagon recounted that in earlier times it was not unusual for birch bark canoes filled with over a thousand men to traverse Lake Michigan. In his 1897 article for the *New York Times*, Pokagon included a reproduction of an engraving of "Chicago in My Grandfather's Days," drawn by Pokagon and printed on birch bark. It depicts a large number of homes clustered about the mouth of what is now known as the Chicago River. In describing the Chi-Kog-Ong (Chicago) of his youth, Pokagon wrote,

> I was present in 1833, at Chicago, though but a small boy, when my father, Leopold Pokagon . . . signed the treaty of which I hold a duplicate, for the site of Chicago and the surrounding country. Well do I remember his telling my mother he would never sign it unless the great chief at Washington would insert in it a promise that he and his band, who had been converted to Christianity, might remain in Michigan, and not be compelled to go West to an unknown land."[2]

For me, as a young person, Chicago was always a place of bright lights, adventure, and danger. I know the impact that the city has had on me personally, and I am interested in exploring in what ways, if any, the Pokagon Potawatomi and the city have affected, influenced, and shaped each other. I am not the only Band member to have a relationship with the city; it has been an integral part of the lives of at least some tribal members since the last cession of lands in the region in the 1833 Treaty of Chicago. In 1893, Simon Pokagon spoke at the World's Columbian Exposition held in the city. Pokagon described his thoughts from the time he rode the Ferris wheel at the fair.

> As we were lifted up a strange sensation came over me, and I thought, the dominant race will yet invent a way for their sinners to reach heaven. For some cause, while our car was at its highest point, the monstrous wheel stood still. My companion said, "Pokagon, it stopped for you to view Chicago." I surveyed the White City, stretching along the lake beneath me. Then, casting my eyes northward, I surveyed the white man's Chicago. But how unlike the Chi-Kog-Ong of the red man! The shore line of the lake, with its fleet of canoes; the marsh and winding river, with flags and rushes fringed; the scattering wigwams and the red men were nowhere to be seen. But in their place rose roof on roof, with steeples tall, smoking towers and masts of ships as far as eye could see. All had changed, except the sun and sky

> above. They had not, because the Great Spirit, in his wisdom, hung them beyond the white man's reach.[3]

Pokagon's remarks reflect the ambivalence that many Pokagon Potawatomi tribal members feel about Chicago to this day. Writing this book has given me an opportunity to explore the connections between my tribal nation/community and Chicago, and in doing that, both have continued to leave their imprint on me.

For the last several decades, scholars have been intrigued with the ways that many American Indians resisted assimilation into the mainstream of the dominant culture of the United States. *Imprints: The Pokagon Band of Potawatomi Indians and the City of Chicago* examines the ways some Pokagon Potawatomi community members found to retain a distinct Indigenous presence in Chicago, as well as the ways their resistance represented both their rejection of assimilation into the mainstream, and their desire for inclusion into the larger contemporary society without forfeiting their Native identities.

Of course, even at the time of the incorporation of Chicago as a city in 1837, there had been American Indians living in the area besides the Potawatomi, including the Miami, Ho-Chunk, Menominee, and Mesquakie. However, for the purposes of this book, I focus on the Pokagon Potawatomi in the city. While few Potawatomi appear to have maintained a residency in the city after 1833 (at least until 1952), this is the story of a people who never lost their connections to that metropolis. Census data or other information to confirm the residency of any Pokagon Potawatomi tribal members before 1950 is difficult to come by because, until the 1890s, Indian identity was not tracked by census record keepers, and tribal affiliation was not noted until the last few decades. As a result, the following chapters focus on a story of presence rather than residence in the city. I am not able to provide a year-by-year report, of course. Family records are scarce, and as is the case with most marginalized peoples, urban American Indians generally, and Potawatomi in Chicago specifically, did not appear often in the press or other archival documents.

This is a narrative about influences, and how the Pokagon Potawatomi and Chicagoans were forever affected and changed by their dialogic interactions even after passage of the Indian Removal Act of 1830 and, in the last land-cession treaty of the region, the 1833 Treaty of Chicago. Native and settler, each community left their imprint on the other. When I offer my "Pokagon Potawatomi perspective," what I share is mine alone; other community members, other Potawatomi generally, and other Native peoples all have their own perspectives. When I speak of oral stories and histories, I refer to those I have been told throughout my lifetime. They originate within my own family and/or from other tribal elders and contemporaries in my community. Other tribal members may have different stories/histories, and other tribes may have other understandings. My intent is to commence a conversation that lifts the veil from the largely hidden history of the Pokagon Potawatomi in Chicago. What I offer here is a series of stories detailing some of the ways in which the Pokagon Potawatomi have remained connected to Chicago. I believe that the essays that follow reveal imprints that the Pokagon Potawatomi and the city have had upon each other over the past 180 plus years. They reveal much about both the character of the Pokagon Potawatomi community and the ever-changing city of Chicago. It is a story full of intrigue, mystery, eccentric characters, promises broken and kept, survival, persistence, revival, and recollection. It is a celebration of a unique relationship between city and tribe that continues to evolve to this day. My wish is that others will continue this conversation with their own unique and valuable perspectives and histories regarding Native peoples and Chicago, as well as other urban places.

The urban Indian experience did not begin after the arrival of Europeans. Places like Cahokia, Mesa Verde, and the large villages of the Mandan on the upper Missouri River are just a few examples that clearly indicate a long history of indigenous peoples building and living in cities. Furthermore, the Chicago urban Indian experience did not begin with the post–World War II federal programs of relocation of American Indians from reservations to urban areas. Rather, the Potawatomi (more specifically the Pokagon Potawatomi) have been a part of Chicago since its founding. In very public expressions of indigeneity, they have refused to hide in plain sight or assimilate. Examining, in roughly chronological order, the literature and rhetoric of Simon Pokagon; the spectacles, performances, and monuments of the Potawatomi; their efforts for the restoration of territory; and their participation in sport and recreation, I show how all reflect activities and practices that preserved and promoted a Pokagon Potawatomi presence in the city. Throughout the city's history, the Pokagon Potawatomi Indians have openly expressed their refusal to be marginalized or forgotten—and in doing so, they have contributed to the fabric and history of the city.

In the chapters that follow, I provide a sketch of the ways in which the Potawatomi remained a part of Chicago even after the removals of the first half of the nineteenth century. I uncover a consistent presence of Potawatomi in Chicago through the stories of notable persons and events. The idea of "urban" Indians before World War II has only relatively recently become a focus of scholarship.[4] That some Indians found ways to retain a distinct "American Indian" identity while choosing to live in urban areas surrounded by non-Natives suggests that resistance, more than a mere rejection of assimilation, could, without forfeiting "Indianness," express a desire for inclusion into a larger contemporary society. The goals of that resistance were varied, as were the ways in which it manifested itself.

Da: To live in a place (Potawatomi)
Chicago édayan: I live in Chicago.
Chicago édat o: He/she lives in Chicago.
Ni pi je édayen?: Where do you live?

Imprints: The Pokagon Band of Potawatomi Indians and the City of Chicago is a Pokagon Potawatomi tribal history of a community whose members have both refused to relinquish their Native identities and maintained a conspicuous and continuous presence in the region. Chapter 1 is an exploration of the Pokagon Band of Potawatomi Indians. Chapter 2 begins with the story of tribal leader Simon Pokagon and his novel *Queen of the Woods*, first published in 1899. In this chapter, I examine the ways in which Pokagon's writing served as a memorial and monument to Native peoples.[5]

Chapter 3 explores a Potawatomi land claim to the Chicago lakefront that proceeded to the U.S. Supreme Court in 1917. Here, the key ideas include cultural geography and critical landscape studies as manifested in treaty rights, land cessions, and land claims by American Indian peoples. The Potawatomi lawsuit for possession of the Chicago lakefront represented a claim to ancestral lands as well as an aggressive move toward the preservation of indigenous identity. Chapter 4 looks at the ways in which the Potawatomi and a non-Native by the name of George Wellington Streeter each played with ideas of discovery and frontier in their respective claims to the Chicago lakefront. I examine why Streeter's claim to the Chicago lakefront is remembered and often written about while the claim by the Potawatomi is not, and what this reveals about collective memories and collective forgettings. Chapter 5 includes a biographical sketch of Leroy Wesaw (Pokagon Band Potawatomi), an early member of the Chicago American Indian Center (the first such urban Indian center in the nation) and founder of the Chicago Canoe Club in 1964. I examine the meanings of canoes and canoeing in post–World War II Chicago, and how the Potawatomi maintained a presence in Chicago through a canoe revival. I introduce what I call a strategy of recollection to resist assimilation as a form of survivance. The catalyst for such movements is the recognition that reengaging with the technology and material culture of the past is an effective way to support individual and community identity as indigenous peoples. The recollection of this traditional knowledge promotes solidarity within the community while protecting the identity boundaries essential to maintaining a distinct sense of what it means to be "Indian." Recollection is not revitalization—it is not an effort to return to an idealized past and has no millenarian/prophetic aspects to it. It is not mere revival—a descriptor that does not capture the memory work, resistance, and identity issues that come into play with recollection. It is not reenactment—those involved are not hobbyists pretending to be something they are not. Rather, recollections are about the ways in which we are agents and not victims, actors and not reactors, proactive and not merely responding or accommodating, as a result of settler immigration and attempts to take our lands and destroy our cultures. Recollections are a reconnecting with traditional practices, places, and things that confirm, for everyone, who we are as peoples. The Pokagon Potawatomi have engaged in such recollections over the last 180 years in their efforts to promote their Indian, and uniquely Potawatomi, identity while participating in the social and political life of the city of Chicago.

I also argue that the Pokagon Potawatomi constructed monuments, when and where they could, in Chicago. Monuments need not be objects constructed of granite, marble, bronze, or similar material; the Potawatomi also promoted and participated in more ephemeral monuments and living memorials, such as the rhetoric of land claims, and the spectacles of encampments, parades, speeches, canoeing, etc., that not only entertained the Chicago public but also maintained the ties of the Pokagon Potawatomi to their Chicago. I conclude with a discussion of the controversy over the so-called "Fort Dearborn Massacre" and how the Pokagon Potawatomi have continued their efforts to remain a part of the city.

This book also dispels the idea that the Pokagon Potawatomi were bound to conceptions of hegemonic masculinities. From Simon Pokagon writing about the Queen of the Woods to Julia Pokagon remonstrating crowds for celebrating events that implicitly marginalized her people, to the women and men of the Chicago Canoe Club—who never equated leadership with gender but with ability, talent, interest, and charisma—to the women who had the vision to start the Black Ash Basket Co-op, the Pokagon Potawatomi people continue to leave imprints upon Chicago that embrace indigenous understandings that counter Eurocentric patriarchal notions of maleness and leadership.

Each chapter contributes to the larger narrative of the imprints of the Pokagon Potawatomi throughout the history of the city of Chicago. While the dominant culture wrestled with its "Indian problem"—whether Indians could be assimilated—Potawatomi peoples themselves were "talking back"[6] by asserting a persistent indigenous identity while expressing a willingness to participate as contemporary Indian peoples in the maelstrom of America.

Perspectives

My intent is to create a work that is valuable both to the Pokagon Potawatomi community and to others who are interested in the history of Chicago, American Indian history generally, and Indian/non-Native relations. This book is not intended to be a comprehensive history of American Indians in Chicago. This is a story of the urban Indian experience of the Pokagon Potawatomi in Chicago from one Pokagon Potawatomi person's perspective. To explore those experiences, I have written what LeAnne Howe calls a "tribalography"—a weaving together of stories—that creates a deeper understanding of Native individual and community experiences. As LeAnne Howe notes, "story creates attitudes and culture, the very glue which binds a society together."[7]

I have chosen to write in a decolonizing style, in a way that is similar to the ways my elders have always told their stories to me. I write in movement, gathering, circling, pausing, retreating, returning, touching, connecting, and ultimately closing the story with the wish that the reader/audience may take the story I tell and come to their own understandings. I think it is essential that Native academics, such as myself, write in a way that is true to the stories and communities with whom we are working. My "research process" has been somewhat auto-ethnographic in method, and the process has given me an opportunity to learn about myself and my place as a human being. My work is in many ways auto-historiographical—an endeavor, as Linda Tuhiwai Smith says, to "research back in the same tradition of 'writing back.'"[8] I weave personal narratives throughout several of the following chapters to engage the past in conversation with the present, in order to enable the reader to better understand the story. My own voice and experiences are seen in places where I felt them to be important to understanding the questions posited in this work. I am convinced that indigenous scholars have an important opportunity, perhaps even an obligation, to add to the deeper understandings and broader histories of their own communities. It is an important act of self- and community expression to do so. I cannot write about the "other" when the other is me. This is a story about us.

Another influence on me has been the work of Craig Womack, who more than a decade ago stressed that valuable histories of Indian peoples are written at the community level.[9] He wrote, "We are not mere victims but active agents in history, innovators of new ways, of Indian ways, of thinking and being and speaking and authoring in this world created by colonial contact. Whatever we might say about the inherent problems concerning what constitutes an Indian viewpoint, we can still reasonably assert that such a viewpoint exists and has been silenced throughout U.S. history to the degree that it finally needs to be heard."[10]

I am an Indigenous[11] storyteller and scholar. I have a BA in American Indian studies from the University of Minnesota, a law degree, and a doctorate in American Culture from the University of Michigan. I can trace the Potawatomi side of my family back four generations to the early 1800s. My great-grandmother, Sarah White, was the daughter of a Pokagon Potawatomi man named Maw Ne Do Gwe We Sause, although I don't think he participated in her upbringing. The oral history of my family is that I am also somehow related to the (Joseph) Bertrand that Simon Pokagon describes in his novel as a good friend. My great grandmother Sarah was "educated" at the Mount Pleasant Indian Industrial Boarding School in north-central Michigan. My grandmother, Goldie White, helped raise me, my uncle Howard Clark was the first Pokagon Band tribal member to serve as our tribal attorney. My childhood was spent in a home across the river from the location of Leopold Pokagon's village in 1830 (his village moved to nearby Sisters Lakes, Michigan, after 1833). As a tribal member and attorney, I have served as the Pokagon Potawatomi tribal attorney, a tribal council member, and was a member of the committee that negotiated the gaming compact with the State of Michigan, I am a co-author of the tribal constitution, and I continue to serve on the Traditions and Repatriation Committee for the community. Writing about the Pokagon Potawatomi from an insider perspective has both advantages and difficulties. I suspect that one advantage is that I have had access to individuals and experiences that a non-tribal member would not. On the other hand, there may have been doors closed to me because of my status that I might not even be aware. Craig Howe writes of the importance of working with Native communities when doing research that involves them.[12] My research, interviewing, and writing have been done with a concerted effort at cooperation and communication while remaining true to tribal traditions of reciprocity and giving back. I have tried to present these stories in an ethical and respectful way.

Also, importantly, I have attempted to maintain my openness to any suggestions and perspectives that might contradict my previous biases or expectations.

Very little has been written about the Pokagon Potawatomi by tribal members, and I feel a great sense of responsibility in chronicling the story of the Pokagon Potawatomi in Chicago. Gail Dana-Sacco, director of the Wabanaki Center in Maine, which supports local Indigenous scholarship, writes, "We Indigenous scholars can exercise more proactive leadership by practicing critical introspection and building strength and capacity from within our communities. By critical introspection I mean a regular, rigorous, reflective self-evaluation process in which we consider our Indigenous research and scholarship practice in the context of our accountability to the collective."[13]

I write reflexively, with sincerity and vulnerability—knowing that what I write will affect both the Pokagon community and the perspectives of outsiders as well. During the course of this project, I have had many elders, from both the Pokagon Potawatomi and Chicago Indian communities, advise me to tell the story of the Potawatomi in Chicago as honestly as I can, to be true to both the community that I write about and the scholarship before me. I fully expect and welcome criticism and amplification from fellow community members and others. My desire is that this book contributes to an ongoing conversation about Pokagon Potawatomi tribal history, the history of American Indians in Chicago, and Indigenous peoples generally in other urban centers around the world.

Acknowledgments

I am indebted to many individuals, institutions, and communities for making this book possible. I apologize if I leave anyone out who deserves special thanks. I owe much to the Williams/Daugherty family (Michaelann Gartner, Frances Dostal, Christine Daugherty, and Kevin Daugherty) who made their grandfather's papers available to me. I am also grateful for the kind assistance of the staffs at the Chicago History Museum archives, the special collections at the Clarke Memorial Library at Central Michigan University, Western Michigan University, the Rackham Graduate Library and the Bentley Library at the University of Michigan, the Harold Washington Library in Chicago, the Grand Rapids Public Museum, the Logan Museum at Beloit College, the Chicago American Indian Center, the Regenstein Library at the University of Chicago, the D'Arcy McNickle Center, and special collections at the Newberry Library in Chicago, Pokagon State Park, and the Great Lakes Regional Branch of the National Archives.

I benefited substantially from the financial support afforded by the award of a five-year Rackham Merit Fellowship at the University of Michigan—without which I could not have pursued my dream of returning to academia. Thank you also to the Education Department of the Pokagon Band of Potawatomi for their financial assistance during my graduate education.

This book has been a work in progress for over a decade, and earlier drafts of some of the materials have appeared in Terry Straus, ed., *Native Chicago* (Brooklyn: Albatross Press, 2002); in articles in J. Randolph Valentine and Monica Macaulay, eds., *Papers of the 44th Algonquian Conference* (Albany: SUNY Press, May 2015); Sara Beth Keough, ed., *Material Culture: The Journal of the Pioneer America Society* 47, no. 1 (Spring 2015); and in the reprint of Simon Pokagon, *O-GÎ-MÄW-KWÈ MIT-Î-GWÄ-KÎ* (*Queen of the Woods*) (East Lansing: Michigan State University Press, 2010).

I want to thank Professor Brenda Child who inspired me to want to continue my work in American Indian and Indigenous studies while I was at the University of Minnesota. While at the University of Chicago, I had the opportunity to be mentored by Professors Ray Fogelson and Terry Straus, both of whom have become dear friends as well as substantial influences on my scholarship. I also wish to thank Morris Fred who supported my work while at the University of Chicago. Steve Nash was also of much help to me while he was at Chicago's Field Museum of Natural History. I am also indebted to Louis Traverzo, Colin Wesaw, Eli Suzukovich, and the late Ralph Frese, for generously sharing their memories of the Chicago American Indian Center Canoe Club with me.

In Ann Arbor, I benefited greatly from the support of classmates in my programs in American Culture and Museum Studies and the members of the graduate student Native Caucus. I have also appreciated the refreshing ideas and insights from the students I have had the honor to teach over the years, including those at the Ohio State University–Newark, the University of Michigan, the University of Chicago, Northeastern Illinois University, Indiana University Northwest, the University of Illinois at Urbana/Champaign, the University of Illinois at Chicago, Northwestern University, and North Central College. During my year as a visiting professor at UIUC, I benefited immensely from the wisdom and insight of Robert Warrior, LeAnne Howe, Robert Parker, Keith Camacho, Jody Bird, Fred Hoxie, and Matthew Gilbert. While a scholar-in-residence at the Newberry Library, I benefited from the assistance of Scott Stevens, A. LaVonne Brown Ruoff, and Helen Tanner. Larry Nesper and Susan Johnson from the University of Wisconsin have also had significant influence on my work beyond what they might imagine, and I thank them for this. The same is true of my friends from Michigan State University, including Susan Sleeper-Smith, Malea Powell, Melissa Rinehart, and Susan Applegate Krouse (who we all dearly miss).

Thank you, Craig Howe, for your insights regarding navigating academia, and thanks for the advice, early on, of N. Scott Momaday regarding my work. Thank you, too, Jean M. O'Brien, Amy Lonetree, and Brian Klopotek for your inspiration through your excellence in scholarship and service, and Charlene Teters, John Trudell, and Winona LaDuke for showing me that scholarship and activism can make a difference.

At the University of Michigan, I was blessed with wonderful professors, including Greg Dowd, Vince Diaz, Phil Deloria, and Ray Silverman. They are incredible scholars and mentors who supported me through every step of the PhD process. I am forever grateful to each of them. I would also like to thank current colleagues at The Ohio State University at Columbus and Newark, particularly in the Departments of Comparative Studies and History, and the Program in American Indian Studies, for their support, including Barry Shank, Chad Allen, Dick Shiels, Lucy Murphy, and Katherine Borland.

This first book has also taught me the value of a great press. Editor in chief/assistant director Julie Loehr and art editor Annette Tanner have been wonderful to work with and essential to my success since they took me and this book on. I am also indebted to my anonymous reviewers who provided helpful suggestions for improvement. In addition, I am most grateful for the invaluable assistance of editors Elise Jajuga, Anastasia Wraight, and Barbara Fitch Cobb. They did a wonderful job!

Back home, I have had the support of members of my tribal community, the Pokagon Band of Potawatomi, which has helped me at every stage of this work. Special thanks go to all the members of the Traditions and Repatriation Committee for their support and assistance. Specifically, I need to say thank you to tribal members Tom Topash, Greg Ballew, Steve Winchester, Majel DeMarsh, Clarence White, Mike Winchester, Jason S. Wesaw, and Marcus Winchester. Tribal member Kevin Daugherty is like a brother to me and was so kind to contribute artwork for the cover. Thank you so much Kevin! You often asked how my "project" was going and have taken a keen interest in my success. Paige Reisser, our director of communications for the tribe, has also been most helpful with images. Wé wé na (thank you to you all).

Thank you too, Grandma Goldie and Great Grandma Sarah, and to all my ancestors. I hope that what I have done honors you for all you endured—when it was sometimes more often a barrier rather than a benefit to be Indian. As a child, I was blessed with parents who encouraged my curiosity and nurtured me. Thank you, Mom and Dad. Lastly, thank you to my wife, Barbara, for your love, patience, and support.

Introduction

> Early the red men gave a name to the river,
> The place of the skunk
> The river of the wild onion smell
> Shee-caw-go
>
> —Carl Sandburg, "The Windy City"

The first peoples of what is now the United States have always engaged in mapping—understanding their relationships to the landscapes around them. Blazed and bent trees often provided directions for fellow travelers when such were available. Birch bark scrolls, petroglyphs and pictographs, oral stories, winter counts on hides, mounds and earthworks, even marks drawn on the land itself—these have always told us where we are from, where we are now, and where we are headed. Thus, it seems most appropriate for me to provide a guide to the reader at the outset of this work.

Many Native American Indian peoples of North America have an intrinsic attachment to their homelands. This might explain, in part, the reluctance of Native peoples to relinquish their traditional lands to the United States government during the treaty-making era. Indians often consider the land, or at least particular sites in the landscape, to be sacred, and traditionally most Indian peoples defined geography, or at least place, via myth, story, and oral history.

When the United States consolidated power over Indians and their lands in the nineteenth century, its agents instituted an alien policy of breaking up Indian lands for commercial agriculture and other economic development. Policymakers in the nineteenth century concluded that dividing up Indian landholdings into parcels of private property would serve to civilize the "savage" Natives.[1] Many Indigenous communities in North America had been planting crops for centuries, often on communally owned lands, because they most often considered their homelands as living networks, not as fragments that could be individually owned. It is hard to overestimate the importance of Indians' relationship to their land, or the importance of their lands to their relationships: sacred, interpersonal, diplomatic, and environmental.[2]

Many, if not most, first peoples of North America lived in ways that were intimately connected to the environment surrounding them. These spaces were not only homelands but also places of either migration or origin. They were also spaces filled with history, teachings, and spiritual importance. Knowledge of one's place upon the land was essential for orientation, navigation, and way-finding. The Potawatomi say, "We walk on the bones of our ancestors" to solemnize our connections to the ones who came before us, as well as to demonstrate our intimate connection to the land. The landscape was known to be a place of promise and of danger, of spirits good and bad—a place that could be one of plenty or poverty. Territory was also defined by use and need. A place worth defending with one's life when necessary; but also a place often shared with Indigenous neighbors. Borders and territories did not arrive with the Europeans. Boundaries existed long before contact with Europeans—in the Indigenous world, those boundaries might be based upon natural features on the landscape, or they might be created by humankind. Like the stargazing seafarers of Oceania and the aboriginal followers of the songlines of what is now called Australia, the Native peoples of North America understood their deep connection to what many referred to as "Mother Earth."[3] North America was a vast series of Indian homelands prior to contact.

Stored memories and instructions were the Indigenous equivalent, in many ways, of European maps.[4] Maps are more than mere directional guides; they are also documents for claims-making, and Indians had alternatives to paper maps to demarcate their borders and territories. Richard Bradley argues that the study of rock art's images and motifs often obscures the significance of the location of pictographs; moreover, such markers often served to signal territory to both community members and outsiders. Stories also served as boundaries.[5] Residence and experience were often the basis for pre-contact claims to the land: "High points and low points on the landscape inscribed Indian sovereignty with both physical and metaphysical boundaries simultaneously. Topographical extremes . . . were points where everyday experience intersects with the supernatural plane."[6] The connection between people and territory lay in the deep and detailed knowledge of the environment and found expression through the naming of, charted movement through, and residence upon that land. Landmarks and geographic knowledge often survive in Euro-American maps.[7] As Keith Basso notes, "[The idea of place is] as old perhaps, as the idea of home, of 'our territory' as opposed to 'their territory,' of entire regions and local landscapes where groups of men and women have invested themselves (their thoughts, their values, their collective sensibilities) and to which they feel they belong."[8]

That the Potawatomi of Chicago would resist the taking of their land, negotiate the best deals possible when cession was the only option, and continue to pursue claims to ancestral lands is not surprising given the common connection of Native peoples to the land. Like many other Indian peoples in North America, the Pokagon Potawatomi are situated upon a landscape embedded with sacred powers and inscribed with social and political meaning and value.

Both treaties and land claims figure significantly in the history of the Pokagon Potawatomi in Chicago. A treaty is generally considered to be a written contract or agreement between two sovereign nations. During early contact between American Indians and Europeans, the newcomers frequently considered the Native tribal/village leaders as having dominion akin to that of the lords and sovereigns of Spain, England, and France, etc., even if they simultaneously undercut this understanding with their pernicious doctrines of discovery, wastelands, or the superior rights of Christians. Despite their legalistic contradictions, European nations initially entered into treaties with the Indian tribes in order to reinforce military and political allegiances, to facilitate trade, and to ensure peace.[9] Before contact with Europeans, Native American tribes such as the Potawatomi did not utilize formal, written treaty agreements in their alliances or agreements with fellow Native American tribes.[10] However, Natives did have formal conferences in which oral contracts were made, and frequently those agreements were memorialized via the use of wampum belts, birch bark scrolls, or similar devices.

With the arrival of the Europeans, American Indian and European customs became interwoven. With the signing of treaties, Europeans and Native Americans held councils, made oral agreements, and wrote treaties that confirmed the details of their arrangements. The United States made use of these particular conventions in its relations with the Natives. In 1778, the United States signed its first treaty with an Indian tribe, the Lenape/Delaware.[11] A little over one hundred years later, in 1871, Congress legislated against making further treaties with the Indian tribes, and the United States has since relied upon official agreements between Native Americans and the federal government.[12] However, in theory, all previously ratified treaties with the Indian tribes remain in full force and effect.[13]

Early on, the United States often used treaties to acquire Indian lands. In treaty negotiations, many tribal leaders requested particular concessions, including specific material items, monetary compensation, specific reserves of lands for tribal members, and guarantees of educational opportunities for their children. In the course of Native Americans relinquishing their lands, many treaties provided them with rights to retain the use of the lands that were ceded to the United States government. Before the sale of these lands, the federal government often formally acknowledged the Natives' original possessory interest in the land. The government sometimes also agreed to the recognition of American Indian usufructuary rights to the ceded territories. These particular rights guaranteed that members of the tribe would continue to be able to hunt, fish, and gather foods and medicines within the ceded lands or on the bodies of water they embraced. At the end of the nineteenth and into the twentieth centuries, these reserved rights, even when not expired by some stipulated limitation, were usually not respected by the states. Indian peoples throughout the United States have had to resort to the courts to compel recognition of their treaty rights. Those claims have often been over land, and as I explore in the following chapters, the Pokagon Potawatomi, earlier than most, advanced their claims in the courts.

In discussing Pokagon Potawatomi land claims to the Chicago lakefront, it is worth noting that there have been numerous works written about claims of the Ojibwe, Hopi, Iroquois, Lakota, and others to their own tribal lands.[14] I also discuss a claim to Chicago that was contemporaneous to that of the Potawatomi, by a man named George Wellington Streeter. Much has been written about Streeter and his claim to "Streeterville" in Chicago.[15] However, no published work considers their competing and yet complementary land claims together—or why Streeter is remembered while the Pokagon claim is largely ignored.

The Nature and Characteristics of Interactions between Peoples

The interactions between American Indians and European settlers have had significant impacts on each group, and these impacts included the cultural transformations of both peoples. The changes often occurred at what has been called "the frontier."[16] A frontier is a geopolitical denotation for areas close to or beyond a certain boundary.[17] In the eighteenth century, a frontier was essentially any segment of hinterland of North America lying at the western edge of existing eastern British or early U.S. settlements.[18] Frederick Jackson Turner popularized the use of the word "frontier" to denote a region at the border of a settled area peculiar to the development of North America. Sometimes a frontier was a zone of interaction among settlers and Natives; sometimes it was marked by formidable geographic barriers, such as the Appalachian and Rocky Mountains.[19] In the Midwest, the Great Lakes became just such a barrier, and this book explores the ways in which the Chicago lakefront, in some ways, became a "frontier" well into the twentieth century.

These areas have also been described as contact zones and borderlands.[20] What these concepts reflect is the recognition that substantial changes are wrought when disparate cultures bump into each other, and that peoples and communities are forever changed by such contact. Contact is not a moment or a geographic region, but rather, an ongoing process and experience.[21] Of course, contact was common long before the arrival of Europeans. Perhaps since the beginning, Native peoples were bumping into and interacting with each other. However, when I refer to "contact" for purposes of this book, I am referring to the collision of European settlers and Native inhabitants in what is now the United States. Vicente M. Diaz has used the term "thick veneers" to describe and explain cultural change and continuity among the Indigenous Chamorro peoples of Guam. "Thick veneers" emphasizes the reality of distinct Indigenous lived experiences while acknowledging the difficulty in separating those differences and mixtures from their non-Indigenous counterparts.[22] Similarly, transculturation characterizes the phenomena of the merger and convergence of cultures.[23] Transculturation describes the effects of colonialism on Indigenous peoples as more than the simple replacement of traditional beliefs with new ones. Key to the theory, as formulated by Fernando Ortiz, is the uprooting of old cultural forms and the creation of new ones that reflect marginalized peoples' relations to mainstream culture. For Ortiz, transculturation included more than simply transition from one culture to another; it entailed not only a mere acquisition of another culture or losing a previously held culture. Rather, transculturation described the amalgamation of cultures into something new. More recently, transculturation has been used to explain the ways in which American Indians navigate through the non-Indian mainstream while retaining a strong sense of cultural heritage and connection to their own tribal identities.[24] Transculturation emerges from colonial subjugation, particularly in a postcolonial era, as Natives strive to retain their perceptions of identity.[25] It is this last iteration of "transculturation" that I find most useful for my work. I look at all of these modes of analysis regarding contact as tools in my toolbox, and I deploy them when most appropriate to help explore the nature of those interactions. The ability of the Pokagon Potawatomi to maintain their indigeneity in the face of colonization is, for example, powerful evidence of transculturational processes at work.

I find it helpful to think of the post-1830 Great Lakes region of the United States as a "scatter zone" to describe the myriad of responses that Native peoples in the area pursued as a result of the ethnic cleansing of the American heartland before and after the passage of the Indian Removal Act of 1830.[26] Those included voluntary emigration, coerced emigration, removal by force, hiding in plain sight, condensing into small groups, negotiating exemption from removal, and fleeing to safer regions (sometimes still in the Midwest), etc.[27] It is important to remember not only how disastrous and deadly implementation of "rules of removal" was to Native peoples living between the bottom of the Great Lakes and north of the Ohio River Valley, but also, importantly, that not all the tribes were successfully pushed out—the Pokagon Band of Potawatomi being one of those that were successful in their refusal to "leave."

In order to explore how the Pokagon Potawatomi Indians have been able to maintain their presence as a unique community in North America generally, and to maintain a presence in Chicago specifically, we can turn to cultural geography as a portal for understanding. A number of significant cultural phenomena examined in the field encompass language, art, various economic and governmental frameworks, religion, music, and other cultural features that provide explanations for the means and reasons for the functioning of a particular group of people in the ways and in the areas in which they reside.[28]

Furthermore, parallel to cultural geography, cultural landscape and critical landscape analysis are also helpful because they relate or connect culture to the physical settings in which people are situated. This is because environment can either impede or foster the development of numerous and distinct cultural attributes. For example, people residing within a particular rural area may have more cultural ties to the natural environment in which they live in comparison to those residing in a large metropolitan region. My focus on Native cultural geography explores indigenous understandings of "land" and homeland.[29]

The Emergence of an "Indigenous" Identity in the United States

Cultural identity, reflected in the beliefs, values, and worldviews of people, has been described as the sharing of a widely parallel conceptual map and mode of interpreting symbols and language.[30] However, it is possible for people to identify themselves in numerous other ways than by their cultures. Identity is also a mixture of such things as class, race, education, religion, region, and gender. The impact of these features of identity on the status of an individual has the capacity to change over time.[31] Colonialism has intensified such changes. Native peoples have become "Indians, "Indigenous" and "First Peoples," both in their own minds and in the minds of non-Natives. Immigrants and their descendants assumed the heroic mantle of settler-pioneer, while Indians were subjected to phases of romanticizing or disdain depending on the prevailing attitudes, agendas, and events of the era.[32]

After the formation of the United States, this process of *othering* continued unabated. The history of relations between Natives and non-Natives has been characterized by a struggle over resources and land and whether Indians can be assimilated into the mainstream. American Indians were often relegated to the margins of American society. Efforts at ethnic cleansing (for example, the Trail of Tears), extermination through military hostilities (the Indian Wars of the nineteenth century), assimilation (missionization and boarding schools), and ossification (literally, into statues) reflected the prevailing assumption that Indians were a "vanishing race." That trope became the settlers' modus operandi, was part of the American Indian experience, and was endured by Indians of the Great Lakes region, including the Potawatomi. Nonetheless, Indians did not vanish and many resisted assimilation. After assuming Indigenous and national identities in response to pressures and expectations from non-Natives, American Indians, including the Pokagon Potawatomi, fought to retain their hard-won community and individual identities. As part of the transculturation process, American Indians across the country—indeed, colonized peoples around the world—often engaged in persistent and creative adaptations to avoid physical, social, political, and personal destruction, and the erasure of their communities. The Pokagon Potawatomi have, through strategies of survivance, maintained a unique identity and presence in the city of Chicago.

Memory Work

Mikwéndek: What is remembered (Potawatomi)
Ni je ga je mikwéndek?: What was remembered?
I yé i émikwéndek: That is what is remembered.

In what ways did the Pokagon Potawatomi remind Chicagoans that they had not disappeared? How did Simon Pokagon's storytelling remind the residents of Chicago of their Native past? How did *tipis*, *wigwams*, and canoes maintain an Indigenous foothold in the collective memories of Chicagoans?[33] How do monuments and memorials manifest, preserve, and promote such memories? How did the Potawatomi lawsuit for the Chicago lakefront undermine the belief that the first urban Indians of Chicago were no more? How did spectacles such as the 1893 World's Columbian Exposition, the encampment of Potawatomi along the lakefront in 1903, and canoes traveling down the Chicago River and elsewhere in the 1960s and 1970s operate as living monuments and memorials to the continued vitality of the Potawatomi?

Collective memory is an idea developed by French sociologist Maurice Halbwachs to separate the concept from individual memory. Collective memory is shared, handed down, and developed by a society or group.[34] The contributions to the function of spaces and places of shared memory, such as monuments and memorials, are significant.[35] The importance of the concepts of collective memory to my work is in framing the question of how the Pokagon Potawatomi have maintained a presence in their ancestral lands, now known as Chicago, and how memory has operated to facilitate that persistence.[36]

According to Halbwachs, individual memory is embedded within the social framework from which it is constructed. He argued that we all belong to many social groups, and that a collective memory is attached to each of them.[37] Pierre Nora has provided an influential attempt to understand the function of collective memory in modernity. For Nora, "sites of memory" have become the fixed, externalized locations of what was once an internal, socialized memory. According to

Nora, History (with a capital H and as a national narrative) seeks to become the official memory.[38] Theoretical differences between individual, collective, social, and historical memory dwell in our understandings of what is saved, preserved, remembered, and retrieved.[39] In addition, how that past is then re-presented is what Emile Durkheim, Barry Schwartz, and others term "collective representation."[40]

Why do traditional art, artifacts, and practices have importance to Native peoples? Their power is not only in the individual memories they convey, but in the collective memories with which they are imbued,[41] and which facilitate the individual and collective need to be connected to a shared past.[42] For Native peoples, memory can be "re-collection." Retrieval of the past is how memory and history are reconfigured.[43] The power is in reconnecting the past to the present and to the future.[44] People can change in many ways, but will often retain the essential markers and memories of identity that are important to them.

Memory serves as a means of producing knowledge, and as an agent in the preservation of the past. Memory is a process by which some things are remembered, forgotten, imagined, and invented. The authority of memory can be institutionalized into religious traditions, legends, songs, and literature, and the memories are stored in places of worship, museums, and archives, where then they can be reified and reinterpreted for new purposes and a multitude of agendas. Memory becomes "evidence" for those who recollect.[45] Collective memories are transferred from one person to another in order to make "remembering in common possible."[46] Rituals, myths, symbols, and practices are all a part of memory-making and memorializing. Collective memory is metaphoric and legitimizing. It can embody a shared past and a national/group identity. It is partly through the collective construction of the past that communal identities emerge.[47] Memory has power because of its multiplicity of interpretations, uses, and transferability.[48]

Unfolding the Map

Pokagon Potawatomi experiences represent an important and understudied example of the ways in which American Indian peoples retained a presence in the urban centers of the United States despite efforts at removal, assimilation, and marginalization. The Pokagon Potawatomi not only maintained their residency in rural areas of southwest Michigan and northwest Indiana, but also retained a position in the city of Chicago—the great urban center of the United States built upon the ancestral lands of the Potawatomi. Simon Pokagon, Julia Pokagon, Michael B. Williams, and Leroy Wesaw are four individuals central to an exploration of the ways in which Chicago remained in the collective memory of the Potawatomi, and how the Potawatomi remained in the collective memory of Chicagoans. But many other Potawatomi contributed to the work. The result can be simply put: since before its incorporation as a city in 1837 to the present, Pokagon Potawatomi Indians have been part of the urban Indian experience in Chicago.

CHAPTER 1

The Potawatomi as Chicago's Early Urban Indians

> There was no glamour about the Potawatomi. He was a real savage. He was lazy, and made his squaw hoe the corn. He had very little regard for women. . . . Like all his race, he was a gambler, playing heavily at his moccasin games and lacrosse. As a general rule, he was cruel, and always had a deadly hatred for the white man. . . . In general appearance the Potawatomi did not compare favorably . . . the Potawatomi were shorter and more thickly set, very dark and squalid. . . . The Potawatomi women were inclined to greasiness and obesity . . . they were not generally of cleanly habits . . . they were true savages, yielding to their animal appetites and desires . . . evidenced by their rapid degeneracy under the influence of whiskey.
>
> —Elmore Barce, *The Land of the Potawatomi*, 1919

The above description of the Potawatomi, authored by a member of the Indiana Historical Society, is indicative of the racist prejudice the Potawatomi have battled against and endured since at least the early nineteenth century. Today, based upon my experience as a college professor, it is evident that very little is taught in middle or high school about American Indians, past or present. People learn about us too often through the myths and stereotypes of popular culture. So this book is an opportunity to "talk back" and give a more accurate depiction of the Pokagon Potawatomi.

The Potawatomi: Chicago's Early Urban Indians

The Potawatomi are Indigenous peoples of North America who are associated at the beginning of the historical era with the upper Mississippi River region of what is now the United States. The Potawatomi language belongs to the Algonquian family. The Potawatomi people refer to themselves as Bodéwadmi, which means "Keepers of the Fire" in the Potawatomi language. This is a name given to them possibly by their Ojibwe cousins. The Potawatomi people originally referred to themselves as Neshnabe, a derivative of the Ojibwe/Odawa word *Anishinabe*, meaning human beings.[1] The Potawatomi people traditionally belonged to an alliance referred to as "the Three Fires Confederacy," along with the Odawa and the Ojibwe. In this alliance, the Potawatomi people were deemed the "youngest brother."[2] At the height of their expansion in the Midwest, some 250 years ago, the Potawatomi people numbered about nine thousand members, and Potawatomi villages covered about 28,000 square miles of territory around the Great Lakes region, stretching east from what is now Green Bay, Wisconsin, south around Lake Michigan to Detroit, and on into Ohio.[3] While the people that would ultimately become "the Pokagon Band of Potawatomi" were primarily located in the St. Joseph River Valley of southwest Michigan and northwest Indiana, the area including what is now Chicago was an intertribal space that would have been routinely traveled to obtain resources, engage in social interaction, and trade.

Some biological/physical anthropologists and archaeologists generally theorize that the direct ancestors of American Indian peoples migrated to North America from eastern Asia, traveling by land across what is now the Bering Strait to Alaska, or by water along the southern coast of the so-called land bridge. Not all academics agree on our origins, and Native oral traditions compete to explain the genesis of the peoples who now call themselves the Potawatomi. We may have migrated west as one people from the mouth of the St. Lawrence River on the Atlantic coastline approximately five hundred years ago, or migrated south from what is now Canada at an even earlier time. Some scholars have placed the precontact Potawatomi in what is now Canada, north of Lakes Superior and Huron, and trace our subsequent migrations south.[4] Or we may have been lowered by the Creator through a hole in

Potawatomi Homelands, ca. 1800. CARTOGRAPHY BY ELLEN R. WHITE.

the sky at the mouth of the Grand River at Lake Michigan, or along the banks of the St. Joseph River near what is now Mishawaka, Indiana. I have heard variants of all these stories my whole life and feel no need to reconcile them. I know which version my Potawatomi grandmother told me as a child, but will not advocate for it here. We are all entitled to our stories, particularly regarding our origins and creation. The Native peoples we now call the Potawatomi may also be the descendants of some of the mound builders of the Great Lakes region, or married into the families of descendants of those peoples already here. Grandma had ideas about that, too. At some point it appears my ancestors may have settled near what is now Sault Ste. Marie before they divided into the Odawa, Ojibwe, and Potawatomi. In any event, the Potawatomi have resided in the Great Lakes region of North America for a long time. Simon Pokagon, discussed at length in chapter 2, wrote that the Great Spirit created the first Potawatomi man and woman after a council with the other spirits;[5] but he does not identify a location for this origin story. Oral histories of the Potawatomi, Odawa, and Ojibwe (collected by writers such as Warren, Johnston, Densmore, Edmunds, and Clifton)[6] also include references to a great flood and earth-diver story in which a cultural hero—Waynabozho, Nanabush, or some other variant—survives along with other creatures of the world by clinging variously to a turtle, log, or canoe.[7] In most versions, Waynabozho settles on the land created on the back of the turtle and comes to teach the Anishinabeg/Neshnabek all important things, including the building of birch bark canoes.[8] Land rising up from the water—in essence what happened at the end of the nineteenth century along the Chicago lakefront—has been a part of Potawatomi tradition from early on.

Life before Contact

The Potawatomi have never been in stasis; they have always interacted with their neighbors, changing both themselves and others as a result. But some general understandings about the Potawatomi, before contact with Europeans, appear to be fair. They lived for thousands of years utilizing the resources around them and securing a balance in their use of the environment. They exchanged their knowledge in canoe building with neighboring tribes for knowledge to grow corn, beans, squash, and tobacco. Once in the Great Lakes region, the Potawatomi developed elaborate agricultural techniques.[9] Food was dried and stored over winter, often in buried birch bark containers. Women and men supplemented their diets with berries and nuts (the latter were often pounded into flour for bread). The making of maple syrup and gathering of wild rice, where available, was also an important activity for the community. Potawatomi homes were most commonly *wigwams* or *tipis*, covered in sheets of elm or birch bark, or mats made of cattails laced together with fibers.[10] The Potawatomi had the advantage of having access to birch trees and the knowledge of how to build canoes from birch bark while also living in a

"Summer Camp," ca. 1837. Potawatomi camp at Crooked Creek, as depicted by artist George Winter. REPRODUCED WITH PERMISSION OF THE TIPPECANOE COUNTY HISTORICAL ASSOCIATION, LAFAYETTE, INDIANA.

relatively mild climate that allowed for extensive farming. Few of their Indigenous neighbors had this combination of transportation technology and opportunity for horticulture to the same degree.[11] Farming and the ability to travel and trade over long distances in birch bark canoes (*wigwas jiman* in Potawatomi) distinguished the Potawatomi from many of their Native neighbors and accounted for the vitality of their communities throughout the Great Lakes.[12]

Material Culture

Traditionally, Potawatomi wore animal skins—deerskin in the summer, and buffalo hide, which was prized for its warmth, in the winter. Breechcloths and moccasins were also made of deerskin. Women tanned the hides and wore dresses or skirts of skins. Clothing was decorated by painting or dyeing it different colors using roots and plants, and embroidering designs onto the item of clothing with porcupine quills. Bird feathers were also frequently used as adornment. Hair was worn long and in braids by women and commonly in scalp locks by men. Both genders used paint from plants to decorate their faces and bodies, and men tattooed themselves. After the arrival of Europeans, beginning in the 1600s, the Potawatomi would trade skins to the white trappers and traders who traveled through the area in return for glass beads, ribbon, and fabrics to add to their clothes. Beadwork became a way of decorating clothing, containers, and more. The Potawatomi became known for their appliqué and beadwork styles, consisting of blocks of color in simple geometric patterns or resembling a flower, tree, or animal. Many of these designs have been passed down through families from one generation to the next, and are still used today. Baskets made from black ash, sweetgrass, and birch bark had utilitarian, social, and ceremonial uses. Pottery was hand coiled and fired. Before contact, the Potawatomi made their tools from material found around their villages. Bows, hoes, and dishes were made from wood; flint was chipped to make arrowheads and used to start fires for cooking and warmth. Needles and fishhooks were carved from animal bone; stones were used for axes and to grind corn and nuts.[13]

Village Life

Villages were usually located on the high ground near lakes, rivers, and streams, near sources of food and drink as well as ways of travel. Single-family dwellings were most common; larger, rectangular multifamily lodges were popular during hot summer months. Durable homes were built from easily obtained materials, and readily movable when the need arose. One to two hundred people inhabited most villages. Each village had a civil chief who led by consensus. The community usually appointed war chiefs in times of threat to the village from outsiders. The status of women as life givers and culture bearers was well established and honored, as was the man's responsibility to provide for and protect his family and village.

Potawatomi communities were divided into clans. Clans or *dodems* were divisions within the village based upon descent from an original nonhuman ancestor, such as a bear, turtle, or sturgeon. The Potawatomi practiced clan exogamy (one had to marry outside of one's own clan). Clan membership established relationships and responsibilities among tribal members and neighbors.[14] The Potawatomi mixed

Scharf map of Indian habitations in the Chicago area, ca. 1804. ORIGINALLY PUBLISHED IN ALBERT F. SCHARF, *INDIAN TRAILS AND VILLAGES OF CHICAGO* (CHICAGO: CHICAGO HISTORICAL SOCIETY, 1901). REPRODUCED WITH PERMISSION OF THE CHICAGO HISTORY MUSEUM (ICHI-31997).

freely with others and often lived in intertribal communities.[15] Village activities were tied to the seasons. Farm fields were tended during the spring and summer; harvesting, hunting, and gathering occupied the fall. Fishing was a year-round activity. Communities gathered during the warm months to socialize. During the winter, much time was spent making and repairing belongings, as well as storytelling. Like many other Native communities in North America, the Potawatomi were engaged in long-range trade for decorative and utilitarian items. Trade networks stretched north to Hudson Bay in what is now Canada, and south to the interior of what is now Mexico.[16]

The Contact Era

First contact between Europeans and the Potawatomi probably occurred in 1634 when a French trader named Jean Nicolet arrived at a place that is now called Red Bank, on the Door Peninsula of Wisconsin, along the western shore of Lake Michigan.[17] Before contact with Europeans, Indigenous national identities were very fluid and sometimes ambiguous. After contact, Native peoples often responded to European expectations by organizing socially and politically into "nations." Relationships based upon affinity (clan, village, family, etc.), reciprocity, and obligation were supplemented with ascribed political statuses to create new social relationships as a result of contact. Historian Michael Witgen writes,

> Algonquian bands that hunted in the western interior and traded at the French posts in the Lake Superior region were central to a new and evolving set of situational identities at the heart of this relationship between the French and their Native allies. By the late seventeenth century these bands, when in the Pays d'en Haut, increasingly assumed identities as Ottawas and Sauteurs. Even as these "national" identities took shape, however, they remained flexible and even interchangeable.[18]

The Potawatomi became entangled in the fur trade, which eventually resulted in overhunting and over-trapping. This soon escalated into armed conflicts—over territory and trading rights—with other Indian peoples and Europeans, and led to an unending assault upon traditional Potawatomi culture and lifeways. During the course of the early fur trade, kinship relationships and intermarriage helped to foster cultural and political connections in which neither party dominated the other. The French learned the Potawatomi language and generally traded according to Native customs. However, competition for depleted resources resulted in warfare between the Potawatomi and the Iroquois and other eastern tribes (the Beaver Wars, 1641). Ultimately, most of the Great Lakes tribes, including the Potawatomi, were forced by the Iroquois to take refuge in northern Michigan, Canada, and on the peninsula now known as Door County, Wisconsin. The Potawatomi fought to retake their traditional homelands back from the Iroquois beginning in 1653, and by 1679 they had expanded throughout the Great Lakes region from what is now Green Bay to Detroit and beyond, and they retained these lands until land-cession treaties with the United States during the nineteenth century.[19]

Unfortunately for the Potawatomi and other Indians, the French and British extended their warfare against each other to North America.[20] The Potawatomi, like most Native peoples living east of the Mississippi at the time, were drawn into the many imperial conflicts that culminated in the "French and Indian War" (1754–63). Many Potawatomi allied themselves with the French during the conflict. When the British ultimately won the war, the Potawatomi and other Indian allies of the French were abandoned at the Treaty of Paris (1763). Subsequently, the Potawatomi would have to deal with the British on their own. After the French departed from the Great Lakes region, the British asserted themselves by terminating the previous kinship relationships established by the French and trading on European terms with an emphasis on maximizing profits. As a result, overhunting and over-trapping continued to increase, and the Indians of the Great Lakes became increasingly dependent upon trade goods. The traditional social and cultural fabric of Potawatomi communities was substantially altered as disease, death, and impoverishment took their toll.[21]

Movements led by Native prophets, such as the Delaware Prophet Neolin, inspired Indians throughout the Great Lakes region to resist the intrusions of the British and American colonists. The Odawa leader Pontiac led an armed resistance, in which many Potawatomi joined, in 1763–64. Although Pontiac and his movement were nearly successful in driving the British from the upper Midwest, they could not overcome the overwhelming numbers of colonists, and the war ended in something of a stalemate.[22] As relations with the British deteriorated, King George III issued a proclamation in 1763 that established a line along the Appalachian Mountains to separate Natives from non-Natives. For a short time, the Potawatomi and other tribes of the Great Lakes would continue to control their traditional homelands.

During the Revolutionary War, most Potawatomi either sided with the British or remained neutral because of their suspicions that the colonists desired their land. Ever-increasing demands by settlers for land and resources conflicted with the Potawatomi desires to retain their ancestral homelands. The situation did not improve for the Potawatomi after the United States secured its independence from Great Britain. It worsened, in fact, as the Americans continued to expand their activities west of the Appalachians and sought the land of the Native peoples rather than only furs or other resources. In 1787, Congress enacted the Northwest Ordinance, which made clear the intent of the United States to take control of the Great Lakes region. The Northwest Ordinance was said to guarantee peace and fair dealing with the Indian tribes in the Midwest. However, the law also established a process for turning the territory into six new states to be added to the Union. The law designated the land bounded by the Ohio River, Mississippi River, the Great Lakes, and Pennsylvania as the Northwest Territory. The intent to settle the Great Lakes and take it from its Native inhabitants was clear. Eventually, the territory would be organized into the states of Ohio, Indiana, Illinois, Michigan, Minnesota, and Wisconsin. The Northwest Ordinance established the framework for United States expansion into the region. This legislation promised, "The utmost good faith shall always be observed towards the Indians; their land and property shall never be taken without their consent; and, in their property, rights, and liberty, they shall never be invaded or disturbed."[23]

Nonetheless, Native resistance in the Great Lakes region continued. At the Battle of Fallen Timbers (1794) a confederacy of Indians, including some Potawatomi, organized by the leaders Blue Jacket (Shawnee), and Mishikinakwa (Little Turtle–Miami) was defeated near Maumee, Ohio. The next year the Potawatomi and the other tribes of the Great Lakes would try to ensure peace with the United States by signing the Treaty of Greenville (1795).[24] In that treaty, much of what is now Ohio was ceded to the United States, and American forts were established throughout the region, including at Chicago and Detroit. The signing of the treaty in 1795 established a temporary peace between the United States and the American Indian tribes that lived in the territory, but encouraged non-Native immigration to the area.[25] Once again, promises were made to the Native signatories to the treaty that they would be treated fairly in future land dealings.

Article 5 of the Treaty of Greenville provided that

> The Indian tribes who have a right to those lands, are quietly to enjoy them, hunting, planting, and dwelling thereon so long as they please, without any molestation from the United States; but when those tribes, or any of them, shall be disposed to sell their lands, or any part of them, they are to be sold only to the United States; and until such sale, the United States will protect all the said Indian tribes in the quiet enjoyment of their lands against all citizens of the United States, and against all other white persons who intrude upon the same.[26]

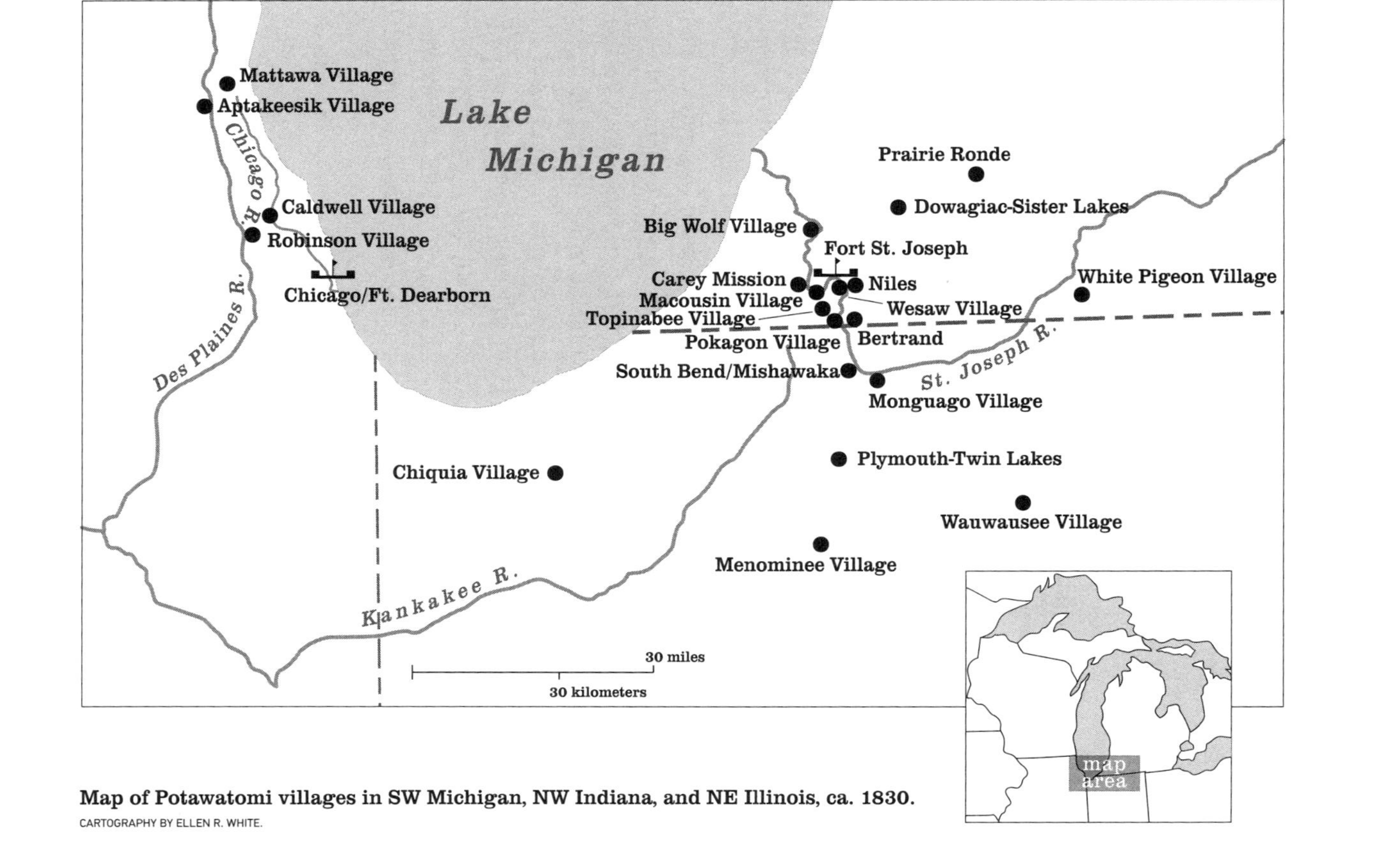

Map of Potawatomi villages in SW Michigan, NW Indiana, and NE Illinois, ca. 1830.

CARTOGRAPHY BY ELLEN R. WHITE.

The map of Potawatomi villages shows the locations of Native villages—including the Potawatomi communities led by Topinabee (Dookmubii, Silent Sitter), Weesaw/ Wesaw, (Leopold) Pokagon (The Rib), and Menominee—circa 1830 at the southern end of Lake Michigan.

Pressures to relinquish more lands to the United States continued, and Indian anger over the constant demands for land mounted as the fur trade came to an end. Dependency on trade goods, and the impact of disease, alcohol, and non-Native technology all contributed to Native frustrations and fears. After 1805, another prophetic movement of resistance swept through the Midwest. The Shawnee Prophet Tenskwatawa and his brother, Tecumseh, promoted a vision of an intertribal Indian resistance to colonization and conquest by the Americans. The Shawnee Prophet ultimately established the intertribal village of Prophetstown, near what is now Battle Ground, Indiana. Tecumseh traveled from Canada to the Gulf Coast attempting to secure an Indian confederacy strong enough to resist the United States. A number of Potawatomi, including some from the St. Joseph River Valley, joined in the movement. The Shawnee Prophet and Tecumseh's vision of a unified resistance ended when the Americans, under the leadership of future president William Henry Harrison, attacked and destroyed Prophetstown at the Battle of Tippecanoe.[27] Shortly afterwards, war broke out between the United States and Britain. Many of the Great Lakes tribes, including many Potawatomi, sided with the British during the War of 1812. In October 1813, Tecumseh was killed in the Battle of the Thames, marking the end of significant armed resistance by the Potawatomi and the other tribes of the region.[28] During the War of 1812, General William Hull ordered the evacuation of Fort Dearborn at present-day Chicago, in August 1812. Captain Nathan Heald oversaw the exit, but on August 15, the evacuees were attacked by about five hundred Potawatomi Indians in the Battle of Fort Dearborn (see chapter 6). The Potawatomi burned the fort to the ground the next day.[29] Although it is far from clear, the Potawatomi of what is now the Pokagon Band may have been involved in the hostilities. One historian of the last century wrote of Topinabee,[30] a leader of one of the villages along the St. Joseph River: "If he did not actually take part in laying the plot, [he] was fully aware of the impending massacre of the troops at Fort Dearborn, or Chicago, on August 15, 1812. . . . The evidence is rather strong that Topenebee [*sic*] was the leader in the whole affair from the beginning."[31]

The Potawatomi, like other Great Lakes tribes, signed many treaties that "sold" their lands to the United States—usually at a fraction of the lands' true value. American negotiators frequently employed chicanery to secure the signatures needed. The scourge of alcohol and its impact upon some Potawatomi leaders is evidenced by the oft-quoted remark of Chief Topinabee to Lewis Cass, territorial governor of Michigan: "Father, we do not care for the land, nor the money, nor the goods; what we want is whiskey; give us whiskey!"[32] In 1825, the Erie Canal was completed, encouraging a flood of non-Native emigration into the Great Lakes region. Potawatomi leaders sought to balance the United States' desire for land with their followers' needs for trade items and good relations with the settlers. Between 1816 and 1833, the Potawatomi were parties in over thirty land-cession treaties.[33] In 1830, Congress passed the Indian Removal Act, a law intended to force all the Indian tribes living east of the Mississippi River to reservations west of the Mississippi. In 1833, the United States government called together all of the Potawatomi tribes of the area to a final treaty negotiation at Chicago. Potawatomi community leaders from villages throughout the Midwest, including Leopold Pokagon, attended with trepidation.[34]

The Indian Removal That Wasn't

After passage of the Indian Removal Act in 1830, some in Chicago may have assumed the days of the Potawatomi in Chicago were numbered; and that belief was likely only strengthened with the negotiation of the Treaty of Chicago in 1833. We who live in Chicago now can imagine what the weather was like that first month of fall 1833. Likely, the days were still warm, though less humid than the previous month. The nights, however, were cooling off; the leaves on the sumacs were probably turning brilliant red and orange, and the water rougher on Lake Michigan. The changes of the season were apparent in the air. So it was in Chicago. For the residents of the Chicago area that fall, the changes would be especially dramatic. The Treaty of Chicago in 1833 ceded the last of the remaining Indian lands in Illinois to the United States, and it is cited as the last great treaty between the United States and American Indians in the Great Lakes region.[35]

We can imagine the weather, but perhaps little else about the situation of 1833. We do have access to eyewitness accounts written by non-Native participants, reflecting their perceptions of what was seen and felt by the parties involved. During his travels through North America, Charles Joseph Latrobe, an Englishman, was present at the treaty negotiations occurring in Chicago that fall of 1833. Latrobe recounts in "The Rambler in North America":

> It is a grievous thing that Government is not strong handed enough to put a stop to the shameful and scandalous sale of whiskey to these poor miserable wretches. But here lie casks of it for sale under the very eye of the Commissioners, met together for purposes which demand that sobriety should be maintained, were it only that no one should be able to lay at their door an accusation of unfair dealing, and of having taken advantage of the helpless Indian in a bargain, whereby the people of the United States were to be greatly the gainers. And such was the state of things day by day. . . .
>
> However anxious I and others might be to exculpate the United States Government from the charge of cold and selfish policy toward the remnant of the Indian tribes, and from that of resorting to unworthy and diabolical means in attaining possession of their lands, as long as it can be said with truth, that drunkenness was not guarded against, and that means were furnished at the very time of the Treaty, and under the very nose of the Commissioners, how can it be expected but a stigma will attend every transaction of this kind. The sin may lie at the door of the individuals more immediately in contact with them; but the character of the people as a nation, it should be guarded against, beyond a possibility of transgression. Who will believe that any act, however formally executed by the chiefs, is valid, as long as it is known that whiskey was one of the parties to the treaty?[36]

We have less widely circulated oral histories that have been passed down among tribal members of the events, as well as parallels in history from which to draw conclusions. The mindset of the original inhabitants of Chicago that September may have been very similar to many other times in history when Indigenous peoples have been dispossessed of their lands at the hands of European colonizers in places like Australia and the Pacific, Africa, India, and the Middle East. The Treaty of Chicago of 1833 began a long period of adjustment for the Indians affected, as they moved from their lifeways of relative independence into a period of persistence and adaptation.

The year 1833 was rife with calls for cession of land and removal of Indians by the ever-increasing American inhabitants of the Chicago region. The Treaty of Chicago and the removal of the Potawatomi reflected a nexus of private desire and federal Indian policy. Often forgotten, by the 1830s some Potawatomi had established themselves in "Chicago society." They were voting in local elections, serving on town councils, and holding positions of public trust. But several separate sets of circumstances contributed to the conclusion that Indians could not be allowed to continue to live in Chicago in substantial numbers.

First, and perhaps foremost, was immigration. With the opening of the Erie Canal, the Great Lakes became a highway of commerce, funneling resources east and moving white "settlers" west. Overland routes over the Appalachians were being opened as well. Chicago, the once quiet area of marsh and onion, then of fur and trade, now was becoming a boomtown for enterprise and American expansion. Many of the Indian residents, for their part, were unenthusiastic about assimilating into agrarian cultures of America. Although the Potawatomi and other Indians had been attracted to, and felt a kinship with, the earlier French trader/trapper lifestyle, they saw a lifeway of farming as full of drudgery and toil. The influx of a population of settlers, miners, developers, and speculators, and the unwillingness of the Indians to join in the tedium of small farming, contributed to their marginalization in the 1830s.

The second factor casting a pall over continued Indian residency in Chicago was the prior warfare between neighboring Indigenous peoples and the newest white intruders onto their lands. One of the legacies of such mobilizations as the 1827 Ho-Chunk Resistance and Black Hawk's War in 1832 was a feeling among non-Natives that *all* Indians had to be removed from the area. The assistance of the Potawatomi to the Americans during Black Hawk's War, and their earlier refusal to participate with the Ho-Chunk were forgotten or ignored as white Chicagoans pressed for removal.

A third factor was economic and political. Subsequent to the War of 1812 with the British Crown, the financially bankrupt American government had established a new fundraising device: buying land from Indians at a fraction of its value through treaties, removing the Indians west, and then selling the land to speculators at big profits. This practice gained particular momentum after the election in 1828 of Andrew Jackson, who ran for the presidency on a platform of removing all of the Indians west of the Mississippi. In 1830, a sharply divided Congress passed the Indian Removal Act. The Treaty of Chicago was one of the first treaties negotiated and ratified under its terms. The act granted the president authority for negotiating the cession of all Indian lands within the states and territories of the United States, and for removal of those Indian peoples to a new "Indian Territory" to be secured for them in parts west of the Mississippi River.

While the requirements of the Indian Removal Act were intended to ameliorate and make more palatable this federal policy of social and ethnic cleansing, it nonetheless is clear that the desire of the United States in 1833 was twofold: acquisition of land, and exclusion of the Indigenous inhabitants. The Treaty of Chicago was only

Leopold Pokagon, painting by Van Sanden, ca. 1820s–30s. FROM THE COLLECTIONS OF THE CENTER FOR HISTORY, OPERATED BY THE NORTHERN INDIANA HISTORICAL SOCIETY. PHOTO BY THE AUTHOR.

partially successful in achieving this goal. A Treaty Council met on September 14, 1833, and the Indian tradition of smoking the "peace" pipe preceded negotiations.[37] Upon the commencement of negotiations with the treaty commissioners, the Potawatomi quickly established that they intended to be no easy mark. Apatakisic (Half Day), a chief from the Fox River in Illinois, told the commissioners that the Potawatomi had no intention of agreeing to any land cession and removal. Apatakisic requested that annuities due the Indians from earlier treaties be paid so that his fellow tribal members could return to their villages and harvest their corn. For several days thereafter, speeches were exchanged.

Finally, on September 19, the Potawatomi notified the Americans that they had selected two Métis spokesmen, Billy Caldwell and Alexander Robinson, as their representatives. More serious negotiations continued for a week, and a treaty agreement was signed on September 26, 1833. Pursuant to that agreement, the Potawatomi were to relinquish five million acres, eight thousand square miles of land, for the promise of the same amount of land along the Missouri River in what are now Iowa and Missouri.

One of the village leaders at the negotiation was Leopold Pokagon (1775?–1841),

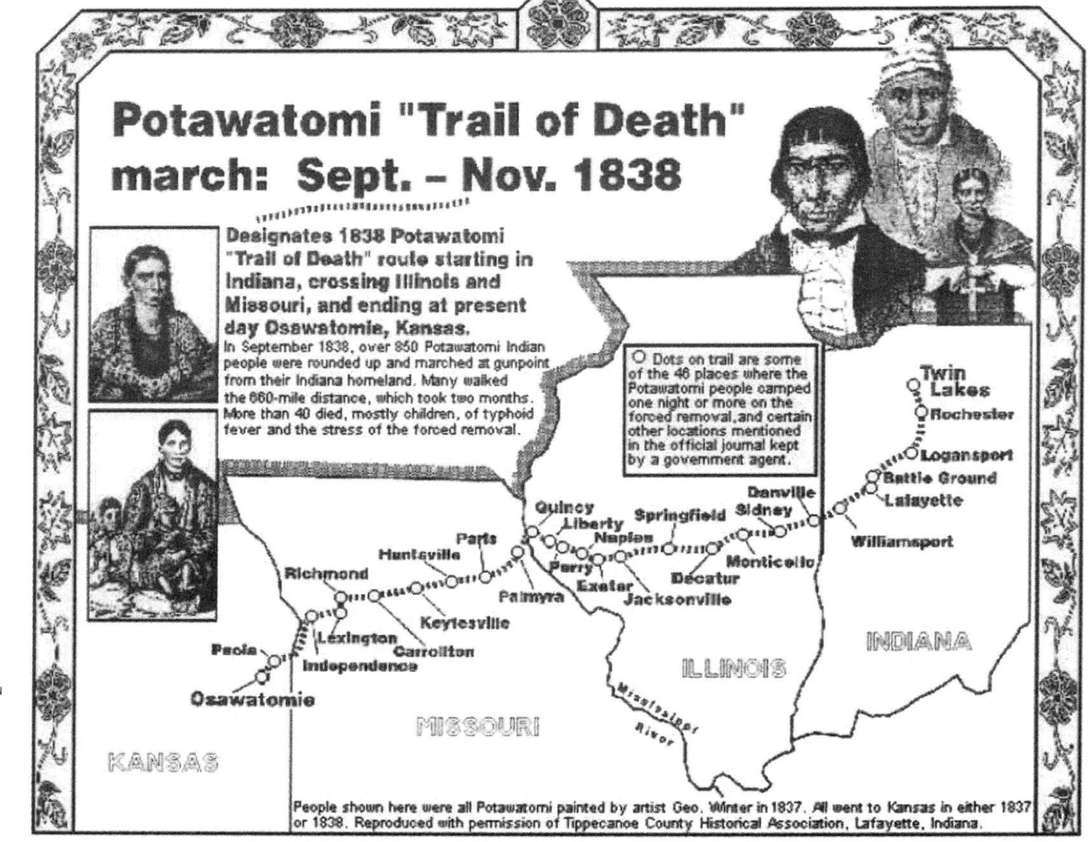

Map of the Potawatomi "Trail of Death," by Tom Hamilton, a member of Citizen Potawatomi Nation. PROPERTY OF THE POTAWATOMI TRAIL OF DEATH ASSN., A BRANCH OF THE FULTON COUNTY HISTORICAL SOCIETY. REPRODUCED WITH PERMISSION OF THE FULTON COUNTY (INDIANA) HISTORICAL SOCIETY.

who was a Potawatomi chief in the first half of the nineteenth century. Taking over for his father-in-law Topinabee, who died in 1826, Pokagon became the head of a Potawatomi village in the St. Joseph River Valley in southwest Michigan. His early life is surrounded by legend, and many details are known only from the oral histories of the tribe. Stories suggest that he was born an Odawa or Ojibwe, but raised from a young age by the Potawatomi. His name, Pokagon, means "The Rib" in the Potawatomi language, an appellation earned, some say, because he was wearing a human rib in his scalp lock when first taken into the tribe.

The scene in Chicago during the 1833 negotiations was carnival-like. James Clifton describes it as "an odd sort of emporium, a strange multi-cultural bazaar, a unique kind of exchange."[38] The air was thick with rumors of a possible windfall for the Americans. Indian land and resources—the prairie, farmland, woods, valleys, streams, marshes, and beaches—were being converted to liquid assets. The Potawatomi brought their families to the negotiations, six thousand setting up camp along the Chicago River just north of what were then the village limits. Potawatomi men, women, and children filled the Chicago streets. Surrounding the Potawatomi was an assortment of characters. Charles Latrobe wrote that most of the whites consisted of

> horse dealers, and horse stealers,—rogues of every description, . . . half breeds, quarter breeds, and men of no breed at all;—dealers in pigs, poultry and potatoes;—men pursuing Indian claims, some for tracts of land, others . . . for pigs which the wolves had eaten;—creditors of the tribe or of particular Indians, who know they have no chance of getting their money, if they do not get it from government agents;—sharpers of every degree; pedlars [*sic*], grog-sellers; Indian agents and Indian traders of every description. . . . The little village [Chicago] was in an uproar from morning to night, and from night to morning.[39]

Clifton points out that for the five days prior to September 26, the treaty journal falls suspiciously silent as to what was transpiring between the parties, a gap in the negotiation record that would lead later to charges of collusion and conspiracy. By the 26th, when the journal restarts its record, the treaty was already written, ready for signing and certification. Tales of negotiation through sophistry, bribery, and the unethical but effective use of alcohol are part of the oral tradition of the Potawatomi. Clifton writes that during these five days of negotiations in Chicago,

> Commissioners Porter and Owens . . . apparently had introduced their own secret weapons, Subagent Ardent Spirits, Colonel John Silver, and Reverend Utmost Chicanery. . . . Exactly what new steps were taken to encourage the Potawatomi to agree to the details of the [treaty] are unknown but on the twenty-sixth Porter indicated that in a general council they had done so.[40]

The treaty was signed by the three commissioners and by seventy-seven headmen of the Potawatomi. The next day, on September 27, supplemental articles reciting the terms of additional agreements between the United States and the Potawatomi Indians of Michigan and Indiana of the St. Joseph River Valley were attached to the treaty. Following signatures to this attachment is the exception that allowed some of the Pokagon Potawatomi to escape removal west.

> And, as since the signing of the treaty a part of the band residing on the reservations in the Territory of Michigan, have requested, on account of their religious creed, permission to remove to the northern part of the peninsula of Michigan, it is agreed that in case of such removal that just proportion of all annuities payable to them under former treaties and that arising from the sale of the reservation on which they now reside shall be paid to them at L'arbre Croche.[41]

According to oral histories of the community that I have heard since childhood, Pokagon moved his followers away from the rest of the Potawatomi gathered at the negotiations so as to avoid the temptations and effects of alcohol. By his temperance and by emphasizing the conversion of himself and his followers to Catholicism, Leopold Pokagon was able to negotiate this amendment to the Treaty of Chicago that allowed Pokagon's Band to remain in Michigan. A year earlier, in the October 1832 Treaty at Tippecanoe, both Pokagon and his wife had each been granted one section of land. Now, from the sale of those parcels and payments pursuant to the terms of the 1833 Treaty, he purchased 874 acres in what is now Silver Creek Township, Cass County, Michigan.[42] The tribe relocated to those lands after the 1833 Treaty.[43] In contrast, almost all the rest of the Potawatomi were slated for removal to west of the Mississippi River by the federal government—as a part of the Indian Removal Act. At the close of the Chicago negotiations, the Potawatomi from Wisconsin would return north to their homes, where they would continue to reside, in Forest County, Wisconsin, and at Hannahville in Menominee County, Michigan. Others returned to their homes near what is now Allegan and Athens, Michigan.

Pokagon Potawatomi gathered near Dowagiac, Michigan, ca. 1910. On the other side of the postcard, presumably written by a nontribal member, is the note "Some of our happy citizens. They are great basket makers as well. We went over to Paw Paw [Michigan] to Chautauqua yesterday." Dated August 23, 1910. FROM THE COLLECTION OF THE AUTHOR.

The great majority by far of Potawatomi gathered at Chicago, however, would be forced to leave the Midwest. Some would flee to Canada, where descendants still live at Walpole Island First Nation and Wasauksing First Nation. Others would escape forced removal by heading south to Mexico.

Those who returned from Chicago and remained in their villages in what we now call Indiana and Illinois were moved west in a series of removals ending in 1838, in what has come to be called the "Trail of Death,"[44] to where their descendants now live as the Prairie Band in Kansas and the Citizen Band of Potawatomi in Oklahoma, respectively.

The Emergence of the Pokagon Band of Potawatomi

During his lifetime, Leopold Pokagon sought to protect and promote the unique position of the Potawatomi communities living in the St. Joseph River Valley. He traveled to Detroit in July 1830, where he visited Father Gabriel Richard to request the services of a priest. Affiliation with the Catholic Church was not only for religious reasons, but also represented an important political alliance in the struggle to avoid removal. That same year, Pokagon was baptized by the vicar general of the Detroit Diocese, Father Frederick Rese. Also in that year, Pokagon, together with three other chiefs, wrote to President Andrew Jackson requesting government support for the provision of a priest for the tribe.[45] In August 1830, Father Stephen Badin arrived to establish a mission to serve the Pokagon Potawatomi. By establishing this affiliation with the Catholic Church, the Potawatomi of the St. Joseph River Valley promoted a new identity as the Pokagon Band of Potawatomi Indians.[46] Catholic Potawatomi throughout southwest Michigan and northwest Indiana acknowledged Leopold Pokagon as their leader. Ever since, villages from Hartford, Rush Lake, Dowagiac, Niles, Buchanan, South Bend, and elsewhere have been united in a common identity: Pokagon's Band of Potawatomi, the Catholic Potawatomi of Michigan and Indiana, and/or the Pokégnek Bodéwadmik.[47] In a movement experienced by many tribes that had previously been loosely organized into small villages under fluid leaderships, the new nation of the Pokagon Band of Potawatomi underwent a reimagi*nation*, if you will, of who they were and how they were organized. The Pokagon Band took on a government-to-government relationship with the U.S. government as a domestic sovereign nation within the boundaries of the United States.[48]

In 1841, Leopold Pokagon had to obtain the assistance of an associate justice of the Michigan Supreme Court, Epaphroditus Ransom, to halt military attempts to remove the Catholic Potawatomi in violation of the 1833 Treaty. After Pokagon's death on July 8, 1841, disputes between his heirs, the community, and the Catholic Church over ownership of the Silver Creek lands resulted in legal battles that painfully disrupted the community. A majority of the residents living at Silver Creek moved to Brush Creek, Rush Lake, and elsewhere in southwest Michigan and northwest Indiana. The community thereafter turned its focus to securing the annuities and other promises owed them under the terms of the many treaties they had signed with the United States.[49]

Simon Pokagon (1830?–January 28, 1899), a son of Leopold Pokagon, was a leader of the community that bears his father's name. He was an early Indian author of numerous articles and one novel, and a popular public speaker of his time. Evidence of his popularity is reflected in the number of his works that were included in the auction of the Daniel F. Appleton library in New York City in 1922,[50] but the city

Pokagon Potawatomi Community Center, 2014. PHOTOGRAPH COURTESY OF THE POKAGON BAND OF POTAWATOMI.

that most felt his presence was Chicago. As will be discussed in chapter 2, he was an early Indian celebrity and widely praised for his rhetorical skills.

Two censuses of tribal members were taken by U.S. government officials in 1895–96 to determine eligibility for treaty annuity payments. Called the "Cadman-Shelby Roll" after the federal officials who tallied the census, it has since been used by the tribe for establishing enrollment and citizenship. In 1896, partial payments were made to the Pokagon Potawatomi for monies owed pursuant to the land-cession treaties of the first half of the nineteenth century. By the turn of the century, the Pokagon Potawatomi also began petitioning for return of lands along the Chicago lakefront. These claims eventually landed in the United States Supreme Court in 1917.[51]

In the 1930s, the Band petitioned for participation in federal programs under the Indian Reorganization Act (1934), but fell victim to the Department of Interior's decision not to extend the IRA's services into much of Lower Michigan, largely due to a lack of personnel and funds.[52]

For the next sixty years, the Pokagon Potawatomi sought to reestablish recognition by the federal government. The Band, particularly under the leadership of tribal chair Michael B. Williams, also proceeded with actions in the Court of Claims for payment of monies still due under the numerous treaties between the tribe and the United States.[53] That effort successfully culminated in payment of monies to tribal members in 1983. Reflecting the tribal leadership's interest in national affairs, Williams and John R. "Dick" Winchester were delegates to the 1961 American Indian Chicago Conference, and Winchester was a delegate to the National Congress of American Indians (NCAI).[54]

In 1981, the Pokagon Band again filed a petition for federal acknowledgment with the secretary of the Interior. Over the next decade, the petition met with continual bureaucratic complications in the Bureau of Indian Affairs' Branch of Acknowledgment and Research. These delays eventually led the Band to abandon the administrative process for federal recognition. The Pokagon Band finally had its federal tribal status restored by the passage of the Pokagon Restoration Act, a congressional act signed into law by President William Clinton on September 21, 1994.

Today, the Pokagon Band is using its reaffirmed sovereignty to reestablish a land base, develop its government and tribal services, and strengthen the tribal community. The Band's headquarters are in Dowagiac, Michigan, and includes Tribal Council offices, a Tribal Court, and Administration and Finance Departments, as well as tribal service programs for Health, Social Services, Housing, and Education. Head Start, language and traditions classes, elders' services and luncheons, commodity distribution, employment training and placement, college scholarships, and youth summer camps are also representative of the services the Band provides to its citizens. The Band maintains a service office satellite in South Bend, Indiana, as well. Federal recognition has also meant access to government grant and loan programs, as well as the protections and opportunities afforded to Indians generally, such as those provided by the Indian Child Welfare Act (ICWA), the Native American Graves Protection and Repatriation Act (NAGPRA), and the Indian Gaming Regulatory Act (IGRA).[55]

The Pokagon Band recently completed Kekyajek Odanek, an elders' village in Dowagiac for which it won an innovative housing award from the U.S. Department of Housing and Urban Development. The Band has developed additional family housing at the site, Pokégnek Édawat, and intends to do the same in the Hartford, Michigan, and South Bend–Mishawaka areas. The tribe has also purchased property

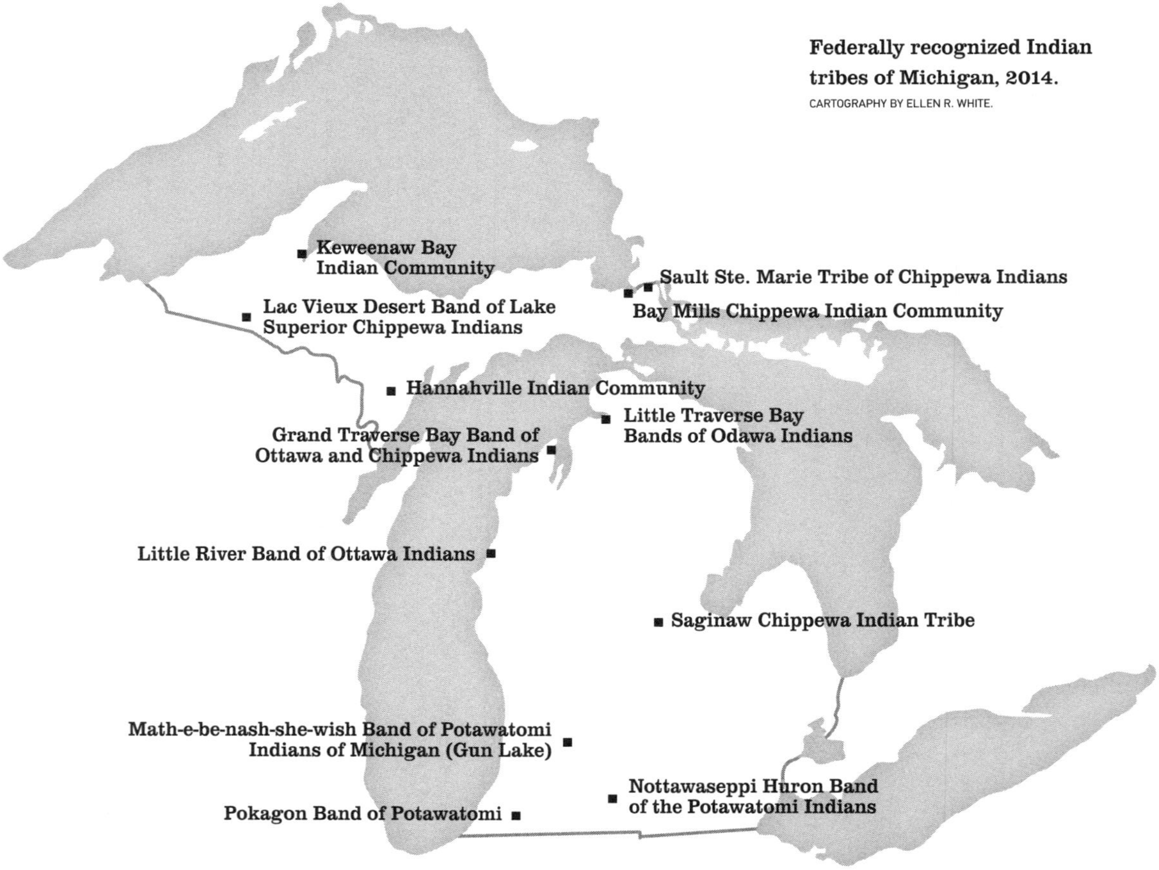

Federally recognized Indian tribes of Michigan, 2014.
CARTOGRAPHY BY ELLEN R. WHITE.

in St. Joseph and La Porte Counties, Indiana, and has enrolled 1,200 of these acres with the U.S. Natural Resource Conservation Service in the Wetland Reserve Program (WRP). This project will restore much of the wetland habitat at this site, which is part of the ancestral Grand Kankakee Marsh.[56]

The Pokagon Band is governed by a democratically elected eleven-member Tribal Council, which is the modern form of the traditional group-based governance. The tribe that bears Leopold Pokagon's name continues as a federally recognized Indian Nation, with over four thousand citizens and a ten-county service area in northwest Indiana and southwest Michigan. Its Indiana service area abuts the city limits of Chicago. Traditional iconography remains important to tribal members, as evidenced by the National Seal of the Pokagon Nation. First unveiled in the 1970s, it depicts the story of how fire was brought to the Neshnabek. Fire is understood to be a gift to the people, brought by the hawk as a piece of the sun. This is particularly important to the Potawatomi since it refers to the role the Potawatomi play as keepers of the fire in the Three Fires Confederacy with the Ojibwe and Odawa. In the center of the seal is a round border, symbolizing the centering of all life within the four directions of Mother Earth.[57]

The Pokagon Band continues efforts to preserve Bodewadmimwen, their native language. In 2003, the Band initiated a cooperative language effort with neighboring Potawatomi, the Match-e-be-nash-she-wish Band of Pottawatomi Indians, and the Nottawaseppi Huron Band of Potawatomi. The project has generated classes in all three tribal communities, as well as developed curriculum and language preservation materials. The Band completed construction of a multimillion-dollar administration building in Dowagiac and has commenced construction of a Cultural Center as well. Pow wows are held throughout the year, the largest being the Kee-Boon-Mein-Kaa celebration, held every Labor Day weekend. Each year the tribe participates in an annual gathering of the dispersed bands of Potawatomi, including the Prairie Band Potawatomi Nation in Kansas, the Citizen Potawatomi Nation in Oklahoma, the Forest County Potawatomi Community in Wisconsin, the Hannahville Indian Community in northern Michigan, the Match-e-be-nash-she-wish Band in Michigan, the Nottawaseppi Huron Band of Potawatomi, also in Michigan, and the Walpole Island First Nation and Wasauksing First Nation, both located in Canada.

The Pokagon Potawatomi operate Four Winds Casino Resort (a $160 million gaming facility in New Buffalo, Michigan, that opened in August 2007)[58] just sixty miles from the Chicago city limits, and in 2011 opened a second casino within its ancestral territory at Hartford, Michigan.[59] A third casino operated by the Band opened in Dowagiac, Michigan, in 2013. Additional economic development and diversification is provided by a program the tribe calls Mno-Bmadsen.[60] There is an active ceremonial and cultural events calendar, in which some members participate,[61] and more than a dozen tribal citizens participate in an artists' collective supported by the tribe. Blackash basketry continues to be a significant artistic endeavor. For instance, Julia Wesaw of Hartford, Michigan, learned traditional blackash basket making from her grandmother and mother. In the 1970s, Wesaw was one of the cofounders of the Pokagon Basket Makers' Exchange/Co-op, which revived the art of basket making in the Pokagon Potawatomi community. In 1989, she was a recipient of a Michigan Heritage Award from the Museum at Michigan State University. John Pigeon, a tribal member from Dorr, Michigan, received the same award for his blackash basketry in 2010. In a 2002 interview while exhibiting at the Eiteljorg Museum of American Indians and Western Art in Indianapolis, Pigeon explained the motivations behind his work.

> The reason I do a lot of the traditional arts is to keep them alive. . . . As Anishinabe people, we try to always think of seven generations. Those seven generations include my grandfather's grandfather all the way to my grandchildren's grandchildren. By making baskets or keeping rituals and ceremonies alive, we're able to give something to our grandchildren's grandchildren.[62]

This interest in tradition and maintaining a distinct Potawatomi identity weaves throughout the course of tribal history.

CHAPTER 2

Simon Pokagon's Claims of Equality and Appeals for Inclusion

> Chief Pokagon, one of the early leaders of conservation, deserves a lasting place among the redmen who worked to save both their people, the white man and the natural life of the country. History will acclaim him more than the past.
>
> —Edward Allen Hyer, "Chief Pokagon, Apostle of Living Beauty"

Unlike his grandfather Chief Topinabee, or his father, Leopold Pokagon, Simon Pokagon did not have the alternatives of armed resistance or treaty to secure peace for himself and his people. A general accord had already been secured by his father, but Simon would spend the majority of his life advocating for Indian equality and inclusion, using the forums available to him: writing, speaking, and performance. During his lifetime, he became the conscience in the ear of the hegemon. Any community, Indian or otherwise, can only survive difficult times if its members retain a sense of meaning, vitality, relevance, and self-respect. Simon Pokagon articulated, to tribal members and the general public alike, that the Potawatomi could (and should) be a part of America's future. The venue where he chose to do his work was primarily in and around Chicago.

Simon Pokagon was a celebrity in Chicago during his lifetime and a featured speaker at the World's Columbian Exposition (WCE) in 1893. His novel, *Queen of the Woods*, serves as a rhetorical monument to the persistence and resiliency of the Potawatomi. His literary and speaking efforts coupled with the materiality of his activities—such as selling his earlier work *The Red Man's Rebuke/The Red Man's Greeting* bound in birch bark—reminded both Natives and non-Natives alike that Chicago is built upon Potawatomi lands.

Pokagon Band Potawatomi tribal history is woven throughout the city's history. This book focuses on Pokagon Potawatomi tribal members of prominence because their voices remain available to us through literature, images, newspapers, and archives. As noted in the previous chapter, the Pokagon Band of Potawatomi avoided removal west after passage of the Indian Removal Act, and members have continued to live in southwest Michigan and northwest Indiana, near Chicago. In the late nineteenth century, Simon Pokagon became a fixture on the Chicago literary and social scene. Utilizing methods, materials, and language from his past, Simon Pokagon spent his time in Chicago communicating his hope that the Potawatomi would be accorded the same rights and privileges as others in modern American society.

The Ancestral Voice of Simon Pokagon

Simon Pokagon—I have heard stories about him all my life. He is cast as both hero and villain. This is in part because the Pokagon community has had deep divisions since the death of his father and tribal patriarch, Leopold Pokagon, in 1853, and subsequent land disputes within the tribe.[1]

Simon Pokagon was not immune from those feelings of ill will. Along with the expectations that came from his being a child of Leopold Pokagon, there were also stories that Simon Pokagon sold the tribe's claims to the Chicago lakefront without appropriate authority and for personal gain.[2] The undercurrent I sensed within the Pokagon community when I was growing up was that some believed he was a lackey—a sort of "Uncle Tom*ahawk*," the Indian equivalent of an "Uncle Tom,"[3] and an overrated representative of the community, someone more interested in impressing the literary circles of his time than in advocating on behalf of his own people.[4] He receives an ambivalent reception from critical literature scholars and historians as well, partly because of questions surrounding his authorship of the novel *Queen of the Woods*.[5]

Frontispiece of Simon Pokagon's novel, published after his death in 1899. FROM THE COLLECTION OF THE AUTHOR.

My intention here is neither to bolster nor to undermine Pokagon's status among either Native or non-Native peoples. My goal is to try to imagine what Simon Pokagon's intentions might have been in writing, and doing, what he did; to reflect upon the contexts in which *Queen of the Woods* and his other works were written; to examine the issue of authorship of the novel; and to explore his influence upon the city of Chicago and vice versa. His essays are a form of written communication more recently acquired by Indian peoples,[6] and his life reflects the continuity of Indian influence in Chicago.

Walter Benjamin noted that libraries are dwellings and books are the foundational stones.[7] So it is with *Queen of the Woods*. Pokagon's only novel serves for some as a touchstone for identity and community. Identity is an edifice that expands when times are good and contracts when they are not; certain acts contribute to that structure or undermine it. New rooms, walls, and windows can be added while others are taken down, moved, or remodeled. These structures can be manifested in buildings, words (written or spoken), images, legal claims, and material culture, and can also be the homes of shared experience, worldviews, and ideology; they house similarly situated and identified members who present a façade of cohesion to the outside world. These structures reflect the fads, fashion, temper, and tone of the times, and if strongly built they will strategically accommodate substantial renovations. Those dwellings form a community held together by its common values and memories. When the familiar is wiped from the earth, new landmarks must be created to hold the memories of the community. Simon Pokagon's writings, and his many references to the landscape and to the language of his ancestors and the material culture of his forebears, created a new landscape for Pokagon tribal community members so that they did not feel entirely lost.

Many libraries of American Indian literature include the novel *Queen of the Woods* in their collections. For Pokagon Potawatomi tribal members, it is not so important that they have read the book. It seems what is important is that it exists and that a fellow tribal member wrote it. There is a pride in his accomplishment, but also sometimes envy within our community. The current interest of some Potawatomi peoples in Simon Pokagon is one example of reengaging with the past as an effective way to enhance individual and community identity while resisting the continued onslaught of non-Native influences upon Indigenous cultures. It reflects an effort by some to mark, reestablish, and assert the uniqueness of the community's history and traditions and the importance of this legacy to their futures. It has the potential to rewrite a history of dispossession with a narrative of pride and survival. It is about the ways memory and history are constructed and deployed.

The Life of Simon Pokagon

Simon Pokagon was an author, and an advocate for American Indians. Born in 1830 near what later became the small village of Bertrand in southwestern Michigan, he died from pneumonia on January 28, 1899, near Hartford, Michigan.[8] As noted above, Pokagon was a son of his tribe's patriarch, Leopold Pokagon. Dubbed by some "the Indian Longfellow" and "the Red Bard," Pokagon was often called the "Hereditary and Last Chief" of the tribe by the press,[9] a title he did not reject. However, despite those common assertions by the press, Pokagon was neither the last nor a hereditary chief of the Potawatomi.[10] The Pokagon community has had leaders since his passing, and that role in the Pokagon Band of Potawatomi is not hereditary.

After receiving an education, he returned to his tribe in 1850, marrying and settling into community life. After the deaths of his two brothers, he was elected leader of his community.[11] In his efforts to collect monies due the tribe pursuant to the land cessions of the 1833 Treaty of Chicago, Pokagon twice visited President Abraham Lincoln, and after the Civil War met with President Ulysses S. Grant, accepting an expression of gratitude from Grant for the Potawatomi volunteers who had served in the Civil War.[12]

The Bureau of American Ethnology provided an early description of the man in its 1910 *Handbook of American Indians North of Mexico.* The handbook was long considered a major academic resource, and the passage bears quoting at length. Although riddled with factual errors, it nonetheless sheds light on his public persona.

> Simon was 10 years of age when his father died, and on reaching his 14th year was sent to school at Notre Dame, Ind. for 3 years; then, encouraged by his mother in his desire for education, attended Oberlin College, Ohio, for a year and next went to Twinsburg, Ohio where he remained 2 years. It is said that he was educated for the priesthood, spoke four or five languages, and bore the reputation of being the best educated full-blood Indian of his time. . . .
>
> He wrote numerous articles for the leading magazines and delivered many addresses of merit during the last quarter of the 19th century. In 1899 he published in book form "O-gî-mäw-kwě mit-i-gwä-kî," "Queen of the Woods," an account of the wooing of his first wife, and at the World's Fair in Chicago, in 1893, "The Red Man's Greeting," a booklet of birch-bark. He was a poet, and the last of his verses, both in its English and Potawatomi versions, appeared in the Chicago Inter-Ocean, Jan 23, 1899, just before his death. Pokagon was credited with ably managing the affairs of his 300 tribesmen scattered through Michigan and inspired by enlightened views, was the means of promoting their welfare. . . . He was a man of sturdy character, unostentatious in manner, of simple habit, and a consistent Catholic. [Actually, he broke from the Church when he married his second wife, who was a divorcée, and Pokagon was denied burial in a Catholic cemetery.[13]] A monument has been erected by the citizens of Chicago in Jackson Park to the memory of Simon and his father. [It never was.[14]]

That Simon Pokagon merited an entry in the handbook is but one indication of his visibility. An interest in Simon Pokagon as an American Indian intellectual, leader, writer, orator, temperance advocate, and environmentalist has remained relatively consistent since his death at the end of the nineteenth century (see appendix 2 for a list of such works).

Pokagon himself was a prolific writer. Besides *Queen of the Woods*, Pokagon's numerous other writings included birch bark booklets and articles in national literary magazines of the day (see appendix 3 for a list of his works). The symbolic importance of the birch bark that clad his little essays merited comment from the beginning. According to an article in the *Chicago Daily Tribune*,

> Bound in Indian Style—These two were wonderful books, superb specimens of the bookbinders' art, bound in "wighassi-makak-wig-wass," or birch bark. The boxes in which they were inclosed [*sic*] were the best efforts of the Pottawatomie tribe's most skillful workmen. They were made of porcupine quills, bound together with small cedar roots—"gijik-ens-obchi-biki." They were tied with "wo-gop" strings, and the mats in the bottoms of the boxes were bordered with "wish-mas-kus-sin," a grass used by the Indians for its fragrance.[15]

Queen of the Woods was also converted, by Pokagon's publisher, into a theatrical production after his death.[16] The volume and visibility of his writings and presence on the national stage are reflected in broadsides and other marketing for *Queen of the Woods*—typical of the promotion surrounding Pokagon.[17]

Where Pokagon was educated remains something of a mystery. He claimed attendance at Notre Dame University and Oberlin College, but that has been challenged, as the schools have no record of his matriculation.[18] It appears more likely that he was educated by the Sisters of St. Mary's Academy near Notre Dame and at the Twinsburg (Ohio) Institute.[19] Although claims of fluency in four of the "classic" European languages may be suspect because of his limited schooling, he nonetheless appears to have been a talented author and an entertaining and persuasive orator given his popularity as a public speaker.[20]

Pokagon was always welcomed by the "progressives" in Chicago's "Gold Coast,"[21] as well as Chautauqua literary and "Friends of Indians" groups nationwide.[22] He was also the subject of many photographs and portraits. He was an early activist for the fair treatment of Indian peoples. He headed the Business Committee of the Pokagon Band of Potawatomi Indians from 1869 until his political fortunes soured and he was removed from office in 1882.[23] He was a complicated individual with what often seemed to be contradictory motivations. For example, while he devoted his efforts to lobbying on behalf of his community for land claims, treaty rights, and annuity payments, he also sold "interests" in the Chicago land claim to non-tribal members, angering some in the Pokagon tribal community and costing himself much political support.[24] A quitclaim deed appears to confirm this allegation.[25] He also made an unsuccessful claim against the federal government for personal fees from an 1895 treaty payment.[26] In fact, almost eight years earlier, in a letter to social activist Joseph Labadie dated October 23, 1888, Pokagon included a note on the receipt for a loan from Labadie that makes clear that Pokagon's repayment was to be accomplished by including his non-Native benefactor in an upcoming treaty settlement payment by the government—as a tribal member.[27] Pokagon was certainly no champion of maintaining the integrity of tribal membership rolls; he did not seem to share a concern for citizenship status or the equitable distribution of tribal monies with other tribal members. Nonetheless, he presented a positive façade to outsiders. According to one contemporary biographer:

> His life was not eventful in the ordinary sense of Indian chieftains, and his fame rests upon the wonderful example which he offered the possibilities of advancement of the Red race in the lines of civilization. Born at a time when all the Indian habits of mind and thought and life were still in full force and vigor, he was able to emerge from these environments and to turn his face and influence towards a different form of life and destiny. He was enabled at an early age to see the great advantage and necessity of laying aside the implements of war and the chase to turn to the cultivation of the soil and the procurement of permanent homes: and it was in this line that he always directed the minds of his people. Otherwise he plainly saw the speedy ending of his race.[28]

In many of his writings, Simon played to national expectations in writing nostalgically of the past, lamenting the passing of a "vanishing" race of Indians.

> The index finger of the past and present is pointing to the future, showing more conclusively that by the middle of the next century all Indian reservations and tribal relations will have passed away. Then our people will begin to scatter; and the result will be a general mixing up of the races. Through intermarriage, the blood of our people, like the waters that flow into the great ocean, will be forever lost in the dominant race; and generations yet unborn will read in history of the red men of the forest, and inquire, "Where are they?"[29]

However, as he well knew, the Pokagon Potawatomi were not vanishing. Intermarriage did not portend the end of the Potawatomi—kinship had long been more important than blood quantum in determining community membership. Pokagon's references to a disappearing people may have been a strategic move by him to garner sympathy and support from outsiders. By the time he made these remarks, the Potawatomi had organized a Business Committee, a traditional, democratically elected tribal council, which governed by consensus and advocated for the rights of tribal members.[30] Meanwhile, most tribal members worked as laborers in local factories and on farms and retained ties to the Catholic Church.[31] According to historian Susan Sleeper-Smith, the Pokagon Potawatomi, as a community, responded to Nativist hysterias against Catholicism during this era by turning inward and presenting a more Indian, and less Catholic, façade. Sleeper-Smith also points out that the neighboring Miami Indians in Indiana chose another strategy and presented façades of whiteness in response to the racialization of "Indianness," and proceeded to "hide in plain view."[32] In many ways, Simon Pokagon seems to have vacillated between these two strategies throughout his adult life and during much of his time in Chicago.

If he sometimes met national expectations, at other times he challenged the marginalization of American Indians in the United States. In a publication originally titled *Red Man's Rebuke* and subsequently retitled *Red Man's Greeting*, Simon wrote in candid terms:

> On behalf of my people, the American Indians, I hereby declare to you, the pale-faced race that has usurped our lands and homes, that we have no spirit to celebrate with you the great Columbian Fair now being held in this Chicago city, the wonder of the world. No; sooner would we hold the high joy day over the graves of our departed than to celebrate our own funeral, the discovery of America. And while . . . your hearts in admiration rejoice over the beauty and grandeur of this young republic and you say, "behold the wonders wrought by our children in this foreign land," do not forget that this success has been at the sacrifice of our homes and a once happy race.[33]

While these words place him as a spokesperson of resistance on behalf of American Indian peoples, his speech at the World's Columbian Exposition on "Chicago Day" reported in the October 4, 1893, edition of the *Chicago Daily Tribune* assumes a much more conciliatory tone while including a plea for inclusion:

> I shall cherish as long as I live the cheering words that have been spoken to me here by the ladies, friends of my race; it has strengthened and encouraged me; I have greater faith in the success of the remaining few of my people than ever before. I now realize the hand of the Great Spirit is open in our behalf; already he has thrown his great search light upon the vault of heaven, and Christian men and women are reading there in characters of fire well understood; "The red man is your brother, and God is the father of all."[34]

Four years later, during celebrations of the founding of Holland, Michigan, Pokagon was again a featured speaker. There, he continued a common theme, lamenting the passing of the Indian and appealing for reconciliation and understanding between the races.

> Our people who sleep beneath your soil came here from the coast of the Atlantic. They were pioneers in their time, as you are today. When they first entered those beautiful woodland plains, they said in their hearts: "we are surely on the border land of the happy hunting grounds beyond." I pray you do not covet the narrow ground they occupy and desecrate and hide their last resting place. For the good of yourselves and your children you had better erect some simple monument over their remains and engrave thereon: "an unknown Red Man lies buried here."[35]

With the understanding that his remarks were often reported in the popular press, it is not surprising that Pokagon spoke in the racialized terms of the dominant culture of the day. As John M. Coward has noted, the othering of American Indians by the press of Pokagon's time was a function of the ideology and hegemonic discourse of the era. The press did not transmit "new" news, but rather confirmed what was already expected.

> News about Indians was created, organized and received in ways that supported Euro-American ideas and challenged or ignored native ones. . . . Social actors (such as Indians) who deviate from social norms . . . are punished or degraded by the media. By creating and organizing the news based on dominant values and assumptions . . . the media has ideological power—the power to define the terms of everyday life. Indian representation in the papers helped create and confirm a social order as well as a racial hierarchy. . . . Indians were explained in the press ethnocentrically; that is, not by their own standards . . . but by those of the press and its readers.[36]

Anyone who would paint Pokagon as a "docile Indian" should take note that he "talked back to civilization," as Frederick J. Hoxie has termed it.[37] In the second half of the nineteenth century, the discourse in America changed from the imperative to "civilize" the Indian to proving the racial inferiority of Indians.[38] Pokagon challenged this ideological turn with his own counter-hegemonic responses.

Simon Pokagon at the Chicago World's Columbian Exposition

During his lifetime, Pokagon certainly left his imprint on the citizens of Chicago. The birch bark booklet *The Red Man's Greeting*, sold by Pokagon on the Midway Plaisance during the World's Columbian Exposition, garnered him much publicity.[39] That little booklet was also a featured item on the fairgrounds at the Michigan State Exposition Building.[40] Years later, a book collector wrote,

> Today every book dealer and antique shop proprietor in Southwestern Michigan is searching for these little booklets to satisfy the demands of their customers. . . . From the publication of the booklet until the end of the Fair, Simon Pokagon and his brethren were recognized. Indeed, Pokagon was lionized and won a fame that was to endure for years after that event.[41]

Another example of Pokagon's ongoing connection to Chicago is an article published in *Harper's Magazine* in 1899 on the taking of Fort Dearborn in 1812 by the Potawatomi. Simon Pokagon was not present at the battle; however, he alludes to traditional tribal accounts of the attack. The article, titled "The Massacre of Fort Dearborn at Chicago—Gathered from the Traditions of the Indian Tribes engaged in the Massacre, and from the published Accounts," reflects his desire to contribute to a fuller understanding of the early history of Chicago.[42] In it, he gives a strong rebuttal to the notion that members of the "civilized" world behaved more humanely than "Indian Savages" during the wars to expel the Indians from their lands.

> They who call themselves civilized cry out against the treachery and cruelty of savages, yet the English generals formed a league with Tecumseh and his warriors, at the beginning of the war of 1812, with a full understanding that they were to

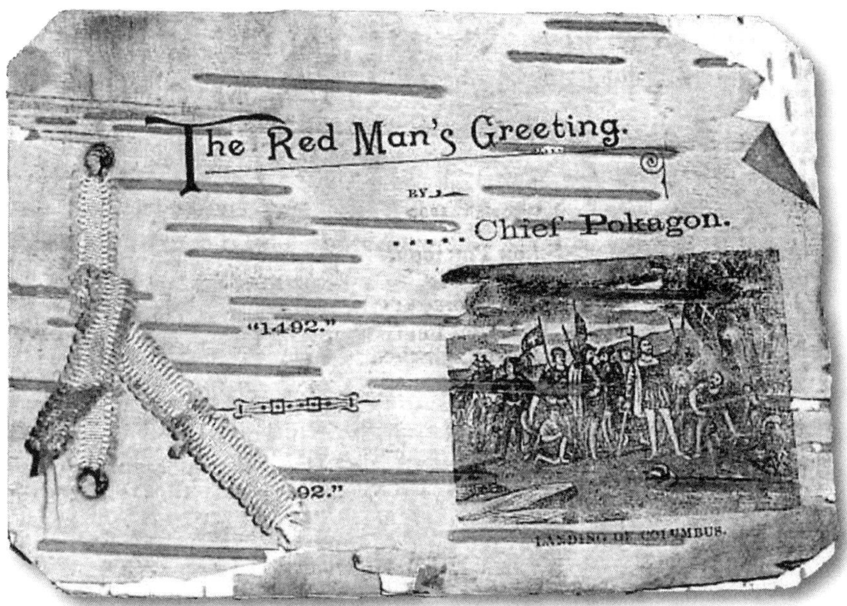

Birch bark booklet distributed by Pokagon at the 1893 World's Columbian Exposition.

FROM THE COLLECTION OF THE AUTHOR.

> take the forts around the Great Lakes, regardless of consequences. The massacre of the Fort Dearborn garrison was but one link in the chain of civilized warfare, deliberately planned and executed. Disguise the fact as the pride of the white man may, when he joins hands with untutored savages in warfare he is a worse savage than they.[43]

Shortly before his death in 1899, Pokagon completed his only novel, *Queen of the Woods*. C. H. Engle, the publisher, states in the preface that Pokagon wanted the book to be published in Hartford, Michigan, so that it would be "circulated among the white people where we have lived and are well known."[44] Multiple audiences, Native and non-Native, were intended. As the publisher of *Queen of the Woods* notes, "His [Pokagon's] greatest desire in publishing the historical sketch of his life has been that the white man and the red man might be brought into closer sympathy with each other."[45]

Authorship of *Queen of the Woods*

Some have doubted the true authorship of the novel, including some Pokagon tribal members and literary scholars; some of these have based their doubts on the remarks of Pokagon's contemporaries who were unconvinced he was able to write such a work, and the scant evidence of his purported education.[46] (The subtitle, *Queen of the Woods*, had already been used a half century earlier as a title for a poem published in *Graham's Magazine*.[47]) Some have suggested that the ghostwriter of *Queen of the Woods* was in fact Sarah Engle, the wife of Pokagon's publisher, C. H. Engle.[48] Pokagon's letters, however, available in the Chicago History Museum, the Newberry Library, the special collections of the University of Michigan and the University of Wisconsin, and the Great Lakes Branch of the National Archives in Chicago, as well as a reprint of one available in the contemporary magazine *The Arena*, reveal a man who was clearly able to write eloquently.[49] A letter to the President of the Chicago Historical Society is typical of both his writing style and his desire to leave a legacy for future Chicagoans.

> Secretary of Chicago Historical Society
>
> Dear Sir: I notice in the Chicago Tribune of Sunday that the surviving infant of Fort Dearborn is still alive—I recall that my father was a chief at that time. I take pleasure in presenting you a copy of my "Red Mans Greeting" printed on birch bark which I wrote in the years of the World's fair—Perhaps you will recall I rode in the Float of 1812 on Chicago Day and was permitted to ring the Liberty Bell in the morning and make a short address.
>
> I am getting to be an old man and wish to leave this greeting with you that it may be read by future generations.
>
> I heard my father say many times before and after he was converted to Christianity if there had been no whiskey, there would had been no Fort Dearborn massacre—I shall write of our side of that sad affair during this winter—hoping this little book will be read with the same spirit in which it is sent I remain yours truly.
>
> [signed] S. Pokagon
> Hartford Mich Dec 29 1896[50]

As a later writer noted,

It may be gratuitous to point out, also that in putting *Queen of the Woods* and his other manuscripts in order for the publisher, Pokagon doubtless had considerable editorial assistance. His handwritten letters which remain show a certain unconcern for the niceties of spelling and punctuation; and the syntax of some of his published work is not beyond reproach. . . . But many otherwise able authors have shown some deficiency in verbal mechanics; and in view of the unusual background from which Pokagon wrote, a syntactical criticism here would be picayune.[51]

According to attorney and publisher Engle, another reason for Simon Pokagon's publishing in Hartford included the fear that some whites might doubt his ability to pen the novel, deny the truth of its narrative, "or perhaps even deny its authorship."[52] In his essay *Burbank among the Indians*, artist E. A. Burbank wrote that Pokagon's autobiography (presumably *Queen of the Woods*) was started by Simon and finished by his son, Charles.

When I went to paint his [Simon Pokagon's] portrait, I drove over to his farm where I found him planting seed in the old way by walking and casting the seed on the ground. I told him of my errand, that I wished to paint his portrait. He asked how much I would pay him, and when I told him two dollars for six hours' sitting, with rest period, he refused, saying that when he worked for the government he was paid three dollars a day. He got the amount he wanted.

I told him I wanted to paint him in his Indian clothes. He said he had no Indian clothes. So I painted him as he was dressed when I met him, in his working clothes.

When it was time for him to rest he would go outdoors and read. I asked him what he was reading. He replied, "Latin." He had studied to be a priest and could read both Latin and Greek. At other times when he was resting he would be talking to some bird. He would say, "Good morning, little bird. I understand what you are saying. You are saying, 'Good morning, Pokagon.' So I say good morning to you."

He made me a present of a little book printed on birch bark and entitled, "The Plea of the Red Man." It was beautifully written. He also gave me a copy of an article on temperance, which he had written. In the article he wrote, "I cannot understand a people who can build a boat that will cross the ocean in safety and comfort, and yet cannot stop this liquor traffic."

I also met Chief Pokagon's wife, a fine old lady. She made Indian baskets, some of which I bought. Their son, Charlie, whose acquaintance I made, lived with them. I stopped with a farmer close to their home.

> Pokagon told me so much about his life and about his father and the Potawatomi Indians that I told him it was his duty to write a book on his life. He replied that it would be a big job.
>
> When I had finished his portrait and was ready to leave, I hired him to take me back to the town where I was to take passage on the boat to Chicago. As we arrived in the town (I think New Haven), I prevailed upon him to go in a store and buy the paper on which to write the story. He did so, and also promised to come and see me in Chicago. But within a few days after I had finished his portrait and bade him good-by, he passed away. He died in January, 1898. He had begun his life story and his son, Charlie, finished it after his death.[53]

Simon Pokagon actually died the following year, on January 28, 1899, so he could have had sufficient time to write the short novel/autobiography with or without the help of his son Charles. If the rest of Burbank's narrative is correct, it appears *Queen of the Woods* was the product of Pokagon (and perhaps his son Charles) rather than non-family members.[54] Another possibility, if indeed his publisher's wife transcribed the work, is that it is in the tradition of "as-told-to" autobiographies, such as *Black Elk Speaks*[55] and others, and deserves consideration as the work and voice of Pokagon rather than the editor/transcriber.[56] There is a substantial difference between ghostwriting and editorial assistance. If Simon Pokagon received only editorial assistance, or if it is a transcription, it makes *Queen of the Woods* no less his work.[57] Having read Pokagon's correspondence, I believe that the best evidence shows that he was more than capable of authoring the novel, although he may have had the assistance of a family member.

In his book *Red on Red: Native American Literary Separatism*, author Craig S. Womack includes Simon Pokagon in a review of important Indian authors, and notes that

> These are some of our ancestral voices, the pioneers, those who came before us whose writings paved the way for what Native authors can do today. Nineteenth-century Indian resistance did not merely take the form of plains warriors on horseback; Indian people authored books that often argued for Indian rights and criticized land theft. In addition to publishing books, many of these authors engaged in other rhetorical acts such as national speaking tours lobbying for Native rights. Their life stories, as well as their literary ideas, provide a useful study of the

Sketch of Simon Pokagon by E. A. Burbank, 1898. A painting of Pokagon by Burbank is in the Ayer Collection at the Newberry Library in Chicago. FROM THE COLLECTION OF THE AUTHOR.

> evolution of Native thought that has led up to contemporary notions of sovereignty and literature.[58]

The evidence for lack of authorship is scant, and was only suggested decades after his death. As an early Indian author at a time when Indians were assumed incapable of literary ability, it may be that the denial of Pokagon's authorship results from a syndrome that Philip J. Deloria has characterized as one consequence of being an "Indian in an unexpected place."[59] Whether intentional or not, those who argue that Pokagon's work is not his run the risk of silencing a Native writer and his voice.[60]

Queen of the Woods: Preserving Community through Storytelling

The first time I held a copy of *Queen of the Woods* left an imprint on me that has never gone away. I made a note of the experience in my own journal, which I share here.

> Holding history in my hands, a portal to a shared past, time speaks to me through this book—its leaves, like worn and delicate sheets of birch bark—its talking pages pass on traditions as I turn them, as I fold the covers in to keep safe the lived experiences of then and now. This small book, a treasure, a memorial to my ancestors, a monument to the resiliency of a people, a tribe—ironically, unexpectedly, and eloquently, written by a man despised by some of his own people, yet embraced by the wealthy of his day. This man insinuated himself and his work into the high culture of America and there recorded our survival. Images and stories of a past I never knew, a title in a language I am ashamed I do not speak. I feel the slight heft of the book in my hands and wonder how many people have read its narrative of love, tragedy, redemption, and survival. How far has it traveled, before, like its author, it returned home?
>
> It is a small book—and he was a man of small physical stature. The cover is burgundy faux Moroccan leather with gold gilt lettering, a mixture of the imitation with the real—replicating in some ways Simon Pokagon's life. A faded inscription inside indicates it was sold some decades ago by a Los Angeles rare books dealer. The bookseller attached a note inside the front cover of the copy I hold in my hand: "This little book is rare, and has become a collector's item, but it has the fault of many such books, it is 'poorly put together.' This is not the fault of the author nor publisher, since his friend, Engle, published it after Pokagon's death."
>
> There is an irony in the book being a collector's item, as Pokagon died penniless. Where did the book go from there? Did it end up on a bookshelf, in an attic, or box? One day, through an online auction, I retrieve it. Now I hold it, ponder its existence, and listen for the memories it holds within.[61]

Like Pierre Nora's sites of memory, *Queen of the Woods* can be considered an attempt to solidify our memory of the past.[62] It is a history Pokagon wishes us to remember, and as such, *Queen of the Woods* serves as an important "site of memory"—a memorial to his people. The fact that Chicago is where he chose to have it sold and exhibited reflects the importance that Pokagon placed on Chicago as a venue for recognition.

The publisher's notes to *Queen of the Woods* include a review of Simon Pokagon's life, his attendance at the World's Columbian Exposition in 1893, his work on behalf of his people, notable historical events such as his visiting Presidents Lincoln and Grant and meeting with Mayor Carter Harrison of Chicago on behalf of the tribe, and the publication of several of his booklets on birch bark. Republished from a local Chicago paper of the day is a review of his first booklet:

> On sale at the American Indian village on the Midway is a little booklet with its leaves and cover made of birch bark. It was written by Simon Pokagon. Its title is "The Red Man's Greeting." . . . No one can read it without realizing the other side of the Indian Question.[63]

Among friends and foes alike, few argued at the end of the nineteenth century for a multicultural respect for Indian peoples and cultures. The "question" most often debated, condensed into the "Indian problem," was whether Indians were capable of improvement, civilization, and assimilation, or just a lost cause. Given that these were the two alternatives being discussed, Pokagon advocated for the education and improvement of his people in lieu of abandonment. This made him very popular among the non-Native Chicagoans who saw themselves as a liberal and enlightened elite. In the parlors at Chicago's Palmer House Hotel, he spoke to an assembled group of wealthy Chicagoans as to the necessity of giving "the educated Indians of the race" an opportunity to attend the World's Columbian Exposition and hold a congress of their own. Pokagon argued that Indians were not the savages caricatured by the war whoops and battle dances performed daily on the Midway Plaisance.

Queen of the Woods concludes with an enumeration of Pokagon's many writings, a commentary on his humble character, and the note that he was called "the red-skin bard, the Longfellow of his race, and the grand old man."[64] Of the two hundred and sixty pages of the 1899 edition of *Queen of the Woods*, somewhat less than two hundred were written by Pokagon; the rest are preface, publisher notes, images, and appendices. Plates inserted after the notes show two images of Pokagon. According to the publisher, the first, a painting, is a representation of how he appeared on Chicago Day.[65] Showing Pokagon dressed in what appears to be Native clothing with an eagle-feather bonnet, it is contradicted by the photographs and other descriptions at the time.[66] On the facing page is a photographic image of Pokagon, dressed in a suit and tie with a ribbon boutonnière, as he appeared at the 50th anniversary of the founding of the city of Holland, Michigan.[67] In conversation with each other, the images convey a theme of *Queen of the Woods*—that Pokagon was a cultural broker able to bridge the worlds of the Native and the non-Native in Chicago. Seeing an Indian dressed like any other Midwestern businessman, one suspects, must have come as a surprise to readers expecting a more "rustic" persona. Together, the images suggest that the author could don whichever identity he preferred—"savage" or "civilized." The ability to cloak himself in multiple identities seemed easy and fluid. Such "situational identities," as Michael Witgen terms them, have had a long history among Great Lakes Indians.[68]

The novel begins with Simon's return from Twinsburg (Ohio) Academy, where he has attended school. During the course of his adventures, Simon meets up with his friend Bertrand. They go hunting and fishing, and head north to an abandoned *wigwam*. While there, Simon makes a birch bark canoe and wears a birch bark cap. *Wigwas* and structures of birch bark figure significantly in the storyline—when Pokagon returns to find his beloved Lonidaw, he comes to her *wigwam*, and they plan a visit to an old man at his *tipi*. Before leaving, they take a birch bark box filled with salt for the elder. He describes the old man's *tipi*/home as a round stockade, about sixteen feet across the base and twelve feet high; the posts leaned inward, leaving "paw-kwe-ne" (a smoke-hole) at the top. Small white birch bark boxes ("wig-was-si ma-kak-ogons") then figure in the teachings he receives from an Odawa elder named Ash-taw.[69]

Wigwams and lodges appear frequently in the narrative as *home* and are material evidence of lived experience. When Simon and Lonidaw marry, he travels to the *wigwam* of his bride. Together they build their new home, a *wigwam* constructed of bark and poles. There they keep their birch canoe for fishing and gathering wild rice. Years later, on the day before their son Olondaw leaves for school, Lonidaw dreams of the *wigwam* of her youth. Three years later the young man returns to their *wigwam* a drunkard. The drowning of their daughter Hazeleye, when her birch canoe capsizes, exacerbates the tragedy of their son returning as an alcoholic. Lonidaw is almost lost, too, when she tries to save her daughter from the water, and Simon is just able to carry his barely breathing wife back to their *wigwam*. Lonidaw dies from grief as Simon wanders the trail to the *wigwam* and watches the fireflies gathering to guide his wife to her spirit home. Later he passes their formerly happy home/*wigwam* but is unable to enter. When a storm comes, he retreats to the home. "Quickly springing to my feet, I rushed into the *wigwam* to avoid the storm without, only to arouse the slumbering storm of sorrow in my soul." Simon pours out all his sorrow to God in that same *wigwam*.[70]

These tragedies, and remembering his commitment to his dying wife to fight against alcohol for the rest of his life, give Pokagon the incentive to carry on. "I am broken down by loss, care and anxiety, feeling that the *wigwam* of my soul is unlocked; that the latch-string has been pulled; that life's latch has been lifted, leaving the door ajar."[71] In deciding what to do, and whether to give up, he asks, "Shall I go forth out of the *wigwam* to join 'nos-sog' (my fathers) and 'nin-gog' (my mothers) to the land beyond"? Yet he is determined, while crossing the "threshold of life's open door," that he will "battle the demon of alcohol that has a chokehold on his race." In *Queen of the Woods*, *wigwams* are more than mere domiciles; they represent structures of youth, leisure, adventure, marriage, family, happiness, trouble, the soul, passages, and containers of memories both good and bad. They convey to the reader a sense of who Potawatomi people are and how they have lived in the past. The insertion of the Potawatomi language into the text of *Queen of the Woods* does the same work. Such references that touch upon memories have the ability to remind the reader that a civilized people occupied Chicago long before the coming of non-Natives. This is particularly important because Pokagon argues at the end of his novel for reconciliation between Natives and non-Natives, as well as the inclusion of Indian peoples in the mainstream of the non-Native world.

As Womack has suggested, Pokagon did not limit his rhetoric to his literary endeavors. About a year before publication of *Queen of the Woods*, Pokagon spoke at the Liberty, Indiana, Hall of the Improved Order of Red Men (IORM), a non-Native fraternal organization dedicated to memorializing the American Indian, at least in imagery and faux ceremonies.[72] At one time a flourishing fraternal organization, the IORM was organized throughout the United States, and represented a peculiar nineteenth-century interactive memorial to Indians in its own way. On January 7, 1898, at the Gem Opera House, Pokagon lectured to the assembly of "Red Men," as members called themselves. Quick to remark on the state of "the vanishing Indian," Pokagon nonetheless also admonished the IORM members that evening:

> Historians have recorded of us that we are vindictive and cruel, because we fought like tigers when our homes were invaded and we were being pushed toward the setting sun. When white men pillaged and burned our villages and slaughtered our families, they called it honorable warfare; but when we retaliated, they called it butchery and murder. . . . But let Pokagon ask, in all that is sacred and dear to mankind, why should the red man be measured by one standard and the white man by another?[73]

In his remarks at that IORM meeting, Pokagon noted that churches, schoolhouses, cottages, and castles had replaced the cabins and *wigwams* of his youth.[74]

Improved Order of Red Men (IORM) leaflet, ca. 1900. FROM THE COLLECTION OF THE AUTHOR.

Throughout his speaking and writing career, Simon Pokagon made clear his conviction that while Indians were "different" from whites, they were no less civilized. While there is no direct evidence, it is fair to speculate that Simon Pokagon made similar arguments for the humanity of Indian peoples while speaking throughout "Chicagoland." In fact, in 1902, the Improved Order of Red Men opened a chapter in the Englewood neighborhood of Chicago and named it the "Pokagon Tribe No. 158," presumably after Simon Pokagon.[75]

Early in his essay on the Algonquin language in *Queen of the Woods*, Pokagon laments the loss of the Potawatomi language by Indian children and notes that the text of the novel was first written in the Algonquin language before being translated to English. He explains the reason for leaving some of the former in the text. "I have retained such Indian words and expressions in 'Queen of the Woods,' as *monuments* along the way" (emphasis added). His use of such language—like his use of birch bark to wrap his early essays, and his obvious pride in Potawatomi traditional material culture—supports his argument that the Potawatomi deserved better than ossification and marginalization. *Queen of the Woods* closes with a section devoted to the skill and artistry of Indian women in working birch bark and black ash into baskets and other items for the tourist trade.[76] In the preface to *Queen of the Woods*, there is a poem, presumably by Pokagon, emphasizing the intersections of materiality, dwelling, and community.

> Is not the red man's wigwam home
> As dear to him as costly dome?
> Is not his loved one's smile as bright
> As the dear ones of the man that's white?
> Freedom—this selfsame freedom you adore—
> Bade him defend his violated shore.

The frequent references to birch bark as both building material and home point to the themes of construction and the reinforcing of community. *Queen of the Woods* is a language lesson, a Victorian melodrama, and a temperance tract; but it is also a story of home and of family and identity in ways that could allow Indians to be different yet recognizable to a predominately non-Native society.[77]

Reading Embedded Meanings

Simon Pokagon's work, like all narratives, is constructed of texts and subtexts. While the text of *Queen of the Woods* might now be viewed as an overwrought Victorian-style lament on the future for Indians, Lucy Maddox argues that these kinds of "performances" by Native intellectuals must be read within their historical context.[78] It can also be argued that the subtext of *Queen of the Woods* is also a plea for pity, itself a convention of Neshnabek rhetoric,[79] and a prodding of the conscience of the nation to treat others more humanely. Pokagon's many references to an iconic material of the Indian (birch bark) and the emphasis in *Queen of the*

Woods on the Algonquin language provide a text of Native authenticity, while the subtext is one of materiality and humanity. The debate over the future of Indians—whether they are hopelessly primitive savages or are capable of assimilation into the dominant culture—is another text of *Queen of the Woods*, while the subtext is one of persistence and survival. Pokagon's references to hostilities between Natives and settlers provide a text that "we were no more savage than you," while the subtext can be read as "this was our land and we had a right to defend it." The many references to Pokagon's attendance at the World's Columbian Exposition provide a text that says it was only fair to include the original inhabitants of Chicago in the festivities. The subtext is that "Indians are Americans too and entitled to the same rights, opportunities, and privileges as others." The extensive collection of reprinted obituaries of Simon included in the appendix to *Queen of the Woods* signals the importance of Simon Pokagon as a man worthy of memorial.

What do Potawatomi peoples—who, according to their oral histories, are descendants of builders of great monuments, the mound builders—do when the mounds and earthworks have been flattened and planted, when the landscape has been unrecognizably altered in their lifetimes? Where does "the wisdom sit"[80] when the countryside is carved into small agrarian farms, the forest is clear-cut, and the wetlands drained?[81] For instance, in Berrien County, Michigan, the location of Leopold Pokagon's village in 1833, half of the original eighty-seven lakes were drained to make arable land by the end of the nineteenth century.[82] Ironically, two of the lakes drained had been named after the Potawatomi: Pottawatomie Lake, located in what is now New Buffalo Township, at one time three miles long and a mile wide, and Topinabee Lake, in Bertrand Township. They were subsequently filled and used as farm fields by the descendants of settler families.[83] Grain, timber, and farmland were key factors in the mass migration of settlers into the region. William Cronon describes the events that took place at the mouth of the Chicago region after the arrival of settlers. Profound changes in the physical, cultural, political, and social landscape occurred throughout the ancestral lands of the Pokagon Potawatomi.

> Chicago is a curiously disembodied place, isolated from its natural landscape much as its inhabitants are isolated from each other . . . natural and cultural landscapes began to shade into and reshape one another. In that mutual reshaping the city's history begins.[84]

Pokagon expressed great dismay that this reshaping did not include the Potawatomi people. He wrote:

> The cyclone of civilization rolled westward; the forests of untold centuries were swept away; streams dried up; lakes fell back from their ancient bounds; all our fathers once loved to gaze upon was destroyed, defaced, or marred, except the sun, moon and starry skies above, which the Great Spirit in his wisdom hung beyond their reach. Still on storm cloud rolled, while before its lightning and thunder the beasts of the field and fowls of the air withered like grass before the lame—were shot for love of power to kill alone, and left, the spoil upon the plains. Their bleaching bones, now scattered far and near, in shame declare the wanton cruelty of pale-faced men. The storm, unsatisfied on land, swept our lakes and streams, while before its clouds of hooks, nets of glistening spears, the fish vanished from our shores like the morning dew before the rising sun. Thus our inheritance was cut off, and we were driven and scattered as sheep before the wolves.[85]

His novel works as a testimonial to the continued struggle he foresaw for us as Pokagon Potawatomi Indian peoples to be accepted as equals.

A Moving Memorial

Simon Pokagon's rhetoric, and his mission to maintain an Indian presence in America, was not limited to his writings. As previously noted, his public appearances were also a part of maintaining a Potawatomi presence in Chicago, most notably as a featured speaker at the 1893 World's Columbian Exposition (WCE) in Chicago. There he presented the mayor of Chicago, Carter H. Harrison, with a facsimile of a deed to Chicago wrapped in birch bark. The mayor got into the spirit of the festivities by emphasizing his own American Indian ancestry. According to one reporter,

> Mayor Carter H. Harrison was an Indian yesterday as he rang the great Columbian Liberty Bell for Chicago day. At least he said he was descended from Pocahontas and the crowd cheered as the man of many nations made the utterance. . . . Before the Mayor made his address he was handed the treaty signed by the father of Chief

> Pokagon of the Pottawatomie tribe. It represented the transfer of 994,000 acres of land at 3 cents an acre, the money for which Chief Pokagon has not received. It was this fact that led the Mayor to reiterate his Indian genealogy.[86]

On a day designated as "Chicago Day," October 9, 1893, over 700,000 fairgoers crowded into the Exposition.[87] Pokagon apparently used this very public opportunity to advocate for the payment of treaty monies owed his people. The festivities included the noontime ringing of the Liberty Bell by Pokagon:

> The venerable chieftain was not able to tug the clapper of the big bell and assistance had to be rendered. It was a double ringing, for on the opposite side of the bell from Chief Pokagon was a husky Indian warrior, decked in his war paint and eagle feathers. He was John Young, the Indian whose father is said to have named Chicago. . . . Thus it appears that the descendant of him who ceded the title to the site of Chicago and the son of the red man who gave the city its name celebrated together the anniversary and the glory of Chicago day at the Exposition.[88]

Among other Exposition activities, Pokagon served as an honorary umpire of an afternoon lacrosse game at the Stock Pavilion Amphitheater featuring Iroquois and Potawatomi players. Before the crowd on that day, Pokagon, dressed in a suit like most of the white men around him, was distinguished by a feathered cap. A photograph of Simon from that day survives. He appears dignified and at ease. In the press, he was described as quiet and self-possessed, with a "look of sadness in his face, showing . . . the weight of years . . . pressed into a moment of time."[89]

On that October morning, nearly 75,000 people crowded into Terminal Plaza at the fair to listen to the Indian man. During his speech, he railed against the evils of alcohol and its devastating effect upon Indians before concluding that his people needed to put aside their tribal allegiances in favor of U.S. citizenship. His calls for temperance were not unlike those of the great Seneca leader Handsome Lake, nearly a century earlier. His wish for the shedding of tribal identity in favor of something greater was not unlike the admonishments of Tecumseh and Tenskwatawa earlier in the century. He never told Indians to stop being Indian; he tried to clear a path for their future.

> What can be done for the best good of . . . our race? Our children must learn that they owe allegiance to no clan or power on earth except these United States . . .

Simon Pokagon at the World's Columbian Exposition, 1893. Pokagon is to the far right. Next to him is Emma Sickels. To the right of Sickels is John Young, the other American Indian invited to the podium that day. PHOTOGRAPH FROM "THE VANISHING WHITE CITY: A SERIES OF BEAUTIFUL AND ARTISTIC VIEWS OF THE GREAT COLUMBIAN EXPOSITION," *COLUMBIAN ART SERIES*, VOL. 1, NO. 12 (CHICAGO: PEACOCK PUBLISHING COMPANY, 1894). COPYRIGHT RENEWED 2007 BY THE AUTHOR, JOHN N. LOW; USE BY PERMISSION ONLY.

> [they] must be educated and learn the . . . trades of the white men . . . [then] they will be able to compete with the dominant race.[90]

Accompanying Pokagon during the day was the activist Emma Sickels. According to an account of the day, "Tomorrow afternoon at 3 o'clock the original treaty which ceded the land on which Chicago now stands to the government will be placed in Mayor Harrison's hands by Miss Emma C. Sickels, the 'woman chief' of the Indians." Sickels headed the fair's Indian Affairs Department before being dismissed for criticizing the treatment and representation of Indians at the Exposition. After her removal from the administration at the WCE, Sickels served as chair of the Indian Committee of the Universal Peace Union, an organization that was critical of the manner in which Indians were represented at the Exposition.[91] She had lobbied for Pokagon's inclusion in the fair program, and had written about the unfair treatment of Indians at residential boarding schools, and against the taking of Indian lands through the Indian Allotment Act of 1887 (Dawes Act).[92]

She also lobbied, along with Pokagon, unsuccessfully, for a congress of Indians to be held at the fair.

> There should be a full and complete delegation of North American Indians, who should have ample opportunity for presenting in their own behalf the . . . condition of their race in the development of their tribal existence and also in the line of modern thought and attainment.[93]

Pokagon had even presented Mayor Harrison with a request for two thousand dollars to help defray the costs of such a congress, arguing, "In making your people rich, we have become poor."[94] Pokagon later wrote to the mayor:

> To His Honor the Mayor: I heard with pleasure that the blood of Pocahontas flows in your veins, and as one of my people I call upon you to help the educated Indians of our great country in their efforts to celebrate this great fair. Many of my people have already come, but have found no place for them in the celebration. The land on which Chicago and the Fair stands still belongs to my people, as it has never been paid for. All we ask from Chicago is that the people help us to come and join our common country. We wish to talk for ourselves. The Pottawatomies have a message to deliver to the world.[95]

However, the congress was never held; the assassination of Mayor Harrison on October 28 and the closing of the Exposition on October 30, 1893, intervened before any assembly of Indians could be organized. Such a congress would have been a respite from the Native "primitiveness and savagery" on display at the Midway Plaisance. While Indians inside the fairgrounds proper were being represented as wards of the federal government capable of being educated,[96] references to the camp of Potawatomi on the Midway as "freaks" were yet another example of the bifurcation of Indians, and this time, rather than noble versus savage, it was a division between those deemed capable of assimilation/civilization versus those who were not.[97] The Chicago World's Columbian Exposition presented these dualities for public consumption on a daily basis. Pokagon's presence served as a third alternative to the "civilized Indians" under government control within the fairgrounds and the "savages" in Buffalo Bill's Wild West show playing just outside the Exposition.

Pokagon would finish "Chicago Day" in 1893 by riding as a special guest on the "History of Chicago" float with a replica of the Black Partridge statue.[98] The float itself became a "moving" monument to the noble savage/savage, uncivilized/civilized dichotomies in its own right. According to a news article preceding the event, Pokagon would be on this third float in the parade.

> Third float—Chicago in 1812—A Trading Post Massacre!—This float bears upon a high platform a group representing the famous Black Partridge in the act of rescuing a white woman from the savage Pottawatomie's tomahawk. This float will be furnished with Native American Indians of historical prominence, including the Pottawatomi Chief Simon Pokagon. . . . Three Cherokee maidens . . . will form a graceful group and sing an Indian song, which will form an unique and authentic historical display.[99]

A parade float with Simon Pokagon waving to the throngs while a group of Cherokee girls sing, presented as an "authentic historic display," sounds far-fetched to us now, but apparently satisfied the expectations of the gathered crowds of spectators, as well as the readers of the newspaper recording the event. Floats represent a unique form of ephemeral monument. Generally constructed for a specific event and use, they are not intended to be permanent. However, they work as monuments for their audience, presenting images that are often meant to celebrate and valorize significant events and individuals while communicating a theme that the viewer is expected to remember and embrace. Pokagon's appearance on the float presumably reflected a juxtaposition of the savage Indians of Chicago's past with the civilized Indians of Chicago of the day. According to a *Chicago Daily Tribune* article about his inclusion in the parade, the newspaper noted,

> The chief interest will lie in one of the people on the float. He is the only man yet discovered who has seen the World's Fair and does not approve of it. Further, he is a royal personage—so royal in fact, that when he came to pay an unofficial visit to the Fair he travelled just as incog as the Archduke Franz Ferdinand von Verterreich d'Este. This old personage is Simon Pokagon, 70 years of age, Chief of the very Pottawatomie Indians who massacred the settlers in 1812 and in 1833 ceded to Uncle Sam the ground on which Chicago stands. But Chief Pokagon's title to fame does not rest upon his illustrious birth. In the vicinity of his residence, Hartford, Mich., he is known as the "Redskin poet."[100]

During his lifetime, in act and deed, this man represented a refusal of Indians generally, and the Pokagon Potawatomi specifically, to be pushed to the sidelines.

Text and Geography

We might think of landscapes as documents that are written upon, and overwritten, by subsequent inhabitants. The landscape can be a story that both consciously and unconsciously conveys what is important to a people. Monuments form chapters in that story. They have overt, covert, and alternate readings as they espouse, advocate, attest, contest, bear witness, and write/rewrite history.[101] In 2006, the Missaukee Earthworks in Michigan were identified as a three-dimensional monument, created by the Indigenous inhabitants of the era, to record and celebrate "Bear's journey" in delivering the Midewiwin set of spiritual beliefs and ceremonial practices to the people. Prior to contact with Europeans, this was a site extensively traveled to by regional residents. After contact, the ability to travel to the earthworks was disrupted, and the Indigenous peoples of the area responded by recording the story of Bear's journey on birch bark scrolls. From storytelling to mounds to birch bark scrolls, from books printed on birch bark to books constructed like others of the dominant culture—each was a progression in the ways in which Potawatomi history and memories have been preserved and passed on.

Like the mound builders before him, Pokagon was an architect building structures of community—in his writings. As its author struggled with the impulses both to be proudly Indian and to hide in plain view, his *Queen of the Woods* presented a public and positive image of what it was to *be* Indian. It also articulated the hurdles facing the Potawatomi, and challenged their exclusion from the rest of American society. Simon Pokagon's writing down of what he thought was an important story had historical precedent; he continued the tradition of transferring memories and memorials of monumental size, transforming them into narratives capable of being carried and shared as opportunity allowed. The stories embedded in the mounds of the ancestors were supplanted with birch bark scrolls inscribed with the history and origins of the people. Leather-bound books replaced birch bark scrolls as the medium. *Queen of the Woods* is the sharing of tradition and knowledge in response to changes in the social, political, cultural, and physical landscapes of America.

Although there were preliminary plans to bury Pokagon in Chicago, after his death in 1899, he was instead interred in a grave next to his beloved wife, in Hartford, Michigan. When others question his motives and his loyalty to the Pokagon Potawatomi, I think it is important to note that he chose to be buried among his people. In the end, he never left us, and his grave is maintained by his descendants to this day.

Simon Pokagon's picture is displayed in many of the tribal offices of the Pokagon Band of Potawatomi Indians today, including the Tribal Council Chambers. *Queen of the Woods* was republished by the Pokagon Potawatomi tribal council in 2008. It is unknown how many tribal members have read the new edition, yet its republication indicates that the Pokagon Potawatomi community is embracing its prodigal son as it repositions itself on the social, political, and cultural map of the United States. The original publication of *Queen of the Woods* in 1899 reflected the use of the prevalent method of communication of the dominant culture, and taking it captive, adopting it, and indigenizing it before returning it back to the mainstream for consideration. Its republication by the tribe reflects a continued effort to do the same, and a renewed pride in the novel itself. This is not to suggest that all Pokagon Potawatomi view Simon Pokagon and his literature in a favorable light, or that maintaining a distinctly Indian identity is important to all of them. However, these beliefs are held by a significant portion of the community, and these reconnections to the Pokagon legacy are arguably fundamental to the community that bears his and his father's name.

Simon Pokagon certainly was a contradiction. He was not only an author, but also a leader and spokesperson for the rights and standing of Indian peoples in the United States. He was also a bit of a narcissist, a trickster, and a chameleon. I prefer to think of him foremost as a pragmatist who used his talents and celebrity status to reach a multiplicity of audiences in support of his people, and who kept the memory of the Potawatomi in Chicago alive.

CHAPTER 3

Claims Making to the Chicago Lakefront

Yankee and voyageur, the Irish and the Dutch, Indian traders and Indian agents, halfbreed and quarter-breed and no breed at all, in the final counting they were all of a single breed. They all had hustler's blood. And kept the old Sauganash hustler's uproar. . . . They hustled the land, they hustled the Indian, hustled by night and they hustled by day. They hustled guns and furs and peltries, grog and the blood-red whiskey-dye; they hustled with dice or a deck or derringer. . . . And decided the Indians were wasting every good hustler's time. Slept till noon and scolded the Indians for being lazy. Paid the Pottawattomies off in cash in the cool of the Indian evening: and had the cash back to the dime by the break of the Indian dawn. They'd do anything under the sun except work for a living, and we remember them reverently, with Balaban and Katz, under such subtitles as "Founding Fathers," "Dauntless Pioneers" or "Far-Visioned Conquerors."

—Nelson Algren, *Chicago: City on the Make*

Nelson Algren may have captured the spirit of the 1830s, an era when the majority of Potawatomi Indians were forced into signing the last of the land-cession treaties for Chicago, and were then marched west beyond the Mississippi River. But the Pokagon Potawatomi were unwilling to concede to the "hustle." At the end of the nineteenth and beginning of the twentieth centuries, utilizing a system of justice created by non-Natives and deploying legal strategies based upon making land claims grounded in treaty rights, the Pokagon Potawatomi fought for possession of ancestral lands along the Chicago lakefront. Not only did they seek to maintain a presence in Chicago; they actually sought to retain a part of the city for themselves. Although the claim ultimately failed, it is indicative of the importance of Chicago to the Pokagon Potawatomi community and their willingness to risk public ridicule, or worse, in order to advance their desire to remain a significant stakeholder in the city of Chicago.

I should explain that there were several reasons for my interest in the Potawatomi lakefront claim, which may also reveal some biases on my part. First, the case involves the history and leadership of the Indian community to which I belong. Secondly, I have a substantial interest in matters involving sovereignty and treaties. Lastly, I find the lakefront land claim compelling because of its intersections, for me, of the oral traditions of my tribe, the legal traditions in which I was schooled, and the traditions that I have been immersed in since my time in academia. I grew up hearing stories from my elders that included an account of how "we," the Potawatomi, had been cheated out of the Chicago lakefront. The narrative was one of a great injustice that had been done to the tribe, and how our tribal leaders had taken our claim "all the way to the U.S. Supreme Court." The story concluded with how justice had been denied us; that wrongly and unfairly, others were on our lakefront land in Chicago. The story always ended with speculation about how life would be for us, "if only . . ." These stories were a part of the oral tradition of my family and our tribe. My legal education taught me that lawsuits could be complicated things, difficult for lay people to decipher. What appear to be losing cases to persons not trained in the law might be winners, and vice versa. Although seemingly "frivolous" cases do not often make it to the Supreme Court, still this case lives on in the collective memories of the Pokagon Potawatomi community. Nonetheless, the matter slipped into my subconscious, pushed into the back of my mind by the many concerns and demands of life that took precedence.

While I was at the University of Chicago beginning in 1999, and upon the advice of my mentor, Professor Raymond Fogelson, I began to read more carefully what ethnohistorian James Clifton had written about the "frivolity" of a Pokagon claim to the Chicago lakefront. Frankly, Clifton's conclusions did not convince me. I considered his assertion that the claim was faulty because "the lands involved did not exist during the treaty era at all." Oddly, this argument had little bearing on the outcome of the case itself, which hinged, for the Supreme Court, on the nature of the Potawatomi possession, or ownership, of the Chicago lands. So it seems at the very least, the Potawatomi claim merits serious reconsideration. After all, the Oneida of New York had successfully pursued their land claims in County of Oneida v. Oneida Indian Nation, 470 U.S. 226 (1985). Water rights of a tribe to Pyramid Lake had been protected in Pyramid Lake Paiute Tribe of Indians v. Morton, 354 F. Supp. 252 (1972). The Passamaquoddy successfully sued the federal government to force it to pursue legal action against the State of Maine for the recovery of tribal lands that were improperly taken in 1794; Joint Tribal Council of Passamaquoddy Tribe v. Morton, 528 F.2d 370 (1975). In a long line of treaty rights cases beginning in the 1970s, the Ojibwe had successfully secured their usufructuary rights to hunt, fish, and gather, and those tribal leaders were rightfully acknowledged for their vision.[1] To understand the claim to the shoreline of Chicago, I also needed to learn more about the city.

A Brief Excursion into Chicago

Chicago, situated at the mouth of the Chicago River on the shores of Lake Michigan, is the third largest city in the United States, with a population within the city limits of more than two and a half million people as of the 2010 U.S. Census.[2] From its beginnings, it was a city of ambitions and aspirations.[3] Located in what is now the State of Illinois, it serves as an economic center of the Midwest, and the surrounding population exceeds nine million. The name Chicago probably comes from *Eschiigwa* or *Chicagou*, which in the language of the Potawatomi Indians refers to the "place of wild onions" or "skunk."[4] The area was likely so named because of the smell of ramps or marshland onions, leeks, or garlic that used to cover it.[5]

Historically an area of intertribal traverse and commerce, by the late eighteenth century the Chicago region was primarily Potawatomi territory. In 1795, the Treaty of Greenville, between the United States and the Indians of the southern Great Lakes region, provided for a six-square-mile area at the mouth of the Chicago River for construction of an American fort. In 1803, Fort Dearborn was built.[6] Jean Baptiste du Sable, a Haitian man of African descent, is acknowledged as the first non-Native resident and a founder of contemporary Chicago.[7] Du Sable married Kittahawaa, a Potawatomi Indian woman from a prominent family, and established a fur-trading business in 1779. By 1837, the city was incorporated, and from the beginning, its location near the southern edge of Lake Michigan made it a transportation hub and population magnet. Early American settlers included its first mayor, William Ogden, and one of its most prominent early entrepreneurs, John Kinzie. According to historian Colin G. Calloway, the canal constructed in 1848 connecting the Chicago and Illinois Rivers made travel possible from the Gulf of Mexico to the Atlantic Ocean via the Mississippi and St. Lawrence Rivers, and made Chicago "the fulcrum of the major east-west and north-south transportation axes serving the interior of the continent."[8] This continued with railroads, and Chicago became a center for nationwide distributors and retailers, including Montgomery Ward, and Sears, Roebuck & Company.[9]

Lake Michigan was not only a source of food and route of travel but also a primary source of fresh water for city residents. As the population grew, the lake water near the city became polluted from the waste being dumped into the Chicago River. The city solved that problem by engineering the reversal of the flow of the river in 1871.[10] Human manipulation of the geography was by then nothing new to Chicago; it had become a hallmark of the urban landscape of Chicago. Speaking of Chicago and other large cities of the American West, historian William Cronon notes,

> The land might have been taken from Indians, its profits might sometimes have been expropriated by absentee landlords, its small farmers might on occasion have suffocated beneath a burden of accumulating debt, but much of what made the land valuable in the first place had little to do with the exploitation of people. The exploitation of nature came first.[11]

Chicago was rich in opportunity and resources ripe for the picking, and economic development was the unofficial motto of the citizenry. By 1871, when much of the city burned in the Great Chicago Fire, the city had grown to a population of over 300,000. After the fire, the rebuilding of the city gave it the atmosphere of a boomtown.

Because of its location in the center of the nation's heartland, yet with the ability to engage in international shipping, Chicago sustained substantial economic growth throughout the first half of the twentieth century.[12] Ships and railroads crowded its lakefront while commerce and the business of doing business occupied the energies of its inhabitants, rich and poor.[13] Chicago was the location of the Pullman Palace Car (rail car) Company and the site of the social experiment of the company town named Pullman. The city exhibited considerable civic pride and investment, including an elaborate city parks system as well as hosting two world's fairs within forty years.

However, it was also a place of substantial labor unrest, including the 1886 strike by the Knights of Labor, one of the first national unions; the infamous Haymarket Riot on May 4 of the same year; and the Pullman rail car strike of 1894, led by labor activist—and later International Workers of the World (IWW) leader and Socialist Party presidential candidate—Eugene Debs.[14] The city wrestled with the misuse of both its resources and its residents during this period. For the latest residents of Chicago, this was a "new world" and the opportunity to "get it right." As geographer Yi-Fu Tuan points out,

> What they [the early immigrants to the United States] really wanted they could have, namely, a participatory form of governing—the right to shape their own destiny. The meaning of landscape (that is, land shape) had subtly shifted; the emphasis was on the shaping of a place into something far better than the one they had left. . . . Ironically, this desire to create a new, utopian community [included] cutting down not only trees but Indians in the process.[15]

The exploitation of nature *and people* is an undercurrent throughout the narrative of the Pokagon Potawatomi land claims. Landscapes, like books with layers of pages, are written and rewritten; when read, landscapes have a multiplicity of meanings. As Donald Mitchell, an early writer in critical geography, noted,

> The degree to which landscapes are made (by hands and minds) and represented (by particular people and classes, and through the accretion of history and myth) indicates that landscapes are in some very important senses "authored." . . . The text metaphor is important, therefore, because it suggests that hegemonic productions—including landscapes—are always undermined by alternative individual and collective readings. In fact, it is the very act of reading that authors.[16]

Mapping the Potawatomi Land Claim

Maps have peculiar political and social powers. For Europeans coming to North America, mapping became a way of claims-making. Land tenure had been in a state of transition in Europe during the seventeenth and eighteenth centuries.

It was during this period, in England, that the open fields and commons of the country were enclosed and passed into private ownership.[17] The move towards the privatization of land ownership in Europe was profound.

> Private landholding added to the European penchant for scientific measurement of land and led to subtle changes in conceptualizing national territory. To cross the Atlantic, Europeans had developed precise systems for navigating distances, but the divvying up land for individual ownership made geometric knowledge even more of a necessity and gave rise to scientific land surveying as a profession. . . . By 1688, surveying had become so commonplace that John Love justified publishing yet another manual by promising to describe surveying in America as well as in England. By the start of the eighteenth century, surveying land for individual ownership had become respectable and widespread.[18]

Maps were routinely drawn by cartographers who had never set foot in North America, yet their renditions of the continent, whether accurate or not, represented an effort at legitimizing colonial claims to the region.[19] Native people had maps too, although their maps were usually based upon firsthand knowledge of the land, and were intended not only to establish territory but also to pass on knowledge and record events. Even Elmore Barce, an Indiana historian of the early twentieth century who cared little for the Potawatomi, noted (quoting a Mrs. J. H. Kinzie):

> Their knowledge of the geography of their country is wonderfully exact. I have seen an Indian sit in his lodge, and draw a map in the ashes of the Northwestern states [the Midwest] not of its statistical, but its geographical features, lakes, rivers and mountains, with the greatest accuracy, giving their relative distances, by days journeys, without hesitancy, and even extending his drawings as far as Kentucky and Tennessee.[20]

European maps are regarded as "non-indexical" in that they are standardized representations intended to be independent of the context in which they are created.[21] Indigenous maps, on the other hand, are considered "indexical" in that they are created for a particular function or reflect a certain context. Non-indexical maps are meant to be comprehendible without reference to any particular knowledge other than general cartographic conventions, although this is an ideal rather than a reality with regard to "Western" maps. In fact, the premise of standardization is the basis for an ideology of maps as "scientific" rather than "political" documents. In reality, all maps are created for a purpose and all require interpretation. As David Turnbull states, "Maps can have a variety of functions: they can make political jokes . . . they can educate and entertain . . . and they can tell lies. All maps also have a latent symbolic function, for example, legitimating and disseminating the state's view of reality."[22] Turnbull concludes,

> European maps are not autonomous. They can only be read through the myths that Europeans tell about their relationship to the land. . . . Maps, like theories, have power in virtue of introducing modes of manipulation and control that are not possible without them. They become evidence of reality in themselves and can only be challenged through the production of other maps or theories.[23]

Early maps of the thirteen colonies show the Chicago area as being within the charter of the colony of Virginia. As referenced in chapter 1, Congress enacted the Northwest Ordinance in 1787, which divided the Great Lakes region into six potential states in anticipation of their eventual settlement and admission into the Union. The first maps of the continent were often inaccurate, but it was the setting down of the topography to paper that gave the map its power, not whether it was accurate.[24] The drawing of the map itself had a performative function, one of making claim to land. When the region that became much of Illinois was ceded by the Indians in the Treaty of St. Louis (1816),[25] the United States government commenced to survey the territory. Platting a region on a map, demarcating its boundary, and publishing the results became part of the ritual of territory-taking in North America. After treaties with the Native inhabitants of Chicago had secured most of northeastern Illinois, the federal government sent surveyors to map out its new territory. According to J. B. Harley, "maps help invent space, and in fact, were an undergirding medium of state power."[26] Using the surveyor's language of metes and bounds, land cessions were dutifully recorded in both written and map form. Doing so was easy when geography did not interfere; however, it could be problematic in places where the landscape was not conducive to neat division by straight lines. Such was the case with Chicago. Because of the meandering border of Lake Michigan, the surveyors for the land-cession treaties with the Indians resorted to using the shoreline as the reference point for boundary. Similarly, the surveyor, John Wall, who completed a survey of northeast Illinois in anticipation of Illinois's admittance into statehood, could only draw an arbitrary line that ran close to the shoreline of 1821. The manipulation of maps coincided with the exploitation of the environment in the colonial project of the United States.

The genius of the Pokagon Potawatomi is that they responded by using maps—the very tools that had been used in earlier times to deprive them of their lands—in their effort to regain some of their territory.

Making a Claim beneath Raven's Wings

In 1914, the Pokagon Band of Potawatomi Indians sued the City of Chicago and other landowners for possession of the Chicago lakefront. The lawsuit arose out of a controversy over ownership of the shorefront that had been "reclaimed" by dumping fill along the lakefront and extending the city east into the lake, a process commencing after the Chicago Fire of 1871 and the need to rid the city of enormous amounts of burnt rubble. Before "The Fire," the shoreline of the city of Chicago ran roughly along what is now Michigan Avenue. Streeterville; the Gold Coast; Lincoln, Grant, and Jackson Parks; the Museum Campus; Soldier Field; the Illinois Central and the Metra lines; and Lakeshore Drive are all on landfill. The filling in and extending of the shoreline continues to this day.

James Clifton was the first, it appears, to have called the Potawatomi claim to the lakebed and reclaimed Chicago lakefront "The Sandbar Case."[27] Clifton further elaborated on the claim in his book *The Pokagons, 1683–1983*. According to Clifton,

> The origins of the Sand Bar Case (or Claim) are somewhat obscure, being neither well documented nor clearly remembered by living Pokagons. But it is plain that this audacious legal action was in large part simply another aspect of the heritage left behind him by the inimitable Simon Pokagon [son of Leopold Pokagon, the Band's negotiator and leader at the Treaty of Chicago in 1833]. Apparently, [the lawsuit] grew out of the relationship between "Chief Simon" and some lesser members of Chicago's elite, who often favored him with their hospitality.[28]

When not writing, Simon Pokagon had spent much of his time involved in tribal politics. Though no longer a leader of the Pokagon Potawatomi by the 1890s, he continued to represent himself as "chief" of the Band. In 1896, the United States Court of Claims awarded tribal members some recompense for the failure of the American government to pay monies promised in treaties in the first half

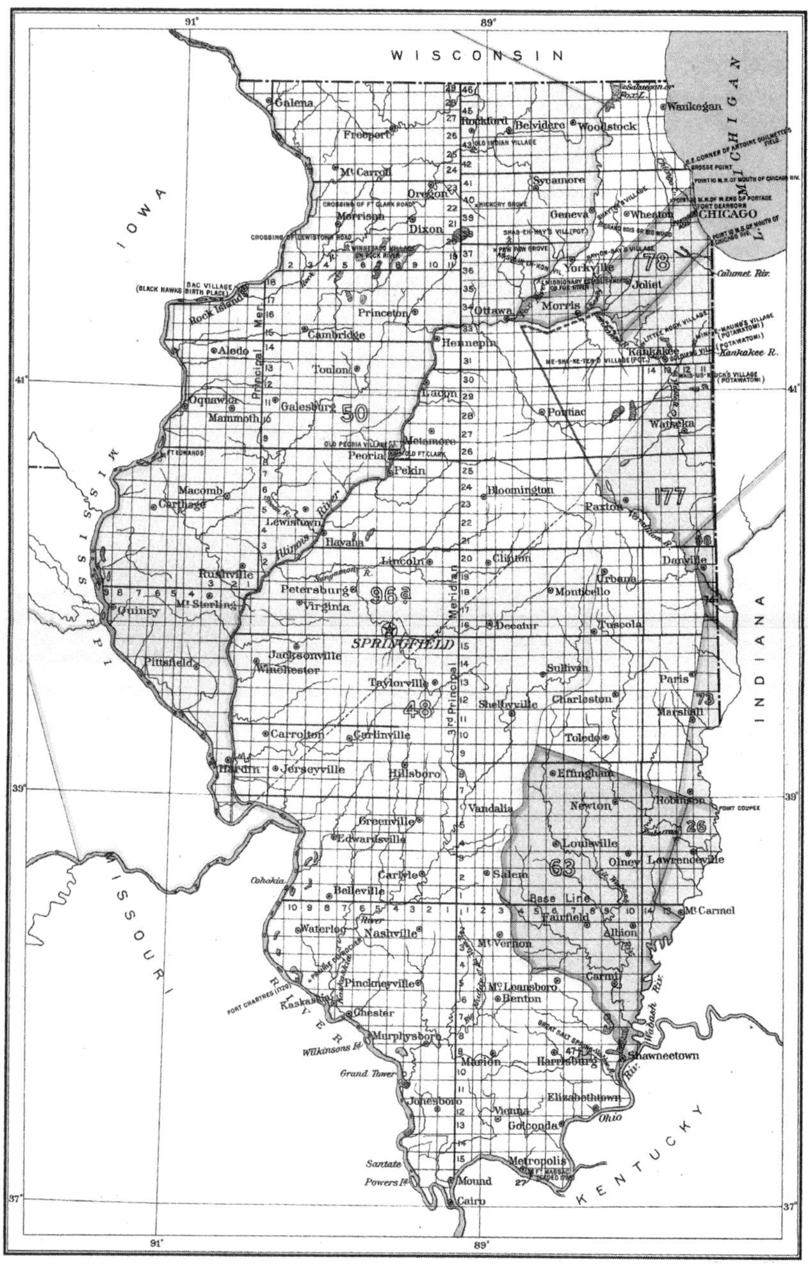

Indian land cessions in Illinois. ORIGINALLY PUBLISHED AS *INDIAN LAND CESSIONS IN THE UNITED STATES*, COMPILED BY CHARLES C. ROYCE AND PRESENTED AS PART 2 OF THE *EIGHTEENTH ANNUAL REPORT OF THE BUREAU OF AMERICAN ETHNOLOGY TO THE SECRETARY OF THE SMITHSONIAN INSTITUTION, 1896–97*. WASHINGTON, DC: GOVERNMENT PRINTING OFFICE, 1899.

of the nineteenth century with the Potawatomi.[29] On the heels of that success, Simon Pokagon was an early supporter of the land claim and commenced selling "interests" in the Chicago lakefront to non-Native real estate speculators.[30] Although he had no authority to sell such interests in this communal claim, Pokagon drew substantial attention to the cause, while making sure to cover his own day-to-day living expenses.

After Simon Pokagon's death in 1899, his son Charles attempted to assert his authority to press forward the claim to the Chicago lakefront, issuing press releases and making public announcements. During this time, the Pokagon Potawatomi also unsuccessfully petitioned Congress to recognize their claim to the lakefront.[31] In 1901, he attempted to organize an "invasion" of the Chicago lakefront, threatening to carry tribal members and their possessions to Chicago by boat or overland by truck.[32] The "invasion" turned out to be something of a publicity stunt, though it surely must have bemused many, both Native and non-Native. Although the lakefront invasion never materialized, the Potawatomi continued to lobby for their claim to the Chicago lakefront.[33] Two years later, Charles also led an encampment of Indians in Lincoln Park, at the invitation of the city, where he continued to assert the Pokagon Potawatomi ownership of the lakefront. Other Potawatomi Indian encampments were held in Chicago in 1922 and 1928.

Efforts were initiated to bring a legal action to the Court of Claims, and a trip was authorized to Washington, DC, to generate support for the claim, although many of the news reports of the day regarding the claim were unsupportive.[34] On occasion the press also reported that the Pokagon Potawatomi had sold their claim.[35] Minutes of the Business Committee of the tribe indicate that they did attempt to sell their claim on at least two occasions.[36] Correspondence after one of their meetings reflects the concern of Business Committee members that one of their own had engaged in self-dealing regarding the lakefront claim.[37] At other meetings, the committee expressed "sincere confidence in our Lake Front Claims in the vicinity of Chicago, Illinois,"[38] sent an appeal to the U.S. President,[39] decided that any committee member who became intoxicated while on tribal business would be expelled,[40] and that committee members would receive compensation equal to 1 percent of any monies recovered on behalf of the tribe.[41] They made provisions that monies received would "be paid to the heads of family [with the] exception of Orphans, [who] must have guardians,"[42] that no less "than ¼ blood be allowed into the Pokagon Band after November 12, 1901,[43] and that each member of the Band be required to pay $3.00 to the committee "for the purpose of maintaining,

Michael B. Williams ca. late 1960s (b. Jan. 29, 1881; d. March 11, 1969). FROM THE MICHAEL B. WILLIAMS PAPERS AND REPRODUCED WITH PERMISSION OF THE HEIRS.

advancing and protecting the property rights and all done and needed to be done past present and future to that end."[44]

From the minutes of the Pokagon Potawatomi Business Committee that are available, it appears that much time and effort was devoted to retaining legal counsel willing and able to prosecute their suit.[45] Finally, in 1914, the Chicago law firm of Burkhalter and Grossberg filed suit in the Federal District Court for the Northern District of Illinois, on behalf of the Pokagon Potawatomi Tribe.[46] Plaintiffs to the action were Chief John Williams; his brother and secretary of the tribe, Michael B. Williams; and the Business Committee of the Band. Defendants included the City of Chicago, the Illinois Central Railroad, the South Park Commissioners, the Lincoln Park Commissioners, the Illinois Steel Company, and the Michigan Central Railroad Company, among others.

The Pokagon lawsuit concluded more than a decade of efforts by the tribe to secure compensation for the lakebed, which was now becoming the most valuable real estate in Chicago. The Federal District Court promptly dismissed the case, and on appeal to the U.S. Supreme Court in 1917, the Indians continued to press their claims without success.[47]

The Court's decision would turn on the nature of the Indians' original ownership interest in the lakefront and whether the Indians had abandoned that space/place. According to historian Richard White, the difference between space and place is human intervention.[48] As Robert Sacks asserts,

> Place-making is essential to both our transformations and to our ideas and images of what really ought to be. Place has a particular meaning. . . . It does not refer simply to a location in space. Rather, it means an area of space that we bound and to some degree control with rules about what can and cannot take place. Place can be any size, from the small-scale of a room or a sacred grove, to the larger scale of a farm or city, to a vast territorial unit such as a nation-state or empire.[49]

Over the last two hundred years, Chicago has witnessed extraordinary intervention from its immigrant residents. Keith Basso authored an important work on the power of place in *Wisdom Sits in Places: Landscape and Language among the Western Apache*, where he noted the lack of attention scholars of the past had paid to Indigenous people's relationships to their environment. Basso concluded,

> Place-based thoughts about the self lead commonly to thoughts about other things—other places, other people, other times, whole networks of associations that ramify unaccountably within the expanding spheres of awareness that they themselves engender. . . . places also provide points from which to look out on life, to grasp one's position in the order of things, to contemplate events from somewhere in particular. . . . places consist in what gets made of them.[50]

According to the belief systems of traditional Potawatomi, Lake Michigan became a place *before* human intervention. The intervention that did take place was a profound supernatural event; after a great flood and the renewal of the world beneath the wings of the great Raven—all the ancestral lands of the Potawatomi became *place*. Thus, while non-Natives might see Lake Michigan as vacant space until it was filled in—for the Potawatomi it was already a place inhabited by the Potawatomi.[51]

From the Potawatomi perspective, there was no difference between the dry place now called Chicago and the wet place now called Lake Michigan. It was all the ancestral lived environment/area of the Potawatomi. By virtue of this supernatural intervention, for the Indian inhabitants of the region, Chicago was a *place* long before Europeans claimed it. While the "new world" to non-Natives was embodied in the discovery of the Western Hemisphere in 1492, to the Potawatomi, it had been a "new world" after the great flood described in their oral histories. Simon Pokagon wrote down this history in 1897, in an article published in the *Forum*, then a popular monthly.

The Great Flood

One very remarkable character reported in our legends, dimly seen through the mist of untold centuries, is Kwi-wi-sens Nenaw-bo-zhoo, meaning, in Algonquin dialect, "The greatest clown-boy in the world."[52] When he became a man, he was not only a great prophet among his people, but a giant of such marvelous strength, that he could wield his war-club with force enough to shatter in pieces the largest pine-tree. His hunting-dog was a monstrous black wolf, as large as a full-grown buffalo, with long, soft hair, and eyes that shone in the night like the moon. The deity of the sea saw the charming beauty of this wolf-dog, and was so extremely jealous of him, that he was determined to take his life. So he appeared before him in the form of a deer; and as the dog rushed to seize him, he was grasped by the deity and drowned in the depths of the sea. He then made a great barbecue and invited as his guests whales, serpents, and all the monsters of the deep, that they might exult and rejoice with him that he had slain the dog of the prophet.

When the seer-clown learned of the fate of his noble dog, through cunning Waw-goosh (the fox), whose keen eyes saw the deception that cost the wolf-dog his life, he sought to take revenge upon the sea-god. So he went at once to the place where the latter was accustomed to come on land with his monster servants to bathe in the sunshine, and there concealed himself among the tall rushes until the "caravan of the deep" came ashore.

When they had fallen fast asleep, he drew his giant bow, twice as long as he was tall, and shot a poisoned arrow that pierced Neben Manito, the water-god, through the heart. Neben Manito rolled into the sea, and cried, "Revenge! Revenge!" Then all the assembled monsters of the deep rushed headlong after the slayer of their king. The prophet fled in consternation before the outraged creatures that hurled after him mountains of water, which swept down the forests like grass before the whirlwind. He continued to flee before the raging flood, but could find no dry land. In sore despair he then called upon the God of Heaven to save him, when there

> appeared before him a great canoe, in which were pairs of all kinds of land-beasts and birds, being rowed by a most beautiful maiden, who let down a rope and drew him up into the boat.
>
> The flood raged on; but, though mountains of water were continually being hurled after the prophet, he was safe. When he had floated on the water many days, he ordered Aw-milk (the beaver) to dive down and, if he could reach the bottom, to bring up some earth. Down the latter plunged, but in a few minutes came floating to the surface lifeless. The prophet pulled him into the boat, blew into his mouth, and he became alive again. He then said to Waw-jashk (the musk-rat), "You are the best diver among all the animal creation. Go down to the bottom and bring me up some earth, out of which I will create a new world; for we cannot much longer live on the face of the deep."
>
> Down plunged the musk-rat; but, like the beaver, he, too, soon came to the surface lifeless, and was drawn into the boat, whereupon the prophet blew into his mouth, and he became alive again. In his paw, however, was found a small quantity of earth, which the prophet rolled into a small ball, and tied to the neck of Ka-ke-gi (the raven), saying, "Go thou, and fly to and fro over the surface of the deep, that dry land may appear." The raven did so; the waters rolled away; the world resumed its former shape; and, in course of time, the maiden and prophet were united and repeopled the world.[53]

These "earth-diver" stories, as they have come to be called, are common among many peoples around the world.[54] The "Great Flood" story has been passed on to each successive generation by storytellers and elders, the keepers of the history, to the next generation. This creation story is still told among the Pokagon Potawatomi and was well known to Potawatomi tribal members back in 1914.

The recitation by Simon Pokagon is an explanation, a teaching, of how the dry land we walk today is a gift from the Creator. The connection of the Potawatomi spiritually to land, water, and lakebed is essential to understanding why the Potawatomi would lay claim to the Chicago lakefront. The Potawatomi have an origin story that explains that until the intervention by their Creator, the world was a space covered by water. The emergence of the Chicago lakefront in the last half of the nineteenth century then was a part of the changeability of their lived environment—at times dry, and other times submerged. But space became place after the Great Flood and the reemergence of dry land. The lake and the lakebed were more than spaces of danger, desolation, or traverse, as they were for Euro-Americans. There were two divergent understandings of water and lakebed—metaphysically and, ultimately, legally—between the settlers and the Potawatomi. Lake Michigan was much more for the Pokagon Potawatomi; the lake and the lakebed are all a place—a part of life essential to our ethnogenesis, an inheritance and birthright, a resource and place of sustenance, a gift from our Creator, and a place to be honored, protected, and utilized.[55]

Custodians of the Land and Water

The Pokagon Potawatomi people were here long before Chicago became incorporated as a city, and they retain a connection to both the land and water. Preceding chapters make clear the connections of the Pokagon Potawatomi people to their environment. Maintaining the health of their environment, both physically and spiritually, continues to be a moral imperative among many Potawatomi and other Indian peoples. The Potawatomi have a long history of caring for the lake and its creatures through their actions, prayers, and ceremonies. Indeed, today the Pokagon Band has their own Department of Natural Resources, which operates a program called Ezh N'bamandamen (How We Think about Caring for the Water).[56] Concern for the land beneath Chicago and the water to its east is important to many Potawatomi tribal members.

Spirits, good and bad, inhabit the deep waters of the lake. The Potawatomi have always had specific ceremonies for the beings living in the waters of Lake Michigan; the performance of those ceremonies ensured safety and balance for all.[57] Women were, and still are, charged with the care of the water—making the necessary prayers and offerings. Ojibwe, Odawa, and Potawatomi women continue to care for the lake with prayer, ceremony, and activism. In 2008 Pokagon tribal members participated in a water walk, circumventing Lake Michigan to pray for the health of the lake. While in Chicago, they stopped periodically to offer prayers for the well-being of the lake.[58]

The traditional belief of the Potawatomi in the Underwater Panther, which resides in such waters as Lake Michigan, is well documented. In 1923, ethnologist Alanson Skinner recorded the belief in the water panther during his study of the Prairie Band of Potawatomi in Kansas; the concept predates European arrival and is general to all Potawatomi prior to contact. According to Skinner, one of these water panthers lived in Lake Michigan, and he describes what he learned in his interviews:

> There is an evil power in the water, who possesses the ability to pass through the earth as well as its natural element. This is the great horned Water-panther called Nampe'shiu, or Nampeshi'k. It is at constant war with the Thunderbirds. When one appears to a man he will become a great warrior. Such panthers maliciously drown people, who are afterwards found with mud in their mouths, eyes, and ears.[59]

In 1938, William Duncan Strong wrote of the Potawatomi conception of the water panther in his treatise on the Indian tribes of the Chicago region: "The evil power in the water was the great horned water-panther . . . who was at constant war with the Thunderbirds." James H. Howard also noted in his study of the panther that depictions are evident in carvings, pictographs, effigy mounds in the Midwest, and other representations of the being. Howard interviewed Prairie Band Potawatomi medicine man James Kagmega, in 1959.[60] Kagmega was the keeper of the Underwater Panther ceremonial bundle and told Howard that the rite was an ancient one for the Potawatomi, one essential to the well-being of the tribe. The teachings of the Underwater Panther included the following:

> We are taught that there is continual warfare between the Powers Above (Thunderbirds and their bird allies) and the Powers Below (Underwater Panthers and their snake and fish allies). Their conflicts affect the lives of the different Indian tribes here on the earth. When they are quiet and at peace, the Indians are peaceful too. When there is battle in the heavens and at the bottom of the waters, then there is warfare among mankind too.[61]

So, taking care of the lake and its beings also takes care of the world. Such ceremonial care of the environment around them reflects the strong connections the Potawatomi continue to have to their ancestral territory, including the places now called Chicago and Lake Michigan.[62] They see themselves as stewards of the water and the lands of their ancestors.

The Potawatomi and the Courts

By the end of the nineteenth century, the Potawatomi had been forced out of Chicago. In the years after the Chicago Treaty of 1833, many had been removed to west of the Mississippi, while others had fled to Wisconsin, Michigan, Mexico,

Potawatomi Indians gathered at Hartford, Michigan, September 4, 1906. According to information accompanying the photograph, Wis-Ki-Ge-Amatyuk, hereditary Principal Pipe carrier and ritual leader of the Potawatomi Indians, sits at center holding traditional Potawatomi pipes. Wis-Ki-Ge-Amatyuk was also known by his American name, John Buckshot. According to Pokagon Potawatomi tribal member Tom Topash, his great-grandmother Mary is in the white blouse next to his great-grandfather Tom Topash in the bowler hat. LIBRARY OF CONGRESS PRINTS AND PHOTOGRAPHS DIVISION, WASHINGTON, DC, 20540 LC-USZ62-132033. (PHOTOGRAPH ATTRIBUTED TO T. R. HAMILTON. SOURCE: GARY WIS-KI-GE-AMATYUK JR., 2009.)

and Canada. The Pokagon Potawatomi stayed in Michigan and Indiana, and they remain the Indian tribe closest to Chicago. The lawsuit on behalf of the Pokagons argued, in short, that none of the land that now constituted the Chicago shoreline had been ceded in any of the treaties signed by their ancestors. That land, which was at the time of the treaties either lakebed or infrequently exposed sandbar, had been filled in and had become dry land on which now stood all sorts of buildings, parks, railroads, industries, and residences. Since the Potawatomi had never ceded that lakebed and sandbar, the Indians were now asserting their ownership over the properties. The implications were stunning, to even the most casual observer. Imagine, if possible, a situation whereby essentially all the land east of Michigan Avenue would revert to the original Indigenous inhabitants. The Pokagon Potawatomi aimed to become the richest landlords in Chicago history.

Clifton summarized the plaintiff Potawatomi's arguments as essentially this: (1) The Pokagon Potawatomi, as the last remnants of the Potawatomi not removed west by the federal government, had a right to assert the claims of the Potawatomi People to the lakefront; (2) that this previously submerged lakebed (and now reclaimed land) had never been ceded by treaty by the Indians to the federal government; (3) and that since the United States had never properly acquired title to the lakefront, neither could the State of Illinois or any subsequent individual, institutions, or corporations. Therefore, these lands now above water were owned by the Pokagon Potawatomi.[63] Clifton concluded that "the brief presented and the attorneys' arguments [for the Potawatomi] were almost grotesquely faulty."

> The serious defects in this argument are apparent, which attorneys for the defendants quickly pointed out. Aside from the fact that the lands involved did not exist during the treaty era at all, the ancestors of the Michigan Potawatomi had not used, resided on, or claimed ownership of even then adjacent tracts in that period. Moreover, the ancestors of the Pokagons were not parties to the treaties in which the adjacent dry-lands were ceded, which cessions the United States negotiated with the Chippewa, Ottawa, and Potawatomi of the Illinois and Milwaukee Rivers. Thus twenty years of high hopes . . . were dashed, leaving behind only a residue of frustrations and bitterness at having been thwarted.[64]

Indeed, the United States Supreme Court finally issued its opinion on January 8, 1917. After reviewing the claims of the Potawatomi, the Court concluded that based upon previous decisions of the Supreme Court, the only property right of the Potawatomi was one of occupancy,[65] and that the Potawatomi had long ago abandoned the right to any occupancy of the Chicago lakefront.[66] But the deed to the city that Simon Pokagon delivered to the mayor of Chicago at the WCE in 1893 is described as being a facsimile of the "treaty deed" signed by his father. Delivering the deed would not constitute a giving up of the claim to the lakefront as it existed in 1893 because the deed would presumably use the metes and bounds of the original treaty along with the boundary line of the shoreline of Lake Michigan as of 1833. One could argue that by giving Mayor Harrison this deed Simon Pokagon was confirming that the Potawatomi he represented claimed a fee title to the lands of Chicago, and that by accepting the deed Mayor Harrison was acknowledging that the Potawatomi indeed had much more than mere Indian/aboriginal right of possession but rather ownership in fee. In fact, when receiving the deed, Harrison is quoted as telling the assembled crowd, "the deed comes from the original possessors—the only people entitled to it."[67] If the Potawatomi did indeed hold title in fee, it is much tougher to claim the Potawatomi abandoned ownership as opposed to "abandoning" their aboriginal right of possession. Although the Potawatomi's attorneys never made this argument in 1914–1917 during the course of the lawsuit, I think it is very helpful to getting over the hurdle that the Potawatomi never possessed any more than a possessory title to the Chicago lakefront. In his article "Simon Pokagon's Sandbar," Clifton wrote, "The [case] did not require much of the Court's time. It was promptly dismissed."[68]

Clifton asserted, "The ancestors of the Michigan Potawatomi had not used, resided on, or claimed ownership of even the adjacent tracts in that period." This assertion is dubious. I was taught by my elders that clan and village affiliations among the Potawatomi had been stronger than any tie to a particular band prior to the Chicago Treaty of 1833. According to tribal leader Michael B. Williams, Potawatomi clan relations extended into and between all of the Potawatomi bands at that time, and population and residency were very fluid.[69] To try to now limit the Potawatomi to specific territories seems to be an effort at forcing Western concepts and ideas of community and nationality onto the Potawatomi—people who lived by their own notions of residence, territory locus, and allegiance. Potawatomi villages were inter- and intratribal communities. What is more, the United States has often treated the Potawatomi as a unified nation.[70] The Potawatomi felt a tie and connection to the land on which they and their fellow Potawatomi lived. So, perhaps the Pokagon Potawatomi could claim an ownership interest, as lawyers would call it, in the lakefront of Chicago. The Pokagon Potawatomi sued on behalf of themselves and all Potawatomi peoples.

In dismissing the legitimacy of the "Sandbar Case," Clifton also said that "the ancestors of the Pokagons were not parties to the treaties in which the adjacent dry-lands were ceded," but that is clearly incorrect. The last of the treaties involving Chicago was the 1833 Treaty of Chicago. In that treaty, supplemental provisions between the United States and Leopold Pokagon's Band made the Michigan Potawatomi parties to the entire treaty in apparent recognition that Potawatomi lands were the lands of all the Potawatomi, without regard to current location or band. In addition, the Pokagon Potawatomi likely participated in the Battle of Fort Dearborn in 1812, and their blood was likely shed in Chicago on that August day. I would argue that the Chicago lakefront could rightfully be called the territory of all of the Potawatomi, including the Pokagon Band.

If the Potawatomi lawsuit had been decided in the tribe's favor, would the case now occupy a place of honor alongside other cases in which other Indian tribes successfully asserted territorial claims? The lawsuit had taken more than three years, from its filing in the Federal District Court in 1914 until its conclusion in the Supreme Court on appeal; the written arguments of the plaintiff Potawatomi were submitted on May 15, 1915, by attorney Jacob (J. G.) Grossberg. In summary, the tribe acknowledged the precedent of *Johnson v. M'Intosh*, 21 U.S. (8 Wheat.) 543 (1823), and the proposition that Indians in North America hold only a possessory interest (often call Indian or aboriginal title) in the land, and a right of occupancy pending cession of any lands to the federal government. However, the tribe argued that the Treaty of Greenville (1795) subsequently gave the Native parties to the treaty an ownership (fee) title to the land not ceded in that treaty. That meant that the Potawatomi became the landowners of much of Michigan, Indiana, and Illinois, including the Chicago region (excluding the six-square-mile parcel at the mouth of the Chicago River reserved for what would include Fort Dearborn). The lawsuit continued with the argument that all of the subsequent land-cession treaties entered into by the Potawatomi post-1795 that included the Chicago region used the then-existing shoreline of Lake Michigan as a boundary. None of those treaties ever ceded Lake Michigan. Therefore, the Potawatomi retained title to the lakebed. As it was filled in after 1871, the new fill extending the shoreline east into the lake was unceded territory and remained the property of the Potawatomi. The lawsuit sought either return of the lakefront or compensation for its taking.[71]

The legal and factual arguments of the Pokagon Band were thoughtful and thought-provoking. Tribal elders had stepped up and asserted treaty rights, and had done so in a very public and forceful way. However, it is problematic that the tribe did not actively include, as co-plaintiffs, the other bands of Potawatomi. Yet, there would have been difficulties in getting so many parties to collaborate on such a substantial venture, particularly when financial resources were very limited in that era, communication was difficult, and some of the tribes had no operating government at the time. J. G. Grossberg's grandson wrote his grandfather's biography in 1994. In it, he included a chapter about Grossberg's involvement in the "Sandbar Case." As recounted in the biography,

> One day in the year 1913 seven American Indians were ushered into J. G.'s office. The leader, Chief John Williams, explained that they represented the Pokagon Band

> of Potawatomi Nation of Indians, and they were seeking redress for the unlawful annexation of certain lands along the shores of Lake Michigan. . . . In essence, the Indians claimed that the land along the shore of Lake Michigan, upon which were built expensive residences, a steel mill, parks, and tracks, and terminals of the Illinois Central Railroad, belonged to them. They had a case. . . . J. G.'s contention was that since the treaty specified that the concession was of land westward from the Lake Michigan shoreline, when the city and the railroad filled in land east of the shoreline, they were encroaching on Indian land.[72]

During the October 1916 term of the United States Supreme Court, attorney Grossberg made his appeal in person before the Court on behalf of the Indians. The justices must have had a difficult decision to make. On the one hand, they had the legal claim of the Indians versus the millions of dollars of property belonging to railroads, park districts, steel companies, and the City of Chicago. The Supreme Court's decision was not published until 1917. The Court concluded that the Treaty of Greenville did *not* give the Native signatories a fee title to the lands they retained. Under federal law, they retained only an aboriginal/Indian title to occupy and use the land, and that right to possession had been abandoned.[73]

> We think it entirely clear that this treaty [of Greenville] did not convey a fee-simple title to the Indians; that under it no tribe could claim more than the right of continued occupancy; that under this was abandoned, all legal right or interest which both tribe and its members had in the territory came to an end.

As Nicholas K. Blomley summarizes,

> Concealed within legal thought and legal practice are a number of representations—or "geographies"—of the spaces of political, social and economic life. In much the same way the law relies in various ways on claims concerning history, so it both defines and draws upon a complex range of geographies and spatial understandings. . . . The legal representation of space must be seen as constituted by—and, in turn constitutive of—complex, normatively charged and often competing visions of social and political life under law. . . . Space, like law, is not an empty or objective category, but has a direct bearing on the way power is deployed and social life structured.[74]

With the Court's decision, the hopes of the Pokagon Potawatomi to a share of the lakefront were dashed.

The Potawatomi land claim was a collision of Indigenous versus immigrant perceptions of the geographies of possession and land tenure.[75] Attorney Grossberg wrote in his brief to the United States Supreme Court: "The future historian who will compile a history of the treatment of the Red Man by this Government is likely to come upon this case." His words were prophetic. After the Court ruled, Grossberg dryly commented, "How submerged lands can be 'abandoned' was not made clear." He further noted, "The Indian tribes were wards of the nation . . . it is difficult to see how they could have voluntarily abandoned their claim . . . the law was with me but the Court was against me."[76]

The Potawatomi claim to the Chicago lakefront deserved a second look. It received one recently. In the case of Ottawa Tribe of Oklahoma v. Sean Logan, Director, Ohio Department of Natural Resources (2009), a case decided by the Sixth Circuit Court of Appeals, the Ottawa Tribe of Oklahoma sued the State of Ohio claiming the Ohio DNR lacked the authority to regulate their fishing in Lake Erie.[77] The court sided with the State of Ohio and relied heavily upon the U.S. Supreme Court ruling in *Williams v. City of Chicago*, 242 U.S. 434 (1917). The court concluded that, as in *Williams*, the Indian tribe had never held fee title to the land, but only "Aboriginal/Indian title,"[78] the right to occupancy of the land. When the land (or water) was abandoned, the federal government was free to take control and divvy it out to the states.[79] In the *Williams* case, the Supreme Court determined the Potawatomi had abandoned the Chicago lakefront, and likewise here, the circuit court concluded that the Ottawa Tribe "abandoned" any legal interest in the lands or water of Ohio when they were removed to Oklahoma in 1831.[80] Reflecting again on the Pokagon claim to the Chicago lakefront, how does one "abandon" their claim to the lake or lakebed, since water usage is often not as obvious and active as the usage of land? Is it not enough to support their claim that they continue to minister to the water? Is it truly abandoned when our origin stories explain our collective connections not only to the dry land, but also to the water and lakebeds that surround us? Don't our origin stories explain how the Creator provided us with dry lands in the past? Aren't drained lands now a reflection of the fluidity and nature of our ancestral homelands? Should our connections to the lake and its lakebed be dismissed as "abandoned" because we don't fish atop or live below the surface? What of our spiritual connections and responsibilities to that lakebed? If the lakebed is drained and built upon, do we somehow forfeit our rights and responsibilities, as the Native peoples of this region, to what emerges? If no treaty cedes the lakebed, how can we rightfully be separated from it?

The year 1917 was a time near the nadir of Indian population in the United States; the "Indian Wars" had been "over" for almost twenty years, and Indians were still expected to either assimilate or die and thus become the "vanishing race." It is not surprising that the United States Supreme Court refused to provide any remedy or recompense to the Potawatomi for the taking of the lakefront without treaty or compensation. However, might there be a different result if a similar claim were made to a more liberal Supreme Court in the future?

If *Williams v. City of Chicago* is settled law, any possibility of a successful claim to the current lakefront is implausible. Yes, the making of the claim was an Indigenous act of resistance to an American history that in the past had focused on Indian land cessions and relinquishment rather than struggle and recovery. The land claim to the lakefront affirmed a Pokagon community memory and worldview reflecting an Indigenous understanding of space and place that differed from the mainstream. As pointed out in a recent essay, whether or not Indian land claims are supported by the law, "Understandings of history shape perceptions of the present, and . . . intensively pursued land claims can provide powerful challenges to inaccurate conceptions of the past. . . . Native Americans are for this reason justified in strategically pursuing land claims that are difficult to justify on other grounds."[81]

The Pokagon Potawatomi land claim was an act of resistance to assimilation as well. Rather than meld into mainstream society or hide in plain sight, the leadership of the Pokagon asserted a bold claim for their territory—a claim that was grounded on tribal traditions and political activism. Although the dominant society may have paid little heed to the sovereign status of the Pokagon nation, *Williams v. City of Chicago* stands as evidence that these Indians were not relinquishing their status as separate and distinct peoples still connected to the ancestral territory of the Potawatomi peoples.

Court opinions can be read as having either broad or narrow applicability, implications, and precedent. The Supreme Court's ruling in *Williams v. City of Chicago* could be interpreted as extinguishing any Indian land claim to the lakefront of Chicago and Lake Michigan forever. If read at its narrowest interpretation, the *Williams* opinion establishes the ownership of the Chicago lakefront as that lakefront existed in 1917. If this interpretation of the decision is accepted, what of other "land" that has been created in Lake Michigan post-1917 as a result of the engineering efforts of non-Natives? For example, Northerly Island, still remembered by many Chicagoans as Meigs Field, is an artificial parcel of land first envisioned in Daniel Burnham's 1909 "Plan for Chicago." Work on creating the "island" however, did not begin until 1920 and finished five years later. The island was created by piling soil and fill onto the lakebed off the lakefront of Chicago until a manmade island emerged from the water. In later years a causeway was extended from the lakefront to the island to allow access to the island by foot or car.

In 1933–34, Northerly Island was the site of some of the celebrations of the city's "Century of Progress Exposition." In 1946, an airport was constructed on the island, and it became known as Meigs Field for nearly the next five decades. In 2003, the airport was closed and the runways dug up. Since then, Northerly Island has been a part of the "Museum Campus" on the city's lakefront—under the jurisdiction of the Chicago Park District. Included in this "campus" are the Field Museum of Natural History, the Shedd Aquarium, and at its north end, the Adler Planetarium. The majority of the island is now being used for a variety of recreational, educational, study of ecology, and entertainment purposes. However, no one has asked the Potawatomi about the place or inquired about their visions for its future use and development. Unlike in 1917, multiculturalism is valued today in America, diversity is celebrated, and Indigenous land claims sometimes have a better reception.

One might argue that it is entirely reasonable and right that the Pokagon Potawatomi, who almost one hundred years ago claimed the Chicago lakefront, ought to be included in the future plans for Northerly Island. Perhaps a cultural center for the Potawatomi (and other first peoples of what is now Chicago) could be created, or some partnership for educational and exhibition spaces could be established with the nearby Field Museum of Natural History. There might be opportunities for some other kind of cultural and/or economic development of Northerly Island that would include partnership and collaboration between the city and the Pokagon Potawatomi. Maybe the Potawatomi would be satisfied with how the island is currently being used, and with any plans for future development by the city, and that would be fine. The important thing is that the Pokagon Potawatomi would have been consulted. Certainly, such bold moves would go a long way towards honoring the sacrifices Native peoples that inhabited Chicago have made since its incorporation in 1837 so that it could thrive, and it would also acknowledge the longstanding connections of the Potawatomi to Chicago.

Indians at 1933 Fort Dearborn Anniversary. A caption with the photo reads, "The Indians here for the Century of Progress attended the Ceremonies in full Indian costume." ACME PHOTOGRAPHY CO. FOR THE *CHICAGO DAILY NEWS*, AUGUST 19, 1933. FROM THE COLLECTION OF THE AUTHOR.

Post–Land Claim in Chicago

Although this book is by design "Potawatomi-centric," they were not the only Indians living in Chicago at the end of the nineteenth and beginning of the twentieth centuries.[82] However, the same difficulty in describing the Indian community in Chicago during this period exists as in uncovering demographic information about the Potawatomi.[83] As one writer for the Library of Congress *American Memory Project* notes, "almost 36 percent of Chicago's population in 1910 were immigrants, and 'native' was a word more often used to differentiate people born within the United States from people who were foreign born."[84] American Indians from around the country came to participate in the 1893 World's Columbian Exposition and the 1933 Century of Progress World's Fair, and it is unknown if any from either stayed.[85] And Indians would invariably be invited to participate in annual celebrations of the Battle of Fort Dearborn.

Olson Park ca. 1940. Note *tipis* in upper right and left corners. FROM THE COLLECTION OF THE AUTHOR.

A 1920 local magazine article identifies that there were around one thousand Indians living in the city by that year. The article itself describes the city's preparations to celebrate its first "Indian Day."[86] The article also includes information about several Indian residents of Chicago, none of them identified as Potawatomi. The celebration was sponsored by the Indian Fellowship League, an intertribal organization of Indians in Chicago dedicated "to bring[ing] about conditions which shall result in better understanding of the American Indian, and true fellowship between his race and the other peoples of our country." Plans for the first "Indian Day" in Chicago included a three-day encampment of Natives and non-Natives.

Probably the best-known Indian residing in Chicago in the early part of the twentieth century was Dr. Carlos Montezuma (Yavapai-Apache), a physician in the city from 1896 to 1922 who was also an activist for Indian rights, a founding member of the Society of American Indians, and founder/editor of the monthly magazine *Wassaja*.[87]

In 1923, the Grand Council Fire of American Indians (after 1932 known as the Indian Council Fire) organized as a group of non-Natives and Natives with a similar purpose as the Indian Fellowship League: to provide legislative, educational, and

Indian mannequin at Olson Park, ca. 1950s? "A Park in Lost Chicago." HTTP://DUENSINGAMERICANA.BLOGSPOT.COM/2010/04/PARK-IN-LOST-CHICAGO.HTML

social services to Indians, but on a national level.[88] In 1935, the Indian Council Fire sponsored the then-annual "Indian Day" with a special celebration. On September 27 of that year, members gathered at the new Olson Rock Garden and Memorial Park to dedicate the grounds. Dr. Henry Roe Cloud, then superintendent of the Haskell Institute for Indians in Lawrence, Kansas, was presented with an "Indian Achievement Award."

The park was located next to the Olson Rug Factory, then at the intersection of Diversey Parkway and Pulaski Road on the near north side. It was conceived by Olson Rug owner Walter E. Olson. The head of the federal Bureau of Indian Affairs, John E. Collier, was even invited to the 1935 event, and a member of the organizing committee optimistically predicted that five to six thousand people would be in attendance, with a national radio audience of up to twenty thousand.[89] A program from that year's "Indian Day" indicates that members of the Potawatomi, Ottawa (Odawa), and Chippewa (Ojibwe) tribes were invited. According to news reports of the day, Mr. Olson symbolically presented them with a deed for the park.[90] While a program from the day of dedication does not identify any Pokagon Potawatomi tribal members by name,[91] it is certainly possible that Mr. Olson's actions hearkened back to the earlier land claim of the Pokagons, and thus important to note that a Pokagon Potawatomi influence on the city through its legal claim might be seen as late as 1935 in this event.

Images of the park after 1935 reflect a place rather reminiscent of the Wisconsin Dells of this era, with Indians posing in eagle-feather headdresses and Plains Indian garb next to their *tipis*. According to several sources, "Throughout the decades, regular events at the park included tribal songs and rituals by Chief Thundercloud of the Ottawa, archery demonstrations from atop the waterfall, a Green Corn Festival (in 1950) when the Great Spirit provided blessings for a bountiful harvest, [and] a recreation (in 1958) of John T. McCutcheon's famous Injun Summer painting using mannequins."[92] There is no indication that Pokagon Potawatomi tribal members participated in these activities or any others at the park; the activities may have been seen as too performative and uncomfortable for Pokagon Potawatomi tribal members to participate.

Nonetheless, leaving their mark on the city has been an ongoing project for the Potawatomi; memories can sometimes fade, and it is convenient for some to want to forget that Indians were here before anyone else. It seems as though nearly every generation of Pokagon Potawatomi has had to reassert their relationship to the city. On occasion, however, the actions of non-Natives have eclipsed the best efforts of the Pokagon Potawatomi. In the next chapter, I will examine the similarities and contradictions between Native and non-Native claims to the Chicago lakefront, and why the claim of George W. Streeter is remembered while those of the Potawatomi seem, for the most part, to be ignored. The competing claims of Streeter and the Pokagon Potawatomi reflect the fact that the interactions between the tribe and the city flowed both ways, and that the Potawatomi were affected by events in Chicago as well.

CHAPTER 4

The Legacies of Turner, Cody, Streeter, and the Pokagon Potawatomi

> He recognized Chicago as Hustler Town from its first prairie morning as the city's fathers hustled the Pottawattomies down to their last moccasin. He recognized it, too, as another place: North Star to Jane Addams to Al Capone, to John Peter Altgeld as to Richard J. Daley, to Clarence Darrow as to Julius Hoffman. He saw it not so much as Janus-faced but as the carny freak show's two-headed boy, one noggin Neanderthal, the other noble-browed. You see, Nelson Algren was a street-corner comic as well as a poet.
>
> —Studs Terkel, *Chicago: City on the Make*

After 1833, the Pokagon Potawatomi strove to maintain some sort of presence in Chicago. Of course, human interaction does not operate only in one direction, and a reciprocal exchange of ideas is to be expected. At times, the activities of non-Native Chicagoans may have even influenced the efforts of the Pokagon Potawatomi in Chicago. There were the competing claims of the Pokagon Potawatomi and non-Natives for the city's lakefront, which would be reflected in highbrow and lowbrow understandings and articulations of frontier, settlement, conquest, civilization, and rights of discovery as advanced by such luminaries as

Frederick Jackson Turner and William F. (Buffalo Bill) Cody. How might we explain the fond remembrance of a Yankee who made claims to the lakefront, while the claims by the Indians to the same lands are absent from the memory of so many Chicagoans.

Chicago is, as Terkel pointed out, a hustler town, and there was one grand hustler who was bold enough to make a claim to the city's most valuable real estate at the end of the nineteenth century. The story of his claim includes the issue of possession versus "right of discovery." The elements that justified the very presence of the immigrant majority in the United States would be turned on their heads by this man. His story returns us to Chicago's lakefront, then extends to Michigan and the Pokagon Potawatomi, includes notions of territory, justice, and creation, and comes back once again to the floor of Lake Michigan.

The Odyssey of George Wellington Streeter

Two events frame the factual parameters in this narrative of claims to territory in Chicago at the end of the nineteenth and beginning of the twentieth centuries: (1) the lawsuit filed by the Pokagon Band of Potawatomi Indians in 1914 (and concluded in 1917) claiming that the Chicago lakefront was Indian land that had never been ceded by act or treaty,[1] and (2) the arrival of George Wellington Streeter in Chicago in 1886, and the claims he proceeded to make to the same lakefront for the next thirty-five years. Taken together, these claims reveal much about territory, boundary, frontier, mapping, claims-making, history, memory, and how we imagine a past that operates to valorize some peoples, events, and things while erasing others.

The ground upon which the city of Chicago rests is a topography of contested land, beliefs, and value systems, and both claims rested upon the power of survey and map. What do these claims suggest about the authority of maps, mapping, and mapmaking? The stories of the land claims, when taken together and in context, have a common history, one of conflicts between rich and poor, landed and homeless, settler and dispossessed, white versus white, white versus Indian, and institutions versus individuals. The analysis of these conflicts reveals contradictions that beg explanation, if not reconciliation. In the nineteenth century, Chicago transformed from an Indigenous community to an early center of trade, to a diasporic site for the Potawatomi, to an industrial capital possessed of enormous wealth alongside desperate poverty. Out of these contradictions and conflicts emerged not only the claims of the Potawatomi, but also the claim of a "Yankee boatman" possessed of his own notions of the doctrines of discovery and conquest. There are parallels between the emergence of Streeterville and the creation story of the Potawatomi Indians. The traditional Potawatomi belief is that the world was consumed by a great flood, and that Chicago, as well as the rest of North America, was resurrected beneath the wings of Raven. Streeter's land claim also rose on topography that was once submerged and now risen from beneath the water and subject to "discovery" and claim. Similarly, both stories are dismissed by the mainstream. Few non-Natives accept the idea that the continent was saved by a muskrat and a raven, and at least two scholars have raised serious questions about the veracity of Streeter's story of running aground on a sandbar (the very premise of his adventure).

The Captain's Invictus

On July 10, 1886, George Wellington Streeter, known as "the Cap" by adversaries and admirers alike, ran his Lake Michigan boat onto a sandbar off the Chicago shore. A lawyer, Civil War veteran, boatman, and prodigious spokesman for the rights of the commoner, Streeter, according to legend, immediately saw an opportunity in this navigational disaster.[2] Disembarking with his wife Maria, he optimistically declared—so the tale goes—that fortune had shone down upon them and blessed them with a new home (albeit a shaky one).[3] The mythologies surrounding Streeter are as complex as they are entertaining, and separating fact from fiction is difficult. In many ways, the myths became more important than the facts as Streeter developed into a Chicago folk hero. Certainly Streeter, and others who were financially and ideologically invested in his legend, encouraged the promotion of that myth. Streeter's adversaries developed their own rhetoric resisting the claims and actions of Streeter and his allies.

Streeter's tale may have been more manufactured romance and hyperbole than reality. A more recent, and much less dramatic, recitation of Streeter's involvement in the shaping of the Chicago lakefront is presented in an article by John W. Stamper.[4] Stamper argues that the development of the shoreline east of what is now Michigan Avenue was the result of the efforts of the Lincoln Park Board of Commissioners and lakeshore property owners; that "George W. Streeter, responsible in legend for the landfill that is now Streeterville, was in fact little more than a nuisance to the tycoons and land barons who literally shaped the shoreline [of Chicago]."[5] Stamper claims, in fact, that Streeter never beached his boat on any sandbar. Rather, Streeter docked the *Reutan* at the foot of Superior Street, where it languished and was about to be destroyed by city officials until Streeter obtained the permission of N. Kellogg Fairbank to haul it onto landfill being dumped in front of the lakefront property of that millionaire businessman. There it sat for five years until 1891, when Fairbank finally asked Streeter to remove it, according to Stamper, at which time the Captain instead responded by claiming ownership of the area and selling lots.[6] Questioning of the Streeter myth is not confined to contemporary writing; at least one newspaper article from the time also appears to cast doubt on the Streeter sandbar story.[7] Nonetheless, the vast majority of the press at the time repeated the story as presented by Streeter as factual.

Stamper's version is certainly not the narrative that continues to capture the imaginations and sympathies of many Chicagoans. Streeter had apparently honed his skills of persuasion during his showman days, and he believed that the truth did not need to get in the way of a good story. Streeter also understood the power of a story that presented him as standing up to the wealthy and elite of Chicago. In the end, at least for Streeter, it made no difference whether his sandbar tale was fact or fiction. What mattered was that it resonated with the citizenry of Chicago and won the battle of public opinion. That public support would make tycoons and land barons, still nervous from the aftermath of the Haymarket Riots and other labor unrest, reluctant to fight Streeter head-on. Instead, they would engage in a strategy that combined intimidation, harassment, and litigation.[8] Today, the version that remains most popular with the public and continues to reside in the historical memory of Chicagoans is Streeter's own version.

The Popular Version of G. W. Streeter in Chicago

An early record of the impressively named George Wellington Streeter is in the 1870 Federal Census, where he is listed as a resident of Genesee County, Michigan, with the profession of boatman.[9] Much of Streeter's early biography comes from *Captain Streeter, Pioneer*, by Everett Guy Ballard. Written as an interview with Streeter himself, it makes for fun reading, but its veracity is suspect (the author was also Streeter's lawyer). Ballard presents a first meeting with Streeter, his subject's early years and ancestry, Streeter's childhood growing up in the Michigan wilderness, travels west, military service in the Civil War, attempts to succeed as a steamboat captain, time spent as a carnival show operator, and ultimately his landing in Chicago and his battles for the lakefront and "rightful due."

Ballard's biography was published in 1914, and appears to have been part of a sort of public relations campaign designed to promote the reputation of Streeter and the claims of his supporters, including the author himself. The populist theme of the book is evident from the outset. The book was dedicated to "the memory of that great patriot and statesman, the Late Governor John P. Altgeld, who shortly before his death, requested that it be written." Altgeld had pardoned Streeter after his conviction for murder in 1902.[10] Whether Altgeld actually asked that a biography of Streeter be written is unknown. Altgeld is best known as the man who pardoned the remaining defendants convicted of complicity in the death of seven police officers during the Haymarket Riot.[11] While the governor received considerable condemnation for the issuance of those pardons from conservatives and anti-labor unionists, Altgeld became a hero in populist and labor circles. Connecting Streeter with Altgeld may have been sleight of hand on Ballard's part, intended to curry the favor of anti-capitalists and to present Streeter as a sort of martyr figure. Certainly, Ballard's intent was to encourage sympathy for Streeter and outrage toward those who opposed his claims.[12] Ballard's introduction includes the admonition that

> [Streeter's adversaries] are conscienceless and inexorable outlaws whose only love is for dollars and luxuries. They have certainly enjoyed their fill, but the day of reckoning is at hand, and the American people will be as merciless and inexorable in their treatment of such scoundrels and inhuman monsters as any people who have ever lived in the past. The lion is only sleeping, but he will awake. I am going to give him a sharp prod and see what will happen.[13]

The polemic that follows then weaves a tale of Streeter, emphasizing his pioneer roots, veteran service, admirable character, courage, and strength. Streeter is presented in mythic proportions as a fearless nemesis to the wealthy of Chicago, who would prosper at the expense of the average woman or man.

> I know of no more grander or no more typical specimen of the real pioneer than Captain George Wellington Streeter. . . . and I know of no more formidable adversary to the Dollar Hogs of America, with whom he has grappled and battled at short range for more than a quarter of a century.[14]

George Wellington Streeter by moonlight. Portrait of Streeter, likely drawn from one of the hundreds of photographs of him, reflects the mythmaking that transformed a small, wiry man into the bayonet-bearing defender of his homeland.
E. G. BALLARD, *CAPTAIN STREETER, PIONEER* (CHICAGO: EMERY PUBLISHING SERVICE, 1914), "FRONTISPIECE."

Simon Pokagon possessed many of the same characteristics of self-promotion and flamboyance as George Streeter. According to Clifton, Simon Pokagon, too, had to be "egocentric, autocratic and self-aggrandizing" to survive for long as a political leader of the Pokagon Potawatomi Band of Indians.[15] Without a doubt, both were showmen in their own right and charismatic characters. There is no direct evidence that the two men met, but their lives and claims to Chicago have significant parallels. One might even speculate that the Pokagon Potawatomi's decision to file a lawsuit claiming the lakefront may have even been inspired by Streeter.

While Streeter's early years are sketchy, the following information from biographies and news articles provides an outline of the life of the man who would challenge Chicago.[16] Streeter was one of eleven children, born near Flint, Michigan, in 1837 to William and Catherine Streeter. His grandfather and great-grandfather were veterans of the War of 1812 and the Revolutionary War, respectively. By age eighteen, Streeter had earned enough money in the lumber business to marry his childhood sweetheart, Minnie. In 1860, suffering from wanderlust, he—along with his wife and two neighbors—struck out for the west. At some point, he apprenticed as a lawyer, and although never making it a formal profession, he learned the law and the art of advocacy. By the time he appeared in Chicago, Streeter had honed his skills at showmanship, self-promotion, and *flim-flam*boyance. While out west, his lawyerly skills were tested when he was commandeered into defending a man charged with murder near Marysville, Kansas. Despite his best efforts, Streeter lost the case and the client was hanged. It would not be the last time the Captain entered a courtroom.

With the commencement of the Civil War, George and Minnie Streeter returned to Michigan, where he mustered into the Fifteenth Michigan volunteers at Flint. According to his biographers, he saw action in more than a dozen battles and acquitted himself well.[17] Returning to Flint after the war, he convinced Minnie to go into show business. In the latter half of the 1860s, Streeter assembled a circus of "wild" animals native to Michigan, including an albino pig that he hawked as "a genuine white elephant."[18] Assuming this is a fairly accurate rendition of Streeter's philosophy on "truth," it appears that the man was convinced that a good story, even if manufactured, was not problematic so long as the public was entertained. This same attitude would prevail in Streeter's pursuit of his land claims in Chicago. It was during this career as a carnival barker that Streeter first donned what would become his signature costume, the ubiquitous silk stovepipe top hat and long, green frock coat.

Streeter arguably played the same game with his claim to the Chicago lakefront as he had with his own traveling show; the audaciousness of his claims left both supporters and detractors with a measure of respect for his sheer brazenness.[19] The "George S. Wellington Shows" made good money the first year as a traveling circus and appeared headed for success until derailed by a disastrous rainy second season. By the fall of 1867, Streeter was bankrupt. He sold out and returned from the road with Minnie to Michigan and his old trade of lumbering. The next year, business was good, and Streeter built his first steamboat for travel on the Great Lakes. He sold that boat, took the profit, and headed south to St. Louis, where he commenced construction of a second craft bearing the name *Minnie E. Streeter*, after his wife. Unfortunately, Minnie had other plans. Taking her husband's seven hundred dollars in savings, she ventured forth to a career in vaudeville.[20] The Captain maintained his composure, secured a divorce, and spent the next three years hauling goods up and down the Mississippi and Ohio Rivers before calling it quits. Eager once again to head west, Streeter bounced from south Chicago to Bedford, Iowa, running a string of enterprises.[21] Bored again, in the mid-1870s he eventually decided to settle in Chicago and return to his showman roots, first buying an interest in the Woods Museum[22] and then the Apollo Theatre, both located at the corners of Randolph and Dearborn Streets in downtown Chicago.[23]

While in Chicago during this time, Captain Streeter met his soul mate, Maria Mulholland. Born in Belfast, she was as rowdy and outrageous as the Captain, and together they made a partnership that fascinated Chicagoans for decades. Hard-drinking and possessed of a fiery temper, Maria Streeter stood by her husband through the hardest years of what would come to be called the Streeterville Wars, until her death in 1905. After committing their lives to each other in a local saloon in 1885, the Streeters joined a gang of gunrunners transporting armaments to Honduran rebels. Maria and George went to work, and finally scouted a wreck of a boat docked near Chicago that they commenced to rehab. Working feverishly, they had her shipshape by the summer of 1886. Christened the *Reutan*, they planned to take her for a shakedown cruise before heading down the Mississippi to the Gulf of Mexico and on to Honduras and some easy money.[24]

On July 10, Maria and the Captain put out from Chicago for Milwaukee under dark and ominous skies. They encountered heavy gales all the way north, and the foul weather continued on the return trip. According to Ballard's interview,

> The waves dashed over the boat hundreds of times with terrific force. I was the only man on deck. My wife and the crew were driven to the berths for safety, and I tied a strong rope about my waist and resolved to witness from the decks whatever happened. Twice I was swept overboard by the tremendous waves, but managed to climb back to deck overhand after the wave had receded.[25]

Streeter's reputation for courage and perseverance, carefully crafted by himself and his supporters, would be a common theme in the retelling of his landfall and subsequent activities. The Captain did his best to navigate the *Reutan* back to port in Chicago, but by 10:00 P.M. the engines had frozen up and the ship was adrift. At 3 A.M., the boat ran aground heavily onto a sandbar, 160 feet offshore and just north of the mouth of the Chicago River. Later that morning, the Captain and his bride were able to disembark and inspect the damage. The ship was in bad shape, with more than a dozen holes in the hull, but the cabin was still reasonably intact. According to one version of the Streeter story, the Captain concluded, "Mebbe we ain't goin' to Honduras at all, Maria. I like the feel of being on a boat and you

Captain Streeter repairing the *Reutan*. E. G. BALLARD, *CAPTAIN STREETER, PIONEER* (CHICAGO: EMERY PUBLISHING SERVICE, 1914), 129.

been talkin' about someday settlin' down in a little house of our own. Looks like we got both right here."[26] A later biographer renders the decision to stay in more pragmatic terms:

> Cap Streeter pondered his cash reserve and his liabilities and decided to stay put. The storm had banked a soggy drift of sand around the sprung bulwarks of the *Reutan*. This promised a degree of temporary safety; the hulk might provide a rent-free shelter until something better turned up.[27]

After he set to making the cabin watertight, Mrs. Streeter commenced housekeeping. The Captain floated timbers out in order to surround and stabilize the sandbar. The bulwark not only protected their new home, but it had the added benefit of causing an accretion of more sand to their homestead sandbar. Within a few months, the situation was so stable that Streeter was able to jack the boat up off the sand and set in a foundation.[28]

By the summer of 1887, Captain Streeter was ready to add a front yard to his homestead. Because of its proximity to downtown and lack of regulation, the shrewd showman convinced refuse haulers to *pay* for the privilege of dumping their loads of "fill" around the *Reutan*. Slowly the area between the sandbar and the shore closed in, and after a while Maria was able to walk from their houseboat to the lakefront along a wooden sidewalk that the Captain built for her. Meanwhile, Captain Streeter secured an old garbage scow and had it towed to their new estate to provide additional living space. Using his experience in lumber and construction, he perched a two-story home on top of the scow. He then pulled the *Reutan* off the sandbar, renamed her *Maria*, and began hauling passengers up and down the lake.[29] Gawkers and tourists began visiting the lakefront to stare at the newly formed land and its appurtenances. The narrative in the Ballard (auto)biography outlines the basis for Streeter's claim to this newly "created" land:

> At the time of the relaunching [*sic*] of the vessel, I had filled in all of the space between my boat and the shore to the west and south and much farther to the northward, as well as more than thirty rods to the east and northeast. This was a territory of one hundred and eighty-six acres, long known to everybody in Chicago as 'Streeterville' and as the 'District of Lake Michigan,' the latter name having been given to the tract by myself, the former by the people of Chicago and vicinity because of *my creation, occupation and ownership of it* [emphasis added]. It bears both names

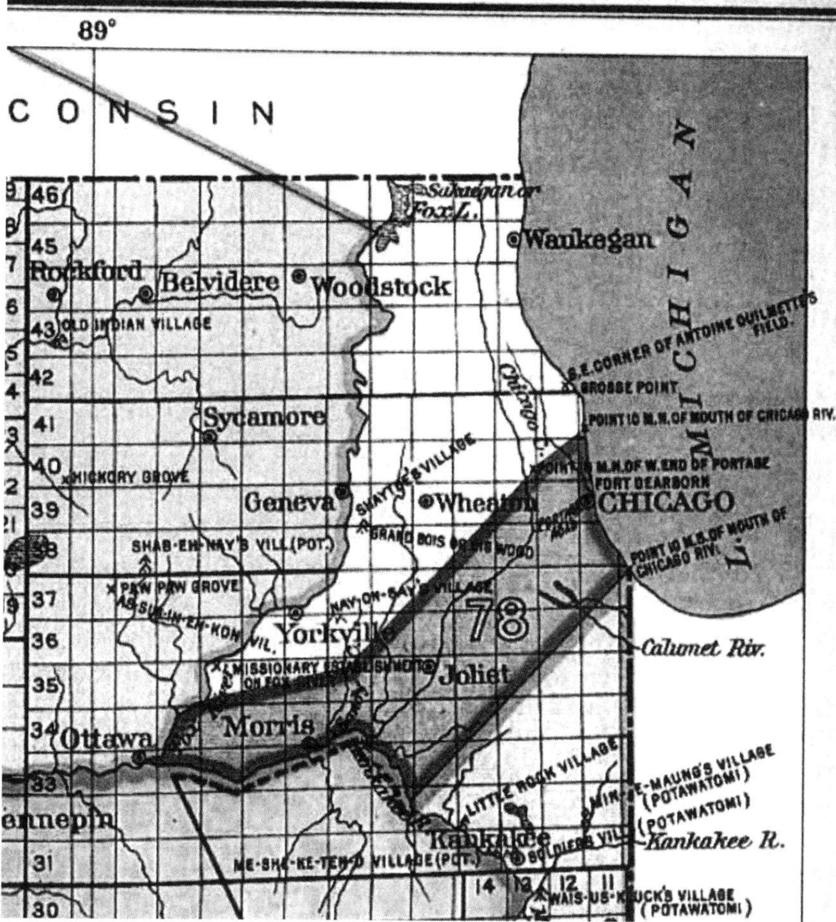

Inset of a map of Indian land cessions in northeastern Illinois. ORIGINALLY PUBLISHED AS *INDIAN LAND CESSIONS IN THE UNITED STATES*, COMPILED BY CHARLES C. ROYCE AND PRESENTED AS PART 2 OF THE *EIGHTEENTH ANNUAL REPORT OF THE BUREAU OF AMERICAN ETHNOLOGY TO THE SECRETARY OF THE SMITHSONIAN INSTITUTION, 1896–97* (WASHINGTON, DC: GOVERNMENT PRINTING OFFICE, 1899).

to this day, not only among the people, but in the daily press, the public records and documents of the city, the county and the legislature of the state of Illinois.[30]

The process of filling and refilling, to which Streeter probably contributed little, continued unabated for six years while the city was immersed in a building boom. Streeter had the entire area surveyed and mapped in 1893; facsimiles of these maps appear in the Ballard biography as well as in earlier pamphlets in support of Streeter.[31] The survey platted the territory into 280 separate lots that Streeter proceeded to rent or sell, and the whole area was populated with an array of shacks and shanties within a few years. Streeter and his supporters disseminated maps of their land claim through pamphlets, books, and legal pleadings.[32] The impulse to create and publicize these maps reflected the power of mapmaking in the promotion and legitimization of the boatman's claim.

Using that shoreline as a boundary, however, causes problems when it fluctuates. Such was the case with Chicago, whose lakefront was moved considerably eastward through the efforts of the city and others, perhaps including George W. Streeter. In many ways, the claim of the Pokagon Potawatomi and the fight over Streeterville were both battles over maps. As others sought to plat, divide, and profit from the new Chicago lakefront, Streeter created his own map and argued that it showed the new lakefront area of Streeterville to be outside the boundaries and jurisdiction of Chicago and Illinois. To legitimize their claim, Streeter and his supporters began publishing copies of a map of the place Streeter dubbed "The District of Lake Michigan" as "proof" of their ownership. Streeter's theory of property law was novel enough, and the power of maps strong enough that adjoining property owners, the press, and the public were unsure of what to make of Streeter's claim. It was a stroke of genius for Streeter to make such a claim by using the very tool that Europeans and Americans had been using for hundreds of years in order to take possession of territory in North America from the Indians. First, you make a map. Then you claim what is on the map. The power of maps reflects the prevailing ideology that underpinned the settlement of the New World—that the world was a place open for the taking so long as the appropriate rituals, formalities, and conventions were followed. Streeter's maps continued this long tradition of cartographic imperialism.

The Pokagon Band of Potawatomi had also used the processes of surveying and boundary making to argue that those lands "unmapped" remained the territory of the tribe. In their pleadings to the Federal District Court filed in 1914, the Potawatomi submitted a map "showing the lines of the land ceded by the Treaty of St. Louis, Aug 6, 1816" (the treaty that included a cession by the Potawatomi of much of the lands constituting Chicago).[33] That government map was introduced as evidence because it purported to show that the eastern boundary of the land cession by the Potawatomi in 1816 did not include the lakefront of Chicago as it existed in 1914. Although both Streeter and the Potawatomi used maps to argue their claims,

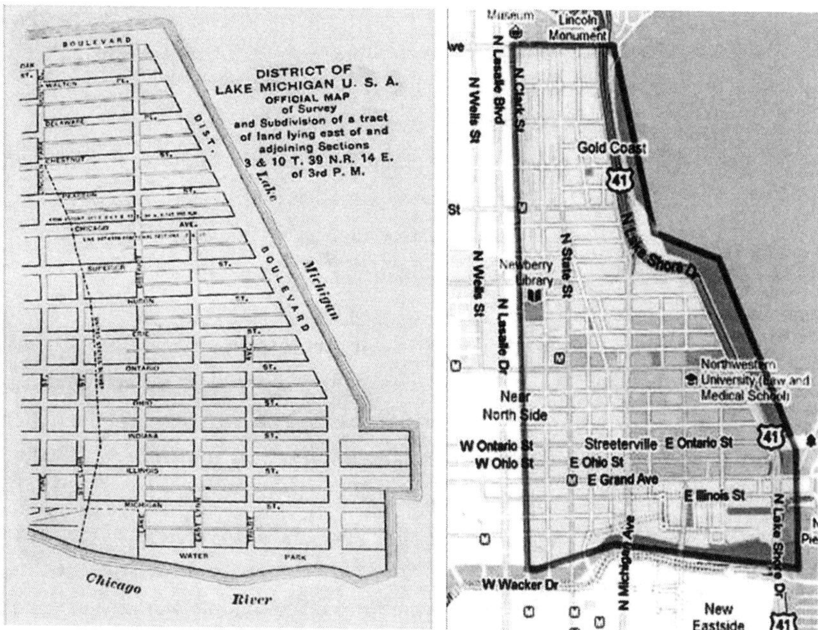

Streeter's mapping of his "District of Lake Michigan" alongside a contemporary map of the Streeterville neighborhood. W. H. NILES, *A BRIEF HISTORY AND THE LEGAL STANDING OF THE DISTRICT OF LAKE MICHIGAN* (CHICAGO: SWANBERG & CO., 1900).

Streeter and his allies created their own map of Streeterville and published it as evidence of their sovereignty, whereas the Potawatomi used an existing map to prove that their land fell outside of the City of Chicago and State of Illinois. The distinction reflects the difference in their perspectives. Streeter needed to create a map to confirm ownership of the territory that he claimed to have created and quickly "discovered." The Potawatomi, on the other hand, as original inhabitants of the region and owners of the land unless and until ceded, sought to bolster their argument by showing that the land they claimed existed outside of the government's mapped boundaries of ceded territory.

Ballard wrote of Streeter's first contact with his lakefront neighbors after he had mapped out his new land:

> After I had virtually completed my filling-in operations . . . I had the tract surveyed and platted, and it was at this juncture that I learned of the displeasure of a lot

> of millionaires who imagined that the time was ripe to engineer a conspiracy to rob me of my hard earned property. . . . At the time I was stranded, the location of some of the homes of the millionaire colony of the North Shore were not particularly valuable . . . the entire frontage . . . was low and swampy, and the location of the present palace or castle of the Palmer family was familiarly known as the 'stink pond' because of the universal use of the pond there to throw garbage and dead animals into. . . . All this was later filled in, but it was for many years an undesirable locality.[34]

Streeter argued with the lakefront property owners over their respective titles to this emerging landscape for the next thirty-five years, they asserting riparian ownership and he claiming squatter's rights, the right of discovery, and the right of creation. Streeter's 1886 "landfall" came at an inopportune time for certain gentry of Chicago. Potter Palmer (whose name now adorns the Palmer House Hilton in Chicago) was moving himself north of the Chicago River to what would become the new Gold Coast of Chicago, adjacent to what is now Lakeshore Drive.[35] Palmer, born of Quaker parents in 1826, had come to Chicago in 1852 to open a dry goods store. Four years later, he hired an assistant by the name of Marshall Field. By 1867, Palmer had made a fortune by combining quality merchandise with personal service, and he sold his interest in the store to Field and others. Palmer took his profits and invested them in Chicago real estate, becoming the premier landlord and developer of the period. In 1868, he built the opulent Palmer House Hotel, which was rebuilt after the Great Chicago Fire of 1871 in even grander style. In 1882, Palmer began buying up real estate along the marshy lakefront north of the Chicago River and had a mansion constructed for himself and his wife, Bertha Honoré Palmer. The mansion had three stories, three thousand feet of frontage facing Lake Michigan, a great hall, an eighty-foot tower, marble mosaic floors, and a grand oak staircase. Potter Palmer subdivided the immediate area around his home into spacious lots for similarly affluent Chicagoans, and he eagerly went about making the development marketable.[36] Because of his status and influence, the Palmer Castle, as it was known, became a catalyst for the city's elite relocating from their previous abodes on Prairie Avenue, south of the central business district, to this area north of the Chicago River.

The Chicago lakefront was no stranger to controversy by the time Streeter arrived. Beginning in the 1830s, the shoreline of gathered driftwood, derelicts, and shanties became a notorious red-light district known as "The Sands."[37] By the 1870s, most of that had been cleared away by civic-minded reformers. During the 1880s, Palmer joined with the city's Lincoln Park Board of Commissioners to improve the lakefront and construct the new boulevard that would become Lakeshore Drive. The drive had been planned since 1875, and the board, comprised mostly of lakefront property owners intent on increasing the size and value of their properties, had been working to extend the lakefront east. In order to accomplish that, they had been issuing bonds, raising funds, and securing and filling the shoreline. Progress was slow, however, and a seawall had to be reconstructed several times.[38] Meanwhile, to the board's chagrin, Streeter had set up housekeeping just offshore.[39] Streeter's presence did not provoke formal action, however, until 1893, when N. Kellogg Fairbank, a neighbor of Palmer's, sued successfully to have Streeter evicted. Streeter lost in court, but simply returned and reestablished his shorefront colony. It was not until 1900, when Palmer consolidated his real estate holdings, that he began to purchase the area claimed by Streeter. The Chicago Title and Trust Company insured the title to those lots and became the institution directly involved in further efforts to evict "the Captain."

Significant similarities between Palmer and Streeter existed; both were "Yankee" entrepreneurs who had come to Chicago seeking their fortunes. Each was flamboyant and charismatic in their own way; both were stubborn and persistent. Palmer had risen within the mercantile system to fabulous wealth, although admittedly, Streeter had not been so successful in his commercial pursuits. They were both attracted to the lakefront entrance to Chicago, but they had substantially differing opinions regarding the utilization of that space. Streeter's conception hearkened back to the frontier; it embodied the vision of earlier Americans who saw the continent as a place open to settlers willing to carve from nature an estate, no matter how large or small.[40] Palmer was much more a product of the Gilded Age, and the belief in capitalist savvy and spirit within which he thrived. Their legacies remain intertwined; the area where Palmer built his "castle" was just north of the neighborhood that retains the name of the boatman land jumper, while the finest hotel in Streeterville carries the name of the capitalist.

Streeter's claims cast a cloud upon the title of the lakefront lots and hampered their development.[41] Over the years, the Chicago Title and Trust Company initiated several lawsuits to eject Streeter and his growing community and clear the title to the land. When the lawsuits didn't work, they resorted to force, using the city police and mercenaries to "motivate" Streeter to move on, according to Streeter's supporters. Streeter would have none of it. He continued claiming the lakefront until his death in 1921, and his heirs pressed their claims in the courts well into the 1930s.

Supporters of Streeter would join in the public discourse regarding the legitimacy of his ownership. One Mrs. L. Edwards authored a small book on behalf of the Streeter claim.

> He was the only person that had any right to the district of Lake Michigan called 'Streeterville.' Three titles, Sovereign of the soil, Right of Discovery, and the *Indians gave him their deeds, which he paid them for* [emphasis added]. . . . Discovery, occupancy and accession, being the means by which Streeter obtained his title, as per custom followed the settlers of the United States generally, to-wit: the very moment the settler sets foot upon unoccupied, unsurveyed public land with purpose, in good faith to make his home thereon, and perfect his title thereto. . . . There are a million people who saw Streeter in possession . . . his was the only right of *Preemption.*[42]

At another point in her short essay, Mrs. Edwards acknowledges the interest of the Indigenous inhabitants in the territory:

> We find [Streeter] here occupying this 226 acres of land which had not been acquired by the United States at the time that Illinois was adopted as a state, into the Union in 1818, land with which the Indians had not parted title but which land by treaty, the Indians especially reserved to themselves under the provisions thereof, being the waters of Lake Michigan and 16 feet above the high water mark forever.[43]

Although that notation reads as though taken from legal pleadings, it is presented as the author's own. Nonetheless, whoever wrote that conclusion was also repeating what essentially formed the basis for the Pokagon Potawatomi Indians' later claim to the same land.

There is other evidence that Streeter and his supporters acknowledged the primacy of the Potawatomi property rights to the lakefront and interacted with the tribe. Streeter himself spoke of entering into "treaties" with the Potawatomi and purchasing the land from them.[44] In 1902, Streeter even appeared on stage with the "Indians." The *Chicago Daily Tribune* reported:

George and "Ma" Streeter at their lakefront home, ca. 1918. *DETROIT NEWS* PHOTOGRAPH, NEGATIVE IN THE COLLECTION OF THE AUTHOR.

> It is worth one's while to see Capt. George Wellington Streeter on the vaudeville stage. The "Cap" made his debut last night at the Metropolitan theater . . . there were supposed Indians clad in red tights and green bodices who sang and danced to ragtime. The good ship Rutan [*sic*] bobbed up and down across the back of the stage while the thunder crashed, and suddenly "Cap" was spilled out of the storm-tossed lake onto the stage. . . . The "Cap" came out of the lake with a telescope and a carpet bag exclaiming "Thank God, that is all I got from the wreck!" and after various spyings of the land he bought 160 acres from Chief Pokagon and proceeded to establish the "district of Lake Michigan."[45]

Interviewed after opening night of the play, Streeter commented on the power of the stage.

> Now take this play of mine. Ain't that a moral document for human rights? Shows how I came into possession of the deestrict and how I bought it from the Indians.[46]

Potter Palmer viewed the relatively uninhabited shoreline north of the Chicago River as an area of opportunity. He bought up the lots just west of Streeterville for a pittance and began constructing rows of fine townhouses, including his own baronial estate. Soon there was a rush among the social elite to rub elbows with each other, and the lots and homes sold quickly at enormous profit.[47] Wealthy lakefront property owners like Palmer envisioned a shoreline that was within the jurisdiction of the city and incorporated into a state that was part of the union comprising the United States. Streeter always argued that his District of Lake Michigan was also a part of the United States. Their visions of a united America may have been similar, but that was the end of their commonality. Palmer's imagined community, the Gold Coast, and Streeter's District of Lake Michigan rested on opposite poles in imaginings about America.

For Streeter, new neighbors on the north shore brought new problems and new complaints. The gentry did not appreciate their view of the lake being "marred" by the converted garbage scow, shanties, outhouses, and throngs of workers and rowdies frequenting the Streeterville saloons. The "silk-stocking set" who would inhabit Palmer's newly created "Gold Coast," as it came to be called, paid a hefty sum to dwell among those they considered their peers. Having the motley crew who resided in Streeterville so nearby was a constant source of aggravation. With the financial crisis of 1893 settling in throughout America, the land barons and industrialists appear to have been reluctant to force Streeter's hand themselves. Mayor Harrison had been assassinated by a deranged and disappointed office-seeker that year; the White City of the World's Columbian Exposition was soon crumbling after its closing, and on July 5, 1894, most of the remaining buildings were burned to the ground by striking railway workers.[48] It was a dicey time to be a "captain of industry"; they needed a proxy to deal with the "Streeter problem" and the Chicago Title and Trust would do just fine.

The Chicago Title and Trust Company had been the guarantor of title for most of the Palmer lots, and for the rest of Streeter's life it would be the behemoth trying to quash his dreams.[49] Established in 1847 as the Rees & Rucker Land Agency, it was renamed the Chicago Title and Trust Company (CT&T) in 1901.[50] In 1888, the company issued the first title-guarantee policy in Illinois, protecting a property owner against loss if the title to his or her land was found to be defective or invalid. The CT&T had an important financial interest, then, in clearing the cloud of Streeter and his land claims from the lakefront. The CT&T took the lead in pressing for the eviction of Streeterville residents. According to Streeter, the company had most of the judges and police in their hire and was not above employing thugs and assassins to do their work; every attempt to oust the residents from Streeterville was invariably attributable to the CT&T or their minions. As the plaintiff in much of the litigation attempting to evict the Streeterville residents, the title company did become a target of animosity for those who sought to preserve the Streeter enclave. Mrs. Edwards wrote,

> The Chicago Title and Trust Company cannot give a clear title [to the lots in Streeterville]. Any title they have to this property is an arrant [*sic*] forgery which should be straightened out, and have Uncle Sam padlock their doors. They are the biggest cut-throats and gangsters that ever infested the globe. I am writing facts that have heretofore been suppressed. They have their gunmen following me on the streets of Chicago for speaking about them. One of them said to me, 'We know you and are going to take you for a ride.' I said to him, 'I'm not afraid of you. I have only one ride to take. It will be my last one and yours too.'[51]

In the summer of 1895, legend has it, the Captain was set upon by a group of roughnecks who had been paid, presumably by CT&T, to evict him and Maria and clear the area. According to the Streeter legend, they were no match for the couple, whose quick wits and loaded musket were said to have convinced the group to leave.

Such sparring continued for several years. In 1898, the Chicago city police actually got involved while trying to serve an eviction notice, but they were also driven off at gunpoint. The next month the local law enforcement returned with an arrest warrant for Streeter, charging him with making an assault upon their fellow officers with a dangerous weapon. Maria was onto them, so the story goes, and she poured scalding water on their heads from the second floor of the scow until her husband could break free and chase them off with the musket. The officers returned with another warrant and finally convinced the old boatman to accompany them to the police station. Held overnight in jail, Streeter pled his case the next morning and persuaded the court that a person's right to defend his or her home prevailed, particularly because the police had acted without the benefit of a warrant during their first arrest attempt. The "Streeterville Wars" had begun.[52]

One might question why the City of Chicago did not take a more active role in addressing the situation with Streeter. One reasonable speculation is that Streeter benefited from the political landscape of the time. For decades, the Chicago mayoral office was dominated by men who cultivated populist followings, and this may have made them reluctant to intervene publicly on behalf of a privileged few. Carter Henry Harrison III was elected to four consecutive terms as mayor of Chicago from 1879 to 1887. He was elected to a fifth term in 1893 and served during the World's Columbian Exposition but was assassinated by a disgruntled office seeker on October 28, 1893.[53] Known for his laissez-faire attitude towards government, his tenure was marked by the tolerance of saloons, brothels, and gambling as an unavoidable part of urban life.[54] The toleration of Streeter's antics by city officials was consistent with the tenor and politics of Chicago during that era.

Carter Harrison's son, Carter Henry Harrison IV, also served five terms as mayor, from 1897 to 1905 and 1911 to 1915. Like his father, he "did not believe in legislating public morality; he advocated instead a populist concept of 'personal liberty.'"[55] According to historian Edward R. Kantowicz, Harrison attracted a broad base of support, including laborers, immigrants, and the wealthy; he was "equally at home in a poker game with party hacks or at a reception on the Gold Coast."[56] Harrison's successor, William "Big Bill" Thompson, was elected mayor three times, in 1915, 1919, and 1927. Rumored to be a close friend of Al Capone and other gangsters, during his final campaign Thompson promised to open ten thousand taverns for every one closed by the previous administration. According to one biographer, racketeering became the biggest business in Chicago during his tenure.[57] While Chicago had its share of reformers, the city exhibited ambivalence

Caricature of G. W. Streeter. Streeter is depicted with his trademark top hat. The cartoon jests at the request of Panamanians for the United States to aid them in their "war for independence," and suggests that Streeter is just the kind of tough "Teddy Roosevelt" sort of character that should be sent down to Panama to represent the United States. *CHICAGO DAILY NEWS*, AUGUST 24, 1901, 1.

and some tolerance towards the kind of independence and individualism that was characteristic of Streeterville.

The story of old man Streeter and his wife besting their millionaire neighbors and the city police made good copy for the local press. Some reporters were openly sympathetic, and the publicity even prompted the sale of a few more lots. Not long after, though, trouble returned when yet another group of thugs, presumably at the behest of adjoining property owners or the title company, showed up at the Streeter residence. Once again, legend has it that the old warrior moved too quickly and drove them off, bloodied and bruised.[58] The resulting publicity brought more newcomers to settle in the District. What Streeter needed now was compelling legal justification to maintain his fledgling community. Using the legal training of his youth, Streeter headed to the Cook County Courthouse. There, he discovered something as important as the original sandbar itself: a legal basis for his right of ownership that might be upheld by the courts.

Streeter's research revealed that President James Monroe had sent a government surveyor named John Wall to Illinois in 1821 to demarcate the state's boundaries. According to the official "map" of Illinois, its eastern boundary lay a few yards east of Michigan Avenue, at what was then the shoreline.[59] Streeter reasoned that everything east of the "Wall Line" thus was outside of Illinois—which was also the argument asserted later by the Pokagon Potawatomi in their legal proceedings. Returning home with this good news, Streeter told an assembled crowd of supporters that he had proof that they were outside the jurisdiction of Illinois and Chicago. Counter to what the Pokagon Potawatomi contended, Streeter never argued that his "District" was not a part of the United States, and he even traveled to Washington, DC, to seek appointment as a congressional representative. While reclamations of submerged lands certainly occurred elsewhere in the United States without results like the Streeter claims, it seems that Streeterville was an odd confluence of the power of mapping, boundaries, land cessions, and personality that resulted in the unique Streeterville saga. The Captain announced to the crowd that they were in "The District of Lake Michigan" and subject only to the laws and jurisdiction of the federal government.[60] A constitutional convention was organized by the Streeterville residents, and according to Streeter,

> We established our government in the District of Lake Michigan without any flourish of authority or blare of trumpets, and, in fact, without any undue demonstration. One of my outhouses was converted into a temple of justice, and a sign placed

> above its door proclaimed its august character. Our deliberations, elections, and other necessary assemblages were held in this building until the police authorities of Chicago regarded it with secret disfavor.[61]

By acclamation of the citizenry assembled, the Captain became the first governor of the District. As the head of a "sovereign government," he duly notified the city, state, and national governments in writing of the District's legal and political status, and the newspapers reported the event widely.[62]

Opportunity attracts opportunists, and the District was no exception. Early to arrive was a dashing young man named William H. Niles. Young, handsome, brash, and educated, Niles volunteered his military experience from five years of service in the U.S. Army and convinced the initially ambivalent Captain to appoint him military governor of the District of Lake Michigan.[63] "Governor" Niles may have penned the following brief (auto)biography written in the third person and ascribed to an unidentified "publisher":

> Governor Niles was born in Lackawanna county, Pennsylvania, March 4, 1860. He received a common school education. His early life on an Illinois farm and five years with the United States regulars laid the foundation for the strength and vigor which now mark his every movement and command.[64]

In 1899, "toughs" hired by North Shore property owners again invaded the District and commenced tearing down and burning everything in sight. Streeter, absent during the initial attack, returned as soon as news of the assault reached him. A battle was waged across Streeterville for three days and nights. The newspapers took to calling it the Streeterville Wars[65] and set up a war correspondents' camp. Immense crowds of supporters gathered at the border to cheer on the underdog District citizenry. As night fell on the third day, Captain Streeter and his forces pulled back, and the occupying hooligans ordered beer wagons in celebration. Once again, the wily boatman was ahead of them, and after letting them have their alcohol for a few hours, he and his followers were able to retake the District from their inebriated foes. Although victorious, the damage to the structures and spirit of the District was substantial.

A second constitutional convention was held in the District on April 5 of that year in order to formally (re)organize a government. One month later, on May 5, all of the citizens and a few hundred onlookers gathered for the raising of the American flag over the territory. Battles with police and thugs, however, continued unabated. An attorney hired by the Captain, carrying what Streeter said would have been irrefutable evidence of the legality of his claim, was murdered on his way back from Evanston, Illinois.[66] On May 25, three hundred police officers massed at the border of Streeterville in order to clear the area, arrest the inhabitants, and end the dispute once and for all. George and Maria were on a tour of the city's saloons at the time, so Governor Niles rallied the citizenry into building breach works and palisades and commandeering cannon from the city parks to load with anything available. Typical of the press coverage of the battle for the District was one headline from the *New York Times*: "Chicago Has Real War, 300 Armed Policemen Sent to Capture Streeter's Force, Squatter's Followers, Backed by Gatling Guns, Were Intrenched [*sic*] on State Land, but Surrendered."[67]

Thousands of Chicagoans rushed to the lakefront to witness the battle as George and Maria returned to discover their home had become a fortress. The first wave of invading officers was repelled with cannon fire. Near the end of the day, and to the rude mockery of the crowd, the police succeeded in arresting Captain Streeter, Niles, and most of the citizens of Streeterville. Streeter was released the next day on grounds that he had not participated in the insurrection. The others remained jailed for several months, until acquitted of anarchy and treason after a weeklong trial. In mid-1900, the Chicago police made another assault on Streeterville. Posing as sightseers, they succeeded in getting into the District and arresting the Captain and Maria. With the Streeters behind bars, resistance abated, and the police concluded the day with a bonfire of shanty wood, furniture, furnishings, and other personal possessions. The Chicago papers declared the end of the Streeterville Wars.[68]

They were not over. Unable to prevent their eviction, the group afterwards issued a "Declaration of Independence," authored in large part by "Governor" Niles.[69] The Declaration, dated May 26, 1900, recited the events of Streeter's arrival in Chicago and the subsequent claim and development of the sandbar area as an independent territory. The next year, the Streeters traveled to Washington, DC, and returned with what was purported to be a land grant to the District, issued to Streeter himself and signed on behalf of President Grover Cleveland by his secretary. The only problem was that it was quickly exposed as a forgery, and the Captain soon found himself under indictment.[70] Streeter secured bail and returned home, where a drunken mob, possibly recruited by the Chicago Title and Trust Company, and led by a ruffian named John Kirk, showed up at Streeter's door. The only casualty in the skirmish that followed was Kirk, who died during an exchange of gunfire. Captain

Streeter and two compatriots were arrested for murder. Press coverage of the affair continued to present the spin of Streeter.[71] The public apparently was hungry for all the details of this dramatic turn of events, and the Chicago newspapers were filled with front-page news of the battle.[72]

It took almost a year for the matter to come to trial. Streeter was found guilty and sentenced to life imprisonment at the state's prison in Joliet. Maria collapsed at the announcement of the verdict and died a few weeks later; Streeter blamed the judicial system for her death. During his incarceration, his sometime ally and sometime rival, William Niles, authored another pamphlet with the rather long title "The Military Government of the District of Lake Michigan, Its legal standing as defined by Official letters and papers, by William H. Niles Military Governor—Captain George Streeter, the American Dreyfus, now in the States Prison at Joliet, Ill."[73]

The reference to Dreyfus is to Alfred Dreyfus, the French military officer who had been wrongfully convicted in 1894 of treason largely due to his being Jewish, and whose release from France's Devil's Island Prison became a worldwide cause. However, in the pamphlet, Niles still accused his ally Streeter of being involved in fraud, selling and reselling lots: "During [Streeter's] trial it was proven that he had sold one lot fourteen Times and it is evident that he sold every lot in the District over three or four times . . . this is why he is so opposed to the military government being established in the District."[74]

Nonetheless, in a more sympathetic tone later in the same document, Niles wrote, "Of course the same influence that sent Streeter to jail will keep him there, for the Board of Pardons owe their political positions to his enemies. Also the fact that a petition for his pardon and signed by 50,000 citizens of Chicago has no effect on the Board of Pardons or the Governor of Illinois."

Astonishingly, nine months after his conviction, the governor of Illinois, John P. Altgeld, issued Streeter a full pardon and he went free.[75] Altgeld was a Democrat who authored *Our Penal Machinery and Its Victims*, and was branded a socialist and a supporter of "radical" causes.[76] Vilified by the press during his lifetime, he became a symbol of good government after his death.[77] By 1902, the press was *not* dismissing Streeter's claim out of hand, unlike their treatment of the Potawatomi claim for the lakefront. Some of the news coverage of Streeter and his allies even questioned the ownership interests of the North Shore property owners.[78]

After his release from the penitentiary, Streeter returned to the District in 1903 and built a brick home, but the flurry of lawsuits over the land continued and additional parties joined the fray, including the family of one of the first white settlers of Chicago, Robert Kinzie. At age sixty-nine, George Streeter remarried and brought to the District his new bride, thirty-six-year-old Alma Lockwood of Wakarusa, Indiana. The new Mrs. Streeter settled into her role as defender of her husband and his dreams, and in return the Captain affectionately called her "Ma."

Little in the situation changed until World War I, when a new ordinance was enacted by the city council closing the city's taverns on Sundays. The Streeters saw a unique business opportunity, and soon liquor was flowing seven days a week in Streeterville. More battles and arrests ensued. In 1915, the police invaded the territory and cleared the area one last time.

> A photographer for the *Chicago Tribune* took a picture of Cap, his little fox terrier, Spot, his wife and (their longtime friend) Mrs. Eddie [presumably the Mrs. L. Edwards who authored the tract previously mentioned], seated on boxes in front of the fire with their belongings piled in the street behind. The picture was blown up and run the next morning with the headline CAP'S DREAMS AGAIN GO UP IN SMOKE. More than one Chicagoan, looking at the pathetic group, swallowed a lump in his throat and cursed the rich.[79]

Later that year the courts finally ruled against Streeter and dismissed any claim that he had to the land. He got another boat and tied it to the municipal pier, and he and "Ma" made ends meet by selling coffee and hot dogs. On January 22, 1921, sick with an infected eye and pneumonia, Captain Streeter died at the age of eighty-four. The obituaries for Streeter reflect some of the valorization of Streeter that had occurred in the papers over the preceding thirty-five years.[80]

"Ma" Streeter and the Streeter heirs tried to carry on the fight, but she died on October 19, 1936, at the age of sixty-six. The newspapers presented her in a nostalgic light and emphasized her meager circumstances at the time of her death.[81] In her obituary in the *Los Angeles Times*, Streeter's widow was described as "the Empress of Streeterville."[82] This exemplifies the penchant of the participants in the Streeterville drama to claim titles of legitimacy that were often repeated in the press. "Captain" emphasized Streeter's authority and experience, "Mayor" and "Empress" were indicative of their status as leaders of a sovereign entity, "Ma" reflected her maternal role over the District, and "Governor" promoted William Niles's authority over the District. Even when repeated tongue-in-cheek, the titles affirmed their public identities and achieved/ascribed statuses. "Ma" Streeter, in

TO MOVE ON CHICAGO.

Entire Tribe of Indians Announce that They Will Invest the Lake Front.

DETROIT, Mich., June 7.—A special to The Tribune from St. Joseph, Mich., says: " tribe of Pottawatomie Indians, living in Van Buren County, held a secret pow-wow at Hartford to-day to listen to a report of scouts sent to Chicago. By a unanimous vote the tribe decided to sail for Chicago June 22 under the leadership of Chief Isaac Quigno, the youngest and most daring full-blooded Indian of the tribe. Chief Charles Pokagon, son of the late Simon Pokagon, was deposed together with his council of seven advisers, because of their lukewarm attitude, and Frank Williams, Frank Sawalk, J. H. Cushway, Stephen Topash, Joseph Motay, Charles Motay, and Andrew Rupp were elected members of the new Council.

"The Pottawatomies propose to invest the lake front of Chicago, and then proceed to prove their claims to their land, which they believe will be sustained.

"If the Chicago claim is established, they will squat on all the lake front from the Indiana line to Grand Haven, Mich., which they say is their land by virtue of the same treaty upon which they base their Chicago claim."

POTTAWATTOMIES TO SQUAT.

Redskins Choose Daring Young Leader and Decide to Invest the Lake Front at Chicago.

[BY THE NEW ASSOCIATED PRESS—A.M.]

ST. JOSEPH (Mich.) June 8.—The tribe of Pottawattomie Indians living in Van Buren county, held a secret powpow at Hartford to listen to a report of scouts sent to Chicago. By a unanimous vote, the tribe decided to sail for Chicago June 22, under the leadership of Chief Isaac Quigno, the youngest and most daring full-blooded Indian of the tribe. Chief Charles Pokagon, son of the late Simon Pokagon, was deposed, together with his council of seven advisors, because of their lukewarm attitude.

The Pottawattomie purpose is to invest the lake front of Chicago, and then proceed to prove their claims to the land, which they believe will be sustained. If the Chicago claim is established, they will squat on all the lake front from the Indiana line to Grand Haven, Mich., which they say is their land by virtue of the same treaty upon which they base their Chicago claim.

Los Angeles Times, January 9, 1901, p. 7 (*left*); *New York Times*, June 8, 1902, p. 8 (*right*).

particular, was eulogized for her devotion to her husband and his dreams despite the hardships they endured.[83]

The Streeters' epic battles are immortalized in the naming of a restaurant, a neighborhood, and a city street after them.[84] Once gone, the city celebrated their eccentricities and glossed over the deeper meanings of what they and their allies had promoted as a populist crusade against the wealthy. Their battle for Streeterville reflected deep divisions in class and identity at the end of the nineteenth and beginning of the twentieth centuries, in Chicago and the rest of the nation. The designation of the neighborhood as "Streeterville," after their deaths, is reminiscent of the way Indian peoples and place names were used by settlers to mark the American landscape after removal of most of the Indians themselves from the territory.

In reports that spanned over forty years, the Streeters earned a substantial amount of publicity in the popular press. Whether good, bad, or indifferent, the news stories conveyed and perpetuated a folksy mythology, an ideology and hegemony of an America where a ne'er-do-well and his supportive spouse were championed as underdogs, even though the likelihood of their success was, if not minimal, then minimized. Much of his success in staying in the public imagination must be credited to Streeter himself, who for decades displayed a Barnumesque ability to put on a show and give his audience the story they wanted. In the end, however, the newspapers confirmed the roles of other institutional forces, including corporations, police, and courts, that in the end denied Streeter or his heirs any claim to the sandbar at the foot of Chicago.

The Potawatomi and George Wellington Streeter crossed paths on numerous occasions throughout Streeter's lifetime. As recounted in his primary biography, as a child in Michigan, Streeter played with other children who were Indian.[85] After Streeter returned to Chicago he told of another connection to his neighboring Potawatomi:

> At one time about fifty Siberians who were on their way to the neighborhood of Houghton Lake [Michigan], where they had purchased considerable land, asked permission to camp on my premises for a few days in order to rest their tired horses and to recuperate a little themselves. I had no objection whatever, and in fact, was pleased to accommodate them, so they settled down peacefully on my homestead without any sort of demonstration whatever. Not long after a swarm of policemen came buzzing curiously about the camp, thinking, as I afterward learned, that these poor people were Indians. Knowing that the Pottawatomies were friends of mine, by

> a great flight of imagination, they came to the conclusion that the Pottawatomies were on deck to aid me in some unknown scheme.[86]

Although no specific date is given for this event, it appears to have been close to the time when Charles Pokagon, chairman of the Business Committee of the Pokagon Band of Potawatomi Indians, was announcing to the newspapers the tribe's intent to move to the lakefront of Chicago and secure their claim to the unceded shoreline.[87] The tribe made news across the nation with the claim; newspaper coverage generally was unsympathetic and reflected negative attitudes of the day towards Indians generally.

As noted earlier, Mrs. Edwards asserted in her treatise that the Indians had sold their right and title to the lakefront to Streeter. Yet the incident points to an understanding, by at least some of the Streeterites, that if the lands east of the Wall Line were not within the jurisdiction of the State of Illinois, then their ownership resided with the original inhabitants of the land, the Potawatomi, until such time as they were divested of such title.[88] The Streeter claim was a counterpart to Indian claims to the same territory; like the Indians, he argued that the newly unsubmerged lakefront was not part of Illinois, then asserting, unlike the Potawatomi, the ideology that it therefore was *terra nullius* and "vacant" land subject to settler homesteading in the grand American tradition of Manifest Destiny.[89]

The Economies of Streeter and the Potawatomi

> Somewhere between the bright carnival of the boulevards and the dark girders of the El, ever so far and ever so faintly between the still grasses and the moving waters, clear as a cat's cry on a midnight wind, the Pottawattomies mourn in the river reeds once more. The Pottawattomies were much too square. They left nothing behind but their dirty river.
>
> —Nelson Algren, *Chicago: City on the Make*

The Pokagon Potawatomi lawsuit made no mention of Streeter and his parallel claim to the Chicago lakefront. Yet, in private correspondence decades later, Michael B. Williams, the secretary of the tribe at the time of the lawsuit, opined that had Streeter allied himself with the Potawatomi, they both might have been successful in their claims. Williams wrote,

Michael B. Williams, ca. 1929, in Niles, Michigan. Williams is to the far left, with other Pokagon Potawatomi tribal members. FROM THE MICHAEL B. WILLIAMS PAPERS AND REPRODUCED WITH PERMISSION OF THE HEIRS.

> I repeat what I once said to you in time past. It is regrettable that "Cap" Streeter was so full of the spirit of physical combativeness he could not see the importance of joining forces with the Indians in the endeavor to resolve the lake front controversy. Together, the two line up: Streeter's priority of occupancy and the Indians with their unrelinquished titles and rights.[90]

However, in that last sentence, Williams succinctly sums up the core of the two claims; while each sought the same land, they were based on mutually exclusive theories of land tenure and there was no way for both to win. Had a court ruled in the favor of either, the claim of the other would be negated. Had the Pokagon

Potawatomi argument that they never relinquished title beyond the "Wall Line" succeeded, then Streeter would have had no room to argue he had the right to newly discovered land. However, the court instead ruled in favor of the status quo, and the Streeter/Pokagon Potawatomi claims share this distinction: while both were based on creative legal theory, both were ultimately unsuccessful.

In the ambitiously titled pamphlet *The Greatest Conspiracy Ever Conceived*, authors and allies of the Potawatomi, W. H. Cox and W. E. Johnson, outlined in fifty-two pages why the Potawatomi were the rightful owners of the Chicago lakefront.[91] It is the same kind of diatribe as those authored by the supporters of Streeter; the arguments are very similar, and their efforts kept the local printers busy. Cox held a quitclaim deed from Simon Pokagon to the lakefront, so the effort appears self-serving since he could argue that he now owned the Indians' interests if their cause prevailed. Still, many of Streeter's supporters were also positioned to benefit financially had his claim been successful. Streeter and the tribe both found themselves in the middle of claims that had far-reaching and substantial implications for supporters and foes alike. While there is scant evidence that Streeter and the Potawatomi ever directly cooperated with each other, they both contributed to the vitality and economy of Chicago by keeping an army of police, lawyers, and judges busy, and providing the fodder to sell a large volume of newspapers detailing their latest activities. The Streeter and Potawatomi claims were even occasionally connected in the press of the day. Representative was this report from 1901:

> Letter from Dowagiac Mich., Announces That Talk of Pottawattomies Trying to Enforce Claims to Lake Shore is "Moonshine." Streeter Would Welcome Allies In the mean time Captain Streeter has announced That he will welcome the Indians, if they as allies, and give them all aid and assistance and a safe harborage in the "District of Lake Michigan."[92]

While the claims of Streeter and the Potawatomi are often cast in an atmosphere of paucity and impoverishment, in fact Streeter and the Potawatomi appear to have done very well financially, even though neither were ultimately successful in the courts. Many in the army of defenders of the District of Lake Michigan and Streeter were in fact lot owners who had purchased the land from Streeter.[93] One report even suggested that Streeter had sold lots to the very Chicago police charged with keeping him under control.[94] Another report announced that Streeter had sold one

Pallbearers at the funeral for George W. Streeter. K. F. BROOMELL AND H. M. CHURCH, "STREETERVILLE SAGA," *JOURNAL OF THE ILLINOIS STATE HISTORICAL SOCIETY* 33, NO. 2 (JUNE 1940): 153–65, BETWEEN 164 AND 165.

lakefront parcel for $30,000, and calculated that the remaining Streeter lots had a total value of $300,000.[95] After his death on January 29, 1923,

> [The Captain] lay in state for three hours in Grace Methodist church . . . while hundreds of persons paid their last tribute, the old hat reposed beside him in the coffin. . . . Reverend Raymond L. Seamans, pastor of the church, preached the funeral sermon, following which the body was taken to Graceland Cemetery for internment [*sic*]. The active pallbearers were all members of the Lake Michigan Land Association, while the honorary pallbearers were the Captain's old comrades in the Civil War. More than forty automobiles, carrying members of the Association and the Grand Army members, followed the hearse to the Cemetery.[96]

As noted in chapter 2, Simon Pokagon appears to have sold his own interests in the lakefront to speculators, and the tribal Business Committee minutes reflect the payment of some $33,900 to the tribe, either as an advance on, or a sale of the tribe's lakefront claim. Tribal members received $100 each for their share of the lakefront (a lot of money in this era).[97] One newspaper of the time reported that purchaser Robert A. Bines, of Chicago, and the Business Committee agreed that each member of the tribe would receive $1,000 "in the event of the successful outcome of the claim."[98] The article continued with an account of the Indians enjoying their new wealth:

> Within an hour the joyful news had spread to every member of the tribe that had camped about Dowagiac for the last three days. . . . Indians who had not exchanged greetings since the government paid them five years ago held reunions on every street corner. The squaws and papooses hung together while the braves and old men held pow wows and exchanged tobacco. The pipe of peace, which was represented by a cheap cigar, was handed about, while the smokers talked of the probabilities of the wheat and corn crops and of the awful possibility of the money never being paid. There was but little drinking; not an Indian was arrested. . . . One Indian family stood in front of the Commercial House last night, and the father and mother and five children divided a quart, each in turn being handed the long black bottle. After the bottle was emptied they all went into the dining-room seemingly greatly refreshed.[99]

Ironically, under federal law, the non-Native purchasers of the Potawatomi land claims could never acquire clear title to their properties since "Indian lands" can only be acquired from the federal government.[100] Without a doubt, however, both claims appealed not only to the imaginations of local residents, but to their coffers as well. The claims provided a financial benefit to Streeter and his supporters as well as to Pokagon Potawatomi tribal members, and in that respect both should be considered a success.

Meaning Making and the Chicago "Frontier"

In the 1890s, others in Chicago were articulating their visions of American expansion and exceptionalism under the rubric of "frontier." Most notably, Frederick Jackson Turner and William F. "Buffalo Bill" Cody presented to Chicagoans and the world their perspectives on the conquest of the North American continent.

Their arguments differed from those of both Streeter and the Potawatomi, and while Potawatomi claims to territory remain largely forgotten by the public, the non-Native narratives of taking survive in the collective memory of Chicagoans.

For more than thirty years, showman William F. Cody manufactured a tale of the "conquest" of the West that has become a part of the collective memory of most Americans. Historian Frederick Jackson Turner's lecture "The Significance of the Frontier in American History," delivered to the American Historical Association in 1893 at the World's Columbian Exposition in Chicago, similarly affected how some Americans thought about themselves. While Turner asserted that the wilds of the United States had been conquered by the axe and plow of settler immigrants, Cody contended that the nation had been wrested from the savagery of its Indigenous inhabitants. The power of Buffalo Bill's Wild West as well as Turner's frontier thesis were not only in the images presented or in the ideas promoted. The most substantial impact was in the unification of the citizenry of the United States under these false hyperrealities. Those metanarratives of destiny and exceptionalism continue to this day.

Turner and Cody offered two distinct representations of four hundred years of American history at the World's Columbian Exposition (WCE) of 1893 in Chicago. Each presented a myth supporting the ideology of Manifest Destiny and justifying Euro-American expansion across the North American continent. Their narratives depended upon differing understandings of the "frontier" to help explain the often difficult interactions between settlers and Indigenous inhabitants. Denied official participation in the fair, William F. Cody set up shop across the street from its main entrance. Cody's Buffalo Bill's Wild West show was located at the western end of the fair on 61st Street. Initially a "report from the front," after the 1890 Wounded Knee Massacre and the final suppression of any significant opportunity for Indian armed resistance, Cody's outdoor extravaganza was reconfigured into an "American History lesson."

Situated in Chicago on fourteen acres, the Wild West show was complete with grandstand seating. It included mock battles between Indians and Cavalry; a reenactment of "Custer's Last Stand"; relics from the events surrounding the Massacre at Wounded Knee, including Sitting Bull's bullet-riddled cabin, erected at the western end of the Midway Plaisance; a rendition of the battle to the death between Buffalo Bill and Yellow Hair; and Indian attacks on wagon trains and settler cabins.[101] The quaint liberal narratives in the Wild West show lamenting the demise of Indian peoples obscured the evidence of Indians' struggles and persistence. This production of imperial nostalgia by Cody, however, made Indians safe enough that active attempts at annihilation ceased.[102] For the price of admission, audiences were transported, in their imaginations, to bear witness to the heroics of the American conquest of the Indian and the settlement of the West. These reenactments were more than mere entertainment; they became a collective historical reality. Buffalo Bill established himself as a physical representation of the Indian fighter, cowboy, and scout who cleared the West for the rest of America.

The self-appointed hero of this metahistory, he became synonymous with all things right and good about America's manifest exploitation of the West. The culture industry packaged a version of American history to create a lasting image product of "how the West was won." Working-class men and women, most of them recent immigrants who were laboring under exploitive situations and living in squalid conditions, could perhaps take comfort that they somehow had a piece of the cultural patrimony, and this proved to them they had earned a place in the metanarrative of the United States. In Cody's shows, the Indians usually played the villains, attacking stagecoaches and wagon trains in order to be driven off by "heroic" cowboys and soldiers. Cody also had the wives and children of his Indian performers travel with the show so that the paying public could see the families of his performers as well. As Philip Deloria has pointed out, many Native performers gladly participated in the Wild West show as an opportunity to escape the poverty and dullness of the reservation.[103] "Buffalo Bill's Wild West" represented a hegemonic discourse where simulation could secure the consent of the subaltern when the real might not suffice.[104]

Through the pageant, Cody engaged in the commodification of memory and history.[105] As George Lipitz points out, audiences engage in a dialogue with the past and the meanings and memories it holds for them. Collective memory becomes part of individual and group identity.[106] The Wild West show helped solidify a collective American identity as rugged individualists, conquerors, and rightful heirs to the North American Continent. The show was a place full of understandings and misunderstandings between performers and audience, but in their interactions, they took those misperceptions and converted them into practices that worked. Performers were allowed to *be* Indian and relieved of the pressures of the era to assimilate into the dominant white culture, while non-Native audiences were able to view the contest between "civilization and savagery" from the safety of their seats. In this arena, Indian performers represented themselves to audiences as proud bearers of the traditional cultures of their communities, while the audience often perceived Indians acting out a history that confirmed the superiority of the white race.[107] According to Greg Dening, "Such an ethnographic moment as encounter, the first product of which is interpretation, an understanding of what is new and unexperienced in the light of what is old and experienced—[opens] a space between cultures filled by interpretation, metamorphic understanding and translation."[108]

Cody's parade through history created a frontier mythology for an audience that sought validation for the colonization of North America. In blurring the lines between fact and fiction and history and melodrama, the spectacle confirmed a "heroic national identity" based upon this frontier crucible.[109] It was an era of claims-making; Streeter and the Pokagon Potawatomi responded by making claim to territory within the boundaries of the United States even as the United States sought to expand beyond it into Hawai'i, Cuba, the Philippines, and elsewhere.

Spectacles and the like are contested sites that often manifest as oppositional displays by those unwilling to embrace the "visions" conjured by the culture industry of showmen and fair planners. Cultural commodities like exhibitions privileged the visual over the textual.[110] Turner's understandings of "frontier" contrasted with Cody's spectacle to best explain the "unique" character of Americans.[111] While Turner resonated with other scholars, Cody was the historian for the masses. Streeter was certainly capable of manufacturing his own spectacles, and his played out both in the courts of law and in public opinion. News reports from 1901 give a flavor of his performative endeavors.

> Accompanied by glistening bayonets and heralded by the music of a band, Captain George W. Streeter will march within the next two days into the territory he claims. It will be a peaceable seizure, though the cohorts of the 'Governor of the District of Lake Michigan' will be ready for trouble. Their arms, deed and the government archives will be under escort of a chosen ten of the army.[112]

The Pokagon Potawatomi also knew how to put on a good show and capture the imagination of the public of the era, as reflected in this newspaper report from later that same year.

> Red Men Prepare to Collect a Bill in Chicago, Grim War to Be Carried to the City's Gates by the Pottawatomies Unless Residents Hand Over Treasure for Lake Front Lands—Subtle Influence of Captain Streeter Seen in the Ultimatum of

Indian encampment, 1903. *CHICAGO DAILY NEWS* PHOTO. FROM THE COLLECTION OF THE AUTHOR.

> the Michigan Residents. . . . the Pottawatomie Indians . . . are preparing to send a warship filed with 200 braves into the harbor of Chicago to collect $45,000 said to be due their tribe for land along the lake shore. The Indians are reputed to be allies of Captain George Wellington Streeter, Governor General of the District of Lake Michigan and defenders of the faith in Streeter. The scheme of parading a menacing gunboat along the lake shore, after the American custom of collecting Turkish and Morocco indemnities, is credited to the fertile brain of General Streeter, who was at his intellectual best during his recent confinement in jail.[113]

Even newspapers outside of Chicago carried news of the gripping events, as is typified by this headlined article from the *Hickman (KY) Courier*: "Michigan Indians: Pottawatomie Tribe Decide at Secret Pow Wow to Invade the Lake Front, Chicago."[114] Although the "invasion" never materialized, by 1903 the Pokagon Potawatomi were back in Chicago. From September 26 to October 1 of that year, the Chicago Centennial Committee hosted an Indian Encampment at Lincoln Park to honor the city.[115] The Pokagon Potawatomi were there, led by Simon Pokagon's son, Charles. A brochure for the fair summarizes the still-strong claim to the lakefront even while introducing the audience to the Native participants in an encampment at Lincoln Park.

> There are those among the chiefs present who still hold to the belief that this land is theirs and that those who have dispossessed them did it by means of that might which makes right. Strange as it may appear to the white possessors of the soil . . . there are those among the temporary sojourners in this village who still have hope that recompense may be made them some day for this land which they yielded up when the ruling race came.[116]

Describing the purpose of the encampment, the brochure continues:

> There are gathered here in the village which makes such a striking feature of the celebration of Chicago's birthday, the representatives of six great tribes of red men who once lived either upon this very spot or its immediate vicinity. Just where these Indians are met to-day there dwelt a century ago, the tribe of Pottawattomies under chiefs Pokagon and Poteneebee [Topinabee].[117]

The description includes the participants' names and their tribal affiliations, identifying their housing in Lincoln Park as a "traditional" village, and describing the "traditional" activities the visitor can plan to see, such as dancing, drumming, lacrosse, canoe racing and portaging, religious ceremonies, council meeting, and bow and arrow shooting.[118] The pamphlet recites again the Pokagon Potawatomi claim:

> The son, [Simon] Pokagon, always insisted that only a part of the territory embraced in the present city was included in the sale and that his tribe is the rightful owner of a large part of the most valuable land in the great city. The Pottawattomies who are present in the Indian village at this centennial celebration believe as did their chief, and it was but little more than a year ago when many of them seriously considered the coming to Chicago to squat upon certain lands, in the hope that such action would call attention to their claim and force its settlement.[119]

For the Potawatomi and for Streeter, claiming the Chicago lakefront was also an imaginative experience and cultural endeavor. Louis Owens has written that discourse takes place within what Mikhail Bakhtin defined as "dialogically agitated space," and what Mary Louise Pratt has called contact zones, "social spaces where disparate cultures meet, clash, and grapple with each other."[120] That sort of *rencontre* between nations and cultures takes place at what are commonly identified as the borderlands.[121]

Owens distinguishes between the conceptualizations of territory and frontier; the former is "clearly mapped, fully imagined as a place of containment, invented to control and subdue." On the other hand, frontier, for Owens, is a "transcultural zone of contact . . . the zone of the trickster, a shimmering, always changing zone of multifaceted contact within which every utterance is challenged and interrogated, all referents put into question. . . . 'Frontier' stands, I would further argue, in neat opposition to the concept of 'territory.'"[122]

The Chicago lakefront was all of these things at the end of the last century. For the wealthy landowners and businesses established on the shore, it was territory, neatly divided squares on a plat map drawn up by surveyors, and whose validity was enforced by lawyers and hirelings of the Chicago Title and Trust Company. For Streeter and his supporters, the space was frontier, a place of complication and contest, where a man could wash up on the shore and commence to build a community. As Streeter himself said, "Streeterville won't never have a Chamber of Commerce until it has the cabaret. This is a frontier town and it's got to go through its red-blooded youth."[123]

For Streeter, the U.S. Census Bureau declaration, in 1890, that the American frontier was "closed" was premature by more than a few decades. For the Potawatomi, the Chicago lakefront was a different place. Still organized as an Indian nation within the borders of the United States, its claim for the Chicago shoreline was the kind of bumping of cultures and nations that happens in contact zones and borderlands. The Potawatomi claim is perhaps best understood as an act of resistance to the hegemony of the United States and its ideology of land, property, and ownership. On the other hand, Streeter embraced that ideology, and turned trickster on Chicago when he invoked the ideologies of land ownership by discovery, creation, and conquest to their detriment.

At the beginning of the twentieth century, Chicago remained a frontier town. This "urban frontier" reflected the physical and mental landscapes in which local and global imaginaries meet and interact—a space filled with transcultural practices, mentalities, relationships, and belief systems.[124] Each side of this urban frontier was inhabited by the "other," who represented radical challenges to models of acceptance, cooperation, rejection, marginalization, violation, love, hatred, and annihilation—represented as the variety of possible responses to the challenged space. Each side of the Native/non-Native divide negotiated their own passages through the culture of the other.[125] How the "other" was treated, when revealed in their irreducibility, when their uniqueness disrupted the neat space of harmonious or contentious interaction narratives, reflected the "contact zones" that occur when disparate peoples meet.[126] This explains how Streeter could claim the lakefront as his personal fiefdom, the Potawatomi could argue that the lakefront remained their ancestral territory, while the majority of Chicago scratched their heads and wondered aloud how what had been under water only a few decades earlier could even be the subject of such controversy.

In this respect, every first encounter with a human from a distinctly different culture reveals itself to be an encounter with one's own internal limits. Provoking an acute crisis of one's identity, a highly tensioned awareness of one's limitations, the other threatens, but also offers, the chance of a boundary transgression and transcendence. The popular captivity narratives of the past recount some of the crossings of that space and attempts at *becoming* the other. Since encounters with one's limits break the space of normality, they complicate the self. They force us to learn the other, to produce some kind of knowledge of the other, and sometimes to learn how to live with the other. This meaning-making of encounter reflects the internal changes and adjustments that occur, and then are manifested, in ongoing responses that in the past were too neatly packaged as temporary coexistence or conflict.

Although we normally think of this interaction as occurring at the moment of direct physical contact, the power of a pageant like the Wild West show was that it preserved the opportunity for re-encounter. Reenactments presented as history become contest points and contact zones in ways not unlike previous direct contacts with the "other." We can engage in the same kind of deep reading of Cody's outdoor drama as we do with a text. Embedded within it is a narrative of power and exchange, identity, authority, obligation, and references to the past and future. We know from the history lesson provided by Cody that Americans connected to his narrative of imperialist impulse and national exceptionalism. In fact, it was Cody who first included a corps of "Rough-Riders," including horsemen from nations around the world, in his later dramas, and Theodore Roosevelt would appropriate the term to describe his troops in the war of opportunity with Spain over Cuba.

While Turner is credited with interpreting the closing of the frontier in America, Cody was busily reenacting a "frontier experience" into the collective memory of the citizens of the United States. Streeter, meanwhile, reenacted his own frontier spectacle, replete with moments of "discovery" and mapping interpreted as ownership. At the same time, the Pokagon Potawatomi created their own spectacle of resistance—creating a borderland within the territory of the nation. At that boundary, along the Chicago lakefront, the Potawatomi sued for what they claimed they had never ceded. What they ultimately never ceded was who they were. Ultimately, one can agree at least that Cody, Turner, Streeter, and the Pokagon Potawatomi all advocated for their perspectives at the lakefront of Chicago.

The frontier for Turner was the boundary between that land already subjugated and the empty wilderness still open to development. Cody, on the other hand, saw the frontier as a boundary between the civilized and the uncivilized. The wilderness was not empty; rather it was full of wild creatures, including Indians, who had to be conquered—not through toil, but through conflict. Streeter interjected an intersectional understanding of frontier as it existed on the Chicago lakefront at the end of the nineteenth century. Streeter's frontier lakefront was empty wilderness available for development à la Turner. However, for Streeter it was also a space that would have to be won through conflict—not with Indians and buffalos, but with the Chicago Title and Trust Company, the Chicago police and judicial system, and Gold Coast neighbors. It is readily acknowledged that all of these frontier myths have been discredited by more recent scholars.[127] Yet the Pokagon Potawatomi land claim was a debunking of the frontier myth six decades prior to scholarly efforts to do so. For the Pokagon Potawatomi, frontier did not represent some boundary between civilized and uncivilized. It was not the edge of the safe and the dangerous or the known and the unknown. It was not that liminal space between development and wilderness. To the Pokagon Potawatomi, there never was a frontier. Their ancestral lands had been their place of abode. Supernatural intervention (the Great Flood) had made this area an Indigenous place long before the arrival of non-Natives. Tribal use of the lands and waters had confirmed this fact to them. For them, the borderland was not a situation of red versus white, civilized versus uncivilized, or urban versus rural, but rather legally ceded versus unceded ancestral lands. While Streeter's frontier mythology borrowed from the most strategic aspects of Turner and Cody, the Pokagon Potawatomi rejected the frontier notion in its entirety in making their claim for return of a part of their homeland.

George "Cap" Wellington Streeter. HTTP://WWW.DOWNESSTUDIO.NET/STREETER.HTML.

Selective Memories

The lingering question in this chapter about memory, meaning, and claims-making is why there is such an abundance of scholarship and popular writing about Turner, Cody, and Streeter while their contemporaries, the Potawatomi, are rarely mentioned. Scholars have understood the power of imagery and symbols in support of myth and ideology for quite some time.[128] Michel Foucault noted the influence of spectacle on memory: "Which utterances are destined to disappear without any trace? Which are destined on the other hand, to enter into human memory through ritual, recitation, pedagogy, amusement, festival and publicity?"[129] The *Indian Encampment, Chicago Centennial of 1903* brochure concluded with prophetic words for the Pokagon Potawatomi:

> There probably never again will be given an opportunity to see a gathering of Indians like the one within the compass of this village. Sadly enough, when Chicago comes to celebrate its second centennial there probably will be left no recognizable remnant of these five assembled tribes. Chicago to-day bids them hail, and hopes that the day long may be deferred before the other and final word, farewell, must be spoken.[130]

The intersections of Turner and Cody have been thoroughly explored. Today, along with the numerous scholarly and popular articles and books, there are several websites devoted to Captain Streeter's claim to the Chicago lakefront.[131] In 2001, there was a stage production of the Streeter legend in a local Chicago theater,[132] and in the fall of 2010, a bronze statue of Streeter was erected at the corner of McClurg Court and East Grand Avenue, at the residential development named Fairbanks [*sic*] Court. It is slightly ironic that Streeter stands so close to a structure named after his adversary N. Kellogg Fairbank. With his stovepipe hat on his head and dachshund in arm, he remains a source of fascination and romanticism for at least some Chicagoans.

Why is the Pokagon Potawatomi claim to the Chicago lakefront rarely acknowledged, and surprising to most people today?[133] I believe that the various frontier narratives of Turner, Cody, and Streeter still resonate in the popular imagination of the American public, and they retain a place among the metanarratives of the American people. The Pokagon Potawatomi claim undermines those frontier mythologies, and so becomes "an inconvenient truth." Even today, Chicago prefers its original Indian inhabitants to be relegated to the past. For example, the website "Frontier to Heartland," sponsored by the Newberry Library, continues the usual narrative about Indians and Chicago:

> Conflict and accommodation between Europeans and the people they called "Indians" dominated life in central North America for much of the three centuries

> following the arrival of Europeans. In the process of settling what they called the frontier, Euro-Americans pushed Indians to the margins. . . . *By then the frontier of settlement between whites and Indians was gone* [emphasis added]. In its place was a new political frontier, the borderline between Canada and the United States.[134]

"Prairie Fire: The Illinois Country, 1673–1818," an Illinois Historical Digitalization Project sponsored by the Newberry Library of Chicago, the University of Chicago, Northern Illinois University, and the Illinois State Library, continues this theme. "Jackson's removal policy [Indian Removal Act of 1830] finalized processes that had been unfolding for centuries before 1830. There had long been changes in which peoples lived in Illinois and what lands each group controlled. With removal, repopulation became depopulation and boundary revisions became total dispossession for the Indians."[135] It is the same with the oddly titled *A Compendium of the Early History of Chicago to the Year 1835 When the Indians Left*.[136] Similarly, the online *Encyclopedia of Chicago* has articles that include "Chicago in the Middle Ground,"[137] "Metropolitan Growth," "Economic Geography," and "Native Americans," although this last article does mention that Indians continued living in Chicago after 1833 but provides few specifics. A timeline in the *Encyclopedia of Chicago* contains no mention of Indians in Chicago after the 1795 and 1812 entries.[138] There *is* an entry for "Streeterville" and the story of George Wellington Streeter,[139] yet the entry for "Potawatomis" begins with contact with Europeans and ends in 1840.[140] This impulse of Euro-Americans to imagine themselves as the inheritors of the land now called Chicago is an example of what Jean M. O'Brien has called "firsting and lasting." Indians are pushed into the background of memory and are presumed extinct.[141] We do have the ability to gather the previously untold stories of marginalized peoples—like the Potawatomi. With that information and knowledge, we can unpack "history" with a more critical eye and in the end acquire a richer history that includes all of us.

CHAPTER 5

Leroy Wesaw and the Chicago Canoe Club

> I have seen Indian boys push their birch-bark canoes into the white-capped waves when, like horses maddened by bit and spur, they would rear and plunge, as if determined to shake them off. Yet, still the youthful monarchs held the reins and safely rode the foaming steeds.
>
> —Simon Pokagon, "The Chi-Kog-Ong of the Red Man," *New York Times*, 1897

After 1950, Americans became aware of a "new" phenomenon, the contemporary urban Indian. With employment opportunities in urban areas and poverty on reservations working as significant motivators, Indians from all over the United States began moving to Chicago after World War II. Federal programs terminating tribal recognition and services, as well as federally sponsored relocation programs, contributed substantially to this migration.[1] In Chicago, urban Indians quickly began to organize into an intertribal community, as evidenced by the founding of the Chicago American Indian Center (AIC) in 1953, the first such urban Indian center in the nation.[2] The AIC served as a social service agency and social center for the community. The population of Indians in Chicago increased dramatically during this decade, as did AIC activities.[3] The AIC sponsored social activities such as pow wows, dances, seasonal festivities, a youth group, a camera club, basketball and softball teams, a boy scout troop, and a canoe club.[4] While other organizations also served the growing American Indian community, including St. Augustine's Center, the AIC became the destination for Indians seeking a sense of community in their often challenging new urban environment.[5]

The AIC's Chicago Canoe Club, organized by Leroy Wesaw, a Pokagon Potawatomi tribal member, promoted in positive and public ways activities that encouraged pride in being Indian in Chicago. From its founding in 1964 to its end in 1972, the Chicago Canoe Club was not only the most popular sport and recreational activity sponsored by the AIC, but it also became the public face of Indians thriving in Chicago. Wesaw, like other Pokagon Potawatomi who came before him, left his own unique mark on the city.

The Potawatomi and sports in Chicago have a long history, and as discussed in chapter 1, sport and recreation have always been a part of Native life. Games such as lacrosse and activities such as canoeing have had both competitive and recreational value to participants. In the nineteenth and twentieth centuries, sport served as both a bridge and a moat—the opportunity to publicly assert the ability to participate in dominant settler society, as well as to signal a distinct Indigenous identity. This chapter chronicles the ways Pokagon Potawatomi Indians used sports and recreation to assert an Indian identity amidst millions of non-Natives in Chicago, and participate in the postwar urban Indian experience in the city.

From Warrior to Worthy Adversary

Lacrosse has been a game played by Indians east of the Mississippi since long before contact with Europeans. The origins of the game are explained in many of the traditional stories of the tribes that play the game.[6] Prior to contact, it served both social and ceremonial purposes and was an intratribal and intertribal competition that allowed families, clans, villages, and communities to assert their physical skills and claim superiority. In the nineteenth century, the sport enjoyed a revival, as non-Natives "discovered" the sport and, in typical fashion of the hegemon, expected American Indians to entertain them with the game.

In Chicago, lacrosse became an opportunity for the Pokagon Potawatomi to maintain their distinct public presence as American Indians within the city. As mentioned in chapter 2, Simon Pokagon presided as honorary umpire of a lacrosse game held as part of World's Columbian Exposition (WCE) festivities.[7] At the time, lacrosse was viewed as a distinctly Indian game. A contemporary news report on the WCE game gives little hint that lacrosse would be embraced by elite non-Natives in the next century, but it does emphasize the way in which the game signaled to the crowd the indigeneity of the players.

> Lacrosse, the oldest known game in the history of America, was played within the gates of the greatest modern monument in civilization this afternoon. . . . Paint, yellow paint, red paint, black paint, all kinds of paint, known and unknown, seemed to meet on an equal footing upon the faces of semi-savage Iroquois and Pottawatomie . . . whose ancestors are mentioned in history as once having owned the present site, and who had hunted and were hunted in turn by their pale face brothers who first found the Chicago River. . . .
>
> The game was between the Canadian Iroquois and the Pottawatomies. Old Chief Pokagon, whose father had much to do with early Chicago history, was the honorary umpire and occupied a seat in the press box.[8]

Although the press emphasized the savage warrior status of the Native players, and while Indian participation served to confirm the fantasies of many non-Natives that Indians were artifacts of the nation's past, the report also provided a counter-narrative to the notion that the Potawatomi were a vanishing race. After all, only three years before the lacrosse exhibition, the same newspaper had reported the demise of the Band.[9]

As noted in the previous chapter, at Chicago's Lincoln Park only ten years later, Simon Pokagon's son, Charles, who had accompanied his father at the lacrosse exhibition of 1893, would lead an camp of "Sacs and Foxes from Iowa, Pottawatomies . . . from Michigan . . . and Winnebagoes . . . Chippewas and Menominees [from Wisconsin]."[10] Ottawa people also came to join the 1903 encampment.[11] The Indians, including the Pokagon Potawatomi, engaged in various "traditional" activities that included holding a lacrosse game for the entertainment of 50,000 spectators.[12] They also participated in canoe portaging, canoe racing, and canoe tilting.[13] The author of a brochure for the 1903 festivities wrote,

> Special mention should be made of the la crosse [*sic*] game which will be played on the baseball ground at Lincoln Park. This game is a favorite with the Indians, and for that matter, with many whites, though it is essentially a red man's game. It is interesting and exciting in the extreme, being full of dash and go from the start. . . . Touching again the matter of sports, it may be said that there have been

> gathered together in this village the Indians known to be the best canoe men in the whole country. . . . Canoe tilting is a favorite water sport of the Indians. They stand in their canoes and each contestant tries by means of his pole to throw his opponent into the water. It is exciting but good humored play.[14]

Once again, the Indians, including the Pokagon Potawatomi, were using the athletic traditions of their ancestors to publicize their presence in the city.

Baseball, which some American Indian nationalists claim is a variation of the lacrosse and stickball games of Indians, was similar to games played in Europe before 1600. Whatever its origins, beginning in the last half of the nineteenth century, a craze for the game swept across the United States. Baseball (along with football and basketball) were seen as civilizing influences at Indian boarding schools, and Native students embraced the game as an opportunity to prove their worth, assert their dignity, and escape the tedium of their schooling.[15] Graduates soon brought baseball to their home reservations, and in communities with often little else happening, baseball became a favorite activity.[16]

White audiences enjoyed watching contests pitting Natives and non-Natives against each other on the playing field. Often the Indians won. Typical is this news report of 1892:

> Indian boys . . . excel in athletic sports, as in the national pastime of baseball. . . . The Haskell Institute nine is a crack team and in its contests with various white clubs in Kansas the Indian boys are almost always victorious.[17]

Another article from the time describes the Ponca tribe's baseball team and the tribal members' enthusiasm for the game.

> They are all picked athletes and fine specimens of manhood. All are exceptionally fleet-footed and can equal in speed almost any man in the National League. They have the baseball fever worse than any Chicago small boy ever dreamed. . . . Should they come it will afford an interesting sight to Chicago fans. All the players wear their hair long and talk in their own language when playing ball.[18]

The Pokagon Potawatomi eagerly embraced baseball. The same Michael B. Williams who led the tribe for five decades was also a manager of the "Famous Pottawatomie Indian Base Ball Club," improbably touted as "the only all Indian team in the Country" and headquartered in Dowagiac, Michigan.[19]

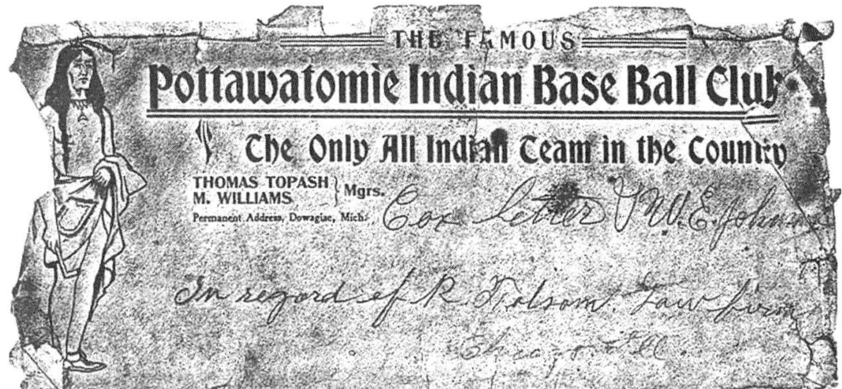

Stationery, ca. 1920. FROM THE MICHAEL B. WILLIAMS PAPERS AND REPRODUCED WITH PERMISSION OF THE HEIRS.

Everett Claspy notes that two Pokagon Potawatomi brothers, Paul and Oliver Hamilton, were stars on the Dowagiac, Michigan, high school baseball team in 1921, and that Oliver played minor-league ball in Lancaster, Pennsylvania, before his untimely death in 1923. His brother Paul played the game while attending Haskell Institute, and later as a pitcher for a St. Louis Browns farm team. Paul also played for factory teams where he worked, including Kawneer Company, National Standard, and Studebaker Automotive. In 1931 he played on the professional Marinette (Wisconsin) baseball team, and in 1932 he pitched for the Nebraska Indians traveling baseball team.[20] While I could find no archival evidence of the Pokagon Potawatomi fielding a team that played specifically in Chicago, it is reasonable to suspect that they participated in games in the Chicago region during the Indian baseball phenomenon that lasted into the World War II era. The sport of baseball would continue the efforts of Indians, including the Pokagon Potawatomi, to resist being pushed into the shadows. Indians were now beating their non-Native neighbors at their own game.

The Power of the Canoe for Potawatomi People

Birch bark canoes (*wigwas jiman* in the Potawatomi language) have figured significantly in the recent histories of the Potawatomi. Some oral histories recount that they were the mode of transport for their great migration west at the behest of prophets five hundred years ago or more from the Atlantic Seaboard to the land where food grows on water (wild rice).[21] Birch bark canoes played a prominent role in the ability of these peoples to dominate their Great Lakes Indigenous neighbors in trade and warfare, including the Mesquakie, Miami, and Kickapoo.[22] The birch bark canoe also was important in the seventeenth century when the Iroquois drove the Algonquin tribes of the Great Lakes from southern Michigan during wars sparked by the colonial fur trade and disease.

James Clifton describes the importance of the canoe to the Potawatomi:

> As older cultural elements, especially bark canoe use, combined with newer ones, particularly horticulture, the Potawatomi economy expanded and the quality of their life was enriched. Few other Indian tribes in the region possessed this exact combination of elements, which gave the Potawatomi their cultural advantage.[23]

Helen Tanner describes a similar value of the canoe to the Ojibwe:

> Canoes were essential items to the Ojibwa. Every family owned several, each weighing from 65 to 125 pounds. Covering the frame and sealed with spruce or pine gum were sheets of birch bark, an indispensable material to the Ojibwa economy. It was tough, light, and easy to peel from the tree in the early spring.[24]

Wigwas jiman is an iconic symbol of Great Lakes Indian identity. The canoe figures prominently in the origin stories of the Potawatomi as told by Simon Pokagon. While it is no longer a routine activity, the Ojibwe, Odawa, and Potawatomi have never ceased building canoes. The Milwaukee Public Museum hired two Ojibwe men in 1947 to construct a traditional birch bark *jiman* while author Robert E. Ritzenthaler documented the steps and the museum staff filmed the process.[25] Ritzenthaler's field notes detail gathering the jack pine roots for sewing; the harvesting of the *wigwas*, and of white cedar for ribs, prows, and gunwales; the shaping of the ribs and prow pieces; gathering cedar branches for flooring; the shaping of the bark and the building of the inner frame; sewing; and the collection of pine pitch and waterproofing.[26] Almost thirty years later, in 1976, Ojibwe canoe builder Earl (Otchingwanigan) Nyholm participated in the making of the film *Earl's Canoe: A Traditional Ojibwe Craft*, which highlights the connection between canoes and identity.[27] Nyholm is an Ojibwe elder who lives in Crystal Falls, Michigan. He has been working with traditional crafts and technology all of his life and learned early the art of canoe construction from tribal elders. According to Nyholm, building canoes "provides a spiritual link to his people—past and present."[28] He explains his point of view in a magazine interview:

> "It's not a hobby for me, it's real life. It's important to hang on to it for some kind of meaning. It's something like an obligation, but different. If life has no meaning, you get lost. I don't want my canoe to get lost." He adds, "In a way, my ancestors talk to me through the canoe. . . . I hear the voices of the old folks." . . . Each time he builds a canoe, he is reminded of his obligation to carry on the traditions of those who came before and to pass them on with reverence and respect. "When I build a canoe, the canoe is in charge of the timing. You can't rush things. You have to do it with respect. You have to thank the trees and the forest for their contributions to the canoe; leave some tobacco as a sacrifice and a token of gratitude."[29]

Canoeing has become a very popular hobby, and there is a canoe rental shop in almost every state in the United States located close to water. People interested in competitive or recreational canoeing often consider canoe building an artful craft. Some Indians in the United States are coming to understand that it is more than skin tone or ancestry that establishes an Indigenous identity separate and distinct from the surrounding non-Native dominant culture. Although spoken regarding a different group of American Indians, the remarks of Creek elder Phillip Deere are illustrative of the connections that some American Indian people are making between their cultures and their survival. In a warning about continuing as "a recognizable people," Deere admonishes,

> We may look like Indians, we have the color of an Indian, but what are we thinking? What are we doing to our own children who are losing their language, their own ways. . . . What are they doing? Are they still trying to be Indians or are they just benefit Indians, a three-day Indian, a clinic Indian, or BIA-school Indian, what kind of Indian are we?[30]

The obfuscation of their cultures has not been lost upon the Indian peoples of the Great Lakes. Subjected to government policies that promoted such things as boarding schools, missionization, language suppression, land loss, allotment, and outlawing of their religions and ceremonies, their cultures were driven underground for several generations until the last several decades of increased plurality. As pressures to assimilate into the "whitestream"[31] continue, Indians are finding new ways and symbols to assert an Indigenous identity. In recent years, Native artisans have been engaging in canoe building. Many of them mix traditional Indian styles of tribal canoes with modern-day designs and construction. Canoe building has also been a part of a renaissance of seafaring among the Indigenous peoples of the Pacific.[32] In discussing the active metaphorical work and communicative agency that canoes engage in, in Malekula, Vanuatu, in the Melanesian Islands of the Pacific, ethnologist Christopher Tilley makes several pertinent points, applicable to canoe building by members of Great Lakes–area Indian communities as well. For example, canoes strengthen individual and community identity. The canoe serves as a utilitarian article of material culture that connects the social life of a community to its past and present as a recognized tradition. The construction and use of canoes promotes a sense of unity, commonality, and community. Canoes also operate as nonverbal communications about relationships within the community, both about themselves and with regard to outsiders. Furthermore, canoes connect peoples to their environment. Tilley concludes:

> Their metaphorical meanings are multifarious, enabling them to combine and embrace contradictory principles and tendencies in social life. The power of imagery resides in the condensation of reference linked with the sensual and tactile qualities of its material form and reference to the human body. The form of the canoe and the metaphorical attributes associated with it permits the creation of vital referential links . . . at the heart of social reproduction.[33]

Whale hunting for the Makah, the canoe revivals of the Tlingit and the Haida, the spearfishing and wild-ricing activities of the Ojibwe, the buffalo herd regeneration efforts of the Lakota and other Plains tribes, and the push for land recovery and sacred site protection are all occurring throughout Indian Country, and all are examples of *recollection* in American Indian communities that are connecting to the past. They also represent efforts of Native inhabitants to embrace their place as Indigenous peoples through connections to natural resources and traditions. Canoe building and canoeing in the Great Lakes region involve the utilization of a natural resource (birch bark) historically claimed as important by the Potawatomi community.

Exemplifying this was the commitment of Pokagon Band members, in the 1980s, to build a birch bark canoe. Tribal elder Mark Alexis; Richard E. "Mike" Daugherty, spouse of tribal elder Rae Daugherty; and others attempted to build a 17-foot canoe, beginning in 1985. Said Alexis, "They were the Mercedes-Benz of the Indian. . . . There was one outside every wigwam." The group used handmade tools, and according to a contemporary news report, such tribal projects as canoe building and basketry "helped to hold the Potawatomi together." That article concludes with the author's opinions about the power of canoes: "There still remains in a corner of the Midwest, a small group of native Americans holding onto their culture, and perhaps more importantly, sharing it willingly with others."[34]

In 2005, recognizing the importance of canoes to Indigenous peoples around the world, and the opportunity for cultural and technological exchange, the University of Michigan sponsored a project, directed by Professor Vicente Diaz, known as "Canoe Crossings." The program brought Ojibwe, Potawatomi, and Odawa Indians to Guam and Hawai'i to meet with navigators and canoe builders, community activists, and Islander scholars.[35]

Unfortunately, in the Pokagon Potawatomi community, the canoe revival paused as a result of the deaths of its principal supporters and participants, Mark Alexis, Mike Daugherty, and Daniel Rapp. However, in 2013, Pokagon Potawatomi tribal member Tom Wood completed a full-size birch bark canoe and donated it to the Pokagon community. Wood, the grandson of Mark Alexis, built the canoe to honor his grandfather and others who had worked so hard to maintain the tradition of canoe building. Says Wood, "When I saw what they did, I thought it was the coolest thing ever." After the passing of Alexis, Daugherty, and Rapp, Wood continued to think about his grandfather's wish that the canoe be completed. "There was a lot of effort to reconnect with Potawatomi culture—language classes, traditional health and bush craft. But no one was building canoes." Wood secured the necessary permits and skill to harvest the bark from Northern Michigan and then commenced the time-consuming process of actual construction. "This was mostly a learn-as-you-go experience. . . . I didn't tell a lot of people what I was doing. I'd never done it before, and didn't know if I could do it." Wood named the finished canoe *Zibi Néktosha* (River Horse). He adds, "As much time as I spent, and as challenging as it was to do, I don't look at this as an individual accomplishment. I finished something Grandpa and Mike didn't have a chance to. They sparked an interest in me about our culture, and always welcomed me to work on their projects with them. This is dedicated to them. We did it."[36]

Native peoples' interest in canoes and canoe building reclaims this item of technology and transportation as a part of Indigenous heritage and inheritance, and places the Native centrally inside the canoe, both literally and symbolically.

This is powerful work. Native peoples who have shared so much of themselves with others are now returning to the needs of their own people and building canoes while they build community.[37]

Canoeing in Chicago and the Legacy of Leroy Wesaw Sr.

As mentioned, the Pokagon had played lacrosse to entertain the non-Natives of Chicago and had established their prowess on the fields of baseball. Canoes would be the next vehicle for Indians to celebrate their heritage. Chicago has a history extending back into the second half of the nineteenth century of "canoe clubs" for the white gentry of the city.[38] Many Americans associated canoes not only with Indians, but also with nostalgia for the past, leisure, and nature. Typical is Walt Whitman's "The Torch."

> On my Northwest coast in the midst of the night a fishermen's group
> stands watching,
> Out on the lake that expands before them, others are spearing salmon,
> The canoe, a dim shadowy thing, moves across the black water,
> Bearing a torch ablaze at the prow.[39]

However, in 1964, the establishment of the Chicago American Indian Center Canoe Club signaled that American Indians were not only going to participate in games and recreation in ways imposed on them by outsiders, or limit themselves to the sports of the hegemon. In that year, Leroy F. Wesaw Sr., a Pokagon Potawatomi tribal member, along with a core group of other American Indian Center members, formed a canoe club that would take this traditionally Indian means of transportation and celebrate their Native identities by canoeing across the waterways of Chicago and elsewhere, and across the imaginations of their non-Native neighbors.

When we think of American Indian resistance to assimilation and/or marginalization, we often think of the confrontational politics of the courts or the streets. But in Chicago, Pokagon Potawatomi tribal member Leroy Wesaw Sr. chose a different path—he took to the water. Using the iconic form of the birch bark canoe, refashioned ironically in the very modern material of fiberglass, he founded a canoe club in the city that traveled the region and country presenting a public face and message that Indians were still in Chicago and still connected to their traditions.

Contemporary in material and construction, the canoe is used by the club as a vessel of memory, imagination, recreation, competition; an identity marker; and a source of individual and community pride. Wesaw's leadership also reconnected the Pokagon Band Potawatomi tribal members to Chicago. That connection and the legacy of the canoe club lives on to this day.

Leroy F. Wesaw Sr. (b. May 26, 1925; d. January 31, 1994) was born near Hartford, Michigan. In his youth, he attended both local public schools and later the Harbor Springs School for Indians until the eighth grade.[40] Childhood memories included all sorts of activities with other Pokagon Potawatomi, including picnics, square dances, and baseball. In 1950, he met his wife Pat (Mohawk and Irish) in Chicago and they married. Unable to find steady work in Michigan, they traveled back and forth between Chicago and Michigan for two years before settling in Chicago.[41] They had three children: Leroy Jr., Dorothy, and Colin. In the early 1950s, Wesaw became involved with the Chicago American Indian community and was an early member of the Chicago American Indian Center (AIC), organized in September 1953.[42] He was very active in many of the activities associated with the Indian Center.[43] Wesaw's son Colin describes his memories of his father's involvement at the AIC.

> My dad became a part of the American Indian Center in Chicago, and we would always be there, I mean always. He was there so much he got a job there and accomplished many things at the Indian Center. He was the Boy Scout Master at the Center, the leader of the American Indian Center Canoe Club, he sat on the board of directors for many years, he would help head up the American Indian Center Pow-Wow, my father's hands were in many if not all functions of the Center. There are too many things my dad did to recall them all but do know he did a lot.[44]

Louis (Bird) Traverzo was a member of the club and remembers Wesaw as being like a second father to him, a traditional man, the head of his household, charismatic, funny, and a natural leader. Traverzo adds that Wesaw was strong, both mentally and physically, well-spoken and respected by the young people at the Indian Center.[45] In 1964, Traverzo's stepfather, Nathan Bird, was working for a Ralph Frese, the founder and owner of the Chicagoland Canoe Base, Inc.[46] At the time, Frese had developed a method for creating canoes and kayaks out of fiberglass. Fiberglass was cheap and relatively easy to work with, and as a result Frese could, with the help of his employees (like Bird), create canoes quickly. It seemed serendipitous that Bird, who was Indian and a friend of Wesaw, would be working at a canoe manufacturing facility. In 1964, Wesaw, Bird, and another AIC member, Dick McPherson, came up with the idea of a canoe club, to be sponsored by the Indian Center. Wanting to use traditional canoes, but unable to secure the materials to build them out of birch bark, and without the time and resources to devote to their construction, they approached Frese. Frese was already creating simulated birch bark canoes out of fiberglass for various Voyageur reenactments he was participating in, and so, according to Frese, it was easy to agree to the idea of building a fleet of similar canoes for the Chicago Canoe Club. In 1964, the club was organized, with Wesaw, Bird, McPherson, and Frese as cofounders. Its address was listed as 4605 N. Paulina Ave., in Chicago, although that was just a side door to the American Indian Center.[47] From the outset, the club garnered much publicity in the city, particularly for a relatively small organization. Although the press often insisted on calling their craft "war canoes," Traverzo reports that the members rarely dressed in ancestral style clothing or worried that their "birch bark" canoes were made of fiberglass. He says, "We were proud to be Indian, happy to be together, and appreciative of the public interest."[48] Wesaw spoke at length about his memories of the club when interviewed for the Newberry Library Oral History Project in the early 1980s:

> With the Canoe Club, we started that coming across Lake Michigan. Sounds like a good idea, why don't we! So we did. And look at how—look at the tremendous popularity that canoe club, when it was in its prime. . . . We had a lot of publicity. We went to New York and whipped the best they had on the east coast. . . . It's—it's been rewarding. I can't look back and say that it hasn't been as I've enjoyed every damn minute of it.[49]

In his essay on the Pokagon Potawatomi, the author Everett Claspy recounts his first meeting with Wesaw and the latter's involvement in affairs both in Chicago and in nearby Michigan:

> I reached the new Indian Center in Chicago at 7 P.M., Jan. 17, 1970 on one of the coldest nights of the year. I thought that something might be going on and Mr. Wesaw was there to take charge of a teenage dance. . . . Leroy and his wife, who is from the Mohawk tribe, have three children. He has kept in close contact with Benton Harbor and Hartford. Last summer he took some Chicago boys on a canoe trip down the Paw Paw River. They camped for several nights on land owned by Jewitt P. Pokagon (grandson of Simon Pokagon). . . . Leroy had recently visited

The Wesaw family (*left to right*): Leroy Wesaw Sr., wife Pat, and their children Colin, Dorothy, and Leroy Jr. FROM "SEEING INDIAN IN CHICAGO" EXHIBITION RECORDS, MIDWEST MANUSCRIPT COLLECTION, THE NEWBERRY LIBRARY, CHICAGO. PHOTO BY ORLANDO CABANBAN. COURTESY OF THE NEWBERRY LIBRARY.

> Oklahoma, and is well acquainted with the Indian groups in Detroit which do not have such a headquarters.[50]

While busy working, and with his many activities at the American Indian Center, including the youth bowling league, the camera club, and of course, the Canoe Club, Wesaw also maintained connections to his tribal community in Michigan. He worked on efforts to establish an Indian Center in southwest Michigan, and to secure restoration of federal recognition for the Pokagon Band.[51]

The Chicago Canoe Club membership dramatically increased when the AIC received a charter for an all-Indian Boy Scout troop. Only the second all-Indian troop in the nation at the time, its scoutmaster was Leroy Wesaw.[52] According to another former club member, Eli Suzukovich, Boy Scout members eagerly joined in the club activities.[53] Club members participated in both competitive and recreational canoeing, which received significant publicity during the club's existence. According to Frese, the club also regularly participated in regional Voyageur reenactments. Typical was the event in April 1968 when club members joined with members of the Prairie Canoe Club and the Illinois Paddling Council to "re-create" the 1675 journey of Father Jacques Marquette down the Illinois River.[54] Although the non-Native participants were "garbed as French woodsmen," the event, to celebrate the Illinois Sesquicentennial, was not only about Voyageur reenactments; once the canoeists arrived at their destination near Starved Rock State Park, the Chicago Canoe Club members erected their own Indian village and held a pow wow in celebration.[55]

Later that same year, Frese, an ardent conservationist, organized a canoe flotilla to journey down the Fox River, to highlight its beauty and need for environmental protection. Chicago Canoe Club members participated, and in the news article covering the event, a photograph of Club members readying the canoes included the following caption:

> Patience—Frese and his assistants, Kluch and [Leroy] Wesaw, begin work on the sitka [*sic*] spruce rim, or gunwale, of a 34-foot fiberglass canoe. . . . He [Frese] designed the simulated birchbark from prints showing the Great Lakes trading canoes used by Indian tribes.[56]

The article includes a second photo, with the caption

> Craftsmanship—Ralph Frese expects quality work from his assistants . . . full blooded Potawatomie, Leroy Wesaw . . . weaves nylon seats on a canoe.[57]

According to Traverzo, activities often focused on family outings and canoe racing.[58] Traverzo remembers the club as being much like the Indian Center—intertribal and social. In fact, he says, non-Indians were always welcome to participate in the club as well. The Canoe Club regularly held family outings, including an annual picnic at Lily Lake located north of Barrington, Illinois, in the far northwest suburbs. Traverzo told me during our interview that his strongest memories of the club are the family and social aspects—the camping, playing, cooking, and competing with each other. He believed the club promoted strong families within the Chicago Indian community by fostering a sense of community and camaraderie. "It reinforced a pride in family and in being Native." Typical of more publicity garnered by the club is this article from the *Chicago Tribune*:

***Ladies of the Lake*, from "Seeing Indian in Chicago" Exhibition Records, Midwest Manuscript Collection, The Newberry Library, Chicago. The text accompanying the image reads, "Winona Factor, Sandy Bird hold down their canoe during a canoe club outing in the mid-1960s."** PHOTO BY ORLANDO CABANBAN. COURTESY OF THE NEWBERRY LIBRARY.

> It's the perfect weather to start the canoe season, or so the American Indian Center Canoe club believes. Four Indian "war" canoes, 26 and 34 feet long, will shove off from Howard street and McCormick boulevard, Evanston today . . . and the club members will paddle down the north branch and pull out of the water at Michigan avenue some three hours later.[59]

During the club's existence, canoeing was the most influential and popular activity sponsored by the AIC, according to Traverzo. Members bought their own canoes or rented them (most often from Frese in either case). Although the canoes were made of fiberglass, the members took great pride in their appearance, according to Traverzo. "We had these really cool jackets with a Chicago Canoe Club logo on the back and when we showed up anywhere with our 'birch bark' canoes, everyone wanted to know who we were and what we were about. It made us feel good." No matter that Frese's fiberglass "birch bark" canoes were twice as heavy as anyone else's and twice as slow, according to Traverzo. "We didn't win many races but we looked good doing it."[60]

Typical of the activities of the club was a trip they made down the Chicago River in 1967. The news account relates the international scope of club events,

> Leroy Wesaw, club president . . . said the trip was a cold-weather warmup [*sic*] for a trip the club is planning to Canada.[61]

Both Traverzo and Frese also remembered racing above Niagara Falls on the St. Lawrence River, later that year. The next year, the club made news when once again they traveled down the Chicago River. A caption under a photograph of members of the club in the water and in their canoes at the State Street Bridge, surrounded by skyscrapers, reports:

> PADDLE PARTY—Members of the Canoe Club of the American Indian center . . . relax after paddling 10 miles down the Chicago river.[62]

In a *Chicago Daily News* photograph from 1971, showing a canoe manned by Ralph Frese and Nathan Bird, among others, the caption reads,

> Chicagoans who found walking cold Tuesday shivered a little more at the sight of these "visitors" paddling in the Chicago River. The icy trip in a 34-foot birchbark craft was aimed to commemorate the 298th anniversary of the discovery of Illinois by Marquette and Joliet and to call attention to the Chicago Boat Show, which opens at the Amphitheatre Friday.[63]

Both Traverzo and Frese confirmed that the Canoe Club's connection to Indian heritage was important for Wesaw and the rest of the members. Indian pride and dignity were at the core of the club. During an event at the American Indian Center in 1967, Wesaw declared, "The Indian is a free man. . . . His spirit is hard to crush."[64] Cultural aspects surrounded club activities, although they were not of the reenactment sort. These were contemporary urban Indians, living their lives in ways that made sense to them. While often public in nature, the activities were not performative or obsessed with the past. For instance, in 1971, the American Indian Center published its first ever *Indian Cook Book*, based upon the foods prepared on Canoe Club outings. Quoting the author, Violet Harper (Ojibwe), the *Tribune* reported:

> She and her husband and children and 10 to 20 other Indian families of the city join a group within the [AIC]—the Canoe Club—to follow a chosen river in canoes almost every weekend, beginning in May, until winter's deep freeze. "The outings are fun and great for families," said Mrs. Harper. "They really give the kids a chance to see what is beyond crowded city streets."[65]

Opportunities to participate in cultural activities sponsored by larger, non-Native institutions also became available.

> Dances, handicraft demonstrations, a canoe race, and a pow-wow will highlight the American Indian festival which opens tomorrow at the Field Museum of Natural History. . . . The canoe race, sponsored by the American Indian center canoe club, will begin at 7 A.M. next Sunday at Wilmette. It will end, after 20 miles of paddling, at Burnham Park harbor. Cruising canoes, kayaks, and war canoes will participate.[66]

The Chicago Canoe Club was also involved in racing and other competitions. The club appears to have begun entering canoe races in 1964. The AIC archives have a photograph taken by Amalia Andujar depicting "Leroy and Pat Wesaw [at] Green Lake, Wisconsin during the big race."[67] The club also participated in the Des Plaines River marathon, the Fox River Valley marathon, and the Lone Rock, Wisconsin, marathon.[68] In June 1966, they won a first-place trophy in the canoe-kayak division at Milwaukee Harbor, completing the five-mile course in 58 minutes and besting fifty-one other teams.[69] Apparently, the weight of the fiberglass did not slow them down that day. Later that summer, the Canoe Club sponsored the "Challenge of the Midwest," a race that traversed a forty-mile course from Zion, Illinois, to Chicago's Roosevelt Road beach.[70] The press noted the club members' preparations for the event with interest.

> A war canoe skims thru Lincoln park lagoon each Saturday as 10 Indians prepare for the "challenge of the Midwest." . . . LeRoy [*sic*] Wesaw, Pottawatomie Indian, guides the 36-foot war canoe with a long-bladed paddle at the stern back as Nathan Bird, Winnebago Indian, sets the pace. . . . "We've got to stay in shape," said Wesaw, club president. "Bird sometimes sets a pace of 60 strokes or more a minute."[71]

According to Wesaw, a large turnout was expected for the event. "'Our only fear is Lake Michigan may get rough, as it often does.' He told me that the Winnebago Indians called the lake Da-wa-shek or 'big, bad water.'"[72] Wesaw added,

Chicago Canoe Club members. The caption to the photograph reads, "8/18/66–CHICAGO: Pictured are part of the American Indian Center Canoe Club's entrants in 'Challenge of the Midwest' Canoe Race for Indians scheduled 8/21. Race will be in Lake Michigan, from Great Lakes Training Center to 12th St. beach here, a distance of 35 miles. . . . Canoes of all classes will be entered, representing six states and ten tribes. Top (*L-R*) Leroy Wesaw, Potawatomi; Joe White, Winnebago; Daniel Battise, Alabama, (*kneeling*) Phil Longie, Sioux and Nathan Bird, Winnebago." According to a *Chicago Sun-Times* article in which members in their canoe were pictured, the AIC Chicago Canoe Club won first place in the "war canoe" class of the race, with a time of 8 hours and 30 minutes. "WINDUP BY LAND, WATER, AND AIR FOR LAKE SHOW," *CHICAGO SUN-TIMES*, AUGUST 22, 1966. UPI TELEPHOTO FROM THE COLLECTION OF THE AUTHOR.

> We started the club to promote canoeing, particularly among the Indian population. . . . Many of us have benefitted from valuable advice from our fathers . . . I'm 41 years old and I'm still learning about canoeing from my father who's in his 80s. He used to pole his way thru Michigan swamps in a canoe.[73]

According to the *Chicago Tribune*,

> In addition to practicing in the war canoe, club members paddle their 18-foot 6-inch, two man canoes two or three times a week. . . . Club members range in age from "two to toothless." They include Sioux, Chippewa, Winnebago, Seminole, Pottawatomie, Mohawk, Coushatta, Oneida, Ottawa, Athabascan, and Menominee Indians and some non Indian members of the center.[74]

The article concludes with a summary of the value of canoeing to the Chicago Indian community. "'Canoeing serves not only as good exercise and fun for the participants,' Wesaw said. 'Like almost everything an Indian family does, it is aimed at preserving our Indian heritage.'"[75]

Ralph Frese remembered another race from New Buffalo to the 95th Street Beach. He recounted to me his memory of a canoe manned by Leroy Wesaw and Nathan Bird that completed the 43-mile journey in just ten and a half hours. Frese witnessed the canoe as it came to shore and remembered the waves being so high that Bird's paddle was barely touching the water at the finish.[76]

Canoe Club members at Lily Lake from "Seeing Indian in Chicago" Exhibition Records, Midwest Manuscript Collection, The Newberry Library, Chicago. According to the label on the photograph, these are "Art Elton, Tony Barker, Archie Blackelk, Paul Goodiron in canoe club race." PHOTO BY ORLANDO CABANBAN. COURTESY OF THE NEWBERRY LIBRARY.

The next year, a highlight of Canoe Club events included a trip to New York and circling Manhattan Island. The race was sponsored by the American Canoe Association and the Olympic Development Committee.[77] In 1969, club members were back in the *Chicago Tribune*, out at Lily Lake, participating in oar races and canoe races. That day, Colin Wesaw and Louis (Bird) Traverzo were the winners.[78]

Elder Joe White (Winnebago) was also interviewed for the Newberry Library Oral History Project. He came to Chicago from Wisconsin in 1948 and was a cofounder of the American Indian Center.[79] He also served as chairman of the Canoe Club and shared memories of the club.

> Leroy Wesaw, and his wife Pat, all the basketball players that were at the center, they were all involved. . . . We had a lot of members then . . . all their wives were involved. . . . We practiced on Lake Michigan, and every weekend we had an outing where we'd paddle down rivers, like Rock River, Aurora River, rivers in Michigan, Indiana and Wisconsin, Black River Falls. . . . We won trophies, did canoe races and won trophies. And there was a canoe race around Manhattan Island. Then we raced in Niagara Falls. We were above [the falls and] the next day were down below. We raced right into the Canadian side.[80]

The Canoe Club lasted until 1972. Its end can be attributed to several things. According to Eli Suzukovich, that period was a time of conflict at the American Indian Center, and many of the programs there faded into the twilight.[81] James LaGrand also notes the difficult times at the AIC during this period and the negative impact on programs and services.[82] In his interview for the Newberry Oral History project, Wesaw himself seemed to connect the decline of the club to his own heart attack in 1972 and the inability of others to continue the club. Nonetheless, during the eight years that the club was active, it provided an opportunity for Indians in Chicago to openly celebrate their heritage, and it reflects the influence that the Pokagon Potawatomi once again asserted on the city.

Can canoeing in "birch bark" canoes constructed of fiberglass be considered a traditional activity that fosters community? The notion of invented tradition calls into question the "authenticity" of a tradition and the depth of Native histories. The literature regarding the "invention of tradition" began with Eric Hobsbawm and Terence Ranger,[83] although it certainly has its roots in the earlier work of Ralph Linton's "Nativistic Movements."[84] Native and non-Native scholars alike have been concerned with the ideological manipulation of heritage. I believe the use of the term "traditional" as articulated by Craig S. Womack—as "anything useful to Indian people in retaining their values and worldviews, no matter how much it deviates from what people did two hundred years ago"—is the best way to understand the Chicago Canoe Club as a traditional activity that publicized the contemporary Indigenous peoples of Chicago.[85]

The canoes themselves were made of fiberglass as a matter of convenience and accessibility—hardly a material invoking Indian identity, like the birch bark–clad books and homes. Wesaw and the Canoe Club favored the craft designed by Ralph Frese to represent the Algonquin canoe because of its affordability and availability. Canoe Club members took great pride in the style of their vessels; it was a celebration of Indian technology and Indian heritage. Frese's fiberglass canoes, complete with simulated pitch, the texture of birch bark, and decorative etchings, were purposefully designed to represent the past. However, the material was contemporary and practical. Fiberglass enabled the production of enough canoes for the club members. Wesaw and the rest of the Canoe Club membership made good use of the opportunity afforded by Frese's canoes. Like the lacrosse players before them at the WCE, they put their Indianness on display, and like Indian baseball players from an earlier era, they successfully competed with non-Natives in the sport. They also used these fiberglass canoes as a means to bind families and community together. Wesaw himself made clear that tradition was important to him. In 1975, he enrolled in Native American Education Services (NAES) College in Chicago, and in 1978 was one of the students of the first graduating class. In his senior field project, titled "Changing Values in the Indian Culture," Wesaw asked,

> Since the Indian tribes east of the Mississippi have been in contact with the dominant society longer than those in the western states, it would be natural to assume the eastern tribes to be more assimilated than those in the west. Have these tribesmen of the east, both rural and urban changed their traditional family and individual roles for a culture that was alien to these shores 300 years ago? Or have they assumed a facile polish of civilization to make their lives easier in the face of the racism that followed the conquest of their lands?[86]

After examining two families and their connections to community and tradition, Wesaw concluded,

Presentation of the Pokagon Potawatomi tribal flag to the Chicago American Indian Center. The image was distributed in the January 2011 Pokagon Potawatomi tribal newsletter. (*Left to right*) Roger Williams, Butch Starrett, tribal chair Matthew Wesaw, and AIC director Joseph Podlasek.

> I could only suggest that in order to fight total assimilation of the Potawatomi into the dominant society, parents must realize they are the connecting link between the old and new. If their heritage and culture are to survive, they must maintain the ties on the reservation and use the resources there. . . . The elders, both rural and urban, must teach as only they can the tradition and mythology of the Pottawatomi people.[87]

What Wesaw may not have been as consciously aware of is that his own activities, specifically the Canoe Club, were not only teaching young Indians who they were. He was also teaching the rest of the Chicago about what it meant to be Indian in the twentieth century.

On November 20, 2010, at the AIC Veteran's Pow Wow, held that year at the Grand Ballroom at Navy Pier, members of the Pokagon Potawatomi community came to formally present the Pokagon Potawatomi national flag to the American

Indian Center of Chicago and to honor the memory and legacy of Leroy Wesaw Sr. According to the tribal newsletter,

> The dedication commemorated the ongoing relationship the tribe has with the City of Chicago. The Pokagon flag takes its place among other tribal flags on display at the Center. Pokagon Chairman Matthew Wesaw spoke at the dedication event. Also in attendance were members of the Tribal Council, Traditions Committee, and the Veterans Group. The flag was escorted by an honor guard composed of veterans from the Pokagon Band. Chairman Wesaw represented the tribe at the ceremony in honoring tribal member Leroy Wesaw, Sr. for his many years of involvement in Native American Affairs.[88]

In his remarks that day, Pokagon Potawatomi tribal chairman Matt Wesaw told the crowd:

> We come here today to honor Leroy Wesaw, a person important to our Nation and to the Chicago American Indian community as well. We present this flag to the Center with the hope that it will be displayed with the flags of all the other tribes that now have members living in Chicago. This is a good thing. It reminds us all that this was ancestral lands of many Native peoples, including the Potawatomi. It reminds us that Chicago is still a part of us.[89]

After the presentation of the flag and remarks by AIC director Joseph Podlasek, the celebration ended with an honor dance in the pow-wow arena in memory of Leroy Wesaw.

Leroy Wesaw's "Potawatomi presence" in the city was different from that of his predecessors; Simon Pokagon, Charles Pokagon, Julia Pokagon, and Michael B. Williams had all been clear with regard to their tribal affiliation and their claims to a place in the city, its history, and its future. Wesaw's activities, on the other hand, reflected the realities of post–World War II experiences for Chicago's urban Indians. After World War II, the organization and focus of the Canoe Club is evidence that specific tribal affiliation was less important than a larger American Indian identity, unity, and community. The Chicago Canoe Club was proudly diverse and intertribal in its membership. While the club was not specifically Pokagon Potawatomi, it probably would not have happened without Pokagon Potawatomi tribal member Leroy Wesaw. In that sense, Wesaw maintained the Pokagon Potawatomi presence in Chicago.

CHAPTER 6

Monuments, Memorials, and the Continued Presence of the Potawatomi in Chicago

> Be it enacted by the Senate and House of Representatives of the Unites States of America in Congress assembled, That there may be erected . . . in the harbor of New York . . . a suitable memorial to the memory of the North American Indian.
>
> —H.R. 1671 62nd Cong. (April 4, 1911)

Decades of settlers cemented their memories of American Indians into statues reflecting a celebration of conquest and nostalgia for a mythical past. These memorials are so numerous that they seem to signal an obsession with rendering Indians immobile, safely ensconced in metal or stone, and in place. Non-Natives created many, some were created in collaboration with Native peoples, and Indians themselves created a few. There are many such landmarks "honoring" the Potawatomi throughout the areas where their communities were located. There are monuments erected by non-Indians to "honor" them, and the Pokagon Potawatomi responded with their own monuments. The writings of Simon Pokagon, his construction of a *tipi* in Chicago, his public appearances there, the activities of his children in and near the city, and more, all point to a desire of the Potawatomi to maintain a place in Chicago civic affairs and in the collective memories of its inhabitants.

There is a profound story embedded in monuments created by non-Natives for non-Natives; they reflect a pathos, guilt, and nostalgia for the disappearing, and now safe, Indian. They are images of Natives in which non-Natives might find comfort and enjoyment; these monuments also allow us to envision how non-Natives of the era were responding to, and thinking about, Indians. Such memorials represent a victory celebration over "the first peoples." They began to appear with gathering frequency after 1890 and the assumed subjugation of the remaining Indian peoples within the boundaries of the nation. No longer perceived as a threat, American Indians were embraced as a part of the national patrimony now worthy of memorialization. According to Philip Deloria, the ideology of pacification that bridged the nineteenth and twentieth centuries represented an affirmation of the "vanishing Indian" trope and an expectation of Indian assimilation. Says Deloria, "All these things added up to either complete domination, with limitless access to Indian lives and cultures, or complete freedom to ignore Indian people altogether."[1]

Very often, memorials and monuments are enduring attempts to stabilize meaning and memory. At the beginning of the twentieth century, a colossal monument was planned to honor "the Indian" in New York City and would have rivaled the Statue of Liberty in size.[2] So many "grand" statues to Indians exist that their presence justified compilation into a book.[3] On the other hand, things created by the Potawatomi—whether structures, writings, treaty claims, or objects of material culture—can also serve as monuments. A book can be a memorial, which can also be physically manifested as a monument. As such, the writings of Simon Pokagon do work as both memorial and monument.

The victims of genocide[4] have, throughout history, resorted to creative ways to memorialize and remember what was perpetrated upon them. During the Holocaust, for example, Jewish peoples used the written word to serve as evidence and testimonial for us all.

> The first "memorials" to the Holocaust period came not in stone, glass, or steel—but in narrative. The Yizkor Bikher—memorial books—remembered both the lives and destruction of European Jewish communities according to the most ancient of Jewish memorial media: words on paper. For a murdered people without graves, without even corpses to inter, these memorial books often came to serve as symbolic tombstones.[5]

Monuments can also be an attempt to insert into the landscape a bookmark of sorts. Landscapes are like libraries; within each are stories reflecting the hopes, fears, aspirations, and lived experiences of human interaction. Like books, places are subject to constructions of a multiplicity of meanings. How we understand and relate to both books and landscapes is ever changing; their meanings are subjective and temporal. The irony is that no matter how heavy the monument, it never stands still. It mirrors the narratives of the hegemon and the counternarratives of the marginalized. Pokagon left signposts for future generations, but how they are read always depends upon the era and the audience. Pokagon affixed a name and a face to his "rhetorical monuments," contributing to the reshaping of an Indigenous landscape that could be recognized by others. *Queen of the Woods* is not merely a nostalgic, Victorian-style romance novel, but also a memorial and monument to the past and future of the Potawatomi people.[6]

Potawatomi Monuments and Memorials

Many Americans, I suspect, assume that American Indians made no monuments or memorials before the arrival of Europeans. Typifying this attitude, historian Elmore Barce wrote in 1919, "They were savages, and have left no enduring temple or lofty fane behind them, but their names still cling to many streams, groves and towns."[7] That, of course, ignores the many mounds, earthworks, petroglyphs, pictographs, etc., that survive on the American landscape to this day.

Indeed, the Potawatomi left their own memorials and constructed them of materials that had significance to them. Simon Pokagon favored birch bark for his monuments. *Wigwas*, known to botanists as *Betula papyrifera Marsh* and to gardeners today as paper or white birch, is a magnificent tree that grows in most of Canada, portions of the Northeast, and most of the Great Lakes region. The uses of *wigwas* reflect the traditions of the people through items of everyday and ceremonial life. *Wigwas* helps to define who the Potawatomi are as a people because they used birch bark so advantageously in much of their traditional daily lives. Birch bark connects to the origin and migration stories of these peoples; it was traditional material for habitation, travel, storage, writing, and recording. Items made from birch bark are not only cultural artifacts but also represent just as much a process, a history, and a narrative of place, name, and people. The people see in birch bark the characteristics they cherish in themselves: self-renewal, strength, adaptability, and dependability.

Traditionally harvested without harm to the plant, the birch trees were a ready and self-renewing resource. Strong, pliable, and available in huge sheets, *wigwas* was also used as material for sacred scrolls that recorded the ceremonies of the Potawatomi, Ojibwe, and Odawa. According to Patty Loew, "The Ojibwe carried the sacred scrolls associated with the Midewiwin [traditional religious ceremonies], the Ottawa organized hunts and organized trade, and the Potawatomi carried and tended the fires. Each responsibility was essential to the group's spiritual, cultural, and physical survival."[8]

Many utilitarian items for the home and for subsistence were also made of birch bark, including the torches used in nighttime spearfishing and the canoes that carried the spearfishers; grave houses; birch bark containers (*makuks*) for gathering and storing berries and wild rice, and storing, collecting, and making maple sugar; trumpet-shaped moose calls; cups, dishes, trays, cases; and floats for fishnets.[9]

Simon Pokagon explained why he chose to use birch bark for the booklet *The Red Man's Greeting* distributed at the World's Columbian Exposition. Birch is not only indigenous and sacred; it is structural, relational, and memorial.

> My object in publishing "The Red Man's Greeting" on the bark of the white birch tree is out of loyalty to my own people, and gratitude to the Great Spirit, who in his wisdom provided for our use for untold generations, this most remarkable tree with manifold bark used by us. . . . Out of the bark of this wonderful tree were made hats, caps and dishes for domestic use, while our maidens tied with it the knot that sealed their marriage vow; wigwams were made of it, as well as large canoes that outrode the violent storms on lake and sea; it was also used for light and fuel at our war councils and spirit dances . . . [like] the red man this tree is vanishing from our forests.[10]

In a review of *The Red Man's Greeting*, reprinted from the *New York Globe*, one critic opined:

> This birch bark book will take its place in the cabinets of admirers of handsome books along with the carved leather bindings and illuminated text of the early German publishers; the heavy oaken-covered books of the first English works; the minute rice paper books of Chinese; the stone tablets of the Phoenicians, and

***Wigwams/tipis* at the World's Columbian Exposition. According to the text accompanying the photograph, "The American Indian village at the fair opened Friday. The Indians are from the tribes of Pottowatomies, Chippewas and Winnebagos, in Northern Wisconsin and Minnesota."** (GRAND HAVEN, MI) *EVENING TRIBUNE*, JULY 3, 1893.

> the parchments of the Greeks, as the representative work of the nationality to which the author belongs. It abounds in all the rich metaphor and eloquence of the aboriginal race.[11]

Pokagon, literally wrapping several of his writings in *wigwas*, invoked the language and lifeways of pre-contact Potawatomi. His writings are an important example of what Malea Powell has called "the rhetoric of survivance"—responding to the hegemon and reimagining what it means to be a contemporary American Indian.[12]

The many structures Pokagon writes about in *Queen of the Woods* have been potent symbols of indigeneity in the United States for the last two hundred years. They have also been appropriated, like much other Indian material culture, as symbols of freedom, individuality, proximity to nature, national patrimony, and

American uniqueness—a process that started at least at the time of the Boston Tea Party and the dressing up as Indians by the colonists.[13] Longfellow's *Song of Hiawatha* takes place at the *wigwam* of Nokomis (grandmother). A search of books on the website of a leading bookseller reveals 14,273 books with the title of "wigwam" in them. Typical are the sorts of books like *Indians of the Wigwams*[14] and the novel by Cornelia Steketee Hulst, *Indian Sketches*, which depicts a *wigwam* on its cover.[15] In fact, Abraham Lincoln was nominated as the Republican Party's presidential candidate in Chicago in 1860 at an auditorium called "The Wigwam." A replica of the Wigwam auditorium was erected at the Century of Progress World's Fair held in Chicago in 1933.

Simon Pokagon not only emphasized and reclaimed the *wigwam* through his writings; he also built a birch bark *tipi/wigwam* at the World's Columbian Exposition in 1893. Although there is no known image of this *tipi*, a photograph from the *Grand Haven Evening Tribune* of that year shows three birch bark *tipis* outside the Anthropology Building in the southeast corner of the fair.

Pokagon's birch bark *tipi* was subsequently re-erected at his Hartford, Michigan, home. Upon his death in 1899, the *tipi* was removed to the front yard of his friend, attorney, and publisher C. H. Engle, where it was a tourist attraction in Hartford, Michigan, for many years. In *The History of Van Buren County*, published in 1912, the author wrote,

> On the preceding page is a picture of Chief Pokagon's last Wigwam. It stood for several years on the lawn of C.H. Engle, opposite the Hartford public park. It is a pyramidic [*sic*] decagon in shape, made of the manifold bark of the white birch tree, being sixteen feet at the base and twenty-four feet high. During the past summer it was procured by the advanced class of the study of nature at Ypsilanti, and now stands on the campus in front of the science building in the grounds of the State Normal School of Michigan.[16]

Simon Pokagon's *wigwam/tipi* and his bark-clad writings are both monuments and memorials. Created so that we will remember who first resided on this continent, they memorialize the shifting of lifeways and of communities that were forever changed by contact with Euro-Americans. They are also monuments to new beginnings—to the potential of Indian peoples in the future of the nation, and to the possibilities that could emerge from their inclusion. The power of Pokagon's work lies, at least in part, in the way that it marks endings and beginnings, and the passages

Simon Pokagon's *wigwam/tipi*. FROM THE COLLECTION OF THE AUTHOR.

between them. Pokagon's son Charles also built a birch bark *tipi* when he headed an encampment of Pokagon Potawatomi Indians on the Chicago lakefront in 1903.[17]

Pokagon was memorialized in death; at one point, it was anticipated that he would be buried in Graceland Cemetery in Chicago and that a monument would be erected in his honor in Jackson Park. Reference to the proposed monument is included in an appendix to *Queen of the Woods* and described in a later biographical sketch.

> The last hereditary chief of the Pottawattamies having died a few weeks ago, an organization has been formed in Chicago to erect a monument to his memory and to that of his father, Pokagon I. . . . The new Indian monument will be erected in Jackson Park, where throngs of visitors may become as familiar with its story as they are with that of the Massacre Monument. The new monument will be erected in memory of the late Simon Pokagon, and will have inscribed upon it his own beautiful words to the children of Chicago, that "the red man and white man are brothers, and God is the Father of all."
>
> Surmounting the pedestal will be a superb statue of the regal figure of Pokagon I in full chieftain's attire. The four bas-reliefs on the pedestal will

> represent events in the history of Chicago's Indian days, which will be decided upon by a committee of pioneers. The names, also, of noted Pottawattamie chiefs who were at the head of bands under Pokagon will be inscribed upon the base of the monument. . . . They have now practically passed away as a separate and distinct race and within a few years, as suggested by Simon Pokagon, the remnant which is left will be absorbed and swallowed up in the blood of the dominant race. That the tincture of their blood will flow on in that of the white race and possibly for its betterment is reasonably certain: but as a distinct race their end is comparatively near at hand.[18]

However, Simon Pokagon was actually buried in a grave near Hartford, Michigan, at Rush Lake Indian Cemetery, and the proposed monument in Jackson Park was never erected. The appendix to *Queen of the Woods* continues:

> It is the wish of the few pioneers left that the closing hour on some one day of Chicago's school days every autumn may be set aside for Indian study, and called Pokagon Day. . . . The Pokagon Monument Association numbers for its advisory committee and patrons the leading pioneers and prominent ladies and gentlemen of the city.[19]

I had read about a monument to Pokagon being in Jackson Park, but was so frustrated by my inability to locate it that in 2010, I finally called the Chicago Park District Office. An employee answered my call, and when I began to inquire about the monument he quickly interrupted. With a bit of an exasperated tone he reported that he regularly receives inquiries about the statue location, but that in fact the truth was that no such memorial had ever been built. His apparent annoyance at once again having to answer a question about "the Simon Pokagon Monument" was matched only by my disappointment that there was nothing to see despite the fact that several writers and websites still refer to it as if it actually exists.

The Potawatomi themselves were rarely consulted about what memorials they might appreciate. Civic leaders made those decisions. After all, these monuments were really not for the Natives, but for the grandchildren of the immigrant-settlers—offered as a kind of apologia in stone. Those monuments that purported to honor the local Indians often reflected a darker message and imagination. Confessed one proponent of such memorials,

> The few monuments that have been erected by white men to commemorate and perpetuate the names and virtues of worthy representatives of the Red race do not at all satisfy the obligations which rest upon us in that behalf. . . . It would seem not only fitting but just that these chiefs and tribes, who were the original occupants and possessors of the soil, should have suitable and enduring monuments to commemorate their names placed in public parks . . . so that our children and our children's children may have kept before them a recollection of a race of men who contended with us for more than two centuries for the possession of the country, but who have been vanquished and almost exterminated by our superior force.[20]

However, on occasion, the Potawatomi were included in the festivities for the unveiling of monuments. For instance, Simon's granddaughter Julia, following the family tradition, re-erected her grandfather's *tipi* at the unveiling of the Chief Menominee Statue on September 4, 1909, at Twin Lakes, Indiana, near Chicago. Julia Pokagon married Michael Quigno, a fellow member of the Pokagon Potawatomi community, and together they lived at Rush Lake in Michigan until her death in 1945.[21] She also assisted the author Cecilia Buechner in writing "The Pokagons."[22]

The Memorialization of Chief Menominee

Menominee, who lived from 1791 to 1841, was the leader of a band of Potawatomi Indians who were tricked into assembling at their church and then forcibly removed to Kansas under order of the governor of the State of Indiana. In 1909, the State of Indiana erected a monument to honor the memory of Chief Menominee. Cornelia Hulst wrote about the man:

> It is not known where Chief Menominee is buried. It is thought that he died on the way to Kansas, or shortly after his tribe reached the new reservation. . . . Just seventy-one years after Menominee and his people were carried captive from their homes, the State of Indiana raised a monument in his honor on the spot where his chapel had stood. It was a tardy recognition, but it does him justice and its inscription in granite will help to tell the future history. . . . This granite figure does, indeed stand as a monument of humanity and appreciation of the courage, devotion, faith, and sorrows of the old chief whom men used despitefully, but it

Unveiling of the Menominee Monument. Julia Pokagon is in the center.

> has a larger aspect also. It is a voice from the present speaking to the future of an injustice done and repented, an appeal from the fathers who erected it to the sons who will follow.[23]

The monument, made of granite and standing twenty feet tall, was unveiled by Julia Quigno Pokagon, who was also invited to address the audience.[24] She said, "It will stand as a monument of humanity, teaching generations yet unborn that the white man and the red man are brothers and God is father of all."[25] That passage is taken almost verbatim from the preface to her grandfather's *Queen of the Woods*, written sixteen years earlier.[26]

A *wigwam* erected by Julia Pokagon at the site of the Chief Menominee statue served as its own monument alongside the stone statue put up by the non-Natives. Following her speech was an address by Daniel McDonald, author of *Removal of the Pottawattomie Indians from Northern Indiana*,[27] and an address by then tribal chairman Michael B. Williams on "Civilization and the Indian Race."[28] At the close of

An early postcard of the Chief Menominee statue issued shortly after its dedication. FROM THE COLLECTION OF THE AUTHOR.

the event, a band played "softly and slowly, 'The Dirge of a Vanished Race (Slumber Song of a Vanished Race).'"[29]

In 1911, the *tipi* was sold to the Eastern Michigan Normal School (now Eastern Michigan University) in Ypsilanti, Michigan, where it was displayed for at least a decade before it was packed away and eventually lost in a subsequent fire.[30] Julia Pokagon continued the family tradition, using the forums available to them during such dedications in order to articulate an agenda for American Indians. In her remarks before the crowd assembled on the campus that day, she demanded respect for her people, as she spoke at the unveiling of her grandfather's *tipi*.

Simon Pokagon's *wigwam* erected at Twin Lakes, Indiana, for the unveiling of the statue of Menominee. His daughter Julia is in the center of the photograph. CORNELIA STEKETEE HULST, *INDIAN SKETCHES: PÈRE MARQUETTE AND THE LAST OF THE POTTAWATOMIE CHIEFS* (NEW YORK: LONGMANS, GREEN AND CO., 1912), 88.

I am glad that I am here; indeed that you have granted to a child of the forest an opportunity to address the teachers and students of the greatest institution of Michigan; am glad this college has honored my race by placing on these grounds the wigwam of my fathers. There is nothing more sacred to our people than 'wigwam.' It is as dear to our hearts as 'home' to the white race. It brings to us all the kindred ties of father, mother, sister, brother, son and daughter. We too can sing with overflowing hearts 'Wigwam, Sweet Wigwam: there is no place like Wigwam!"

About one year since I was honored, by making the unveiling address of an Indian statue [of Chief Menominee at Twin Lakes, Indiana] erected in memory of the unjust banishment of my people from the state of Indiana in 1838. As I there stood in the presence of a great multitude gathered to atone as far as possible

> for the wrongs their fathers had dealt out to our people through the influence of bad men, my heart mourned.[31]

Julia Pokagon did not perceive the earlier monument in Indiana solely as an honor to Chief Menominee, but also as a marker of the wrongs done to the Potawatomi people—another example of how the Potawatomi might "read" these granite markers differently than their non-Native neighbors.

In the fall of 2009, a rededication of the Chief Menominee statue was held, and I attended the public event. My memories of that day, written down in my personal journal, provide some insight into the reading of monuments for and by the Potawatomi in the past and present.

Installation of Pokagon's birch bark *tipi* at Ypsilanti, Michigan. In Native dress to the left is Julia Pokagon, with her daughter and husband. "Recalls Big Chief; Birch Bark Wigwam Dedicated at Ypsilanti; Pokagon Built It; Head of Pottawatomics Honored at Normal School," *GRAND RAPIDS PRESS*, JUNE 15, 1911, 1.

I am driving from Champaign, Illinois to Twin Lakes, Indiana, the car cuts through the center of the two states. Illinois, named after the peoples of the Illini Confederacy with a French appendage, Indiana being a Greek reference to the lands of the Indians. The irony is that many of the original Indians were removed west out of both places in the 1830s.

The car moves past long, flat fields of soy and corn—another irony is that the landscape has been changed as much as the inhabitants. Wetlands drained and controlled, forests clear-cut so that planted fields of cash crops extend to the horizon.

Traveling—Friday, September 18, 2009, to the "Chief Menominee 100th Anniversary Rededication Ceremony." A celebration of sorts—a commemoration of the dedication of the Chief Menominee statue that was erected by the State of Indiana in 1909. Originally an honoring of the Potawatomi chief; carved of granite, it is an engraved plea for forgiveness of the sin of ethnic cleansing and removal of the Potawatomi to places west—a process and policy that even by 1909 folks were uncomfortable with.

One hundred years ago, Julia Pokagon and Michael B. Williams, spokespeople from the Pokagon Potawatomi community—the closest Potawatomi to Twin Lakes—were invited to participate. In 2009, Potawatomi from Oklahoma and Kansas are in attendance. No Pokagon Potawatomi are here this day but me. Whether the Pokagon Potawatomi were officially invited I do not know. The Pokagon Band of Potawatomi were not removed, and members of the tribe are this day more interested in upcoming fall ceremonies than statuary-centric events.

Most of those in attendance are non-Natives; children from the local elementary school, boy scouts, pastors, musicians, orators, politicians, and members of the Trail of Death Association—the latter folks putting signposts along the route that Chief Menominee and his Twin Lakes Band were forced to walk in 1838 during their removal.

The statue (missing some fingers and thumbs) is tall—and framed by the shining sun on a nearly cloudless day. Old oaks surround the park-like parcel of ground, and fields across the street gleam with soon to be harvested corn. The monument itself looks today much as it does in the old photographs I have seen showing Julia Pokagon on that first dedication day. This white men's monument to their own bad behavior; is there pleasure in the pathos? Pokagon's *Red Man's Greeting* has been called *The Red Man's Book of Lamentations.* This statue to the memory of Chief Menominee is perhaps then the settlers' monument of lamentations.

The festivities continue with pomp and circumstance and conclude with an elderly pastor raising his arms to the sky and offering an "Indian prayer." The Indians in attendance lay tobacco onto the earth near the monument and offer their own prayers in the old language.

An instructor from the nearby Culver Academy Preparatory School invites Eddie Joe Mitchell, a Prairie Band Potawatomi member from Kansas, to return later in the year to instruct the young students on the "real ways" of the Indian. Mitchell seems to take the request in stride and smiles slightly. "Indian ways" are now worthy of instruction to the descendants of settlers who saw no value in Indians or their ways. Eddie looks at me and it seems the irony is not lost on either of us. Nearby, George Godfrey, a Citizen Band Potawatomi, who before retirement taught entomology at the University of Illinois, is dressed as the Potawatomi of Indiana did in 1838, looking as though he has stepped out of a George Winter watercolor.

The non-Native organizers of the event are dressed also in their imaginings of what the Potawatomi of the 1830s wore—lots of buckskin and beads—non-Natives, playing Indian in what appears to be a sincere attempt to honor those long-removed Twin Lakes Indians. Toward the end of the outdoor festivities a gathering of musicians sing odes to the good Chief Menominee in Gordon Lightfootesque seriousness. As dinnertime approaches, the gathered adjourn to the nearby Menominee Elementary School for a chili supper and a feel good moment—history is pain free so long as it has an aura of solemnity. Time helps heal the wounds and it is safe to remember the atrocities of the past.

I eat the chili and engage in small talk with tablemates. However, I am left wondering about the erasure of the first dedication, the lack of reference to it and the missing remonstrations that Julia Pokagon voiced at the first commemoration. Today, unlike the first time, there is no talk of bitterness or responsibility.

I am struck by the multiplicity of meanings that can be "read" from this monument. I leave feeling a sense of melancholy that there is for me no feeling of reconciliation. I suspect, however, that most leave feeling better for having celebrated the memory of a great Indian chief and the passing of his people and their ways. My angst contrasts with their nostalgia.

Back at the monument, all is quiet. The simulacrum of Chief Menominee stands silent and still, in repose, frozen in time. After the crowd has gone: who remembers, what do they remember, and why? I am reminded that the dominant culture and the Potawatomi each have their own ways of memorializing the past for future generations. The power and wonder of monuments, memorials and commemorative events is that every audience member will read what they experience based upon their own experiences, expectations and biases.[32]

Memorials and monuments to the Potawatomi dot the landscape surrounding Chicago. In Shipshewana, Indiana, not far from Chicago, Memorial Day 1931 was proclaimed Chief Shipshewana Day. The Shipshewana, Indiana, Chamber of Commerce organized the event, which included the unveiling of a monument in the chief's memory. According to a program from the event,

> On the south side of the lake stands the monument which has been erected in the chieftain's honor, bearing the following inscription: 'In memory of Chief Shipshewana and his band of Pottawatomie Indians removed from this reservation Sept. 4, 1838, and escorted to Kansas by a company of soldiers. One year later the heart-broken chief was allowed to return to his old camping grounds on the banks of beautiful Shipshewana Lake where he died in 1841.[33]

Included on the program for that day were music and talk by Rev. Joe C. Pamp-to-pee, direct descendant of Chief Shipshewana, and an address by Rev. William Soney (described as an Indian Orator), who spoke on the "Attitude and Gratitude of the Indian Today." That afternoon, a baseball game pitting the Elkhart, Indiana, Giants vs. the "Shipshewana Indians" at 4 P.M. was also held. According to the day's program, "Mr. Dalby of South Bend will have his collection of Indian relics on display the entire day. A delegation of Indians from the reservation at Athens, Michigan, will be present."[34]

Prior to "removal," some of the Potawatomi lived in the Fox Valley area of Illinois, near Chicago, during the summers, and wintered in southern Illinois. To honor the legacy of the Potawatomi people there, a statue was erected near Chicago, at Pottawatomie Park in St. Charles, Illinois, in 1915. Vandalism during the 1960s damaged the statue beyond repair and it had to be removed. In the 1980s, a new statue was sculpted by Guy Bellaver, dedicated in memory of the Potawatomi, and erected by the community on the same site. The fifteen-foot bronze statue stands looking westward over the Fox River.[35]

Installed on May 22, 1988, the statue cost an estimated $90,000. Members of four bands of Potawatomi were invited to the dedication, including those from the Pokagon Band. A year later, the statue received its name.[36] Potawatomi tribal members, believing that it was important to name the statue to give it a protective

***Ekwabet*, St. Charles, Illinois.** PHOTOGRAPH BY THE AUTHOR.

spirit—something that the 1915 statue did not have—named the statue *Ekwabet* or "watching over." According to at least one tribal member, the sculptor told them that it is modeled after Leopold Pokagon, the patriarch of the Pokagon Band of Potawatomi and Simon Pokagon's father.[37] I remember tribal member Rae Daugherty telling me several years later about the dedication, and that she hadn't known how to tell the sculptor that for her *Ekwabet* was facing in the wrong direction; that he should be facing east to greet each morning rather than facing west.

Another, earlier statue dedicated to the memory of the Potawatomi is the memorial to Black Partridge.[38] Sculpted by Carl Rohl-Smith and dedicated on June 22, 1893, it depicts an image of Black Partridge saving a Mrs. Helm during what has come to be called "the Fort Dearborn Massacre."[39] The famous industrialist G. W. Pullman of Pullman railway car wealth, who commissioned the statue, had it erected in front of his mansion at 18th St. and Prairie Avenue in Chicago. The statue was originally located near the site of the battle between Potawatomi warriors and a group of Americans fleeing Fort Dearborn in 1812. The plaque at the front of Rohl-Smith's sculpture describes the tableau. This description was recorded in the *Chicago Daily Tribune*:

> Black Partridge, the Pottawattomie chief, saving Mrs. Helm from death by . . . tomahawk. At the back of the group Dr. Van Voorhees, the post surgeon [meets] his death . . . an Indian . . . thrusting a spear through his breast.[40]

The design appears to have been inspired by Juliette Magill Kinzie's account of the destruction of Fort Dearborn.[41]

Fort Dearborn and the Potawatomi

On June 18, 1812, the United States declared war against Great Britain and its allies. Many Indians of the Great Lakes region had already been engaged in a struggle against American expansion under the leadership of Tecumseh since 1811, and that conflict merged into the War of 1812.[42] The Battle of Fort Dearborn occurred on August 15, 1812, near the mouth of the Chicago River. Indians allied with Great Britain were encouraged by the latter to engage in military actions against the United States. Fort Dearborn was ordered evacuated by the United States military. The fort's commander, Captain Nathan Heald, had negotiated with the surrounding Indians, mostly Potawatomi, for safe passage. In return, the Indians were promised the provisions in the fort, including all of the alcohol and ammunition. However, on the day of the evacuation, Heald reneged on the promise and destroyed the provisions, agitating the Potawatomi, who needed the gunpowder in particular for their weapons—not just for war, but also to hunt and provide for their families.[43] A timeline of the events leading up to the Battle of Fort Dearborn is included in appendix 4.

As the garrison of soldiers and families commenced their evacuation, they were escorted by Potawatomi and Miami Indians to a point about a mile and a half south of the fort. There, near what is now 18th Street and Calumet Avenue, shots rang out. Ultimately the Potawatomi prevailed, killing most of the militia as well as two women and twelve children. Who fired the first shot is unclear, as we are left primarily with the subjective written accounts of the non-Native survivors and their descendants.[44] However, it is quite possible that the Americans attacked the Potawatomi first.[45] The only written account of the battle from an Indian perspective comes from Simon Pokagon. A Potawatomi Indian, he recounted sixty years after the conflict some of the stories his elders who had participated in the battle had told him. His version of the events of the battle emphasizes provocations by the United States as the cause of the confrontation.[46] He intended to write a longer account, but his death prevented this.[47] However, before his passing, Simon was interviewed about the battle by the *Chicago Daily Tribune* where he wryly noted "when whites are killed it is a massacre . . . when Indians are killed it is a fight."[48]

During the battle, Captain Heald is reported to have attempted to ride into a nearby Potawatomi village to attack the women and children there. However, he was killed before he was able to do so.[49] The remaining non-Natives from the fort were taken prisoner and delivered to the British at Detroit. The fort was burned to the ground, and the area remained free of U.S. citizens until after the war.[50] Typical of the dominant attitude about the impact of the battle, however, are the remarks of historian Milo M. Quaife:

> For nine years the garrison of Fort Dearborn upheld the banner of civilization west of Lake Michigan—a tiny island engulfed in a sea of savagery. Then, as an incident in a world-wide convulsion, having its center four thousand miles away in distant Europe, garrison and community were blotted out, and the forces of barbarism again reigned supreme at Chicago.[51]

This memorial to Black Partridge provided an example of "the good Indian," in contrast to his savage comrades, and typifies the bifurcation that was common to the era, which categorized Indians as either noble or ignoble.

In 1896, magazine editor B. O. Flowers noted the irony of the installation of the Black Partridge statue in the then most expensive neighborhood of Chicago by one of the wealthiest members of the upper class.[52] Flowers provided a helpful description of the area.

> Mr. George M. Pullman's stately mansion stands in the shade of the cottonwood tree, his conservatory is erected upon the battle-field. . . . Within an area of five blocks forty of the sixty members of the Commercial Club have established their homes. Mr. Marshall Field and Mr. Phillip Armour live near together on the east

side of the avenue a little further south. Probably there are as many millions of dollars to the square inch of this residential district as are to be found for any equal area on the world's surface. It is the very Mecca of Mammon, the Olympus of the great gods of Chicago.[53]

The mansions that surrounded that statue in 1893 were monuments as well—to conquest, power, and the unequal distribution of wealth, made possible through the rise of capitalism and industrialization. The statue, which was moved sometime after the demographics of the neighborhood shifted from wealthy white to lower-income and African American, was later housed in the rotunda of the Chicago History Society (now Museum) and is now stored in a Chicago Park District Warehouse.

The Politics of the Battle of Fort Dearborn Park

In 2007, the Prairie District Neighborhood Association (PDNA) sought to create a green space from a gravel- and weed-covered parcel of land owned by the city. The PDNA initiated an effort to commemorate "The Fort Dearborn Massacre" by naming the small park located near the site of the original attack in 1812 after Black Partridge and reinstalling the statue of him. The Prairie Avenue neighborhood itself was undergoing substantial gentrification at the time, and expensive townhomes and high-rise condominiums were replacing underused and empty businesses and residences. However, reinstallation of the statue of Black Partridge met with staunch resistance from the Chicago American Indian Center, according to a 2007 article in the *Chicago Reader*.[54]

The greatest potential problem is public reaction, especially from the Native American community, which may object to the depiction of the Indians as aggressors. . . . The day after he took the Black Partridge name to the Park Board, [Mark] Kieras [a member of the local neighborhood association] placed a call to Joseph Podlasek, director of Chicago's American Indian Center. "Hopefully they'll be interested in having it too," Kieras says. "We feel if we get their support, it'll be a slam dunk." That doesn't seem likely. After getting a look at a photo of the statue this week, Podlasek said the name for the park might be OK (though he'd have to see the research to be sure), but they'd need a different piece of art. "This is clearly the image that our

"Black Partridge Saving Mrs. Helm," a.k.a. "The Fort Dearborn Massacre Monument."

FROM THE COLLECTION OF THE AUTHOR.

> elders had removed from the Chicago Historical Society many years ago," he said. "We will not support this coming out of storage. Ever."

In addition to whether the statute should be reinstalled was the issue of what to name the park. The Chicago American Indian community and others voiced objections to naming the park after the so-called Fort Dearborn "Massacre." Back in 1943, an Illinois historian had advocated for renaming the conflict as a battle rather than a massacre.

> H. A. Musham, Chicago naval architect, chairman of the Fort Dearborn Memorial commission and for many years a student of Chicago and Illinois' history, recently declared in an article in the Journal of the Illinois Historical society that the Fort Dearborn action should be called the Battle of Chicago and not the Fort Dearborn massacre or Chicago massacre. "It was not a massacre for it was not an indiscriminate killing," Musham said. "Those who perished were killed in the fighting or soon afterward in accordance with Indian customs, or died because of the privations of their captivity. It was, in fact, a minor engagement, a physical struggle between two opposing forces, American and Indian. While it did take place at Chicago, it did not occur at Fort Dearborn. It is therefore correct to call it the battle of Chicago.[55]

The Prairie District Neighborhood Association again suggested that the park be named after Chief Black Partridge. At subsequent meetings, which I was invited to attend as a representative of the Pokagon Potawatomi Traditions and Repatriation Committee (of which I am a member), I made clear my belief that a park in honor of Black Partridge was insufficient for the magnitude of the events that occurred there and too closely hearkened back to the memory of the Pullman statue. Instead, I suggested that the park be named "Battle of Fort Dearborn Park" to better reflect the events of that day in 1812, and that a plaque rather than the statue be placed at the park. The precinct alderman's office, the PDNA, the Chicago American Indian Center, and others ultimately came to a consensus, embracing my suggestion for the park's name and forgoing the installation of the Black Partridge statue.[56]

Why was it important to participate in the statue and park-name controversy? For too long, only one side was being heard about the so-called "massacre" at Fort Dearborn in 1812. The statue and the name only served to confirm the stereotypes that too many non-Natives hold against American Indians generally, and the

Potawatomi specifically. Typical of that prejudicial attitude are the remarks a historian made back in 1919 when commenting on the events of that day in 1812.

> [The Potawatomi] brained innocent children, clinging to their mother's knees, and then struck down the mothers, and with hands reeking with blood, tore their scalps from their heads even before death had put an end to their sufferings. . . . Such was the horrible fate that innocents often met, at the hands of these cruel and relentless savages.[57]

The Pokagon Potawatomi, the Chicago American Indian Center, local politicians, a grassroots neighborhood association, and scholars from around the area both Native and non-Native took this opportunity to demythologize an important aspect of early city history. All the participants in the naming of the park hoped that it would allow future generations to see the combatants in the struggle for control of the region as human beings, rather than villains.

On August 15, 2009, the park was dedicated with participation from members of the neighborhood association and other residents of Chicago, members of the American Indian Center, representatives of the local Illinois National Guard, and members of the Pokagon Band of Potawatomi.[58] According to press reports,

> During the dedication, [Pokagon] Potawatomi elder Roger Williams blessed the site. To commemorate its history, an Illinois National Guard honor guard presented the colors, and ritual performers offered traditional Native American singing, drumming, and dancing. . . .
>
> Second Ward Alderman Robert Fioretti noted the dedication day focused on unity and healing, and Williams said the City's invitation to the Potawatomi to join the dedication "completed the circle" linking the past and the present. . . . During the planning process, participants decided against naming the site after Potawatomi chief Black Partridge, who warned the soldiers and pioneers about the planned attack. The American Indian Center supported naming the park after Black Partridge but opposed the statue, as did Fioretti. The statue "doesn't symbolize how people can come together," he said, noting it "portrays Native Americans in the wrong light."[59]

Roger Williams, a leader of the Pokagon Potawatomi veterans group Ogichidaw, outlined the reasons for their presence:

Dedication of the Battle of Fort Dearborn Park. Potawatomi veteran Roger Williams is to the left. PHOTOGRAPH COURTESY OF THE PRAIRIE DISTRICT NEIGHBORHOOD ASSOCIATION.

> Chicago is a part of the Potawatomi and the Potawatomi will always be a part of Chicago. Our Ancestors fought at the Battle of Fort Dearborn. We come today to honor those who died on that day in August, 1812, and also to honor all those who have fought to protect our traditions and way of life.[60]

Lively debate about the name of the park, and whether the event was a massacre or a battle, appeared in the local online newspaper the *Chicago Examiner*, *Chicago Magazine*, the *Chicago Tribune*, and on local public radio station WBEZ.[61] Explaining the objection to naming the park after Black Partridge, James Grossman, vice president for research and education at the Newberry Library, senior research associate in the Department of History at the University of Chicago, and coeditor of *The Encyclopedia of Chicago*, said, "From their [Native] perspective, Black Partridge was a traitor."[62] At the dedication of the park, Russell Lewis, executive vice president and chief historian of the Chicago History Museum, pointed out that Simon Pokagon had criticized the battle being called a massacre: quoting Pokagon, "When whites are killed, it is a massacre; when Indians are killed, it is a fight."[63]

Some bemoaned the failure to reinstall the statue; more comments focused on the naming issue. One person posted on an online site about the controversy:

> I have followed articles about the controversy of the naming of the park with great interest. I find it ridiculous that Chicago's history is allowed to be distorted to mollify those who want to stand in the way of truth.
>
> Who is John N. Low and why should we care what he thinks? Why should the statue that honors Black Partridge be warehoused when he valiantly saved a white woman from being killed? It's because some Native Americans still see him as a traitor for doing so. Isn't that a sad commentary that any American would still feel that way today?
>
> Nearly 200 years have passed, but time doesn't change facts. The American public is sick to death of political correctness getting in the way of truth. It's time to tell it like it is and stop catering to fringe groups who want to retell history to their own satisfaction.
>
> Were there any descendants of the victims of the Fort Dearborn Massacre on this board that decided the name of the park? I doubt it. I'm surprised our government hasn't apologized for building the fort there in the first place. Maybe that's next.
>
> Nancy Margraff, Chicago[64]

Some predicted trouble for the new name. According to one *Chicago Tribune* columnist,

> A tragic chapter in Windy City history known to generations of schoolchildren as "The Ft. Dearborn Massacre" will be renamed by the Chicago Park District on Saturday. With a military honor guard and Native American dancers, a patch of green at 18th Street and Calumet Avenue is to be dedicated the "Battle of Ft. Dearborn Park." That apparent nod to political correctness won't go down well with many Chicagoans who from bar stools to seminar tables, cherish their city's legend and lore.[65]

However, the new name stuck.[66] Arguably, the park's new designation recognizes that lives were lost on both sides, and better reflects the complex nature of the overall war, with American Indians and early settlers battling over land and westward expansion, resources, and a multitude of other issues and grievances.

It seems that the difficulty in accepting the new title for the conflict stems from the notion, held by some, that "history" should be a single, unchanging narrative.[67] Perhaps this would be ameliorated if we designated the study of the past as *histories*, rather than the singular *history*. The controversy over the demise of the "Fort Dearborn Massacre" narrative sparked anew in 2012 with the 200th anniversary of the Battle of Fort Dearborn. Once again, those in favor of and against the "name change" and the statue debated in the press and on Internet blogs/websites. Some of the comments were very supportive of what had been started in 2009. Lindsay Prossnitz wrote for the *Chicago Tonight* blog,

> I get a little annoyed when people say it's political correctness, as a practicing historian. For history to have value in our society, it's great when you can find it does more than entertain, but actually does something. When history is an agent for reconciliation, it's a powerful and wonderful thing.[68]

The *Chicago Tribune* and the *Chicago Sun-Times*, major newspapers in Chicago, embraced the designation of the "Battle of Fort Dearborn." However, one opinion editor in particular was strident in his call for Chicagoans to rise up in support of the massacre moniker and reinstallation of the Black Partridge statue.[69] Thus far, nothing has come from this call to arms.

In 2012, the Chicago City Council approved a resolution marking the anniversary of the Battle of Fort Dearborn. The resolution included a request for city officials to "encourage thoughtful and inclusive discussion and education involving Native American history and culture." The council's resolution reflected the power in securing a clearer understanding of our shared past. Its message highlighted the still-contested struggle over the "history" of Native/non-Native relations in early Chicago, how the struggle over memory of those events mimicked in some ways the struggle for the land two hundred years ago, and how an opportunity for reconciliation between contemporary non-Native and Native peoples was secured by those willing to reconsider a metanarrative for the "founding of Chicago."

Historian Ann Durkin Keating concludes that "[the battle] was not a 'massacre' but part of a declared war that the United States waged against Great Britain and their Indian allies." However, Keating also advocates for reinstallation of Pullman's Black Partridge monument, either at the Fort Dearborn Park site, the administration building for the former Pullman Palace Car Company on the far south side, or in a public display at the Chicago History Museum. She advocates renaming the statue after Black Partridge and including a "reinterpretation" (presumably with some accompanying label).[70] However, the problem with reinstallation of the statue with some form of textual reinterpretation is that most viewers of the statue will only see the worn-out caricature of the noble red man saving the helpless white woman from the hands of another savage Indian. One wonders if any amount of labeling can overcome that visual message.[71]

On August 11, 2012, the Chicago History Museum held a commemoration day for the "Battle of Fort Dearborn Bicentennial," complete with groups of War of 1812 reenactors and a "Reconciliation and Memorial Program." On September 8 of that year, the Prairie District Neighborhood Association held its annual South Loop festival with a 200th Year Anniversary commemoration of the Battle of Fort Dearborn. American Indian musicians, educators, artists, and storytellers from the Chicago area participated, as did the Pokagon Potawatomi—led, as in 2009, by tribal member and head veteran Roger Williams.

Heid Erdrich (2008) reminds us that Native peoples had monuments long before contact with non-Natives.[72] But for the last several hundred years, the mainstream of settler-colonists and their descendants in the United States have erected a multitude of monuments celebrating their "conquest" of North America. It is a rare occurrence when both Natives and non-Natives can share a commemorative space that acknowledges the difficulties and complexities of early contact between the two. It is a good sign that Natives and non-Natives can share such a place in Chicago. The battle over "The Battle of Fort Dearborn Park" represents a milestone for the city and the nation. Not only were members of the Pokagon Potawatomi Indians and the Chicago American Indian Center invited to participate in the process of creating a memorial; they also had a significant voice in how Chicago history was reinterpreted.

Black Ash Basketry and Winter Storytelling

In recent decades, basketry and storytelling have also been ways for the Pokagon Potawatomi to contribute to the social and cultural life of Chicago. In the 1980s, the Pokagon Potawatomi Black Ash Basket Co-op was organized to maintain, promote, and pass on the art of basket making. The Co-op became a very visible institution for cultural revival, and its members made numerous trips to Chicago to teach basketry and to display and sell their wares. Well-publicized visits to the Mitchell Museum of the American Indian and the Chicago Botanic Gardens reflected their efforts to promote their art and identity in Chicago.[73]

The Pokagon Potawatomi have also participated in other public events in Chicago in recent years. On January 26, 2001, elders from the community together with other members, tribal council representatives, and the general public joined in the sixth annual celebration of "Winter: A Time of Telling," held at the Newberry Library.[74] Founded by the American Indian Economic Development Association (AIEDA) of Chicago in 1995, the storytelling is sponsored by the D'Arcy McNickle Center for American Indian and Indigenous Studies. According to the Newberry Library website,

> Since 1995, *Winter: A Time of Telling*, Chicago's only annual public program of its kind, has brought members of Chicago's diverse American Indian community to the Newberry Library to celebrate and share their living cultures. Oral tradition is an integral aspect of Native cultures. Identity, history, spirituality, and values are passed down through stories. The traditional storytelling season for many American Indians falls between the first and last frosts when animals featured in their stories are hibernating.

Bernd Peyer notes that during the event that year, Simon Pokagon was honored for his contributions in literature and conservation of oral traditions. Baskets from the Co-op were also sold at the event.[75] This connection between stories and material culture is reminiscent of Pokagon's *Queen of the Woods*, which closes with pictures of black-ash baskets and other art of the Pokagon Potawatomi. I had the opportunity to emcee that celebration and helped one of the basket makers and sellers, Judy Augusta, set up her table before the event. When the doors to the Newberry Library opened that evening, I noticed a crush of people around her table. A bit later I came out to the lobby where her table was and saw that she looked sad. I asked her what was wrong, and she replied, "I sold a year's worth of baskets in five minutes! Now what do I do for the rest of the night?" We both laughed. So, it seems, the fascination with the cultural productions of the Potawatomi continues unabated in Chicago.

The Bricolage at the Foster Avenue Underpass of Lakeshore Drive

Further evidence that the presence of the Pokagon Potawatomi continues in Chicago is reflected in a recent public art installation in the Edgewater/Uptown neighborhoods of the city. In 2009, 48th Ward alderwoman Mary Ann Smith proposed using $107,770 of discretionary infrastructure funds to create a 3,400-square-foot mural on Foster Avenue at the Lakeshore Drive underpass "to honor Chicago's Native American heritage."[76] Inspired by a trip to Alaska and the Native art there, the city council member coordinated the creation of a bricolage detailing Chicago's Native past and present.[77] The bricolage is a multimedia mosaic, composed of materials that include ceramic tiles and plaster that have both original art and historical and contemporary images painted and printed onto the tiles.

The project was the result of a collaboration between Alderwoman Smith, her office and staff, an organization called the Chicago Public Art Group (CPAG), the Chicago American Indian Center, the Trickster Gallery in Schaumburg, Illinois, the Mitchell Museum of the American Indian in Evanston, Illinois, American Indian scholars, members of the Chicago Indian arts community, youth volunteers from Alternatives, Inc. (a youth and family agency), and the After School Matters program of Chicago.[78] The bricolage, titled *Indian Land Dancing* after a poem by Ojibwe artist E. Donald Two-Rivers, is located ten minutes from the American Indian Center and the Uptown neighborhood, which was the area where Indians coming to Chicago after World War II primarily located. The power of such public art is noted by Mary Ann Jacobs, a former instructor at the School of the Art Institute of Chicago and now the chair of American Indian Studies and an associate professor at the University of North Carolina at Pembroke. "Art in public space has been enabling in a community . . . the work becomes embraced and that grows richer over time. . . . It grounds people within their own consciousness of place."[79]

Amidst the symbolic images on the murals—which include a rising sun of welcome, a hand covering a giant turtle, a thunderbird, cattails along the Lake Michigan shoreline, an eagle soaring, and a circle of life—are also images of Mohawk ironworkers, family photographs, a lithograph reproduction of Black Hawk, a new painting of world-renowned ballerina Maria Tallchief, and images of other notable Indian residents of Chicago. The tiles are interspersed with pieces of mirror that allow the viewers to see themselves within the mural. Included in the montage, which embraces both sides of Foster Avenue, are the visages of

The mural on Foster Avenue, Chicago (detail). PHOTOGRAPH FROM THE COLLECTION OF THE AUTHOR.

Leopold and Simon Pokagon, as well as a quote from the latter Pokagon's *The Red Man's Greeting*, and a listing of the land-cession treaties involving Chicago in which the Potawatomi participated.[80] Additional images of the Potawatomi include a reproduction of a montage of Potawatomi chiefs painted by George Winter in the first half of the nineteenth century, and a map of the "Trail of Death," the route taken by Potawatomi of Indiana and Illinois when forcibly removed to the west in 1838 by the federal government. One section of the wall includes a rendering of a *tipi* and books, painted by Chicago artist Robert Wapahi (Dakota) to "symbolize local tribes' transition from oral to written storytelling."[81] Wapahi's image is evocative of the contributions of Simon Pokagon to the intellectual and real landscape of Chicago.

Indian Land Dancing was dedicated on August 22, 2009, with the attendance of then mayor Richard M. Daley, the alderwoman, many of the project's participants,

Detail from the Foster Avenue bricolage in Chicago. The image of Simon Pokagon is in the center row to the far right. To his left is an image of his father, Leopold Pokagon. PHOTOGRAPH FROM THE COLLECTION OF THE AUTHOR.

and the general public. After the ceremony, the Chicago Indian community held a pow wow to honor the bricolage and the effort and collaboration that made it possible.[82] The bricolage is a public and proud demonstration that the Chicago Indian community and the City of Chicago both recognize the continued vitality of the Native community.

Monuments and memorials to the Potawatomi abound in the greater Chicago area. Most recently, there has been a shift to collaboration with tribal members, and that has resulted in a different representation of the peoples who are intended to be honored and memorialized. The non-Native newcomers initially created their architectural renderings to commemorate the Indigenous peoples they had supplanted. However, Native peoples have talked back, including Pokagon tribal members, by rendering their own memorials, whether in literature, performance, or structure. Today, a resident or visitor to Chicago has the opportunity to read these memorials like chapters in a book—each chapter reflecting the course of Indian experience in Chicago and the evolution of Native/non-Native relations in the city.

The Pokagon Potawatomi never accepted the new world forced upon them passively. Through a combination of the written and spoken word, joined with the symbolism of material culture, Simon Pokagon restored to ancestral lands a familiarity that reminded Natives and non-Natives alike that American Indians wished to participate in the social, political, and cultural milieu/maelstrom of America. This visibility confirmed that the Potawatomi were neither totally assimilated nor exterminated. Monuments proposed to honor Simon Pokagon in Chicago immediately after his death (for example, his proposed burial at Graceland Cemetery and a Jackson Park Statue) reflect his popularity in the city, even though they never came to pass.[83] Simon Pokagon worked to clear a space for the Pokagon Potawatomi to allow them to do much more than withdraw from their non-Native neighbors in Chicago. Other Pokagon Potawatomi tribal members followed his lead. Evidence of the Pokagons' continued "presence" in Chicago is reflected in the bricolage mural on Foster Avenue and attendance of tribal members at events throughout the city in recent times, which provide testimonial to the fact that even though most Pokagon Potawatomi have not resided within the city for more than 160 years, they have never acceded to their estrangement from their lands at the mouth of the Chicago River.

Chicagou/Chicago: Today and Tomorrow

The presence of Pokagon Potawatomi tribal members in the life of the City continues to this day. For example, on June 15, 2015, Marine and Army veteran Anthony Foerster found himself on center ice at the United Center in Chicago. Chicago's Blackhawks professional hockey team would in a few hours win the Stanley Cup Championship. Foerster was identified by the emcee as a member of the Pokagon Band of Potawatomi Indians as he represented his community in the color guard during the singing of the national anthem at the commencement of the game. Dressed in a ribbon shirt, he held the eagle staff of the Pokagon Potawatomi nation of which he is a citizen. Once again, this time on national television, in prime time, broadcast internationally, the world was reminded that the Pokagon Potawatomi are still participants in the life in Chicago.

The reasons behind the efforts of Pokagon Potawatomi tribal members to maintain a connection with Chicago are as varied as the lives and experiences of the individuals documented in this book. The actions of Leopold, Simon, Charles, and Julia Pokagon; of Michael B. Williams and the tribe's Business Committee; of Leroy Wesaw Sr. and many others all reflected a demand for respect as fellow citizens of the United States. There are also elements in their actions of opposition, especially a refusal to be marginalized by non-Native neighbors, and a desire for inclusion in the life of the city. An acknowledgment that this was still Indian land as well as a metropolitan center also seems to weave its way through their stories. Money was also a motivator; as the city became a center of incredible wealth, some Pokagon Potawatomi saw the opportunity to benefit themselves and fellow tribal members by making claims to a piece of it. Chicago has served as a stage to reach large audiences—whether the desire was for individual celebrity or the confirmation of individual and community identity. A common thread in these stories is that tribal members continued to insert themselves into the collective memory of Chicagoans through reference to traditional activities and materials. Living as contemporary peoples, they laid claim not only to the past, but also to the present.

Today, there are four stars on the flag of the City of Chicago, each representing a watershed moment in the history of the city. The first represents Fort Dearborn, the second the Great Fire of 1871, the third the World's Columbian Exposition, and the fourth the 1933 Century of Progress Exposition. We know that the Pokagon Potawatomi played important roles in the first and third and were connected to the second because tribal land claims were a consequence of the conflagration.

They were also a part of many other important moments in the history of the city. Chicago never was the sole territory of the Potawatomi; there were many other Native peoples living here before contact with Europeans. And since the arrival of settlers, the Potawatomi have never been the only Indians living in the city we now call Chicago. Nonetheless, the Potawatomi, particularly the Pokagon Band, have played an important part in the city's history.

So what is at stake in efforts by Pokagon Potawatomi to retain a place in Chicago? Do they reflect an inability to accept that their ancestral lands have been taken from them? Is it nostalgia for the past, or is it something deeper and more common to the human experience? For settler-colonists the frontier "closed" in 1890, and in the twentieth century Chicago became the homeland for millions of immigrants from all over the globe as it grew from a border town into an urban metropolis. Chicago history reflects a transition from frontier to heartland in the imaginings of the hegemon, and the city remains, in metaphorical terms, at the very heart of the nation.[84] The Pokagon Potawatomi have a similar relationship to the land they call Nokmeskignan or Grandmother Earth, a familial and enduring relationship. The Potawatomi also have a strong affinity to the lake adjacent to the city.[85] Non-Natives, who may not understand the ethos of the Potawatomi to care for and retain a place in their ancestral lands, need only look to their affection for their own heartland to understand why the Potawatomi will never relinquish a place they still consider home.

APPENDIX 1

Transcription of *Pottawattamie Book of Genesis: Legend of the Creation of Man*

There is an old tradition among our people dimly seen through the mists of time, that Ki-ji Man-i-to (The Great Spirit), after he had created nomash (The Fish) of ni-bi-nong (the waters) and b-nes-sig (the fowls) of no-din (the air), and mo-naw-to-auk, the beasts of a-ki (the land). His work still failed to satisfy the grand conception of His soul. Hence He called a great Counsel of man-i-to-og (the spirits) that ruled over land and seas, His agents, and revealed unto them how it was the great desire of Nin o-daw (His heart) to create a new being that should stand erect upon his hind legs, and to possess the combined intelligence of all the living creatures He had made.

Most of those spirits whom He had permitted to hold do-minion over the earth, when they met in the great Council, encouraged His Divine plans, but Man-i-to O-gi-maw-og (the spiritual Chief) when they considered the great power the proposed being might wield, quietly withdrew themselves from the Council, and held a private pow wow of their own, to frustrate, if possible, the plans of How-waw-tuck (the Almighty). The loyal Mon-i-tog who remained at the grand Council stood aghast as Ki-ji Man-i-to revealed unto them His Divine plan, explaining the great possibilities that awaited the new creature He had conceived in His heart to create.

The Divine Council was prolonged by debate from the set of sun until morning dawn. Ke-sus (the sun) arose in greater brilliancy than ever before. The Spirits anxiously began to inquire of His Maj-esty, "How many suns and moons would pass before He could accomplish His wonderful work?" While yet the inquiry hung on ki o-don-og (their lips), He said unto them "Follow me." He led them into a great wilderness to Sa-gi-i-gan, a beautiful inland lake. And as He stood upon the shores thereof in the presence of them all, His eyes flashed waw-sawmo-win (lightning)! The lake became boiling water! He then spake in a voice of thunder; "COME FORTH YE LORDS OF AU-KEE (the world)!" The ground opened! And from out of the red clay that lined the lake came forth Au-ne-ne gaie Ik-we (man and woman) like kego (flying fish) from out the water! In presence of the new born pair all was still as death! A dark cloud hung over the lake! It began to boil again! The awful silence was then broken! The earth shook! And Ki-ji Man-i-to said: "Come forth ye servants of An-nish-naw-be (man)!" Forth leaped at once from out the lake Ni-ji wa-be gon o-nim-og (a pair of snow-white dogs) and laid down where stood the new made pair kissing their feet and hands.

The bride and groom then each other fondly kissed as hand in hand they stood, in naked innocence, in their full bloom of youth, perfect in make and mould, of body and of limb. Ki-gi-nos maw-kaw mis-taw-kaw (their long black hair) almost reached the ground, which, gently waving in nip-nong oden (the morning breeze) in contrast with their rich color, grace, and forms erect, outrivaled in beauty all other creatures He had made. They looked all about them in wonder and surprise. Surveyed all living creatures that moved in sight. Gazed upon the towering trees. The grass. The flowers. The lake. The sunshine and the shade. And again each other fondly kissed as their eyes looked love to eyes, with no other language their feelings to express.

At length I-kwe (the maiden fair) slyly let go Os-ki-nawe o-ning-i-maw (the young man's hand) and stole away into the dark shades and hid, where she might watch to test his love, and learn thereby if his feelings were akin to hers. Long he sought in vain to find his mate, until at length the snow-white dogs, following on her track, joyfully howled out: "We have found her."

Now when mau-tchi Man-i-tog (the spiritual Chiefs) first learned that Ki-ji Man-i-to had finished His Crowning works, as He had proposed to do, sought diligently for the new made pair until they found them. And as they surveyed the beauty of their forms erect and the surpassing loveliness of body and limb, their wonder and admiration was unbounded. But when they saw the soul of the Divine shining in their faces, like the noon-day sun, their hearts were stung through and through by maw-tchi a-mog (the cruel wasps) of envy and jealousy. Hence they resolved, in nin o-daw (their hearts), that in-stead of trying to live in peace with them, as they had done with the first creation, they would do all they could to make them discontented, un-happy and miserable.

As time rolled on, the first o-nig-go-maw (parents) and generations after them, began to realize there were man-tchi dash meno Mandito (bad spirits and good spirits) that exercised dominion over mountains, lakes, streams and plains, and that they were in a measure controlled by them. They also began to learn that au-nish-i-naw-be (man) possessed the nature and the intelligence of all the animal creation; and that he was endowed with a spiritual nature which was given him by mi-si ge-go ga-gi-ji-tod (the Creator of all things) in waw-kwing dash Au-kee (in heaven and on earth). Hence when they were unfortunate in securing game, or unsuccessful in battle, it was all attributed to the bad spirits that held Dominion over the country wherein they dwelt.

And when game was plenty, and they were successful in battle, this they attributed to the good spirits that controlled the land in which they lived. Sometimes in order to appease bad spirits, they made offerings of fruits and grains. But they sacrificed animals only to Ki-ji Man-i-to waw-quin (the God of Heaven) who alone they recognized as the great Creator and Ruler of all things in heaven and on earth.

Our fathers and mothers in their primeval state, did not name their children as do the civilized races, simply that they might be known and designated by them. But when their children were born, whatever animal or bird they imagined they must resemble they were called by that name; and as strange as it may appear to the white race, in after generations those bearing the name of some animal believed, at least they claimed, to have descended from such animal whose name they bore. It might be, maw-qua (the bear), or waw-goosh (the fox) or mi-gi-si (the eagle). The same rule followed in each individual case. And so it was in succeeding generations, each tribe or clan adopted as their "to-tum" the animal or thing whose name the patriarch of the tribe was called when a child.

Sometimes when at war, the animal was taken with them alive, but generally it was painted on a tanned hide and used as white men use their flags.

It was an emblem of royalty as well as a symbol of loyalty, and when engaged in battle a warrior would rather die than surrender his totem.

It matters not how foolish our legends may appear to those races who call themselves civilized, still they were as sacred to us as holy writ to them.

APPENDIX 2

Selected Essays, Articles, and Monographs Regarding Simon Pokagon

Berliner, Jonathan. "Discursive Ground: Naturalization in American Literature, 1836–1918." PhD diss. Chicago: University of Chicago, 2008.

Buechner, Cecilia Bain. "The Pokagons." (*Indianapolis*) *Indiana Historical Soc. Publications* 10, no. 5 (1933).

Claspy, Everett. *The Potawatomi Indians of Southwestern Michigan*. Ann Arbor, MI: Braun-Brumfield, Inc., 1966.

———. *The Dowagiac–Sister Lakes Resort Area and More about Its Potawatomi Indians*. Dowagiac, MI: Self-published, 1970.

Clifton, James A. *The Pokagons, 1683–1983: Catholic Potawatomi Indians of the St. Joseph River Valley*. Lanham, MD: University Press of America, 1984.

———. "Simon Pokagon's Sandbar Claim to the Chicago Lakefront." *Michigan History Magazine* (September/October 1987): 14.

Colonese, Tom. *American Indian Novelists: An Annotated Critical Bibliography*. New York: Garland Press, 1985, 771.

Corey, Alex. "Fair Material: Birch Bark, Politics, and the Market in Simon Pokagon's 'The Red Man's Rebuke' and 'The Red Man's Greeting.'" *Dartmouth Master of Arts in Liberal Studies Quarterly* (Spring 2010): 5–21.

Deloria, Philip J. *Indians in Unexpected Places*. Lawrence: University Press of

Kansas, 2004, 104.

Dickason, David H. "Chief Simon Pokagon: The Indian Longfellow." *Indiana Magazine of History* 52 (1961): 127–40.

Flowers, B. O. "An Interesting Representative of a Vanishing Race." *The Arena* 26 (1896): 240–50.

Hodge, Frederick W., ed. *Handbook of American Indians North of Mexico*. Vol. 2. Bureau of American Ethnology: Washington, DC, 1907–1910, 274.

Hochbruck, Wolfgang. "Between Victorian Tract and Native American Novel: Simon Pokagon's Ogi-mäw-kwe Mit-i-gwä-ki (1899)." In *Victorian Brand, Indian Brand: The White Shadow on the Native Image*, ed. Naila Clerici, 13–29. Turin: Il Segnalibro, 1993.

Hoxie, Frederick E. *Talking Back to Civilization: Indian Voices from the Progressive Era*. Boston: Bedford-St. Martin's Press, 2001, 29–35.

Hulst, Cornelia Steketee. *Indian Sketches: Père Marquette and the Last of the Pottawatomie Chiefs*. New York: Longmans, Green and Co., 1912.

Hyer, Edward Allen. *A Twentieth Century History of Marshall County, Indiana*. Vol. 1. Chicago: The Lewis Company, 1908, 30.

———. "Chief Pokagon: Apostle of Living Beauty." *Nature Magazine* 15, no. 1 (January 1930): 44–46.

"An Indian Idyll of Love, Sorrow and Death: Being the Story of Chief Pokagon and Lonidaw." *Indian's Friend* 19 (August 1907): 2.

Lamb, E. Wendell, and Lawrence W. Schultz. *Indian Lore*. Winona Lake, IN: Light and Life Press, 1964.

Larson, Charles R. *American Indian Fiction*. Albuquerque: University of New Mexico, 1978, 37–46.

Maddox, Lucy. *Citizen Indians: Native American Intellectuals, Race, and Reform*. Ithaca, NY: Cornell University Press, 2005, 1–3.

"Magazines." *Rosary Magazine* 14 (January–June 1899).

Marble, C. C. "Chief Simon Pokagon." *Birds and All Nature* 5, no. 4 (April 1899).

Martin, Lawrence T. "Simon Pokagon: Charlatan or Authentic Spokesman for the 19th-Century Anishinaabeg?," *Papers of the 29th Algonquin Conference*, ed. David H. Pentland (Winnipeg: University of Manitoba Press, 1998), 29:182–91.

McDonald, Daniel. *Removal of the Pottawatomie Indians from Northern Indiana, Embracing also a Brief Statement of the Indian Policy of the Government, and Other Historical Matter Relating to the Indian Question*. Plymouth, IN: D. McDonald Co., 1899, 31–32.

Peyer, Bernd C. *"The Thinking Indian": Native American Writers, 1850s–1920s.* Frankfurt: Peter Lang, 2007.

Pokagon, Simon. "To the Michigan Ornithological Club." *Bulletin of the Michigan Ornithological Club*, no. 3 (1897).

———. "The Happiness of Singing Birds." *Grand Rapids Review* (Fall/Winter 1982): 25–30.

Rigal-Cellard, Bernadette. "Simon Pokagon's O-gî-mäw-kwe Mit-i-gwä-kî (Queen of the Woods): A Deceptively Simple and Charming Romance of Love and Death in the Wild Woods." In *Before Yesterday: The Long History of Native American Writing*, ed. Simone Pellerin. Pessac, France: Presses Universitaires de Bordeaux, 2009.

Roland, Captain O. W. *A History of Van Buren County Michigan: A Narrative Account of Its Historical Progress, Its People, and Its Principal Interests.* Vol. 1. Chicago: Lewis Publishing Co., 1912, 1–52.

Ruoff, A. LaVonne Brown. "Simon Pokagon, Ogi-maw-kwe Mit-I-Gwa Ki, Queen of the Woods." *American Literary Realism* 13 (1980): 317–19.

———. "American Indian Authors, 1774–1899." In *Critical Essays on Native American Literature*, ed. Andrew Wiget. Boston: Twayne, 1985.

———. "Simon Pokagon (1830–January 1899)." In *Dictionary of Native American Literature*, ed. Andrew Wiget. Vol. 1815. New York: Garland Publishing, 1994, 277–79.

Smith, Susan Harris, and Melanie Dawson, eds. *The American 1890s: A Cultural Reader.* Durham, NC: Duke University Press, 2000.

Taylor, Edward Livingston. "Monuments to Historical Indian Chiefs." *Ohio Archaeological and Historical Publication.* Vol. 11. Columbus: Ohio Archaeological and Historical Society/Fred J. Heer, 1903, 1–29.

Tigerman, Kathleen, ed. "Queen of the Woods." In *Wisconsin Indian Literature: Anthology of Native Voices.* Madison: University of Wisconsin Press, 2006, 183–88.

Trachtenberg, Alan. *Shades of Hiawatha: Staging Indians, Making Americans, 1880–1930.* New York: Hill & Wang, 2004, 47–48.

Walker, Cheryl L. "Indian Nation." In *Native American Literature and Nineteenth-Century Nationalisms.* Durham, NC: Duke University Press, 1997.

Winger, Otho. *The Potawatomi Indians.* Elgin, IL: Elgin Press, 1939.

Zolla, Elemire. *The Writer and the Shaman.* New York: Harcourt, 1973, 240.

APPENDIX 3

List of Works by Simon Pokagon

Algonquin Legends of Paw Paw. Hartford, MI: C.H. Engle, ca. 1900.

Algonquin Legends of South Haven. Hartford, MI: C.H. Engle, 1900.

"The Chi-Kog-Ong of the Red Man." *New York Times, Sunday Magazine*. December 5, 1897, 7–10.

"The Future of the Red Man." *Forum* 23 (1897): 698–708.

"A Grateful Friend." *Indian's Friend* 10 (June 1898): 8.

"Hazeleye's Lullaby." In *Queen of the Woods*, appendix, 232–33.

"How the Terrible Slaughter by White Men Caused Extermination of the 'Me-Me-Og,' or Wild Pigeon." Special insert, Michigan Tales, The State in Review, *Detroit Tribune*, April 19, 1914, 1.

"Indian Native Skill." *Chautauquan* 26 (1898): 540–42.

"An Indian on the Problems of His Race." *Review of Reviews* 12 (1895): 694–95.

"Indian Superstitions and Legends." *Forum* 25 (1898): 618–29.

"Our Indian Women." *Chautauquan* 22 (1896): 732–34.

"An Indian's Observation on the Mating of Geese." *Arena* 16 (1896): 245–48.

"An Indian's Plea for Prohibition." *The Red Man* 15, no. 2 (October/November 1898): 5.

"KI-TCHI GI-OS-SE WAW-BE AN-NE-WE-OG: The Big Hunt of the White Men." *Recreation* 19, no. 6 (December 1903): 431.

"Massacre at Fort Dearborn at Chicago." *Harper's New Monthly Magazine* 98 (1899): 649–56.

"To the Michigan Ornithological Club." *Bulletin of the Michigan Ornithological Club* 1, no. 3 (Grand Rapids, 1897).

O-GÎ-MÄW-KWĚ MIT-Î-GWÄ-KÎ (Queen of the Woods), Also a Brief Sketch of the Algaic Language. Hartford, MI: C.H. Engle, 1899.

O-GÎ-MÄW-KWĚ MIT-Î-GWÄ-KÎ (Queen of the Woods), Also a Brief Sketch of the Algaic Language. Hartford, MI: C.H. Engle, 1901.

Pottawattomie Book of Genesis: Legend of the Creation of Man, Dibangomowin Pottawattamie Ejitodwin Aunishnawbebe. Hartford, MI: C.H. Engle, 1901.

"The Pottawatomies in the War of 1812." *Arena* 26 (1901): 48–55.

"Queen of the Woods." In *Queen of the Woods*, appendix, 235–37.

The Red Man's Greeting. Hartford, MI: C.H. Engle, 1893.

The Red Man's Rebuke. Hartford, MI: C.H. Engle, 1893.

"Simon Pokagon on Naming the Indians." *Review of Reviews* 26 (September 1897), 320–21.

"The Wild Pigeon of North America." *Chautauquan* 22 (1895): 202–6.

Timeline of the 1812 Battle of Fort Dearborn

Before August 1812

Fort Dearborn, a United States military outpost established in 1803, was populated with four officers (two with wives), fifty plus soldiers (some with wives), and servants (some enslaved). It had been built in 1803 near the mouth of the Chicago River. The fort was named in honor of Henry Dearborn, then U.S. secretary of war.

John Kinzie lived at his nearby trading post with his wife Eleanor Kinzie, their four children, a nurse, clerks, and servants. In the area were also French and American fur traders, with wives and families. Some of these traders and children were Métis. Regularly trading at the Kinzie trading post and visiting the fort were members of the Potawatomi, Ho-Chunk, Mesquakie (Fox), Ilini, Wea, Kickapoo, Miami, Ojibwe, and Odawa tribes.

November 7, 1811

Preceding the Battle of Fort Dearborn was the Battle of Tippecanoe. The Shawnee Prophet Tenskwatawa, and sibling Tecumseh, organized an intertribal confederation intended to revitalize and reenergize traditional Indian life and spirituality in the region and resist further colonial/settler encroachment by Americans. Their "headquarters," Prophetstown, was located just north of what is now Lafayette, Indiana, near the confluence of the Tippecanoe and Wabash Rivers. On November 7, 1811, the village was approached by military forces led by Indiana territorial governor William Henry Harrison. Tenskwatawa's followers mounted an unsuccessful attack in defense of the village, and the town was burned to the ground by the Americans the next day. Already tense relations between American Indian supporters of the confederation and whites were greatly aggravated by this provocation. Many Indians of the Great Lakes had already been engaged in a struggle against American expansion under the leadership of Tecumseh, and that conflict merged into the War of 1812.[1]

April 7, 1812

An intertribal group of Indians attacked a settler homestead south of Fort Dearborn on the Chicago River—a farm known as Lee's Place or Hardscrabble. Learning of the attack, settlers in Chicago took refuge in Fort Dearborn.

Spring 1812

The United States prepared for war with Great Britain. President James Madison placed Michigan territorial governor William Hull in charge of leading an invasion of Canada. Indian tribes in the Great Lakes allied themselves with the British, who had been providing them with guns and ammunition. Indians allied with Great Britain were encouraged by the latter to engage in military actions against the United States.

June 18, 1812

The United States declared war on Great Britain.

July 12, 1812

General Hull invaded Canada. On July 17, the British captured the United States fort at Mackinac.

August 7–8, 1812

Hull retreated from Canada back to Detroit. Hull wrote to the commander of Fort Dearborn, Captain Nathan Heald, and advised him of the state of war with Great Britain and its Indian allies, and that Fort Mackinac had been lost to the British; he ordered Heald to evacuate Fort Dearborn and proceed to Fort Wayne in northwest Indiana.

August 1812

Captain Heald negotiated with the surrounding Indians, mostly Potawatomi, for safe passage to Fort Wayne. Despite his promises to the contrary to the Indians, Captain Heald had the ammunition and alcohol at Fort Dearborn destroyed before commencing the evacuation. This gravely agitated the Potawatomi, who needed the gunpowder in particular for their weapons, not just for war, but also to hunt and provide for their families.[2]

August 12 or 13, 1812

Captain William Wells arrived from Fort Wayne, accompanied by some Miami warriors, with the intent to escort the evacuation. Wells was the son-in-law of Chief Little Turtle of the Miami Indians. Wells had been taken captive by that tribe at age twelve and lived with the Miami during the majority of his life—ultimately serving as a confidant of tribal leaders, an Indian agent for the U.S. government, and enlisting in the U.S. military, where he rose to the rank of captain.

August 14, 1812

Black Partridge, a chief of one of the nearby Potawatomi villages, is said to have warned Heald of an impending attack the night before the battle took place. While away from his Peoria Lake village, it was burned to the ground by Illinois militia, and his daughter and granddaughter were murdered.[3]

August 15, 1812

The evacuees left Fort Dearborn for Fort Wayne. After heading south along the shoreline of Lake Michigan, it appears the Miami "escort" distanced themselves from the evacuation party. Shortly thereafter, near what is now Prairie Avenue and 18th Street in Chicago, more than five hundred Indians (mostly Potawatomi) attacked the Americans, killing, wounding, and capturing most. During the short and fierce battle, twenty-eight regular soldiers and fourteen civilians were killed. Thirty-eight soldiers and thirteen civilians were captured. Approximately fifteen Indians are also believed to have died in the battle. Most of the captives were later delivered by the Indians to the British at Detroit.

During the battle, Captain Heald is reported to have attempted to ride into a nearby Potawatomi village to respond to the attack on civilian evacuees by killing women and children there; however, he was killed before he was able to do so.[4]

August 16, 1812

The day after the battle, the American Indians razed Fort Dearborn. The War of 1812 ultimately concluded with no clear victor, except that the British distanced themselves from, and no longer provided assistance to, their Indian allies.

1816

John Kinzie returned to rebuild his trading house, and the United States rebuilt Fort Dearborn. After 1816, settlers returned in droves to the Chicago area.[5] The United States government continued to exact land-cession treaties from the Indians, so that by 1833 all the native lands in Illinois had been taken. By 1838, most of the Indians of Illinois had either fled north to Canada or Wisconsin, or been forcibly removed west of the Mississippi. Small communities of Potawatomi and Miami continued to live in Michigan and Indiana.

Notes

Preface

1. Simon Pokagon, "The Chi-Kog-Ong of the Red Man," *New York Times, Sunday Magazine*, December 5, 1897, 7–10, 7.
2. Ibid., 9.
3. Ibid., 10.
4. Nancy Shoemaker, "Urban Indians and Ethnic Choices: American Indian Organizations in Minneapolis, 1920–1950," *Western Historical Quarterly* 19, no. 4 (1988): 431–47; Edmund Danzinger, *Survival and Regeneration: Detroit's American Indian Community* (Detroit: Wayne State University Press, 1991); David R. M. Beck, "The Chicago American Indian Community, an 'Invisible Minority,'" in *Beyond Black and White: New Voices, New Faces in United States Schools*, ed. Maxine S. Seller and Lois Weis (Albany, NY: SUNY Press, 1997); David R. M. Beck, "Native American Education in Chicago: Teach Them the Truth," *Education and Urban Society* 32 (February 2000): 243; David R. M. Beck, "Developing a Voice: The Evolution of Self-Determination in an Urban Indian Community," *Wicazo Sa Review* 17, no. 2 (2002): 117–41; Rosalyn R. LaPier, "'We Are Not Savages, but a Civilized Race': American Indian Activism and the Development of Chicago's First American Indian Organizations, 1919–1934" (master's thesis, DePaul University, 2000); James B. LaGrand, *Indian Metropolis: Native Americans in Chicago, 1945–75* (Urbana: University

of Illinois Press, 2002); Coll Thrush, *Native Seattle: Histories from the Crossing-Over Place* (Seattle: University of Washington Press, 2008); S. K. Adam, *Extinction or Survival? The Remarkable Story of the Tigua, an Urban American Indian Tribe* (Boulder, CO: Paradigm Publishers, 2009); Nicolas Rosenthal, *Reimagining Indian Country: Native American Migration and Identity in Twentieth-Century Los Angeles* (Chapel Hill: University of North Carolina Press, 2012); David R. M. Beck and Rosalyn R. LaPier, "Crossroads for a Culture: American Indians in Progressive Era Chicago," *Chicago History* 38, no. 1 (2012): 22–43.

5. Edward Livingston Taylor, "Monuments to Historical Indian Chiefs," *Ohio Archaeological and Historical Publications* 11 (Columbus: Ohio Archaeological and Historical Society/ Fred J. Heer) (1903): 1–29; Marion E. Gridley, *America's Indian Statues* (Chicago: Amerindian/Towertown Press, 1966).
6. Frederick Hoxie first used this descriptor of Indian responses to Anglo expectations in his book *Talking Back to Civilization: Indian Voices from the Progressive Era* (Boston: Bedford/ St. Martin's Press, 2001), 29–35.
7. LeAnne Howe, "Tribalography: The Power of Native Stories," *Journal of Dramatic Theory and Criticism* 14 (1999): 117–25.
8. Linda Tuhiwai Smith, *Decolonizing Methodologies: Research and Indigenous Peoples*, 2nd ed. (London: Zed Books, 2012), 17. See also Norman K. Denzin, *Handbook of Critical and Indigenous Methodologies* (Thousand Oaks, CA: Sage Publications, 2008), 348–51.
9. Craig S. Womack, *Red on Red: Native American Indian Separatism* (Minneapolis: University of Minnesota Press, 1999).
10. Ibid., 6.
11. I use the terms "Indigenous" and "Indigeneity" in this book to refer to those peoples and communities who, after contact with outsiders, either adopted an identity as, or were labeled, the first upon the land. The term is particularly important in this work, as length of residency and connection to the land often has defined the legal, political, and social status and rights of American Indian people in the United States.
12. Howe, "Keep Your Thoughts above the Trees," 161–73.
13. Gail Dana-Sacco, "The Indigenous Researcher as Individual and Collective: Building a Research Practice Ethic within the Context of Indigenous Languages," *American Indian Quarterly* 34, no. 1 (2010): 6.

Introduction

1. Richard White and Patricia Nelson Limerick, "Frederick Jackson Turner and Buffalo Bill," in *The Frontier in American Culture*, ed. James R. Grossman (Berkeley: University of California Press, 1994), 28.

2. Alan Taylor, *Divided Ground: Indians, Settlers, and the Northern Borderland of the American Revolution* (New York: Alfred A. Knopf, 2006), 69.
3. Juliana Barr, "Geographies of Power: Mapping Indian Borders in the 'Borderlands' of the Early Southwest," *William and Mary Quarterly*, 3rd ser., 68, no. 1 (January 2011): 5–46. See also Philip J. Deloria, "From Nation to Neighborhood: Land, Policy, Culture, Colonialism, and Empire in U.S.-Indian Relations," in *The Cultural Turn in U.S. History*, ed. James W. Cook, Lawrence B. Glickman, and Michael O'Malley (Chicago: University of Chicago Press, 2008), 353, 359. For twentieth-century Indian responses to the political applications of cartography, see Peter Nabokov, "Orientations from Their Side: Dimensions of Native American Cartographic Discourse," in *Cartographic Encounters: Perspectives on Native American Mapmaking and Map Use*, ed. G. Malcolm Lewis (Chicago: University of Chicago Press, 1998), 241–69; Claudio Saunt, "'Our Indians': European Empires and the History of the Native American South," in *The Atlantic in Global History, 1500–2000*, ed. Jorge Cañizares-Esguerra and Erik R. Seeman (Upper Saddle River, NJ: Pearson Prentice Hall, 2007), 61. Colin G. Calloway makes a similar argument, pointing out that North America is "not a canvas for a single national narrative; it is a series of Indian homelands. It may also witness 'a series of frontiers, zones of interaction,'" but they "formed, overlapped, and re-formed around those homelands." Colin G. Calloway, *One Vast Winter Count: The Native American West before Lewis and Clark* (Lincoln: University of Nebraska Press, 2003), 2. See also Taylor, *Divided Ground*; Richard White, *The Middle Ground: Indians, Empires, and Republics in the Great Lakes Region, 1650–1815* (New York: Cambridge University Press, 1991); Patricia Albers and Jeanne Kay, "Sharing the Land: A Study in American Indian Territoriality," in *A Cultural Geography of North American Indians*, ed. Thomas E. Ross and Tyrel G. Moore (Boulder, CO: Westview Press, 1987), 47–91, 50; Peter J. Usher, Frank J. Tough, and Robert M. Galois, "Reclaiming the Land: Aboriginal Title, Treaty Rights and Land Claims in Canada," *Applied Geography* 12 (1992): 112. For a discussion of the defense of social and economic boundaries, see Nancy Shoemaker, *A Strange Likeness: Becoming Red and White in Eighteenth-Century North America* (New York: Oxford University Press, 2004), 4–8; James Taylor Carson, "Ethnogeography and the Native American Past," *Ethnohistory* 49 (Fall 2002): 783; Cecilia Sheridan, "Social Control and Native Territoriality in Northeastern New Spain," in *Choice, Persuasion, and Coercion: Social Control on Spain's North American Frontiers*, ed. Jesús F. de la Teja and Ross Frank, trans. Ned F. Brierley (Albuquerque: University of New Mexico Press, 2005), 123; and Imre Sutton, "Cartographic Review of Indian Land Tenure and Territoriality: A Schematic Approach," *American Indian Culture and Research Journal* 26 (2002): 69.

4. Barr, "Geographies of Power," 9–19. See also Imre Sutton, *Indian Land Tenure: Bibliographical Essays and a Guide to the Literature* (Orofino, ID: Clearwater Publishing Co., 1975).
5. Richard Bradley, *An Archaeology of Natural Places* (New York: Routledge, 2000), 38–39, 69; Harry J. Shafer, "Art and Territoriality in the Lower Pecos Archaic," *Plains Anthropologist* 22, no. 75 (February 1977): 16. See also Mark Warhus, *Another America: Native American Maps and the History of Our Land* (New York: St. Martin's Press, 1997), 19–22, for a discussion of a connection between petroglyphs and Indian mapping. See also David J. Wishart, "The Dispossession of the Pawnee," *Annals of the Association of American Geographers* 69 (September 1979): 383; Bénard de la Harpe, "Account of the Journey of Bénard de la Harpe: Discovery Made by Him of Several Nations Situated in the West," trans. Ralph A. Smith, *Southwestern Historical Quarterly* 62 (October 1958): 253; and Denis Wood, *The Power of Maps* (New York: Guilford Press, 1992), 147. For Indian mapping and map-making, see Louis De Vorsey Jr., "Silent Witnesses: Native American Maps," *Georgia Review* 46 (Winter 1992): 709–26; Barbara E. Mundy, *The Mapping of New Spain: Indigenous Cartography and the Maps of the Relaciones Geográficas* (Chicago: University of Chicago Press, 1996); Renée Fossett, "Mapping Inuktut: Inuit Views of the Real World," in *Reading beyond Words: Contexts for Native History*, ed. Jennifer S. H. Brown and Elizabeth Vibert (Orchard Park, NY: Broadview Press, 1996), 74–94; John C. Ewers, "The Making and Uses of Maps by Plains Indian Warriors," in *Plains Indian History and Culture: Essays on Continuity and Change* (Norman: University of Oklahoma Press, 1997), 180–90; G. Malcolm Lewis, *Cartographic Encounters: Perspectives on Native American Mapmaking and Map Use* (Chicago: University of Chicago Press, 1998); and Gustavo Verdesio, "Forgotten Territorialities: The Materiality of Indigenous Pasts," *Nephantla: View from the South* 2 (2001): 85–114.
6. Barr, "Geographies of Power," 33. Craig Howe adds, "The social dimension of tribalism relates land and identity to the concept of 'peoplehood,' a unique community identity differentiated from other tribes and from individual persons. The relationship between a specific people and a particular landscape is not a relationship between an individual and the land or between 'Indians' and the land. Instead, it is a relationship between a distinct community and their remembered landscape, it is a relationship often encoded in stories about particular past events that their ancestors experienced. . . . Event-centered tribal histories are based on the idea that 'identity is a conception of and feelings about events which a people have lived. It is the meaning of events in which one's ancestors took part, in ways that make one proud, which differentiate people into ethnic groups.'. . . tribal histories are community-based and tribally specific. Therefore,

tribal histories from an indigenous tribal perspective focus on historical experiences that are meaningful to each community as a whole and on the places where a community's epitomizing events occurred. Furthermore, the communication of these experiences rests firmly on the foundation of oral tradition in general and specific tribal languages in particular." Craig Howe, "Keep Your Thoughts above the Trees: Ideas on Developing and Presenting Tribal Histories," in *Clearing a Path: Theorizing the Past in Native American Studies*, ed. Nancy Shoemaker (New York: Routledge, 2002), 161–80, 165.

7. Barr, "Geographies of Power," 42. See also J. B. Harley, "Rereading the Maps of the Columbian Encounter," *Annals of the Association of American Geographers* 82 (1992): 522–42; Chip Colwell-Chanthaphonh and J. Brett Hill, "Mapping History: Cartography and the Construction of the San Pedro Valley," *History and Anthropology* 15 (2004): 175–200; and Lewis, *Cartographic Encounters*, 45.
8. Keith Basso, *Wisdom Sits in Places: Landscape and Language among the Western Apache* (Albuquerque: University of New Mexico Press, 1996), xiii. For continental (and hemispheric) approaches to early American history, see Felipe Fernández-Armesto, *The Americas: A Hemispheric History* (New York: Modern Library, 2003); Calloway, *One Vast Winter Count*; Paul Mapp, "Atlantic History from Imperial, Continental, and Pacific Perspectives," *William and Mary Quarterly*, 3rd ser., 63 (October 1996): 713–24; and Daniel Richter, *Facing East from Indian Country: A Native History of Early America* (Cambridge, MA: Harvard University Press, 2003).
9. Ronald N. Satz, *Chippewa Treaty Rights: The Reserved Rights of Wisconsin's Chippewa Indians in Historical Perspective* (Madison: Wisconsin Academy of Science, 1996), 48.
10. Lawrence C. Kelly, *Federal Indian Policy: Well-illustrated Survey of Federal Government Policy toward the Native American Population* (New York: Chelsea House, 1989), 32.
11. Charles J. Kappler, *Indian Affairs: Laws and Treaties* (Washington, DC: Government Printing Office, 1904–1941), vols. 1–5; E. B. O'Callaghan, *Documents Relative to the Colonial History of the State of New York* (Albany, NY: Weed, Parsons and Co. 1857), 8:111–37.
12. The 1871 act reads in part, " No Indian nation or tribe . . . shall be acknowledged or recognized as an independent nation, tribe, or power with whom the United States may contract by treaty" (25 U.S.C.A. § 71); Larry Nesper, *The Walleye War: The Struggle for Ojibwe Spearfishing and Treaty Rights* (Lincoln: University of Nebraska Press, 2002), 88.
13. Kelly, *Federal Indian Policy*, 54.
14. Patty Loew, "Hidden Transcripts in the Chippewa Treaty Rights Struggle: A Twice Told Story, Race, Resistance, and the Politics of Power," *American Indian Quarterly* 21, no. 2 (Fall 1997); Satz, *Chippewa Treaty Rights*; James M. McClurken, ed., *Fish in the Lakes, Wild Rice, and Game in Abundance: Testimony on Behalf of Mille Lacs Ojibwe Hunting*

and Fishing Rights (East Lansing: Michigan State University Press, 2000); Larry Nesper, "Ogitchida at Waswagonning: Conflict in the Revitalization of Flambeau Anishinaabe Identity," in *Reassessing Revitalization Movements: Perspectives from North America and the Pacific Islands*, ed., Michael Harkin (Lincoln: University of Nebraska Press, 2004), 225–46; Paul Brodeur, *Restitution: The Land Claims of the Mashpee, Passamaquoddy, and Penobscot Indians of New England* (Boston: Northeastern University Press, 1985); Edward Lazarus, *Black Hills/White Justice: The Sioux Nation versus the United States, 1775 to the Present* (Lincoln: University of Nebraska Press, 1999); Donald Mitchell, *Take My Land, Take My Life: The Story of Congress's Historic Settlement of Alaska Native Land Claims, 1960–1971* (Juneau: University of Alaska Press, 2001); E. Richard Hart, ed., *Zuni and the Courts: A Struggle for Sovereign Land Rights* (Lawrence: University of Kansas Press, 1995); Burke A. Hendrix, *Ownership, Authority, and Self-Determination: Moral Principles and Indigenous Rights Claims* (University Park: Penn State University Press, 2008); and Burke A. Hendrix, "Memory in Native American Land Claims," *Political Theory* 33, no. 6 (December 2005): 763–85.

15. W. H. Niles, *A Brief History and the Legal Standing of the District of Lake Michigan* (Chicago: Swanberg & Co., 1900), 15; Frederick D. C. Langdon, "The Wreck of the '*Reutan*' and What Came of It," *Wide World Magazine* 7 (April–September, 1901): 539–43; Edward B. Clark, "The Amazing History of the Streeterville War," *Women's Home Companion* 29, no. 12 (December 1902); William H. Niles, *The Military Government of the District of Lake Michigan, Its legal standing as defined by Official letters and papers, by William H. Niles Military Governor—Captain George Streeter, the American Dreyfus, now in the States Prison at Joliet, Ill.* (Chicago: Hufford & Co., 1903); Edward Bergstrom, "Cap Streeter: Squatter King," *Tradition* 4, no. 10 (October 1961): 23; Everett Guy Ballard, *Captain Streeter, Pioneer* (Chicago: Emery Publishing Service, 1914), 218; Robert Shackleton, "A Modern Corsair," in *The Book of Chicago* (Philadelphia: Penn Publishing Company, 1920), chap. 13; "Captain George Wellington Streeter, Battling Hero of the 'Deestrick of Lake Michigan,'" *Journal of the Illinois State Historical Society* 13, no. 4 (January 1921): 571–74; Kenneth F. Broomell and Harlow M. Church, "Streeterville Saga," *Journal of the Illinois State Historical Society* 33, no. 2 (June 1940): 153–65; Mrs. L. Edwards, *My Twenty Years Experience in Streeterville District of Lake Michigan* (Chicago[?]: N.p., ca. 1940); Francesca Miller, *The Sands: The Story of Chicago's Front Yard* (Chicago: Valentine-Newman Publishers, 1948); Patricia Bronte, *Vittles and Vice* (Chicago: Henry Regency Co., 1952), 29–32; Joseph Millard, "George Wellington Streeter—All This Out Here Is My Land," in *No Law But Their Own* (Evanston, IL: Regency Books, 1963), 111–58; Lois Willie, *Forever Open, Clear, and Free: The Struggle for Chicago's Lakefront* (Chicago: Henry Regency Co., 1972), 58–61; K. C.

Tessendorf, "Captain Streeter's District of Lake Michigan," *Chicago History* 5, no. 3 (1976): 152–60; John W. Stamper, "Shaping Chicago's Shoreline," *Chicago History* 14, no. 4 (1985–1986): 44–55; June Skinner Sawyers, *Chicago Portraits: Biographies of 250 Famous Chicagoans* (Chicago: Loyola University Press, 1991), 202; June Skinner Sawyers, "The Eccentric Captain of Streeterville," in *Chicago Sketches: Urban Tales, Stories, and Legends from Chicago History* (Chicago: Loyola Press/Wild Onion Books, 1995), 9–40; Ursula Bielski, *More Chicago Haunts: Scenes from Myth and Memory* (Chicago: Lake Claremont Press, 2000), 296–300; Joshua Salzman, "The Chicago Lakefront's Last Frontier: The Turnerian Mythology of Streeterville, 1886–1961," *Journal of Illinois History* 9 (Autumn 2006): 201–14; and Scotti Cohn, "The Captain's War," in *It Happened in Chicago* (Guilford, CT: Morris Book Publishing, 2009), 66–70.

16. Frederick J. Turner, "The Significance of the Frontier in American History," in the *Annual Report of the American Historical Association for the Year 1893* (Washington, DC: Government Printing Office and American Historical Association, 1894), 199–227. In 1893, Turner addressed a historical association assembled at the World's Columbian Exposition in Chicago and presented his famous "frontier thesis," which was published the next year.
17. White, *The Middle Ground*, 40; Stephen Aron, "Pioneers and Profiteers: Land Speculation and the Homestead Ethic in Frontier Kentucky," *Western Historical Quarterly* 23, no. 2 (1992): 179.
18. Of course, in the eighteenth century, other frontiers also existed at the northern edge of Spanish settlements in the Southwest and the southern edge of French Canadian settlements to the north. There are numerous iterations of "frontier" (e.g., Gloria Anzaldúa, *Borderlands/La Frontera: The New Mestiza* [San Francisco: Aunt Lute Books, 1987]), and some of these ideas and concepts are seeded throughout the following chapters. However, the idea of frontier in westward expansion, as defined by F. J. Turner and others, has particular relevance to this story, particularly in its physical representation/presentation, a convergence of ideas, of sorts, at the very urban space that is the topic of this book—the city of Chicago. See also Jorge Capetillo-Ponce, "Exploring Gloria Anzaldúa's Methodology in Borderlands/La Frontera—The New Mestiza," *Human Architecture: Journal of the Sociology of Self-Knowledge* 4, no. 3, special issue (Summer 2006).
19. Richard Slotkin, *Gunfighter Nation: The Myth of the Frontier in Twentieth-Century America* (New York: Athenaeum, 1992), 38.
20. Mary Louise Pratt, "Arts of the Contact Zone," *Profession* 91 (1991): 3–40; Mary Louise Pratt, *Imperial Eyes: Travel Writing and Transculturation* (London: Routledge, 1992). See

also Carlos G. Vélez-Ibáñez, *Border Visions: Mexican Cultures of the Southwest United States* (Tucson: University of Arizona Press, 1996), 4–6.

21. Robert Maxwell Brown, "Backcountry Rebellions and the Homestead Ethic in America, 1740–1799," in *Tradition, Conflict, and Modernization: Perspectives on the American Revolution*, ed. Robert Maxwell Brown and Don E. Fehrenbacher (Academic Press: New York, 1977), 73–98; and Eviatar Zerubavael, *Terra Cognita: The Mental Discovery of America* (New Brunswick, NJ: Rutgers University Press, 1992).
22. Vicente M. Diaz, *Repositioning the Missionary: Rewriting the Histories of Colonialism, Native Catholicism, and Indigeneity in Guam* (Honolulu: University of Hawai'i Press, 2010), 26–32, 27.
23. Fernando Ortiz, *Cuban Counterpoint: Tobacco and Sugar* (Durham, NC: Duke University Press, 1995).
24. T. Huffman, "Resistance Theory and the Transculturation Hypothesis as Explanations of College Attrition and Persistence among Culturally Traditional American Indian Students," *Journal of American Indian Education* 40, no. 3 (2011): 1–23; T. Huffman, "Plans to Live on a Reservation Following College among American Indian Students: An Examination of Transculturation Theory," in *Journal of Research in Rural Education* 26, no. 3 (2001): 1–12.
25. Zerubavael, *Terra Cognita*, 65.
26. Particularly in places we now identify as Indiana, Ohio, Illinois, and southern Michigan.
27. The idea of "scatter zone" to describe these responses stems from my reading and thinking about the recent work *Mapping the Mississippian Shatter Zone: The Colonial Indian Slave Trade and Regional Instability in the American South*, ed. Robbie Ethridge and Sheri M. Shuck-Hal (Lincoln: University of Nebraska Press, 2009).
28. Carl Sauer, "The Morphology of Landscape," *University of California Publications in Geography* 2 (1925): 19. See also Philip L. Wagner and Marvin W. Mikesell, *Readings in Cultural Geography* (Chicago: University of Chicago Press, 1962).
29. For a variety of discussions of the meanings of "homeland" and "homeland theory," see Richard L. Norstrand and Lawrence E. Estaville, eds., *Homelands: A Geography of Culture and Place across America* (Baltimore: Johns Hopkins University Press, 2001); Douglas A. Hurt, "Defining American Homelands: A Creek Nation Example, 1828–1907," *Journal of Cultural Geography* 21, no. 1 (2003): 19–21; Dawn Marsh, "Creating Delaware Homelands in the Ohio Country," *Ohio History* 116 (2009): 26–40; and Stephen Warren, *The Worlds the Shawnee Made: Migration and Violence in Early America* (Chapel Hill: University of North Carolina Press, 2014).
30. Clifford Geertz, *The Interpretation of Culture* (New York: Basic Books, 1973).

31. William S. Penn, *As We Are Now: Mixblood Essays on Race and Identity* (Berkeley: University of California Press, 1997), 22.
32. Robert F. Berkhofer, *The White Man's Indian: Images of the American Indian from Columbus to the Present* (New York: Random House, 1978); Peter Nabokov, *Native American Testimony: A Chronicle of Indian-White Relations from Prophecy to the Present, 1497–2000* (New York: Penguin Books, 1999); and Philip J. Deloria, *Playing Indian* (New Haven, CT: Yale University Press, 1999).
33. I have italicized Algonquian words throughout my text to emphasize that these are our words, no matter how commonly they are used by non-Native speakers.
34. Jan Assmann, *Religion and Cultural Memory: Ten Studies* (Stanford, CA: Stanford University Press, 2005).
35. Maurice Halbwachs, *On Collective Memory*, ed. and trans. Lewis A. Coser (Chicago: University of Chicago Press, 1992), 37.
36. Patrick Geary, *Phantoms of Remembrance: Memory and Oblivion in the First Millennium* (Princeton, NJ: Princeton University Press, 1994), 3–23, 7. See also L. G. Moses, "Performative Traditions in American Indian History," in *A Companion to American Indian History*, ed. Philip J. Deloria and Neal Salisbury (Malden, MA: Blackwell Publishing, 2004), 193–208.
37. Maurice Halbwachs, *The Collective Memory*, trans. Francis J. Ditter Jr. and Vida Yazdi Ditter (New York: Harper and Row, 1980), 65.
38. Pierre Nora, "Between History and Memory: *Les Lieux de Mémoire*," *Representations* 26 (Spring 1989): 7–25.
39. See Paul Ricoeur, *Memory, History, Forgetting*, trans. Kathleen Blamey and David Pellauer (Chicago: University of Chicago Press, 2004); Alison Landsberg, *Prosthetic Memory: The Transformation of American Remembrance in the Age of Mass Culture* (New York: Columbia University Press, 2004); and Susannah Radstone and Bill Schwarz, ed. *Memory: Histories, Theories, Debates* (New York: Fordham University Press, 2010).
40. Emile Durkheim, "The Cultural Logic of Collective Representations," in *Social Theory: The Multicultural and Classic Readings*, ed. C. Lemert (Boulder, CO: Westview Press, 2010), 94–103. See also Barry Schwartz, "The Social Context of Commemoration: A Study in Collective Memory," *Social Forces* 61, no. 2 (December 1982): 374–402.
41. "Nearly all the most resilient oppositional cultures have been rooted in collective memory, in precipitates of past historical experience." Jackson Lears, "Power, Culture, and Memory," *Journal of American History* 75, no. 1 (June 1988): 137–40, 138.
42. "Objects matter in cultural process, especially among peoples who have not relied on written texts for the recording of knowledge. Stripped bare of their traditional objects

of use, beauty and power, Native American communities have suffered interruptions of historical memory, paralyzing failures in the generational transfer of political and sacred power and the cessation of organic growth in many ancient stylistic and iconographic traditions." Janet C. Berlo and Ruth B. Phillips, "Our (Museum) World Turned Upside Down: Re-presenting Native American Arts," *Art Bulletin* 77, no. 1 (1995): 6–10, 9.

43. According to Carolyn Steedman, "A modern 'identity,' constructed through the process of identification, is at once a claim for absolute sameness, a coincidence and matching with the desired object, group, or person (perhaps a historical identity, located in the historical past) and at the same time, in the enclosed circuit of meaning, is a process of individuation, the modern making of an individuality and a unique personality. In the project of finding an identity through the processes of historical identification, the past is searched for something (someone, some group, some series of events) that confirms the searcher in his or her sense of self, confirms them as they want to be, and feel in some measure that they already are." Carolyn Steedman, *The Archive and Cultural History* (New Brunswick, NJ: Rutgers University Press, 2001), 77.

44. LeAnne Howe writes, "Native stories are power. They create people. They author tribes. America is a tribal creation story, a tribalography . . . [that] achieves a new understanding in theorizing on Native studies. This is a tall order for a storyteller, but here goes. Native stories, no matter what form they take (novel, poem, drama, memoir, film, history) seem to pull all the elements together of the storyteller's tribe, meaning the people, the land, and multiple characters and all their manifestations and revelations, and connect these in past, present, and future milieus (present and future milieus mean non-Indians). . . . tribalography comes from the Native propensity for bringing things together, for making consensus, and for symbiotically connecting one thing to another." LeAnne Howe, "The Story of America: A Tribalography," in *Clearing a Path: Theorizing the Past in Native American Studies*, ed. Nancy Shoemaker (New York: Routledge, 2002), 29–50.

45. Schwartz, "Social Context of Commemoration," 374–402; George Lipitz, *Time Passages: Collective Memory and American Popular Culture* (Minneapolis: University of Minnesota Press, 1990); Michel Foucault, "Politics and the Study of Discourse," in *The Foucault Effect: Studies in Governmentality*, ed. Graham Burchell, Colin Gordon, and Peter Miller (Chicago: University of Chicago Press, 1991), 59–60; Stuart Hall, ed., *Representation: Cultural Representations and Signifying Practices* (London: Sage Publications, 1997); Marita Sturken, *Tangled Memories: The Vietnam War, the AIDS Epidemic and the Politics of Remembering* (Berkeley: University of California Press, 1997); Susan A. Crane, "Writing the Individual Back into Collective Memory," *American Historical Review* 102, no. 5 (December 1997): 1372–85; Allan Megill, "History, Memory, Identity," *History of the*

Human Sciences 11, no. 3 (1998): 37–62; and Amy Ku'uleialoha Stillman, "Re-Membering the History of the Hawaiian Hula," in *Cultural Memory: Reconfiguring History and Identity in the Postcolonial Pacific*, ed. J. M. Mageo (Honolulu: University of Hawai'i Press, 2001), 187–204.

46. Paul Connerton, *How Societies Remember* (New York: Cambridge University Press, 2004).
47. Edwina Taborsky, "The Discursive Object," in *Objects of Knowledge*, ed. S. M. Pearce (London: Athlone Press, 2002), 50–70.
48. James E. Young introduced the idea of "collected" memory to better describe memory's inherently fragmented, collected, and individual character. James E. Young, *The Texture of Memory: Holocaust, Memorials, and Meaning* (New Haven: Yale University Press, 1993), 7. Michael Rothberg argues that the connections between collective memory and group identity are dialogic, what he terms a theory of multidirectional memory, in which memories of multiple peoples and events interact productively in much the same ways peoples accept, accommodate, incorporate, and/or reject all sorts of outsider influences. Michael Rothberg, *Multidirectional Memory: Remembering the Holocaust in the Age of Decolonization*, Cultural Memory in the Present Series (Stanford, CA: Stanford University Press, 2009). As Marita Sturken notes, "Memory is crucial to the understanding of a culture precisely because it indicates collective desires, needs and self-identification." Sturken, *Tangled Memories*, 8.

Chapter 1. The Potawatomi as Chicago's Early Urban Indians

1. James A. Clifton, *The Prairie People: Continuity and Change in Potawatomi Indian Culture, 1665–1965* (Iowa City: University of Iowa Press, 1998), 11–18; R. David Edmunds, *The Potawatomis: Keepers of the Fire* (Norman: University of Oklahoma Press, 1978), 3.
2. James A. Clifton, George L. Cornell, and James M. McClurken, *People of the Three Fires: The Ottawa, Potawatomi, and Ojibway of Michigan* (Grand Rapids: Michigan Indian Press, 1986), v.
3. Ibid., xxii.
4. James A. Clifton, *The Potawatomi*, Indians of North America Series (New York: Chelsea House Publishers, 1987), 16; Helen Hornbeck Tanner, ed., *Atlas of Great Lakes Indian History* (Norman: University of Oklahoma Press, 1987), 3.
5. Simon Pokagon, *Pottawattamie Book of Genesis: Legend of the Creation of Man* (Hartford, MI: C.H. Engle, 1900). Although several of Pokagon's writings, specifically *The Red Man's Greeting* and *Queen of the Woods*, are readily available to the public, this booklet is not, so the text is reproduced in appendix 1. There is a possibility that *Pottawattamie Book of Genesis*, although generally assumed to be the work of Simon Pokagon, may actually

be the work of his son Charles. My reason for suggesting this is that the booklet was published in 1901, two years after Simon Pokagon's death; the cover of the booklet identifies the author only as "Chief Pokagon," and after his father's death, Charles Pokagon was sometimes identified as a chief. Even if authored by Charles, it reflects the passing on from father to son of the tradition of transcribing Potawatomi stories onto birch bark for the public.

6. William W. Warren, *History of the Ojibway People, Based upon Traditions and Oral Statements* (St. Paul: Minnesota Historical Society, 1885); Basil H. Johnston, *Ojibway Heritage* (New York: Columbia University Press, 1976); Basil H. Johnston, *Ojibway Ceremonies* (Toronto: McClelland and Stewart, 1987); Frances Densmore, *Chippewa Customs* (Washington, DC: U.S. Government Printing Office, 1929); R. David Edmunds, *Kinsmen through Time: An Annotated Bibliography of Potawatomi History* (Metuchen, NJ: Scarecrow Press, 1987); Edmunds, *Potawatomis: Keepers of the Fire*; Clifton, *The Potawatomi*; James A. Clifton, *The Pokagons, 1683–1983: Catholic Potawatomi Indians of the St. Joseph River Valley* (Lanham, MD: University Press of America, 1984).
7. Charles E. Cleland, *Rites of Conquest: The History and Culture of Michigan's Native Americans* (Ann Arbor: University of Michigan Press, 1992), 39.
8. Simon Pokagon, "Indian Superstitions and Legends," *Forum* 25 (1898): 618–29. Such teachings were also transcribed by Europeans and Americans having contact with the Native peoples, including the German traveler Johann Georg Kohl, who wrote in 1860 that "Even the Indians seem to honour their own invention greatly, and impart to it a divine origin. They say that Menaboju (their Prometheus, or Hercules) invented the canoe. They even point to some half-dozen lumps of stone, on the shore of one of these Apostle Islands [in Lake Superior] and say that Menaboju built his canoe between them, and hung it to dry upon them." Johann Georg Kohl, *Kitchi-Gami: Life among the Lake Superior Ojibway* (1860; St. Paul: Minnesota Historical Society Press, 1985), 33–34. See also Clifton, *The Potawatomi*, 20; and Johnston, *Ojibway Heritage*, 17–20.
9. Emerson F. Greenman, *The Indians of Michigan* (Lansing: Michigan Historical Commission, 1961), 17; Bela Hubbard, *Ancient Garden Beds of Michigan*, 1878, reprinted in Susan Sleeper-Smith, *Indian Women and French Men: Rethinking Cultural Encounter in the Great Lakes* (Amherst: University of Massachusetts Press, 2001).
10. Edmunds, *The Potawatomis: Keepers of the Fire*, 13–22.
11. Clifton, Cornell, and McClurken, *People of the Three Fires*, 40–41.
12. Clifton, *The Potawatomi*, 17–20.
13. Ibid., 32–46.
14. Clifton, Cornell, and McClurken, *People of the Three Fires*, 45–48.

15. Tanner, *Atlas of Great Lakes Indian History*, 3.
16. Ibid., 43–49; William Duncan Strong, *The Indian Tribes of the Chicago Region, With Special Reference to the Illinois and the Potawatomi*, Leaflet 24 (Chicago: Field Museum of Natural History, 1926), 16–22.
17. Clifton, *The Prairie People*, 35; Clifton, *The Potawatomi*, 20–21.
18. Michael Witgen, "The Rituals of Possession: Native Identity and the Invention of Empire in Seventeenth-Century Western North America," *Ethnohistory* 54, no. 4 (2007): 639–68.
19. Ibid.; Clifton, *The Pokagons, 1683–1983*, 15–28.
20. Edmunds, *The Potawatomis: Keepers of the Fire*, 3–58.
21. Clifton, Cornell, and McClurken, *People of the Three Fires*, 49–51.
22. For a sophisticated work on Pontiac and his war of resistance, see Gregory E. Dowd, *War under Heaven: Pontiac, the Indian Nations, and the British Empire* (Baltimore: Johns Hopkins University Press, 2004).
23. "An Ordinance for the Government of the Territory of the United States North-West of the River Ohio" (College Park, MD: National Archives and Records Administration, 1787).
24. Clifton, *The Pokagons, 1683–1983*, 29–42.
25. Clifton, Cornell, and McClurken, *People of the Three Fires*, 55–58.
26. Charles J. Kappler, *Indian Affairs and Treaties*, vol. 2, *Treaties* (Washington, DC: Government Printing Office, 1904).
27. See Gregory E. Dowd's analysis of prophetic movements and resistance during this era in Dowd, *A Spirited Resistance: The North American Indian Struggle for Unity, 1745–1815* (Baltimore: Johns Hopkins University Press, 1993).
28. Clifton, Cornell, and McClurken, *People of the Three Fires*, 57–58.
29. Ibid., 53–58; Milo M. Quaife, *Checagou: From Indian Wigwam to Modern City, 1673–1835* (Chicago: University of Chicago Press, 1933).
30. Also spelled variously as Toop-Peen-Bee, Thu-pe-ne bu, Tuthinipee, Topeeneebee, Topenibe, Topanepee, Topnibe, Topinebe, Topinebi, and Topineby, he was born in the St. Joseph River Valley in 1758 and died in 1826. He was succeeded in leadership of his village by Leopold Pokagon, who had married his daughter.
31. Elmore Barce, *The Land of the Potawatomi, (by a) Member of Indiana Historical Society* (Fowler, IN: Benton Review, 1919), 54–55.
32. Michigan State Historical Society, Michigan Historical Commission, *Collections and Researches, Michigan Pioneer and Historical Society*, reprint (Lansing: Wynkoop, Hallenbeck, Crawford Co., 1908), 14:260; Barce, *The Land of the Potawatomi*, 48.
33. Clifton, Cornell, and McClurken, *People of the Three Fires*, 58.
34. Clifton, *The Pokagons, 1683–1983*, 29–52.

35. James A. Clifton, "Chicago, September 14, 1833: The Last Great Indian Treaty of the Old Northwest," *Chicago History* 9 no. 2 (Summer 1980), 86–97.
36. Charles Joseph Latrobe, "The Rambler in North America," reprinted in *As Others See Chicago*, comp. and ed. Bessie Louise Pierce (Charleston, SC: Nabu Press, 2012), 55.
37. Anselm J. Gerwing, "The Chicago Treaty of 1833," *Journal of the Illinois State Historical Society* 57 (1964): 117–42, 125.
38. Clifton, "Chicago, September 14, 1833," 88.
39. Latrobe, "The Rambler in North America," 55.
40. Clifton, *The Prairie People*, 240–41.
41. Kappler, *Indian Affairs: Laws and Treaties*, vol. 2, *Treaties*, 402–15, 413.
42. Sleeper-Smith, *Indian Women and French Men*, 69.
43. Ibid., 53–76. In 2006, an entire issue of the *Midcontinental Journal of Archaeology* was devoted to the Removal Era of the Potawatomi. Articles include Mark R. Schurr, "Untangling Removal Period Archaeology: The Complexity of Potawatomi Sites"; W. Ben Secunda, "To Cede or Seed? Risk and Identity among the Woodland Potawatomi during the Removal Period"; Elizabeth Bollwerk, "Controlling Acculturation: A Potawatomi Strategy for Avoiding Removal"; Mark R. Schurr, Terrance J. Martin, and W. Ben Secunda, "How the Pokagon Band Avoided Removal: Archaeological Evidence from the Faunal Assemblage of the Pokagon Village Site (20BE13)." *MCJA* 31, no. 1 (Spring 2006).
44. Shirley Willard, Susan Campbell, and Benjamin Marie Petit, *Potawatomi Trail of Death: 1838 Removal from Indiana to Kansas* (Rochester, IN: Fulton County Historical Society, 2003).
45. In the *Petition to President Andrew Jackson from four chiefs of the Pokagon Potawatomi along the St. Joseph River*, the chiefs protest the takeover of the local mission site by the federal Indian agent and request that the president allow the black robes "to occupy the mission and instruct the Potawatomi and their children in the worship of the Great Spirit." The petition was signed (marked) by Pagagen (presumably Leopold Pokagon), Wapanto, Noakota, and Sanguinai. "Petition to President Andrew Jackson from four chiefs of the Pokagon Potawatomi along the St. Joseph River," in *Berichte der Leopoldinen-Stiftung im Kaiserthum Oesterreich*, vol. 9 (Vienna, 1836).
46. The Pokagon Band has also been known since this time as the Catholic Potawatomi of Indiana and Michigan.
47. James A. Clifton, "Chicago Was Theirs," *Chicago History* 1, no. 1 (Spring 1970): 4–17; Clifton, "Chicago, September 14, 1833," 86–97; James A. Clifton, "Leopold Pokagon: Transformative Leadership on the St. Joseph River Frontier," *Michigan History* 69, no. 5 (September/October 1985): 16–23.

48. For A. Irving Hallowell, transculturation is more than the creation of hybrid new cultures; in his view, transculturation describes the socialization process by which peoples learn to function in a new culture. A. I. Hallowell, "American Indians, White and Black: The Phenomenon of Transculturation," *Current Anthropology* 4 (1963): 519–31. Transculturation seems a helpful way to consider the changes that the people were going through as they reimagined themselves as a sovereign nation called the Pokagon Band of Potawatomi.
49. Clifton, *The Pokagons, 1683–1983*, 90.
50. *Sale Catalogues, Issues 1631–1654* (New York: American Art Association, Anderson Galleries, 1922), 104.
51. Ibid., 112–15; James A. Clifton, "Simon Pokagon's Sandbar: Potawatomi Claims to Chicago's Lakefront," *Michigan History* 71, no. 5 (September/October 1987): 12–17.
52. Ibid., 120–21.
53. Ibid., 126–31.
54. "Michigan Delegate," *Dowagiac Daily News*, June 13, 1961, 3. Williams also corresponded directly with Sol Tax, professor at the University of Chicago and facilitator of the conference, regarding the tribe. Letter dated June 4, 1961, Michael B. Williams Papers, Dowagiac, MI.
55. From the tribal website at http://www.pokagon.com.
56. From the tribal website at http://www.pokagon.com.
57. "Seal Use Act," *Pokagon Band of Potawatomi*, http://www.pokagon.com/government/codes-and-ordinances.
58. James Pritchard, "New Buffalo Casino Boosts Tourism," *Detroit Free Press*, June 28, 2008, 12.
59. From the tribal website at www.pokagon.com.
60. Alex Wesaw, "Mno-Bmadsen Featured in Business Publication," *Pokégnek Yajdanawa*, July 2013, 2.
61. For instance, in the January 2011 issue of *Pokégnek Yajdanawa*, the Pokagon Band's Department of Language and Culture sponsored a "Storytelling and Traditional Snow Snake Games," led by John Pigeon. *Pokégnek Yajdanawa*, January 2011, 12.
62. John Pigeon, quoted at http://www.turtletrack.org/Issues02/Co06152002/CO_06152002_Mihtohseenionki.htm.

Chapter 2. Simon Pokagon's Claims of Equality and Appeals for Inclusion

1. For discussions of the specifics of the rupture in the Pokagon Potawatomi community, see James Clifton, *The Pokagons, 1683–1983: Catholic Potawatomi Indians of the St. Joseph*

River Valley (Lanham, MD: American University Press), 73–76; and Cecilia Bain Buechner, "The Pokagons," *Indiana Magazine of History* 10, no. 5 (1933).

2. See chapter 3 for a thorough discussion of the intrigue involved in the Pokagon Potawatomi claim to the Chicago lakefront.
3. Win Blevins, *The Dictionary of the American West* (College Station: Texas A&M University Press, 2008).
4. Everett Claspy, *The Potawatomi Indians of Southwestern Michigan* (Ann Arbor, MI: Braun-Brumfield, Inc., 1966), 23.
5. Simon Pokagon, *O-GÎ-MÄW-KWÈ MIT-Î-GWÄ-KÎ (Queen of the Woods), Also a Brief Sketch of the Algaic Language* (Hartford, MI: C.H. Engle, 1899, 1901).
6. When I use the term "indigeneity" I am not using it as a synonym for American Indian. Rather, I am influenced by a course I took with Philip Deloria and Gustavo Verdesio at the University of Michigan, "Rethinking Indigeneity." I use it to denote those peoples around the world that were first inhabitants of lands at the moment of contact with outside settler-colonists after 1492. See also Robert Dale Parker, *The Invention of Native American Literature* (Ithaca, NY: Cornell University Press, 2003); and Craig S. Womack, *Red on Red: Native American Literary Separatism* (Minneapolis: University of Minnesota Press, 1999), 2–4.
7. Walter Benjamin, "Unpacking My Library," in *Illuminations, Essays, and Reflections*, ed. Hannah Arendt (New York: Schocken Books, 1968), 67.
8. Buechner, "The Pokagons," 327; "Will Bury Pokagon Today," *Chicago Daily Tribune*, January 30, 1899, 7.
9. David A. Dickason, "Chief Simon Pokagon: The Indian Longfellow," *Indiana Magazine of History* 57 (June 1961): 127–40; "Prose Idyll by Red Bard," *Chicago Daily Tribune*, May 7, 1899, 35; "Death Notice of Simon Pokagon," *South Bend Tribune*, January 28, 1899. In the latter article the author wrote, "The story of Chief Simon Pokagon's life, if correctly written, would make one of the most interesting, as well as one of the most thrilling and pathetic tales to be told in all Indian history." In the appendix to *Queen of the Woods* are several other obituaries for Simon Pokagon from the Chicago press. The cover of the magazine that printed Pokagon's "The Future of the Red Man" describes him as the "Last Chief of the Pottawattamie Pokagon Band." Simon Pokagon, "The Future of the Red Man," in *The Forum*, ed. J. M. Rice (New York: Forum Publishing Company, August 1897).
10. Some newspapers took to calling Simon Pokagon the last chief of the Pokagon Potawatomi because after 1866, the tribe was governed by a Business Committee rather than council, and the head of the committee was designated the chair rather than chief. However, many subsequent chairmen continued to call themselves, or be

identified as, chief, including Simon Pokagon's son Charles. The Pokagon Potawatomi, like most Algonquin tribes, did not determine leadership by ancestry. There was no hereditary right to being chief. Rather, leaders were selected based upon the consensus of tribal members. James Clifton points out that after 1866, the roles of principal chief and chairman of the Business Committee were often indistinct. Clifton, *The Pokagons, 1683–1983*, 92.

11. Buechner, "The Pokagons," 318.
12. Pokagon, *Queen of the Woods*, 7–9. Pokagon was able to secure, according to him, a partial payment of $39,000 in 1866. However, the balance of $150,000 was not paid until 1896 after an appeal to the United States Supreme Court.
13. "Pokagon in a Pauper's Grave," *Chicago Daily Tribune*, January 31, 1899, 2. According to the article, "The funeral of Simon Pokagon at Hartford today was a sad disappointment to his people. Upon inquiry of Father Joos, Bishop Foley of the Diocese of Detroit dispatched word that the body of the Pottawatomie Chief could not be buried in a Catholic cemetery, and neither could the services be held in the Catholic Church, because the chief's second wife was a divorced woman. It was the wish of the tribe that Pokagon's body be placed in the cemetery with other members of his tribe."
14. Cyrus Thomas, "Pokagon, Simon," Smithsonian Institute, Bureau of American Ethnology, Bulletin 30, *Handbook of American Indians North of Mexico* (Washington, DC: Government Printing Office, 1910), 274–75.
15. "Bound in Indian Style," *Chicago Daily Tribune*, July 15, 1900, 4.
16. "'O-Gi'-Maw-Kwe Mit-I-Gwa-Ki' Big Chief's Poem Has Been Dramatized and Will Be Played," *New York Times*, May 5, 1904, 1. The article continues: "Chicago, May 4—The late Chief Pokagon's poem, 'O-gi-maw-kwe mit-i-gwa-ki, the Queen of the Woods,' has been dramatized by C. H. Engle of Hartford, Mich., and will have its 'first production on any stage' at Watervliet, in the home State of the dead Pottawattamie chief next Wednesday night. Pokagon's work is a poem of love and lamentation. The old fellow was lamenting all his life, and there is the chief's word for it that love for the queen of the woods kept pace with his sorrowing [*sic*] over the wrongs of his race." In the published play, C. H. Engle makes clear that he, Engle, is the author. He makes no such inference in the original novel. Engle, *Indian Drama . . . "Queen of the Woods,"* dramatized and published by C. H. Engle (Hartford, MI: Day Spring Power Presses, 1904).
17. After his death, his son Charles Pokagon sent copies of *Queen of the Woods* to notables including the president of the Chicago Board of Education, the Queen of the Netherlands, and the wife of President McKinley. "Prose Idyll by Red Bard," *Chicago Daily Tribune*, May 7, 1899, 35; "Van Schaack Gives to Queen," *Chicago Daily Tribune*, July 15,

1900, 4.

18. Bernd C. Peyer, *The Thinking Indian: Native American Writers, 1850s–1920s* (Frankfurt: Peter Lang, 2007), 149 n. 26.
19. James A. Clifton, “Simon Pokagon's Sandbar Claim to the Chicago Lakefront,” *Michigan History Magazine* (September/October 1987), 13–14; A. LaVonne Brown Ruoff, “Simon Pokagon (1830–January 1899),” in *Dictionary of Native American Literature*, ed. Andrew Wiget, Garland Reference Library of the Humanities, vol. 1815 (New York: Garland Publishing, 1994), 277–79, 277; Lawrence T. Martin, “Simon Pokagon: Charlatan or Authentic Spokesman for the 19th-Century Anishinaabeg?,” in *Papers of the 29th Algonquin Conference*, ed. David H. Pentland (Winnipeg: University of Manitoba Press, 1998), 29:182–91, 185; Peyer, *The Thinking Indian*, 149. Available from the Oberlin College Archives is correspondence from both Oberlin College (dated 1959) and Notre Dame University (dated 1972) indicating that neither school has a record of Simon's enrollment at their respective institutions. Oberlin College Archives, Group 28/1, Alumni—non grad files, Simon Pokagon folder, box 203.
20. Peyer, *The Thinking Indian*, 149. For a partial list of his public appearances, see Buechner, “The Pokagons,” 340.
21. So called because the rich and powerful elite congregated their homes on the near northside neighborhood along the lake at the end of the nineteenth century.
22. Clifton, “Simon Pokagon's Sandbar,” 12–13.
23. Peyer, *The Thinking Indian*, 150–51; Clifton, *The Pokagons, 1683–1983*, 95–98.
24. Clifton, *The Pokagons, 1683–1983*, 97. However, a contemporary account had a different take on the reasons for Pokagon's fall from grace among tribal members. “[Pokagon] spent many of the best years of his life in trying to collect a Pottawatomie claim of $100,000 from the government, and he lived long enough to see it distributed among his people—and to get their ill-will because he did not procure more for them after they had drank and gambled that away. The almost utter isolation of the old chief, who was far above the abject specimens of his tribe to whom he devoted so much of his energy, appealed strongly to all who knew him.” “Death of Chief Pokagon,” *Chicago Daily Tribune*, January 29, 1899, 30.
25. An individual by the name of Jody Skrtic contacted this author in 2009 and provided a copy of a quitclaim deed bearing the signature of Simon Pokagon and purporting to transfer claim of ownership to a part of the Chicago lakefront to a William H. Cox, dated April 5, 1897. Pokagon signed the document on behalf of “himself and as the chief of the Indian tribe of Pottawattomies.” Reference to this deed is also made in Peyer, *The Thinking Indian*, fn. 33.

26. Great Lakes Branch of the National Archives, folder 81—Simon Pokagon letters.
27. "Received of Francis Labadie $250 paid for J. A. Labadie (a member of my band) as a donation to assist me in defraying expenses to secure the Indian payment in which the said Labadie is to share. Yours, Simon Pokagon, Chief." Joseph Labadie Papers, Special Collections Library, University of Michigan, Ann Arbor, MI.
28. Edward Livingston Taylor, "Monuments to Historical Indian Chiefs," *Ohio Archaeological and Historical Publications* 11 (Columbus: Ohio Archaeological and Historical Society/ Fred J. Heer, 1903): 1–29, 23.
29. Pokagon, "The Future of the Red Man," 708.
30. Clifton, *The Pokagons, 1683–1983*, 92.
31. Taylor, "Monuments to Historical Indian Chiefs," 116.
32. Susan Sleeper-Smith, *Indian Women and French Men: Rethinking Cultural Encounter in the Great Lakes* (Amherst: University of Massachusetts Press, 2001), 112–16. According to Sleeper-Smith, "Increasingly, the Pokagon Potawatomi withdrew into their own separate community—they became publicly more Indian and less Catholic. Ironically, it was probably that withdrawal from the larger Catholic community and from the institutional structure of the Catholic Church that preserved their distinctive Potawatomi traditions and rituals." Ibid., 112.
33. *The Red Man's Rebuke*, by Chief Pokagon (Pottawattamie Chief). It was subsequently reprinted with a new title that same year as Simon Pokagon, The Red Man's Greeting (Hartford, MI: C.H. Engle Publisher, 1893). The little booklet, printed on birch bark paper, is relatively scarce, but it has been reprinted several times. According to the contemporary press, The Red Man's Rebuke occupied "a prominent place in the Michigan exhibit" at the 1893 World's Columbian Exposition in Chicago. "Poem by an Indian Chief," Chicago Daily Tribune, May 4, 1893, 9.
34. "Pokagon the Poet," *Chicago Daily Tribune*, October 4, 1893, 1.
35. "Held by the Dutch," *Chicago Daily Tribune*, August 26, 1897, 5.
36. John M. Coward, *The Newspaper Indian: Native American Identity in the Press, 1820–90* (Urbana: University of Illinois Press, 1999), 9–12.
37. Frederick E. Hoxie, *Talking Back to Civilization: Indian Voices from the Progressive Era*, Bedford Series in History and Culture (New York: Bedford-St. Martin's Press, 2001).
38. Sleeper-Smith, *Indian Women and French Men*, 139. See also Mona Domosh, "A 'Civilized' Commerce: Gender, 'Race' and Empire at the 1893 Chicago Exposition," *Cultural Geographies* 9 (2002): 181–201.
39. For a discussion of the complexity of representing the "civilized" versus the "savage" native at the WCE, see Melissa Rinehart. "To Hell with the Wigs! Native American

Representation and Resistance at the World's Columbian Exposition," *American Indian Quarterly* 36, no. 4 (2012): 403–42.

40. "Probably the most unique exhibit is the poem 'The Red Man's Rebuke,' composed by the last chief of the Pottawatomies, and printed on birch bark." Rand McNally & Co., *Handbook of the World's Columbian Exposition: With Special Descriptive Articles*, contributor Mrs. Potter Palmer (Chicago: Rand McNally and Co., 1893), 188–89.
41. John Cumming, "Pokagon's Birch Bark Books," in *The American Book Collector*, ed. and pub. William B. Thorsen (Chicago: William B. Thorsen, 1968), 18:14–17, 15.
42. Simon Pokagon, "Massacre of Fort Dearborn at Chicago," *Harper's New Monthly Magazine* 98 (1899): 649–56. The name of the article might seem contradictory to his argument; however, it may have been that the editor of the magazine chose the title rather than Pokagon.
43. Ibid. Simon also disputed that the 1812 battle was a massacre in an interview with a reporter from the *Chicago Daily Tribune* in "Fort Dearborn Massacre from an Indian's Point of View," *Chicago Daily Tribune,* Feb. 7, 1897, 37.
44. Pokagon, *Queen of the Woods*, preface, ii.
45. Ibid., i. Simon Pokagon was not the only tribal member to publish a book before World War II. DA-MACK (John D. Williams) who was a plaintiff in the tribe's lawsuit for the Chicago Lakefront also was an author. DA-MACK (John D. Williams), *The American Indian and His Origin* (Benton Harbor, MI: C.A. Spradling, Pub., 1933). A copy is in the Michael B. Williams Papers, Dowagiac, MI.
46. See, for instance, Parker, *The Invention of Native American Literature*, 48.
47. L. Incommce, "The Queen of the Woods, My Lida," *Grahams Magazine* 36 (January–June 1850).
48. As mentioned previously, James A. Clifton was perhaps the strongest voice questioning the authorship of *Queen of the Woods*. See Clifton, *The Prairie People: Continuity and Change in Potawatomi Indian Culture, 1665–1965* (Iowa City: University of Iowa Press, 1998). Clifton wrote that it was Pokagon's attorney's wife who "was the most likely 'ghost writer' of what he calls a "cloying romantic frontier fantasy." See also Clifton, *The Pokagons, 1683–1983,* 104. Clifton echoes this sentiment in "Simon Pokagon's Sandbar: Potawatomi Claims to Chicago's Lakefront," *Michigan History* 71, no. 5 (September/October 1987): 12–17, 14. However, even Clifton appears to have been willing to reconsider the issue according to a personal communication cited in a 1999 dissertation: Tracey Sue Jordan, "Braving New Worlds: Breed Fictions, Mixedblood Identities," PhD diss. (New York: Columbia University, 1999), n. 13. Everett Claspy quoted Michael B. Williams, then chair of the Pokagon Potawatomi Tribal Business Committee, for the opinion that Cyrus

Engle's wife did much of the writing of *Queen of the Woods*. Claspy, *The Potawatomi Indians of Southwestern Michigan*, 23. Others who weighed in on whether Simon Pokagon was the author of *Queen of the Woods* include A. LaVonne Brown Ruoff, "Simon Pokagon (1830–January 1899)," 277–79; Wolfgang Hochbruck, "Between Victorian Tract and Native American Novel: Simon Pokagon's Ogi-mäw-kwe Mit-i-gwä-ki (1899)," in *Victorian Brand, Indian Brand: The White Shadow on the Native Image*, ed. Naila Clerici (Torino: Il Segnalibro, 1993), 13–29; Martin, "Simon Pokagon: Charlatan or Authentic Spokesman?," 182–91; and Parker, *The Invention of Native American Literature*, 48. A website devoted to Native American authors, hosted by Drexel University, repeats the assertion by Clifton that "his autobiography was largely a work of fiction written by the wife of his personal attorney." Http://www.ipl.org/div/natam/bin/browse.pl/A85.

49. B. O. Flowers, "An Interesting Representative of a Vanishing Race," *The Arena* 16 (Boston: Arena Publishing Co., 1896): 240–50.
50. Correspondence to the Secretary of the Chicago Historical Society—Simon Pokagon Collection, box 32, Chicago History Museum, Chicago, IL.
51. Dickason, "Chief Simon Pokagon: The Indian Longfellow," 129.
52. Ibid., ii. A denial of authorship and authenticity was not the concern of Simon Pokagon alone. For instance, in his history of the Ottawa and Chippewa Indians of Michigan, the Ottawa author Andrew J. Blackbird included the names of nine non-Natives who attested to his "reliability." Andrew J. Blackbird, *History of the Ottawa and Chippewa Indians of Michigan: A Grammar of Their Language, and Personal and Family History* (Ypsilanti, MI: Ypsilanti Job Printing House, 1887), 4.
53. E. A. Burbank, *Burbank among the Indians: As Told by Ernest Royce* (New York: Caxton Printers, 1944), fig. 90. The painting by Burbank is in the Ayers Collection of the Newberry Library, Chicago. The text accompanying the portrait explains: "In 1898 Pokagon's last portrait was painted, at the request of the Field Museum, by E. A. Burbank. It shows us the old chief's face weakened by age, but full of character, radiant with interest, direct and noble in its gaze, gentle and friendly in its general expression." According to Cecilia B. Buechner, "A portrait that represented him [Pokagon] as he looked in his home during the last summer of his life was painted by E. A. Burbank for the Field Museum and a duplicate for the Ayer's Room of Indian History in the Newberry Library in Chicago, at the request of Edward E. Ayer, the donor." Buechner, "The Pokagons," 32–33.
54. *Queen of the Woods* was advertised for sale throughout the country with broadsides. One broadside includes a three-paragraph statement by the publisher about the book, beginning: "The latest work of Chief Pokagon entitled, 'Queen of the Woods,' is just

ready to be placed on sale." Following are an additional three paragraphs written by the publisher, including a brief biography of the author, and information about Pokagon's attendance at the Chicago World's Columbian Exposition. The circular was included in a letter originating from Hartford, Michigan, February 16, 1899—eighteen lines in neat pencil holograph. The letter, to "A. O. Robinson," states (in part): "My father chief Pokagon, author of 'The Redman's Greeting,' suddenly died last month just as his book 'Queen of the Woods' was in type. . . . Sincerely yours [signed] C. L. Pokagon." From the collection of the author. Another copy of the circular and similar letter is available at the Chicago History Museum, Simon Pokagon folder, Letter to E. G. Mason, dated March 15, 1899, written by Pokagon's son Charles.

55. Nicholas Black Elk (author), John G. Neihardt (collaborator), *Black Elk Speaks: Being the Life Story of a Holy Man of the Oglala Sioux*, 3rd ed. (1932; Lincoln: University of Nebraska Press, 2004).

56. Beginning in August 2009, I began a correspondence with Kenneth Hakken, the great-grandson of C. H. Engle. He lives in Dunnellon, Florida, and retains two copies of *Queen of the Woods*. In a September 20, 2009, e-mail to me, he wrote, "I've read that some people believe that Cyrus [Engle] had a large part in writing the book. I don't believe this. The story of the Osprey and the fish could only have been written by Simon. I think that Cyrus only helped him edit and publish the manuscript. All good authors have editors to help them organize. The story was all Simon."

57. Bernd C. Peyer also noted in his 2007 work, *The Thinking Indian: Native American Writers, 1850s–1920s*, that several of Pokagon's biographers questioned the authorship of *Queen of the Woods*. Peyer, *The Thinking Indian*, fn., 40–44. Peyer ultimately concluded that the narrative was essentially written by Simon Pokagon. Peyer and others have lamented the lack of a surviving manuscript to settle the speculation regarding the authorship issue. However, Bernadette Rigal-Cellard, who maintained a friendship with James Clifton, writes that Clifton told her that he had discovered a manuscript apparently written by Pokagon that alluded to the novel. She continues that Clifton told her that he was at the time of their conversation of the opinion that Pokagon had at least written a draft of the publication. Rigal-Cellard also reports that A. LaVonne Brown Ruoff "knew of someone who has seen the manuscript." Bernadette Rigal-Cellard, "Simon Pokagon's *O-gî-mäw-kwe Mit-i-gwä-kî* (*Queen of the Woods*): A Deceptively Simple and Charming Romance of Love and Death in the Wild Woods," in *Before Yesterday: The Long History of Native American Writing*, ed. Simone Pellerin (Pessac, France: Presses Universitaires de Bordeaux, 2009), 83–84. However, in a conversation with Brown Ruoff on March 24, 2011, she advised me that the hoped-for "manuscript" that she ultimately located was in fact a copy of the

manuscript for a biography of Pokagon, written by C. H. Engle, for the preface of *Queen of the Woods*, which she found in the University of Michigan library.

58. Womack, *Red on Red*, 2–3.
59. Philip J. Deloria, *Indians in Unexpected Places* (Lawrence: University Press of Kansas, 2004).
60. Pokagon's 1899 text serves as the source material for a 1912 publication by Marietta Walker entitled *Object-Lessons on Temperance, or, The Indian Maiden and Her White Deer* (Lamoni, IA: Herald Pub. House, 1912). The text not only duplicates the central narrative of *Queen of the Woods* but also reproduces entire sections of Pokagon's novel. This was the subject of a presentation by Dr. Kathleen Washburn, assistant professor of English, University of New Mexico at the 2014 Native American & Indigenous Studies Association (NAISA) Conference, "Pokagon without Pokagon: Queen of the Woods, Marietta Walker, and Indian Temperance."
61. John N. Low, Personal journal, 1982.
62. Pierre Nora, "Between Memory and History: *Les Lieux de Mémoire*," *Representations* 26 (Spring 1989): 7–25.
63. Reprinted in Pokagon, *Queen of the Woods*, 11.
64. Pokagon, *Queen of the Woods*, 33.
65. Ibid., unnumbered, following 33.
66. The headdress is not appropriate to the Great Lakes tribes, and seems to have been the result of artistic license. See, for instance, the photograph of Simon Pokagon ringing the Liberty Bell on Chicago Day at the Exposition. "The Vanishing White City: A Series of Beautiful and Artistic Views of the Great Columbian Exposition," *Columbian Art Series*, vol. 1, no. 12 (Chicago: Peacock Publishing Company, March 21, 1894).
67. Pokagon, *Queen of the Woods*, unnumbered, following 33. That photo is also used for the 2007 edition of Bernd C. Peyer's *The Thinking Indian: Native American Writers, 1850s–1920s*.
68. Michael Witgen, "The Rituals of Possession: Native Identity and the Invention of Empire in Seventeenth-Century Western North America," *Ethnohistory* 54, no. 4 (2007): 641.
69. Pokagon, *Queen of the Woods*, 49, 52, 64–65, 116, 123, 128, 135.
70. Ibid., 160, 163, 170, 175–78, 184, 188, 189, 190.
71. Ibid., 198.
72. According to Deloria, Indians of this era sometimes "[donned] a literary headdress" that allowed them the opportunity to pursue their own agendas while meeting the expectations of their non-Native audiences. Philip J. Deloria, *Playing Indian* (New Haven: Yale University Press, 1999), 126.

73. Pokagon, *Queen of the Woods*, appendix, 224–25.
74. Ibid., 223.
75. *The Illinois Red Man* 1, no. 1 (Bloomington: Official Paper of the Great Council of Illinois Imp. O.R.M., October 1902): 7.
76. Pokagon, *Queen of the Woods*, 35, 36, 254.
77. Temperance was not only a concern of Victorian society and such national organizations as the Woman's Christian Temperance Union (WCTU). American Indian prophets, including Neolin, Handsome Lake, and Tenskwatawa, had also admonished their followers regarding the debilitating effects of alcohol on Native communities. In that regard, then, Pokagon continues this tradition of temperance advocacy.
78. Lucy Maddox, *Citizen Indians: Native American Intellectuals, Race, and Reform* (Ithaca, NY: Cornell University Press, 2005), 4–5.
79. Richard White notes that expectations of reciprocity and "the ritual Algonquin language designed to evoke pity and generosity" were a part of the mutual misunderstandings prevalent in interactions between Great Lakes Indians and non-Natives early on. Richard White, *The Middle Ground: Indians, Empires, and Republics in the Great Lakes Region, 1650–1815* (Cambridge: Cambridge University Press, 1991), 96.
80. Keith Basso, *Wisdom Sits in Places: Landscape and Language among the Western Apache* (Albuquerque: University of New Mexico Press, 1996).
81. George R. Fox, "Place Names of Berrien County," *Michigan History Magazine* 8, no. 1 (January 1924): 6–35.
82. Ibid. Sleeper-Smith writes, "The landscape evidence . . . has not been incorporated into Great Lakes Indian history. Instead, historians have relied on the rather scornful letters of settlers and territorial officials who conveyed the impression that agriculture was a part-time endeavor, with Indian women tending small household gardens rather than cultivated fields." Sleeper-Smith, *Indian Women and French Men*, 83.
83. Ibid., 8–9, 34–35.
84. William Cronon, *Nature's Metropolis: Chicago and the Great West* (New York: W.W. Norton, 1992), 16.
85. Pokagon, *The Red Man's Greeting*, reprinted in Buechner, "The Pokagons," 331–37.
86. "Triumph of Peace," *Chicago Daily Tribune*, October 11, 1893, 9.
87. "Chicago's Great Day," *Chicago Daily Tribune*, October 11, 1893, 1. Chicago History Society website, "Official Chicago-Day Program," display ad, *Chicago Daily Tribune*, October 9, 1893, 1, http://www. chicagohs.org/history/expo.html.
88. "Chicago's Great Day," *Chicago Daily Tribune*, October 11, 1893, 1.
89. Cornelia Steketee Hulst, *Indian Sketches: Père Marquette and the Last of the Pottawatomie*

Chiefs (New York: Longmans, Green and Co., 1912), 97; Pokagon, *O-gî-mäw-kwè Mit-i-gwä-kî (Queen of the Woods)*, 19.

90. "Triumph of Peace," *Chicago Daily Tribune*, October 10, 1893, 9.
91. "Ready for Crowds," *Chicago Daily Tribune*, October 8, 1893; Peyer, *The Thinking Indian*, 161, and fn. 66. Sickels is sometimes spelled Sickles, although the former appears to be the correct spelling.
92. "Triumph of Peace," *Chicago Daily Tribune*, October 10, 1893, 51.
93. "Work of the Women," *Chicago Daily Tribune*, September 10, 1892, 13.
94. "Chief Pokagon Wants an Even $2,000," *Chicago Daily Tribune*, October 15, 1893, 7.
95. Ibid.
96. Robert A. Trennert Jr., "Selling Indian Education at World's Fairs and Expositions, 1893–1904," *American Indian Quarterly* 11, no. 3 (Summer 1987): 204.
97. "Return as Freaks," *Chicago Daily Tribune*, July 1, 1893, 1.
98. G. L. Dybwad and Joy V. Bliss, *Chicago Day at the World's Columbian Exposition: Illustrated with Candid Photographs* (Albuquerque: The Book Stops Here, 1997), 20. "Pokagon and his staff of warriors were in full tribal regalia, designed for the occasion from old pictures of Indian ceremonial attire. Pokagon held the original deed loaned by the war department, which he tendered to the United States officials, whose uniforms of buff and blue and tri-cornered hats made a striking contrast to the gorgeous colors of the Indian representatives from Michigan and Illinois. This tableau was the fourth float. Pokagon II was there, nearly seventy years old."
99. "Makeup of the Pageant," *Chicago Daily Tribune*, October 7, 1893, 1; Dybwad and Bliss, *Chicago Day at the World's Columbian Exposition*, 23, 29, 49–51, 55, 58.
100. "Pokagon the Poet," *Chicago Daily Tribune*, October 4, 1893, 1.
101. Chris Wilson and Paul Groth, eds., *Everyday America: Cultural Landscape Studies after J. B. Jackson* (Berkeley: University of California Press, 2003), 86–91, 103.

Chapter 3. Claims Making to the Chicago Lakefront

1. In the Great Lakes region, beginning in the 1970s, protests and lawsuits became the battleground for defending treaty rights. In 1974, Judge Boldt issued an opinion in United States v. Washington, 384 F. Supp. 312 (1974) that upheld the rights of the tribes in the Northwest to fish off-reservation and manage fisheries. The opinion also gave plaintiff tribes an equal share in the harvest of fish in their traditional fishing areas on ceded land. Those rights had been guaranteed in a treaty in the previous century. On March 8, 1974, Fred and Mike Tribble of the Lac Courte Oreilles (LCO) Band of Ojibwe in Wisconsin were arrested by the Wisconsin Department of Natural Resources for possession of a

spear and for the taking of off-reservation, inland-water fish. In 1980, Judge Fox rendered his decision in United States v. Michigan, 623 F.2d 448 (1980). The Fox decision upheld the rights of Michigan Ojibwe tribes to fish in ceded areas of the Great Lakes within the boundaries of the state, based upon an 1836 treaty reserving that right. That ruling was followed in 1983 with the decision by Judge Voigt. In that case, Lac Courte Oreilles v. Wisconsin, 700 F2d. 341 (1983), Judge Voigt affirmed that hunting, fishing, and gathering rights were reserved by the Ojibwe in treaties of 1837, 1842, and 1854. The case involved the Tribble brothers and represented a vindication some nine years after their initial arrest. The final decision affirming the rights of Indian peoples in the Great Lakes to the usufructuary rights guaranteed in treaties with the United States was issued in 1999. In Mille Lacs v. Minnesota, 526 U.S. 172 (1999), a counterpart to the Voigt decision in Wisconsin and the Fox decision in Michigan, the U.S. Supreme Court ruled that the 1837 treaty ceding most of northern Minnesota, reserving the right of the Ojibwe to hunt, fish, and gather on ceded territory, was still valid.

2. United States Census Bureau data online, http://www.census.gov/2010census/.
3. From early on in its history, Chicago was self-consciously impressed with its own importance in the world. The city would have the opportunity to showcase itself for the world beginning in 1893 with the Columbian Exposition. See, for instance, the civic boosterism evident in a typical tourist guidebook, J. F. Martin, *Martin's World's Fair Album-Atlas and Family Souvenir* (Chicago: C. Ropp & Sons, 1892), 1. The introduction reads, "Chicago of 1892 is the attraction of the world. Going back a few brief years, we find a small village, forming the nucleus from which has grown, like magic, a mighty city. . . . on October 8th, 1871, the world was electrified by the news that the rapidly growing City of Chicago was laid in ashes."
4. James R. Grossman, Ann Durkin Keating, and Janice L. Reiff, ed., *The Encyclopedia of Chicago* (Chicago: University of Chicago Press, 2004).
5. Jay Miller, "Land and Lifeway in the Chicago Area: Chicago and the Illinois-Miami," in *Indians of the Chicago Area*, ed. Terry Straus (Chicago: NAES College Press, 1989); Milo M. Quaife, *Checagou: From Indian Wigwam to Modern City, 1673–1835* (Chicago: University of Chicago Press, 1933), 17–20; William Cronon, *Nature's Metropolis: Chicago and the Great West* (New York: W.W. Norton, 1991), 23; Virgil J. Vogel, "Indian Place Names in Illinois," *Journal of the Illinois State Historical Society* 55, no. 2 (1962): 157–89; Edward Callary, *Place Names of Illinois* (Urbana: University of Illinois Press, 2008), 68–69. According to Callary, there are at least thirteen explanations for the origins and meaning of "Chicago." See also Milo M. Quaife, "Garlic River Beginnings," in *Lake Michigan* (Indianapolis: Bobbs-Merrill Co., 1944), chap. 6; and John F. Swenson, "Chicagoua/Chicago: The Origin, Meaning, and

Etymology of a Place Name," *Illinois Historical Journal* 84, no. 4 (1991): 235–48.

6. A. T. Andreas, *History of Chicago from the Earliest Period to the Present Time* (Chicago, 1884).
7. Quaife, *Checagou, 1673–1835*, 38.
8. Colin G. Calloway, *One Vast Winter Count: The Native American West before Lewis and Clark* (Lincoln: University of Nebraska Press, 2003), 218. Milo M. Quaife noted, "The prosperity of Chicago and her possibilities of future growth have alike been conditioned, at every period of her existence as a city, by the character and extent of her highway systems. These have been of threefold character, comprising waterways, country thoroughfares, and railroads." Milo M. Quaife, *Chicago's Highways Old and New* (Chicago: D.F. Keller and Co., 1923), 14.
9. Edwin O. Gale, *Chicago and Vicinity* (Chicago: Fleming H. Revell, 1902). See also Bessie Louise Pierce, *A History of Chicago, 1673–1848* (New York: A.A. Knopf, 1937).
10. Grossman, Keating, and Reiff, eds., *The Encyclopedia of Chicago*. See also Harold M. Mayer and Richard C. Wade, *Chicago: Growth of a Metropolis* (Chicago: University of Chicago Press, 1969).
11. Cronon, *Nature's Metropolis*, 150.
12. "Chicago would be a metropolis—not the central city of the continent as the boosters had hoped but the gateway city to the Great West, with a vast reach and dominance that flowed from its control over that region's trade with the rest of the world." Cronon, *Nature's Metropolis*, 92.
13. Typical of the civic pride of the time is the declaration "He who would study America must come to Chicago, where beats the heart of this great, nervous, fast growing and ambitious nation. From out this whirlpool of business, old Father Time emerges, battle-scarred and bruised, for here his passage is jealously contended and every step vigorously opposed. No mere idler can be happy in Chicago; here is the spirit of *work*, and every man, woman and child feels it" (emphasis original). *Chicago: Souvenir of Chicago in Colors* (1892; Chicago: V.O. Hammon Publishing Co., 1908), 1.
14. Grossman, Keating, and Reiff, ed., *The Encyclopedia of Chicago*, 61.
15. Yi-Fu Tuan, "Foreword," in *Landscape, Nature and the Body Politic: From Britain's Renaissance to America's New World*, by Kenneth Robert Olwig (Madison: University of Wisconsin Press, 2002), xvii–xviii.
16. Donald Mitchell, *Cultural Geography: A Critical Introduction* (Malden, MA: Blackwell Publishing, 2000), 121, 123.
17. Nancy Shoemaker, *A Strange Likeness: Becoming Red and White in Eighteenth Century North America* (New York: Oxford University Press, 2004), 20.

18. Ibid., 21.
19. For a review of the three-hundred-year process by which Europeans came to understand the Western Hemisphere as a *place*, see Eviatar Zerubavael, *Terra Cognita: The Mental Discovery of America* (New Brunswick, NJ: Rutgers University Press, 1992).
20. Elmore Barce, *The Land of the Potawatomi, (by a) Member of Indiana Historical Society* (Fowler, IN: Benton Review, 1919), 61.
21. David Turnbull, *Maps Are Territories: Science Is an Atlas* (Chicago: University of Chicago Press, 1989), 19, 20.
22. Ibid., 44.
23. Ibid.
24. "The Portuguese cartographer Diego Ribero's map of the world (1529) [depicted] Pope Alexander VI's 'line of demarcation,' dividing the undiscovered world between Spain and Portugal following the Treaty of Tordesillas in 1494. Despite the fact that no one had either the instruments or the techniques to locate or define the line with any accuracy, the mere fact of having a map enabled a division of the world with immense political ramifications." Ibid., 58.
25. In a treaty executed on August 24, 1816, in St. Louis, the Potawatomi Indians ceded a strip of land twenty miles wide, which reached from Lake Michigan south to the Illinois River, the northern boundary located ten miles north of the Chicago River. The land ceded by the treaty would become a large part of the City of Chicago.
26. J. B. Harley, "Maps, Knowledge and Power," in *The Iconography of Landscape: Essays on the Symbolic Representation, Design, and Use of Past Environments*, ed. D. Cosgrove and S. Daniels (New York: Cambridge University Press, 1989), 277–312.
27. James A. Clifton, "Simon Pokagon's Sandbar: Potawatomi Claims to Chicago's Lakefront," *Michigan Historical Review* 71, no. 5 (1987): 12–17.
28. James A. Clifton, *The Pokagons, 1683–1983: Catholic Potawatomi Indians of the St. Joseph River Valley* (Lanham, MD: University Press of America and Potawatomi Indian Nation Inc., 1984), 112.
29. Clifton wrote that "In January of 1890 . . . the House and Senate approved legislation enabling the Potawatomi of Michigan and Indiana to bring suit against the United States in the Court of Claims. Congress practically dictated most terms of a finding to the Court." Clifton, *The Pokagons, 1683–1983*, 100. The Court of Claims ruled in favor of the Potawatomi and awarded them $104,626 for unpaid back treaty annuities plus interest. This payment, however, caused a rift within the tribe concerning payment of the tribal attorneys and exacerbated an already complicated political scene within the community, as evidenced by the substantial discord over legal fees. "Claims of J. B. Shipman and J.

Critcher for Legal Services to the Pokagon Potawatomi," NARA microfilm roll 80, Office of Indian Affairs (OIA) Special Files, National Archives and Records Administration, Great Lakes Region, Chicago, IL.

30. "Own 130 Acres in Chicago: Claim of the Pottawatomie Indians—Agents of the Tribe to See about It," *New York Times*, September 22, 1897, 1. The article discloses, "Benton Harbor, Mich., Sept 21,—Simon Pokagon, Chief of the Pottawatomie tribe of Indians, and Lawyer Ingalls of Hartford, Mich., were here this morning on their way to Chicago to see W. H. Cox, a Chicago capitalist, in relation to a claim that the Pottawatomie tribe hold title to 130 acres of land in the heart of Chicago, which land is mostly in the possession of Mr. Cox." In Pokagon's obituary it was reported, "Pokagon made frequent trips to Chicago, hired a special lawyer to look into the matter, but just before his death became convinced there was nothing to it." See also "Death of Simon Pokagon," *Chicago Daily Tribune*, January 28, 1899, 5. If Pokagon did give up any claim to the lakefront, it may have been because he knew he had already attempted to quitclaim any interest of the tribe's to real estate speculators. However, any quitclaim deed signed by Simon Pokagon could only have served to legally tender his own interests in the realty, since he had no authority to sign such a deed on behalf of the Pokagon people in toto.
31. "End of Po-Ka-Gon Claim, House Committee Decides against Demand of Indians, All Rights to Lake Michigan and Other Illinois Lands Ceded Long Ago," *Chicago Daily Tribune*, June 1, 1900, 5.
32. "Indians to Take Lake Front, Pottawatomies Decide to Go to Chicago and Occupy the Disputed Land," *Washington Post*, January 8, 1901; "Pottawatomies to Squat, Redskins Chose Daring Young Leader and Decide to Invade the Lake Front of Chicago," *Los Angeles Times*, January 9, 1901, 1; and "Indians to Seize Lakefront Lands, Pottawatomies to Descend upon the Windy City, Chief Pokagon's Secy Asks for Terms for Transport of Men, Women and Children, Ponies, Cats, Dogs, Pet Deer and 'Tame' Wild Animals," *Los Angeles Times*, May 29, 1901, 3.
33. "Indians Claim to Lake Front," *Chicago Daily Tribune*, May 27, 1900, 9; "To Settle Land Rights of Pottawatomies," *Chicago Daily Tribune*, February 13, 1900, 7; "Indians Appeal to President," *Washington Post*, February 19, 1905, 4; and "Indians Claiming Submerged Land, Pokagon Tribe Appeals to Legislature in Fight for Made Ground Near Lake Michigan," *Christian Science Monitor*, April 8, 1909, 1.
34. "Indians Have No Title to Sell," *Chicago Daily Tribune*, January 22, 1902, 1; "State May Seize Lake Front Land, Title to 'Streeterville,' Chicago Beach Hotel, and Shore Club Questioned," *Chicago Daily Tribune*, August 11, 1909, 1; and "Ignores Indians' Claim to Shore," *Chicago Daily Tribune*, May 27, 1909, 9.

35. "Indians Sell Chicago Claims, Robert Bines of This City Buys Supposed Rights of Pottawatomies to Lake Shore Land, Pays $100 to Each One," *Chicago Daily Tribune*, January 18, 1902, 1. Minutes of the Business Committee appear to confirm that they entered into a contract with Bines and were paid a lump sum of $33,900.00 by him. Minutes of the Pokagon Potawatomi Business Committee, June 22, 1902, Michael B. Williams Papers, Dowagiac, Michigan.
36. Minutes of the Pokagon Potawatomi Business Committee, December 27, 1899, and August 5, 1901, Michael B. Williams Papers. Other minutes indicate that several years later, the Business Committee was working with W. H. Cox (Cox had obtained a quitclaim deed signed by Simon Pokagon "on behalf of himself and as Chief of the Indian Tribe of Pottawattomies" on April 5, 1897). Apparently, this did not prevent Cox from working with the Business Committee on their claim; Minutes of the Pokagon Potawatomi Business Committee, March 25, 1909, Michael B. Williams Papers. W. E. Johnson appeared at a later Business Committee meeting to discuss the "fact [*sic*] and documents of our Chicago Lake front lands"; Minutes of the Pokagon Potawatomi Business Committee, March 25, 1909, Michael B. Williams Papers. Just prior to filing suit in federal court, the Business Committee continued to work with Cox and Johnson. On June 8, 1912, the committee reviewed correspondence from Johnson and Cox, who were described as "our representatives" in the minutes; Minutes of the Pokagon Potawatomi Business Committee, June 8, 1912, Michael B. Williams Papers. Cox was present at the committee meeting of June 17, 1912, to "make a partial report of their progressing to our Chicago Lake front lands"; Minutes, Michael B. Williams Papers. His partner W. E. Johnson also submitted a written letter to the committee with the stirring conclusion "Therefore, let our single purpose be—regardless of whom it may please or offend among men—to speak the truth in its simplicity and power, not to conceal danger or fill over crimes, or screen the wrong-doer"; Johnson to Chief, Chairman Secretary and Members of the Business Committee, September 28, 1912, Michael B. Williams Papers.
37. Correspondence from J. H. Cushway to Michael B. Williams, February 19, 1903, Michael B. Williams Papers.
38. October 21, 1911, Michael B. Williams Papers.
39. Minutes of the Pokagon Potawatomi Business Committee, November 17, 1900, Michael B. Williams Papers.
40. Minutes of the Pokagon Potawatomi Business Committee, June 4, 1901, Michael B. Williams Papers.
41. Ibid.
42. Minutes of the Pokagon Potawatomi Business Committee, undated, Michael B. Williams

Papers.

43. Minutes of the Pokagon Potawatomi Business Committee, November 12, 1901, Michael B. Williams Papers.
44. Minutes of the Pokagon Potawatomi Business Committee, November 12 and 13, 1901, Michael B. Williams Papers. See also Clifton, *The Pokagons, 1683–1983*, 92–107.
45. Minutes of the Pokagon Potawatomi Business Committee, August 6, 1900; January 5, 1901; August 15, 1901; April 21, 1901; April 24, 1901; June 4, 1901; June 5, 1901; June 8, 1901; June 15, 1901; November 12, 1901; November 21, 1901; December 20, 1901; January 17, 1902, Michael B. Williams Papers.
46. "Indians Claim Lake Front, Descendants of Many Tribes Sue under Old Grant," *New York Times*, November 13, 1913, 1.
47. Williams v. City of Chicago, 242 US 434 (1917).
48. Richard White, "The Spatial Turn: The Parameters of a Digital History," lecture, Illinois Program for Research in the Humanities, April 12, 2010, at University of Illinois, Urbana-Champaign. Put another way, according to Yi-Fu Tuan, "The meaning of space often merges with that of place. 'Space' is more abstract than 'place.' What begins as undifferentiated space becomes place as we get to know it better and endow it with value." Yi-Fu Tuan, *Space and Place: The Perspective of Experience* (Minneapolis: University of Minnesota Press, 1977), 6. For additional discussions of space and place, see David Harvey, *Justice, Nature and the Geography of Difference* (Oxford: Blackwell Publishing, 1996), chap. 9, "The Social Construction of Space and Time," and chap. 11, "From Space to Place and Back Again."
49. Robert Sack, *A Geographical Guide to the Real and the Good* (New York: Routledge, 2003), 4.
50. Keith Basso, *Wisdom Sits in Places: Landscape and Language among the Western Apache* (Albuquerque: University of New Mexico Press, 1996), 106, 107, 109.
51. Similar to European perceptions of the Pacific as being filled with small dots of land surrounded by a desert of water, the Indigenous inhabitants of Oceania view their islands as interconnected, and the water as highways rather than boundaries or borders. See Eric Waddell, Vijay Naidu, and Epeli Hau'ofa, eds., *A New Oceania: Rediscovering Our Sea of Islands* (Fiji: School of Social and Economic Development, University of the South Pacific in Association with Beake House, 1993).
52. Spelled in different ways and interpreted in different ways, Kwi-wi-sens Nenaw-bo-zhoo, Waynabozho, Nanabozho, Nannabush, Waynabush, Winabojo, etc., all represent the cultural hero and spirit being of the Potawatomi, Ojibwe, and Odawa. "Kitche Manido, the Great Spirit, was . . . responsible for Nanabush or Wenebojo. Nanabush was born

of an Earth Mother and Father Sun, so he belonged to both the earth and spirit worlds. A Trickster who could change form to become other beings, animals or even a rock, he brought all manner of knowledge to the Anishinabe. Nanabush also served as an intermediary between the Anishinabe and the spirit world." Helen Hornbeck Tanner, *The Ojibwa* (Philadelphia: Chelsea House Publishers, 1992), 13–14. See also Basil Johnston, *Ojibwe Heritage* (Lincoln: University of Nebraska Press, 1976), 17–20.

53. Simon Pokagon, "Indian Superstitions and Legends," *Forum* 25 (1898): 618–29.
54. Dawn E. Bastian and Judy K. Mitchell, *Handbook of Native American Mythology* (Santa Barbara, CA: ABC-CLIO, 2004).
55. Patty Loew, "Hidden Transcripts in the Chippewa Treaty Rights Struggle: A Twice Told Story, Race, Resistance, and the Politics of Power," *American Indian Quarterly* 21, no. 4 (1997): 713. Loew recites a similar version of the creation story of the Ojibwe, Odawa, and Potawatomi. "After the Great Flood, Waynaboojo (a spirit being, cultural hero and trickster figure) found himself resting on a log with the other animals. There was no land to be found. Waynaboojo asked each animal to dive under the water to bring up some muck, from which Waynaboojo would make the New Earth. Each animal tried and failed except muskrat, who gave his life in the effort. Turtle offered his back to receive the spreading muck and in this way Waynaboojo was able to fashion the new world, which the Potawatomi call Turtle Island [North America]." See also the recitation by Edward Benton-Banai, *The Mishomis Book: The Voice of the Ojibway* (Haywood, WI: Indian Country Communications, Inc., 1988), chap. 5.
56. Pokagon Potawatomi Tribal Newsletter, *Pokégnek Yajdanawa*, Dowagiac, MI, July 2013, 16.
57. "[A] ritual was held in honor of a mythical creature, prominent in the lore of the tribe, called Nambi-zac in Potawatomi and the 'Underwater Panther' in English. Although generally considered an evil creature, the Underwater Panther is greatly feared and respected by all of the groups having the creature in their pantheon. Among the Ojibwa and Potawatomi the monster is especially venerated by the members of the Midewiwin or Grand Medicine society." James H. Howard, "When They Worship the Underwater Panther: A Prairie Potawatomi Bundle Ceremony," *Southwestern Journal of Anthropology* 16, no. 2 (1960): 217–24.
58. *Mother Earth Water Walk*, http://motherearthwaterwalk.com/index.php?option=com_content&view=article&id=72&Itemid=83.
59. Alanson Skinner, "The Mascoutens or Prairie Potawatomi Indians: Part I, Social Life and Ceremonies," *Bulletin, Public Museum of the City of Milwaukee* 6, no. 1 (1923): 1–262, 47–48.
60. The Prairie Band of Potawatomi were relocated from Illinois beginning in the 1830s.

61. Howard, "When They Worship the Underwater Panther," 217–24.
62. According to the Mother Earth Water Walk Project, "Two Anishinawbe Grandmothers, and a group of Anishinawbe Women and Men have taken action regarding the water issue by walking the perimeter of the Great Lakes. Along with a group of Anishinabe-que and supports, they walked around Lake Superior in 2003, around Lake Michigan in 2004, Lake Huron in 2005, Lake Ontario in 2006 and Lake Erie in 2007." A website describes their activities: http://motherearthwaterwalk.com/index.php.
63. Clifton, *The Pokagon Potawatomi, 1683–1983*, 115.
64. Ibid.
65. Johnson v. M'Intosh, 8 Wheat. 543 (1823).
66. Williams v. City of Chicago 242 U.S. 434 (1917), 437–438.
67. Pokagon, *Queen of the Woods*, 16–17.
68. Clifton, "Simon Pokagon's Sandbar," 17.
69. Michael B. Williams Papers. Mr. Williams was secretary of the Pokagon Potawatomi Business Committee when they filed suit for the Chicago lakefront. Throughout his life he was the acknowledged historian of the tribe, a popular public speaker, painstaking record keeper, tribal leader, and advocate for tribal claims. While some of his conclusions are not possible to verify with other sources, they are a valuable transcription of the oral history of the community.
70. Throughout his correspondence and notes, Williams writes that prior to contact with Europeans, the Potawatomi were unified peoples, and that the claim of any branch of the Potawatomi is a claim available to all of the Potawatomi. Michael B. Williams Papers. The Indian Claims Commission also concluded that in the time period between the Treaty of Greenville in August 1795 and the Treaty of Chicago in 1833, the Potawatomi were a single overall political entity known as the Potawatomi tribe or nation, with an overriding interest in all Potawatomi lands; that during this period the federal government recognized this fact and dealt with the Potawatomi as a single political entity; and that during this period, when a certain group of Potawatomi entered into a treaty with the United States, they acted on behalf of the whole Potawatomi nation or tribe. Citizen Band of Potawatomi Indians v. United States, Docket 71, et al., 27 Ind. Cl. Comm. 187 (1972). See also Helen Hornbeck Tanner, *Atlas of Great Lakes Indian History* (Norman: University of Oklahoma Press, 1987).
71. The case was initiated in the Federal District Court for the Northern District of Illinois in January 1914. The suit was dismissed by the District Court in May of the same year. See http://caselaw.lp.findlaw.com/scripts/getcase.pl?court=US&vol=242&invol=434.
72. Edmund Jess Grossberg, *J.G.'s Legacy, with foreword by Walter Roth, President, Chicago*

Jewish Historical Society (Glencoe, IL: Published by the Author, 1994).

73. Williams v. City of Chicago, (1917) 242 U.S. 434, 438. The Court cited to Johnson v. M'Intosh, (1823) 8 Wheat. 543, 584, 586, 588; Mitchel v. United States, (1835) 9 Pet. 711, 745; United States v. Cook, (1873) 19 Wall. 591, 592, 22; and Beecher v. Wetherby, (1877) 95 U.S. 517, 525.
74. Nicholas K. Bromley, *Law, Space, and the Geographies of Power* (New York: Guilford Press, 1994), xi–xii.
75. Ibid., 51–56.
76. Ibid.
77. No. 08-3621, decided and filed August 18, 2009.
78. Johnson v. M'Intosh, 8 Wheat. 543 (1823).
79. I am unable to ascertain at this time whether this decision will be appealed to a higher court.
80. Ottawa Tribe of Oklahoma v. Logan, No. 08–3621, United States Court of Appeals, 6th Circ., decided August 18, 2009, 7.
81. Burke A. Hendrix, "Memory in Native American Land Claims," *Political Theory* 33, no. 6 (December 2005): 763–85.
82. See Terry Straus, *Indians of the Chicago Area* (Chicago: NAES College Press, 1989); Terry Straus and Grant P. Ardnt, eds., *Native Chicago*. Chicago: *Native Chicago*, 1998., Terry Straus, ed. *Native Chicago*. 2nd ed. San Francisco: Albatross Press, 2002.
83. Odette Yousef, "Do Descendants of Chicago's Native American Tribes Live in the City Today?" *WBEZ 91.5*, July 11, 2012, http://www.wbez.org/series/curious-city/do-descendants-chicagos-native-american-tribes-live-city-today-100217.
84. "Photographs from the *Chicago Daily News*, 1902–1933, American Indians/Native Americans," *Library of Congress, American Memory*, http://memory.loc.gov.
85. "American Indians at Chicago's Columbian Exposition," Dept. of Anthropology, University of Illinois, http://www.ao.uiuc.edu/courses/aiiopcmpss/essays/exposition/expo1.htm.
86. Mabel McIlvaine, "Chicago to Celebrate Indian Day," *Fort Dearborn Magazine*, September 1920, 3–4. There are also articles about the hostilities at Fort Dearborn in 1812 (the article refers to it as a "battle" rather than a "massacre") as well as the Potawatomi Chief Shabbona in that issue of the *Fort Dearborn Magazine*, which has on its cover a painting of an anonymous Indian viewing the metropolis of Chicago.
87. Peter Iverson, *Carlos Montezuma and the Changing World of American Indians* (Albuquerque: University of New Mexico Press, 1982). Simon Pokagon corresponded with Montezuma and presented him with a copy of his *Red Man's Greeting*. Carlos Montezuma

Papers at the Newberry Library, Chicago, http://mms.newberry.org/ html/montezuma.html.

88. Telegram from the American Indian Day Committee to Commissioner John E. Collier, September 12, 1935, Indian Council Fire Records, 1920–1990, Papers, correspondence, scrapbooks, clippings, photographs, and publications of the Indian Council Fire, a Chicago-based organization supporting educational, legislative, and social services for urban and reservation Indians, Newberry Library, Chicago.
89. Robert E. Lester, ed., *Native Americans and the New Deal: The Office Files of John Collier, 1933–1945* (Bethesda, MD: University Publications of America, 1994), microfilm, reel 6.
90. "Relic of Treaty Elm to Figure in Indian Ceremony: Giant Boulder to Be Base," *Chicago Daily Tribune*, September 22, 1935, 10. See also "Olson Rug Co. Plans $10,000 Rock Garden," *Chicago Daily Tribune*, August 11, 1935, A12. For websites recording memories of the park, see "History of Olson Rug of Chicago," http://www.olsonrug.com/History-of-Olson-Rug.asp; John R. Schmidt, "Olson Rug Park, Former Chicago Landmark, Now Parking Lot," http://www.wbez.org/blog/john-r-schmidt/2011-09-02/olson-rug-park-91037; "Olson Rug Factory Rock Garden," http://dimbeautyofchicago.blogspot.com/2007/10/olson-rug-factory-rock-garden.html; "Olson Waterfall, Diversey Avenue and Pulaski Road," *WTTW Chicago Time Machine*, http://interactive.wttw.com/timemachine/olson-waterfall; Ron Grossman, "Chicago's Seven Lost Wonders," http://www.chicagotribune.com/chi-0508290065aug29-story.html#page=1; "Paving the Way to 'Progress': Olson Park Then and Now," http://reliablerascal.com/avondale/2012/09/olson-park/; "A Park in Lost Chicago," http://duensingamericana.blogspot.com/2010/04/park-in-lost-chicago.html; Daniel Pogorzelski, "Olson Waterfall," *Forgotten Chicago*, http://forgottenchicago.com/columns/northwest/olson-waterfall/.
91. The program is titled "Program, 17th Annual Celebration, under the auspices of the Indian Council Fire and the American Indian Day Committee . . . Olson Memorial Park." From the collection of the author.
92. "Paving the Way to 'Progress': Olson Park Then and Now," http://reliablerascal.com/avondale/2012/09/olson-park/.

Chapter 4. The Legacies of Turner, Cody, Streeter, and the Pokagon Potawatomi

1. Williams v. City of Chicago, 242 U.S. 434 (1917).
2. Various versions of the scuttling of Streeter's boat and his resting on a sandbar a short distance north of the Chicago River are recited in K. C. Tessendorf, "Captain Streeter's District of Lake Michigan," *Chicago History* 5, no. 3 (1976): 155; Edward Bergstrom, "Cap

Streeter: Squatter King," *Tradition* 10 (October 1961): 23; Everett Guy Ballard, *Captain Streeter, Pioneer* (Chicago: Emery Publishing Service, 1914), 218; and Joseph Millard, "George Wellington Streeter—All This Out Here Is My Land," in *No Law But Their Own* (Evanston, IL: Regency Books, 1963), 120.

3. Tessendorf, "Captain Streeter's District of Lake Michigan," 155.
4. John W. Stamper, "Shaping Chicago's Shoreline," *Chicago History* 14, no. 4 (1985–1986): 44–55. See also the recent article affirming the Stamper version of events in Joshua Salzman, "The Chicago Lakefront's Last Frontier: The Turnerian Mythology of Streeterville, 1886–1961," *Journal of Illinois History* 9 (Autumn 2006): 201–2, 208.
5. Stamper, "Shaping Chicago's Shoreline," 44.
6. Ibid., 47.
7. Unidentified newspaper fragment from the George W. Streeter Archives of the Chicago Public Library, "Streeter Legend Shattered: Famous Craft of the Captain Wrecked While Tied to a Pier," Chicago Public Library, Special Collections and Preservation Division, Neighborhood History Research Collection, Streeterville Collection, Call numbers: Archives_STR.
8. Bergstrom, "Cap Streeter: Squatter King," 23–27.
9. 1870 United States Federal Census, National Archives and Records Administration (NARA), Washington, DC, M 593_671, 309.
10. "Prison Is Streeter's Fate: Verdict of Guilty Is Returned in the Kirk Murder Trial, Three Defendants Must Serve Terms, Jury Decides upon Conviction for Manslaughter, 'Captain' Streeter Says That Millionaires Conspired against Him," *Chicago Chronicle*, December 4, 1902, 1.
11. According to June Sawyers, "On May 4, 1886, a crowd gathered in Haymarket Square on the near west side of Chicago to protest the treatment by police of striking workers at the McCormick Harvesting plant. During the gathering, someone threw a bomb into the crowd, which resulted in the death of a police officer. In a controversial trial, seven men were convicted and on November 11, 1887, four were executed. On June 26, 1893, Governor Altgeld pardoned the three remaining defendants." June Skinner Sawyers, *Chicago Portraits: Biographies of 250 Famous Chicagoans* (Chicago: Loyola University Press, 1991), 11–12.
12. In a dramatic flair, Ballard followed the dedication with a quote from Oliver Goldsmith, to wit: "Ill fares the land, to hastening ills a prey. Where wealth accumulates, and men decay." Ballard, *Captain Streeter, Pioneer*, 4.
13. Ibid., 5–6.
14. Ibid., 6.

15. Ibid., 14.
16. Scotti Cohn, "The Captain's War," in *It Happened in Chicago* (Guilford, CT: Morris Book Publishing, 2009), 66–70; Ursula Bielski, *More Chicago Haunts: Scenes from Myth and Memory* (Chicago: Lake Claremont Press, 2000), 296–300; June Skinner Sawyers, "The Eccentric Captain of Streeterville," in *Chicago Sketches: Urban Tales, Stories, and Legends from Chicago History* (Chicago: Loyola Press/Wild Onion Books, 1995), 9–40; Joseph Millard, "George Wellington Streeter—All This Out Here Is My Land," in *No Law But Their Own* (Evanston, IL: Regency Books, 1963), 111–58; Mrs. L. Edwards, *My Twenty Years Experience in Streeterville District of Lake Michigan* (N.p., ca. 1940); Patricia Bronte, *Vittles and Vice* (Chicago: Henry Regency Company, 1952), 29–32; Lois Willie, *Forever Open, Clear, and Free: The Struggle for Chicago's Lakefront* (Chicago: Henry Regency Co., 1972), 58–61; Francesca Falk Miller, *The Sands: The Story of Chicago's Front Yard* (Chicago: Valentine-Newman Publishers, 1948); Robert Shackleton, "A Modern Corsair," in *The Book of Chicago* (Philadelphia: Penn Publishing Co., 1920), chap. 13; "Captain George Wellington Streeter, Battling Hero of the 'Deestrick of Lake Michigan,'" *Journal of the Illinois State Historical Society* 13, no. 4 (January 1921): 571–74; Kenneth F. Broomell and Harlow M. Church, "Streeterville Saga," *Journal of the Illinois State Historical Society* 33, no. 2 (June 1940): 153–65; Frederick D. C. Langdon, "The Wreck of the 'Reutan' and What Came of It," *Wide World Magazine* 7 (April–September 1901): 539–43; and Edward B. Clark, "The Amazing History of the Streeterville War," *Women's Home Companion* 29, no. 12 (December 1902).
17. Ballard devotes an entire chapter to his military service. Ballard, *Captain Streeter, Pioneer*, 131–78.
18. Millard, "George Wellington Streeter," 115.
19. According to James W. Cook, such traveling exhibitions were common in nineteenth-century America. Cook writes that the showman P. T. Barnum was the most famous and adroit in this era at exhibiting curiosities and spectacles that challenged the audience to ascertain the legitimacy of what they were viewing. These exhibition frauds fooled some, but just as importantly, they intrigued many others bent on exposing the hoax. Either way, P. T. Barnum's show was a popular cultural phenomenon. James W. Cook, *The Arts of Deception: Playing with Fraud in the Age of Barnum* (Cambridge, MA: Harvard University Press, 2001), introduction.
20. According to the Ballard biography, "During the winter of 1869 and 1870 I built a steamboat, and in the spring of the latter year christened her the 'Minnie E. Streeter,' in honor of my wife, who did not long thereafter honor me by her presence, for she decamped suddenly without notice . . . and accepted an engagement on a vaudeville

circuit." Ballard, *Captain Streeter, Pioneer*, 190.

21. Ibid., 210.
22. Ballard, "quoting" Streeter, writes, "On my return to Chicago I . . . finally purchased an interest in the old 'Woods Museum,' already famous as a place of local entertainment. During the six months that I was half owner of this place, such famous personages as . . . Tenny C. Claflin . . . appeared there. . . . [who] afterwards married a member of the English House of Lords. . . . She was one of the pioneer advocates of women suffrage, and created quite a furore [*sic*] in Chicago when the doctrine was then new." Ballard, *Captain Streeter, Pioneer*, 210.
23. A later biographer writes, "Cap Streeter quickly established himself as a raffish personality, circulating garrulously amid the bars and shores of the city's entertainment district. He was a rather small man, sporting a flowing red mane, shaggy eyebrows, and a mussy moustache, which framed a face turned brick red by prolonged exposure to the outdoor elements and indoor spirits. The wiry Streeter was a memorable sartorial spectacle in his ever-present top hat and the 'tobacco-stained, rusty green frock coat several sizes too large' that dangled from his lean shoulders to his ankles." Tessendorf, "Captain Streeter's District of Lake Michigan," 153–54.
24. Ibid., 154.
25. Ballard, *Captain Streeter, Pioneer*, 216.
26. Millard, "George Wellington Streeter," 120.
27. Tessendorf, "Captain Streeter's District of Lake Michigan," 155.
28. Ibid.
29. Ballard, *Captain Streeter, Pioneer*, 420.
30. Ibid.
31. Ballard, *Captain Streeter, Pioneer*, between 224 and 225; W. H. Niles, *A Brief History and the Legal Standing of the District of Lake Michigan* (Chicago: Swanberg & Co., 1900), 15; and W. H. Niles, *The Military Government of the District of Lake Michigan* (Chicago: Hufford & Co., 1903), 24–25.
32. Ibid.
33. Williams v. City of Chicago (1917).
34. Ballard, *Captain Streeter, Pioneer*, 222–23.
35. The Palmer residence became an instant tourist attraction for the city and the center of social life in Chicago in the era of the captains of industry. A typical souvenir book of the period contains a color photo of the castle-like manor, with the caption "Mrs. Potter Palmer's Residence, Located on the Lake Shore Drive. One of the finest residences in the city." *Chicago: Souvenir of Chicago in Colors* (Chicago: V.O. Hammon Publishing Co., 1908).

36. Sawyers, *Chicago Portraits*, 201–3.
37. For a fascinating, albeit far from objective, depiction of the place "where the Chicago River oozed into Lake Michigan [and] the Sands began," see Miller, *The Sands.*
38. Stamper, "Shaping Chicago's Shoreline," 53.
39. Ballard, *Captain Streeter, Pioneer*, 220. Although born and raised in Michigan, Streeter was consistently portrayed as having a "foreign" accent and colorful oratory that added to his eccentricity and set him apart. For instance, in "Streeterspeak," the area he claimed as his own was the "Deestrick" of Lake Michigan. Oftentimes the press emphasized his accent as a part of the folklore/myth in their headlines. As examples, see "'Captain' Streeter's Heirs Battle for 'Deestrict' Today: Appeal to Come Up in U.S. Court, Hundreds of Millions Involved, Widow Is Not Party to Suit, Fought for Fifty years, Recalls Old Houseboat and Shipwreck on Shore of Lake; Craft Sunk by the Police," *Chicago Herald and Examiner*, January 3, 1928, 1; "'Deestrict' Heirs Fight for Estate," *Chicago Daily News*, January 3, 1928, 1; "Streeter Heirs Go to Court Jan 18 to Push Claim: 'Captain's' Kin Want to Carry on Fight for 'Deestrict,'" *Chicago Evening Post*, January 3, 1928, 1; "Blow from Streeter Falls on Streeter: Three Claimants to 64 Lots in 'Deestrict' of Lake Michigan Will Sue; 'Stolen' Cries the 'Cap,' Deeds Which Are Basis of the Demand Declared 'Illegally Obtained,'" *Chicago Record*, January 31, 1911, 3; and "Streeter's Big Coup, Transfers Fight for 'Deestrict of Lake Michigan' to Milwaukee, in United States Court," *Chicago Record-Examiner*, August 1, 1902, 1.
40. This kind of rhetoric is apparent in a piece of newspaper fragment in the Streeter Archives in the Special Collections at the Chicago Public Library. "'New Pilgrim Home' Is What Streeter Will Now Call District of Lake Michigan, Streeterville," unidentified newspaper scrap, May 6, 1902, 3.
41. "Court Rule Ends the Long Fought Streeter Case," *Chicago Evening Post*, April 18, 1928, 1. In reporting the dismissal of an appeal of a federal court denying the claim of the heirs, the *Evening Post* noted, "Capt. Streeter claimed the new land was his. Shore owners said it was theirs by virtue of riparian rights. Streeter's claim was good enough to frighten off the title companies for a time. Also, it was good enough to secure him some financial backing." Another example of the story that the Streeter claim had slowed development of the area is reflected in a news report: "Purchase of nine acres [for Northwestern University's downtown campus] was made possible by the long retarded growth of this section of the lakefront called 'Streeterville,'" *Christian Science Monitor*, November 22, 1926, 1.
42. Mrs. L. Edwards, *My Twenty Years Experience in Streeterville District of Lake Michigan*, 1, 16.
43. Ibid., 16.

44. Broomell and Church, "Streeterville Saga," 157.
45. "'Cap' Streeter on the Stage: Discoverer of District of Lake Michigan Appears in Vaudeville at the Metropolitan," *Chicago Daily Tribune*, November 11, 1902, 4.
46. "Streeter Shows His Art," *Chicago Daily Tribune*, November 13, 1902, 3.
47. "Although Lake Shore Drive in the 1890s was still home to fewer millionaires than Prairie Avenue, it quickly became the richest street on the North Side. It had many attractions: a view of Lake Michigan, the roar of the surf, and clean air. The Palmer mansion advertised the development of upper Lake Shore Drive. It attracted so much attention that Palmer could be choosy about buyers for his lots in the blocks north and south of him. He sold only to those he considered his peers, and thus the neighborhood became the most elegant part of town. Among those who bought property on or near Lake Shore Drive were . . . Robert Todd Lincoln and Harold and Edith McCormick." Stamper, "Shaping Chicago's Shoreline," 53. The area quickly came to be called Chicago's "Gold Coast."
48. Raymond D. Fogelson, "The Red Man in the White City," in *Columbian Consequences: The Spanish Borderlands in Pan-American Perspective*, ed. David Hurst Thomas, vol. 3 (Washington DC: Smithsonian Press, 1991), chap. 4.
49. Edwards, *My Twenty Years Experience in Streeterville District of Lake Michigan*, 10.
50. Homer Hoyt, *One Hundred Years of Land Values in Chicago* (Chicago: University of Chicago, 1933), 437.
51. Ibid.
52. Sawyers, "The Eccentric Captain of Streeterville, 39.
53. The exposition closed shortly afterward without fanfare.
54. Ibid., 114–15.
55. Ibid., 116.
56. Edward R. Kantowicz, "Carter H. Harrison II: The Politics of Balance," in *The Mayors: The Chicago Political Tradition*, ed. Paul M. Green and Melvin G. Holli (Carbondale: Southern Illinois University Press, 1995).
57. Ibid. For more information on ward politics of Chicago at the end of the nineteenth and beginning of the twentieth centuries and the story of John "Bathhouse" Coughlin and Michael "Hinky Dink" Kenna, prototypes of the saloon-keeper aldermen and influence peddlers of Chicago, see Herman Kogan and Lloyd Wendt, *Lords of the Levee: The Story of Bathhouse John and Hinky Dink* (Evanston, IL: Northwestern University Press, 2005).
58. Salzman, "The Chicago Lakefront's Last Frontier, 157.
59. Michigan Avenue up to almost the end of the nineteenth century was known as Pine Street. Stamper, "Shaping Chicago's Shoreline," 46.
60. Millard, *No Law But Their Own*, 132.

61. Tessendorf, "Captain Streeter's District of Lake Michigan," 157.
62. Niles, *The Military Government of the District of Lake Michigan*, 8–9.
63. Later disputes in authority and strategy would emerge as evidenced by the following public statements of Niles: "February 16th, 1900, G.W. Streeter reports that he has collected money for taxes, about $70.00, but none has been turned over to W. H. Niles for public use, and as W. H. Niles has received no money for taxes, therefore, in accordance with the act of January 8th, 1900, all lots upon which the taxes have not been paid . . . are hereby declared to be the property of the Government of the District of Lake Michigan. May 26th, 1900, District of Lake Michigan. Know all men by these acts that W. H. Niles has this day on the soil of the District of Lake Michigan and by an armed assembly of the property holders, been nominated and elected Military Governor of the District of Lake Michigan for as long a time as a military government is necessary in the district by the unanimous vote of all the property holders present, with the power to do all things pertaining to the peace and prosperity of the district." Niles, *A Brief History and the Legal Standing of the District of Lake Michigan*, 21. Streeter wrote of Niles, "One of my warmest friends and defenders, William H. Niles, conceived the idea that he could declare himself military governor of the territory without the necessary appointment by the chief executive of the nation. In this move I had no part, and it was done without my knowledge or consent. I admired his nerve and fighting spirit, but I did not approve his judgment, for I knew full well that he was making a mistake from a legal standpoint. His declaration of authority over the territory, which was purely civil and had no relation whatever to the title to the land itself, was undertaken under the cover of darkness, which does not bode good to any cause." Ballard, *Captain Streeter, Pioneer*, 264.
64. Niles, *The Military Government of the District of Lake Michigan*, 4.
65. This article is typical of the casting of the land dispute in military terms, which was done both by the press and the supporters of Streeter: "Streeter War Looms Again, Ald. Cullerton's Efforts to Secure Building Permit May Lead to Renewal of District Troubles," *Chicago Journal*, March 4, 1902, 2.
66. Mrs. L. Edwards wrote, "Captain Streeter's attorney, a man by the name of Ed Bailey, was waylaid and murdered on his way home from Evanston. Captain had sent him out to his friend's house to get some valuable papers, some deeds. Captain often told me about it, as well as other people . . . his dead body was found near Chicago on the outer drive. His pockets had been torn, his coat was open, and his papers were taken. Near his dead body lay a monkey wrench and his head had been split open. The stolen papers were used against Streeter at the trial where the deeds of Streeterville had been in dispute." Edwards, *My Twenty Years Experience in Streeterville District of Lake Michigan*, 9.

67. *New York Times*, May 27, 1900, 15.
68. "Drive Streeter off Lake Front," *Chicago Daily Tribune*, September 21, 1901, 1.
69. A copy of the Declaration of Independence was published in Niles, *A Brief History and the Legal Standing of the District of Lake Michigan*, 2–4. In the booklet, Niles writes, "The object of this book will be to present to the *thinking* public a brief history of our case and to show we have been deprived of our property and political rights by the power of money." Ibid., 1 (emphasis original).
70. "'Captain' Streeter Indicted," *New York Times*, February 1, 1902, 1. See also Salzman, "The Chicago Lakefront's Last Frontier," 208.
71. "Women Hold for Streeter Disputed Land, Where Fatal Battle Took Place Last Night, Police Seek to Learn Who Started Fight, Each Side Accuses the Other; No Disinterested Witnesses Saw Opening Shot, Squatters Were in Ambush," *Chicago Evening American*, January 12, 1902, 1. The article, with details of the death of John Kirk, continues with the banner "Their [the elite's] only hope to get possession of the property included within the boundaries of the District of Lake Michigan is to keep 'Cap' Streeter in jail or hang him. They will do neither . . . the main conspirators were willing to sacrifice the life of one of their hirelings to land the Streeter forces behind bars . . . —Statement by Captain George Wellington Streeter."
72. Examples include "Here Is a Diagram Illustrating the Streeterville Shooting and a Picture of the Scene of the Fight," *Hearst's Chicago American*, February 12, 1902, 1; "To Corner Streeter, Authorities Will Push Murder Prosecution against Lake Front Claimant, Exemption Plea Ignored, Evidence Secured That Captain Was an Active Combatant in the Battle, Land Claimed by 'Captain' Streeter—Scene of Tuesday Night's Tragedy," *Chicago Record-Herald*, February 12, 1902, 1; "Streeter Guards Kill an 'Invader,' Pitched Battle in the Dark, Forces Line Up and Send Bullet after Bullet through the Night Shadows," *Chicago Accord Herald*, February 2, 1902, 1.
73. Niles, *The Military Government of the District of Lake Michigan*, 44.
74. Ibid., 45.
75. Sawyers, "The Eccentric Captain of Streeterville," 38.
76. Sawyers, *Chicago Portraits*, 11–12.
77. Ibid.
78. "Is This $25,000,000 Tract Ownerless?—Cap'n Streeter's Claim," *Chicago Daily Morning*, March 9, 1902, 1; and "Who Owns the Lake Front and Other Chicago Gossip," *Pekin (Ill.) Times*, February 20, 1902, 1.
79. Millard, *No Law But Their Own*, 156.
80. "Fighting 'Cap' Streeter Dead, End Comes for Aged Squatter on Houseboat, Battled for

Years to Enforce Claim to 186 Acres on 'Gold Coast,'" "Squatter's spectacular career full of clashes with armed forces of the law, [widow] plans to carry on fight, [Streeter] often arrested as bootlegger, tribute from opposing counsel." *Chicago Daily Journal*, January 24, 1921, 1. The article concludes: "'Capt. Streeter was one of the most picturesque characters Chicago has ever produced, and his death will remove one of the most constant sources of entertainment the courts have had' said Robert Humphrey, an attorney for the Chicago Title and Trust company, which contested to annul the captain's claims in Streeterville property. 'His opponents must admit that he has been a game and persistent fighter.'" See also "Noted 'Mayor' Is Dead, Capt. Streeter, Who Carried on a Long Fight for Land, Passes Away," *Los Angeles Times*, January 25, 1921, 11.

81. In this article featuring a photograph of a coy-looking "Ma," Streeter's widow is described as having at her ready "shotgun and bulldogs to battle for her rights." "'Captain' Streeter's Heirs Battle for 'Deestrict' Today, Appeal to Come Up in U.S. Court, Hundreds of Millions Involved, Widow Is Not Party to Suit; Fought for Fifty Years, Recalls Old Houseboat and Shipwreck on Shore of Lake; Craft Sunk by the Police," *Chicago Herald and Examiner*, January 3, 1928, 1. In a subsequent article in the same newspaper, "'Ma' Streeter Ready to Battle Invaders," *Chicago Herald and Examiner*, July 28, 1922, 1, the writer notes that "[The Captain's] last words to 'Ma' Streeter and other heirs were, 'Keep up the faith. Don't give up the ship.' They are fulfilling his adjurations." See also "Labor Seeks Site in Streeterville, Backs Fight of Captain's Widow on Promise of Land Bequest," *Chicago Daily News*, April 5, 1928, 1. The article announces, "Inspired by the deeding of a considerable plot of land for a proposed 'labor temple' and a permanent home for the WCFL (Chicago Federation of Labor) in what is known as 'Streeterville,' on the near north side, labor delegates present took up the Streeter cause with a whoop of delight at the picture of a state 'temple' in the midst of that exclusive settlement."
82. "Death Comes to 'Ma' Streeter," *Los Angeles Times*, October 19, 1936, 9.
83. "'Ma' Streeter Dies; Claimed Millions, Shouldered Shotgun to Help Squatter Husband Defend Chicago Lake Front, Had Planned a Utopia, but Courts Held Her 'Sovereign State' Did Not Exist—Had Peddled Aprons for Living," *New York Times*, October 19, 1936, 19; "'Ma' Streeter Dies in Chicago, Destitute, Alone, Helped Husband Fight for $350,000,000 Gold Coast Property," *Washington Post*, October 18, 1936, 24.
84. As previously mentioned, the so-called "Gold Coast" of Chicago, the wealthiest residential neighborhood in the city, retains the unofficial designation of "Streeterville." During a recent rehab of Navy Pier, one of the service drives was christened Streeter Drive. In the 1980s, one of the restaurants at the Hyatt Regency in Chicago was named "Captain Streeters" (oddly enough, it advertised as specializing in Mexican fare). Display

ad, *New York Times*, June 19, 1980, 207.

85. Ballard, *Captain Streeter, Pioneer*, 106.
86. Ibid., 267–68.
87. See for instance "Indians to Take Lakefront, Pottawatomies Decide to Go to Chicago and Occupy the Disputed Land," *Washington Post*, June 8, 1901, 1.
88. Streeter and his advocates circumvented the argument that the Federal Trade and Intercourse Acts and the holding of the United States Supreme Court in Johnson v. M'Intosh (1823)—which made clear that Indian tribes have no authority to sell land to individuals, only to the federal government, and that any individual sale is void on its face—by arguing, like the Potawatomi did in their suit, that the Treaty of Greenville (1795) gave the Indians a fee title to the unceded lands, including Chicago, which could then be sold to individuals.
89. Beginning in 1862, the United States passed a series of laws that allowed for citizens to gain title to parcels of land in exchange for settling upon and improving that land. This mixture of habitation and labor was seen as legitimizing the claim to the land. Earlier, preemption acts had pointed in the same direction. The ideology dated to the eighteenth century. Robert Maxwell Brown details the homestead ethic that underpinned the ideology of settler privilege in the United States. Robert Maxwell Brown, "Backcountry Rebellions and the Homestead Ethic in America, 1740–1799," in *Tradition, Conflict, and Modernization: Perspectives on the American Revolution*, ed. Robert Maxwell Brown and Don E. Fehrenbacher (New York: Academic Press, 1977), 73–98. See also Stephen Aron, "Pioneers and Profiteers: Land Speculation and the Homestead Ethic in Frontier Kentucky," *Western Historical Quarterly* 23, no. 2 (May 1992): 179–98, 181.
90. Correspondence from Michael B. Williams to C. E. Caple of Los Angeles, California, dated September 2, 1964. Michael B. Williams Papers, Dowagiac, MI.
91. W. H. Cox and W. E. Johnson, *The Greatest Conspiracy Ever Conceived, By any class of human beings in this Conspiracy, by a class of people who are devising by every way and means illegal and unjust to rob the legal owners of their Chicago Lake Front Lands and of their title and rights to quiet possession secured to them by treaty with the United States* (Chicago, December 1908). This treatise was found in the Michael B. Williams Papers, Dowagiac, MI.
92. "Indian Invasion a Dream," *Chicago Daily Tribune*, May 30, 1901, 9.
93. Salzman, "The Chicago Lakefront's Last Frontier," fn. 38.
94. "Streeter Sells to the Police, Thirty Patrolmen Are Purchasers of Lots in His 'District of Lake Michigan,'" *Chicago Daily Tribune*, July 13, 1900, 1.
95. "Capt. Streeter in Luck, A Shipwreck Caused Him to Blossom Out as a Capitalist," *New*

York Times, December 4, 1892, 1.

96. "Captain George Wellington Streeter," editorial, *Journal of the Illinois Historical Society* 13, no. 4 (January 1922): 571–74, 574.
97. "Indians Sell Chicago Claims, Robert Bines of This City Buys Supposed Rights of Pottawatomies to Lake Shore Land, Pays $100 to Each One," *Chicago Daily Tribune*, January 18, 1902, 1. Minutes of the Business Committee appear to confirm that they entered into a contract with Bines and were paid a lump sum of $33,900 by him. Minutes of the Pokagon Potawatomi Business Committee, June 22, 1902, Michael B. Williams Papers, Dowagiac, MI.
98. "Indians Sell Chicago Claims," 1.
99. Ibid.
100. Johnson v. M'Intosh, 21 U.S. (8 Wheat.) 543 (1823).
101. Paul Redden, *Wild West Shows* (Urbana: University of Illinois Press, 1999), 119.
102. Frederick E. Hoxie, *A Final Promise: The Campaign to Assimilate the Indians, 1880–1920* (Lincoln: University of Nebraska Press, 1984); Vine Deloria Jr., "The Indians," in *Buffalo Bill and the Wild West*, ed. David H. Katzive et al. (New York: Brooklyn Museum, 1981), 56–58; L. G. Moses, *Wild West Shows and the Images of American Indians, 1883–1933* (Albuquerque: University of New Mexico Press, 1996); L. G. Moses, "Performative Traditions in American Indian History," in *A Companion to American Indian History*, ed. Philip J. Deloria and Neal Salisbury (Malden, MA: Blackwell Publishing, 2004), 193–208; and Robert W. Rydell, *All the World's a Fair: Visions of Empire at American International Expositions, 1876–1916* (Chicago: University of Chicago Press, 1984).
103. Philip J. Deloria, *Indians in Unexpected Places* (Lawrence: University of Kansas Press, 2004).
104. Meenakshi Gigi Durham and Douglas M. Kellner, eds., *Media and Cultural Studies: KeyWorks* (New York: Wiley-Blackwell, 2006), xv; and Antonio Gramsci, "(i) History of the Subaltern Classes; (ii) The Concept of "Ideology"; (iii) Cultural Themes: Ideological Material," in ibid., 14–16.
105. Richard Slotkin, *Gunfighter Nation: The Myth of the Frontier in Twentieth-Century America* (New York: Athenaeum, 1992), 5–6. Slotkin discusses the intersections of ideology and myth. Ideology is the basic system of concepts, beliefs, and values that define a society's way of interpreting its cosmos and the meaning of its history. Myth is contrasted as the stories that have acquired the power to symbolize a society's ideology. Myth is an expression of ideology in narrative form.
106. George Lipitz, *Time Passages: Collective Memory and American Popular Culture* (Minneapolis: University of Minnesota Press, 1990).

107. As David Roediger points out, this stratification of the social order and placement of others below the newly arrived immigrant classes came at a heavy price for everyone. David A. Roediger, *Wages of Whiteness: Race and the Making of the American Working Class*, rev. ed. (New York: Verso Books, 1999). However, one could argue that perhaps some of the performers and audience took a different view; that the show was about healing the wounds left over from the "Indian Wars," making Indians more approachable to White Americans, transferring real hatred to staged hatred, real experiences into fantasy, real gulfs between cultures into bridged experiences, conquest into collaboration, and guilt into atonement.
108. Greg Dening, as quoted in Roslyn Poignant, *Professional Savages: Captive Lives and Western Spectacle* (New Haven, CT: Yale University Press, 2004), 275.
109. Ibid., 242–43.
110. Gail Bederman, *Manliness and Civilization* (Chicago: University of Chicago Press, 1995); and Richard White and Patricia Nelson Limerick, "Frederick Jackson Turner and Buffalo Bill," in *The Frontier in American Culture*, ed. James Grossman (Berkeley: University of California Press, 1994), 7–66.
111. Frederick J. Turner, "The Significance of the Frontier in American History," in *Annual Report of the American Historical Association for the Year 1893* (Washington, DC: GPO and American Historical Association, 1894), 199–227.
112. "Align Tribe for Invasion," *Chicago Daily Tribune*, January 8, 1901, 3.
113. "Cash or the Tomahawk," *Chicago Daily Tribune*, April 28, 1901, 1.
114. "Michigan Indians," *Hickman (KY) Courier*, Friday, June 14, 1901, 1.
115. Edward B. Clark, *Indian Encampment, Chicago Centennial of 1903: In Honor of the City's Centennial Anniversary* (Chicago: Chicago Centennial Committee, 1903). This brochure promotes the activities of the festival events.
116. Ibid., unnumbered page 3.
117. Ibid.
118. Ibid., unnumbered back page of brochure.
119. Ibid., unnumbered page 10.
120. Mary Louise Pratt, *Imperial Eyes: Travel Writing and Transculturation* (London: Routledge, 1992).
121. Carlos G. Vélez-Ibáñez, *Border Visions: Mexican Cultures of the Southwest United States* (Tucson: University of Arizona Press, 1996), 4–6.
122. Louis Owens, *Mixedblood Messages: Literature, Film, Family, Place* (Norman: University of Oklahoma Press, 2001), 26.
123. Broomell and Church, "Streeterville Saga," 164, quoting Streeter.

124. Fernando Ortiz, *Cuban Counterpoint: Tobacco and Sugar* (Durham, NC: Duke University Press, 1995).
125. A. I. Hallowell, "American Indians, White and Black: The Phenomenon of Transculturation," *Current Anthropology* 4 (1963): 519–31.
126. "Contact zone" is a term first articulated by Mary Louise Pratt to describe the often-contentious interactions that occur when peoples of different cultures clash, struggle, resist, and accommodate each other. Mary Louise Pratt, "Arts of the Contact Zone," *Profession* (1991): 3–40.
127. These "new Western historians" include William Cronon, *Nature's Metropolis: Chicago and the Great West* (New York: W.W. Norton, 1991); Patricia Nelson Limerick, *The Legacy of Conquest: The Unbroken Past of the American West* (New York: W.W. Norton, 1987); Richard White, *"It's Your Misfortune and None of My Own": A History of the American West* (Norman: University of Oklahoma Press, 1991); and James R. Grossman, ed., The Frontier in American Culture (Berkeley: University of California Press, 1994).
128. Alan Trachtenberg, *Brooklyn Bridge* (New York: Oxford University Press, 1965). See also Robert Berkhofer, *The White Man's Indian* (New York: Knopf, 1978).
129. Michel Foucault, "Politics and the Study of Discourse," in *The Foucault Effect: Studies in Governmentality*, ed. Graham Burchell, Colin Gordon, and Peter Miller (Chicago: University of Chicago Press), 59–60.
130. Clark, *Indian Encampment*, unnumbered page 13.
131. *Streeterville—A Play by Ralph Covert and Griley Mills*, at http://www.waterdogmusic.com/ralphcovert/streeterville.html#; and *George Wellington "Cap" Streeter*, at http://www.capstreeter.com. A radio show devoted to Streeter was produced by Archie H. Jones, "The Squatter," WAAF Radio Program, January 15, 1961, Archie H. Jones Papers, Chicago History Museum.
132. *Streeterville—A Play by Ralph Covert and Griley Mills*. The play had its world premiere at TimeLine Theatre, from February 15 through March 18, 2001, http://www.waterdogmusic.com/ralphcovert/streeterville.html.
133. For instance, a recent publication by the Streeterville Organization of Active Residents includes an entire page devoted to George Wellington Streeter while only mentioning that the "Potawatomi were removed from Chicago in 1824." Rolf Achilles, *Pride of Place: The Streeterville Story* (Chicago: SOAR, 2005), 4.
134. "Introduction," *Frontier to Heartland*, http://publications.newberry.org/frontiertoheartland/exhibits/show/perspectives/fourcenturies.
135. James E. Lewis Jr., "American Settlement, 1783–1819," *Prairiefire: The Illinois Country Before 1818*, http://prairiefire.lib.niu.edu/settlement.

136. Ulrich Danckers, Jane Meredith, and John F. Swenson, *A Compendium of the Early History of Chicago to the Year 1835 When the Indians Left* (River Forest, IL: Early Chicago, Inc., 1999).
137. R. David Edmunds, "Chicago in the Middle Ground," *Encyclopedia of Chicago*, http://encyclopedia.chicagohistory.org/pages/254.html; Ann Durkin Keating, "Metropolitan Growth," *Encyclopedia of Chicago*, http://encyclopedia.chicagohistory.org/pages/821.html. "While humans have inhabited this area for thousands of years, most of our local history begins with the Potawatomi presence in the eighteenth and early nineteenth centuries. Potawatomi farmed, hunted, and traded in this area, locating along trails and water routes." The Potawatomi are spoken of in the past tense throughout the website; Susan E. Hirsch, "Economic Geography," *Encyclopedia of Chicago*, http://encyclopedia.chicagohistory.org/pages/409.html; Louis Delgado, "Native Americans," *Encyclopedia of Chicago*, http://www.encyclopedia.chicagohistory.org/pages/874.html.
138. See *Encyclopedia of Chicago* at http://encyclopedia.chicagohistory.org/pages/500001.html; and http://encyclopedia.chicagohistory.org/pages/500002.html.
139. Amanda Seligman, "Streeterville," *Encyclopedia of Chicago*, http://encyclopedia.chicagohistory.org/pages/1208.html.
140. R. David Edmunds, "Potawatomis," *Encyclopedia of Chicago*, http://encyclopedia.chicagohistory.org/pages/1001.html.
141. Jean M. O'Brien, *Firsting and Lasting: Writing Indians out of Existence in New England* (Minneapolis: University of Minnesota Press, 2010), introduction.

Chapter 5. Leroy Wesaw and the Chicago Canoe Club

1. Donald L. Fixico, *Termination and Relocation: Federal Indian Policy, 1945–1960* (Albuquerque: University of New Mexico Press, 1990).
2. Donald L. Fixico, "The Relocation Program and Urbanization," in *Indians of the Chicago Area*, ed. Terry Straus (Chicago: NAES College Press, 1989), 143–64.
3. James B. LaGrand, *Indian Metropolis: Native Americans in Chicago, 1945–75* (Urbana: University of Illinois Press, 2002), 138–47.
4. Donald Fixico, *The Urban Indian Experience in America* (Albuquerque: University of New Mexico Press, 2000), 133.
5. LaGrand, *Indian Metropolis*, 218–20; David Beck, "Chronological Index of Community History—Chicago," in *Indians of the Chicago Area*, ed. Terry Straus (Chicago: NAES College Press, 1989), 197–202.
6. Thomas Vennum Jr., *American Indian Lacrosse: Little Brother of War* (Washington, DC: Smithsonian Institution Press, 1994), 301–18.

7. "Red Men Play a Game of Lacrosse," *Chicago Daily Tribune*, October 10, 1893, 9.
8. Ibid.
9. Nora Marks, "Fading from the Earth: The Pottawatomies of the Michigan Hunting Ground, Dissipation and Their Inability to Live in Civilization Too Strong for the Remnant of the Once Mighty Tribe . . . ," *Chicago Daily Tribune*, February 15, 1890, 7.
10. "Chicago Day to Revere the Past," *Chicago Daily Tribune*, September 26, 1903, 2.
11. Edward B. Clark, *Indian Encampment at Lincoln Park, Chicago, Sept. 26 to Oct. 1, 1903: In Honor of the City's Centennial Anniversary* (Chicago: Chicago Centennial Committee, 1903), unnumbered last page of the brochure.
12. "Chicago Day to Revere the Past," 2.
13. Clark, *Indian Encampment at Lincoln Park, Chicago, Sept. 26 to Oct. 1, 1903*, unnumbered last page of the brochure.
14. Ibid., unnumbered pages 6–8.
15. John Bloom, *To Show What an Indian Can Do* (Minneapolis: University of Minnesota Press, 2000).
16. "Now that the Indian has caught the base-ball craze, who knows but Mr. Anson's next team will be the American Reds against all the other colors in the field," no title, *Chicago Daily Tribune*, August 4, 1891, 4. "Cap" Adrian Anson was one of the first professional baseball superstars and was a first baseman and manager for the Chicago White Stockings/Cubs. Born in 1852 and dying in 1922, he is perhaps most remembered for being among many white ball players of the time who refused to take the field against African Americans. David L. Fleitz, *Cap Anson: The Grand Old Man of Baseball* (Jefferson, NC: McFarland and Co., 2005).
17. "Winning Their Way," *Chicago Daily Tribune*, August 14, 1892, 25.
18. "Camp on Anson's Trail," *Chicago Daily Tribune*, June 8, 1896, 4.
19. According to Everett Claspy, Williams attended the St. Joseph College for Boys in Rensselaer, Indiana, and worked as a bookkeeper at the Dowagiac Drill Works from where he retired. "In 1913 he was Secretary of the Silver Creek Base Ball team." Everett Claspy, *The Potawatomi Indians of Southwestern Michigan* (Ann Arbor: Braun-Brumfield, 1966), 34.
20. Everett Claspy, *The Dowagiac–Sister Lakes Resort Area and More about Its Potawatomi Indians* (Dowagiac, MI: Self-published, 1970), 130, 134–36.
21. James A. Clifton, George L. Cornell, and James M. McClurken, *People of the Three Fires: The Ottawa, Potawatomi and Ojibway of Michigan* (Grand Rapids: Grand Rapids Inter-Tribal Council, 1986), 41; William W. Warren, *History of the Ojibway People*, reprint (1885; St. Paul: Minnesota Historical Press, 1984), 146–47.

22. James A. Clifton, *The Pokagons, 1683–1983: Catholic Potawatomi Indians of the St. Joseph River Valley* (Lanham, MD: University Press of America, 1984), 2.
23. Clifton, Cornell, and McClurken, *People of the Three Fires*, 40–41.
24. Helen Hornbeck Tanner, *The Ojibwa*, Indians of North America Series, ed. Frank W. Porter III (Philadelphia: Chelsea House Publishers, 1992), 24.
25. Robert E. Ritzenthaler, "The Building of a Chippewa Indian Birch-Bark Canoe," *Bulletin of the Public Museum of Milwaukee* 19, no. 2 (1950): 1–33; reprinted in 1972.
26. Ibid. In the 1971 film *César's Bark Canoe*, sixty-seven-year-old Attikamek Indian Cesar Newashish builds a birch bark canoe. According to the liner notes, "With a sure hand he works methodically to fashion a craft unsurpassed in function or beauty of design." *César's Bark Canoe*, VHS, directed by Bernard Gosselin (Montreal: National Film Board of Canada, 1971).
27. Thomas Vennum Jr., *Earl's Canoe: A Traditional Ojibwe Craft*, VHS, directed by Thomas Vennum and Charles Weber with participation by Earl Nyholm (Watertown, MA: Documentary Educational Resources, 1999).
28. C. Ted Behne, "The BirchBark Canoe: Back from the Brink," *Native Peoples Magazine* (July/August 2001): 53–54.
29. Ibid.
30. Craig S. Womack, *Red on Red: Native American Indian Separatism* (Minneapolis: University of Minnesota Press, 1999), 55.
31. For more on the "whitestreaming" of American Indians into the mainstream of the hegemony of white America, see Sandy Grande, *Red Pedagogy: Native American Social and Political Thought* (Lanham, MD: Rowman and Littlefield, 2004), 9.
32. Blake Edgar, "The Polynesian Connection," *Archaeology* 58, issue 2 (March/April 2005); Ben R. Finney, *Sailing in the Wake of the Ancestors* (Honolulu: Bishop Museum Press, 2003); Michael E. Harkin, ed., *Reassessing Revitalization Movements: Perspectives from North America and the Pacific Islands* (Lincoln: University of Nebraska Press, 2005); David Lewis, *We, the Navigators: The Ancient Art of Landfinding in the Pacific*, 2nd ed. (Honolulu: University of Hawai'i Press, 1994); and Lawrence J. Cunningham, Ward Kranz, and Manny Sikau, "Restoring Traditional Seafaring and Navigation in Guam," *Micronesian Journal of the Humanities and Social Sciences* 5, nos. 1/2 (November 2006).
33. Christopher Tilly, "Metaphor, Materiality and Interpretation: Introduction and the Metaphorical Transformation of Wala Canoes," in *The Material Culture Reader*, ed. V. Buchli (Oxford: Berg Press, 2002), 23–55. Tilly adds, "The enduring symbolic and social significance of the canoe for Wala islanders has always principally resided in its use as a vehicle of power, and in the social relationships that it engenders. . . . On another and

more abstract plane of meaning the canoes are a dynamic symbolic manifestation of the strength and *power* of the past in the present" (53).

34. Michael Becker and George W. Wilson, "Tribal Leaders Seek to Maintain Traditional Potawatomi Skills," *South Bend Tribune*, September 29, 1985, 3–4.
35. "Everywhere, Canoes," in "Faculty," *LSA Newsletter* (Ann Arbor: University of Michigan, Spring 2009): 38–39. I participated in the program while a graduate student at the university and served as a liaison with the Pokagon Potawatomi. Daniel Rapp, another member and elder of the Pokagon Band, also made the journey.
36. *Pokégnek Yajdanawa* (As the Pokagons Tell It), monthly newsletter of the Pokagon Band of Potawatomi (Dowagiac, MI), November 2013, 2.
37. Early depictions by non-Natives of Chicago include images of Indians (presumably Potawatomi) canoeing along the lakeshore. See for example the engraving titled "Chicago in 1820" (Illinois State Historical Library) and "Chicago in 1820, from an Old View, after a drawing by Henry Rowe Schoolcraft" (Chicago Historical Society), reprinted in R. David Edmunds, *The Potawatomis: Keepers of the Fire* (Norman: University of Oklahoma Press, 1987), 147, and also in William D. Strong, *Indian Tribes of the Chicago Region, with Special Reference to the Illinois and the Potawatomi* (Chicago: Field Museum of Natural History, 1938), plate 2.
38. For example, in 1891 a group of canoe enthusiasts formed the "Chicago Canoe Club," headed by Commodore D. H. Crane. "Canoeists of Chicago," *Chicago Daily Tribune*, May 3, 1891, 9. An industry of canoe makers emerged, typified by the success of the Old Town Canoe Company and J.H. Rushton, Inc. In the Rushton catalog of 1910, the "Indian Girl Canoe" was a featured item. *Rushton Indian Girl Canoes* (Canton, NY: J.H. Rushton, Inc., 1910).
39. Walt Whitman (1819–1892), *Leaves of Grass* (Philadelphia: David McKay, 1900).
40. Interview with Leroy Wesaw Sr., Chicago American Indian Oral History Project, December 16, 1982, box 2, folder 5, Newberry Library and NAES (Native American Education Services) College Library, Chicago, Illinois, 1. His memories of early education were not good. He was kicked out of the local public school. "In the 1930s there was a lot of racism, their culture was strictly alien to me" (15). At the Harbor Springs school, sponsored by the Catholic Church, there was little tolerance for Indian traditions or language. He recounts how one of the Sisters caught him speaking Potawatomi and gave him a licking, while exclaiming, "I'll make you—I'll civilize you, you heathen you" (16).
41. Ibid., 15, 18.
42. LaGrand, *Indian Metropolis*, 139.
43. Interview with Leroy Wesaw Sr., 6.

44. Letter from Colin Wesaw to the author, November 10, 2010. Colin Wesaw was a cultural presenter in Minnesota and Wisconsin at the time of his correspondence and interview with me.
45. Louis Traverzo, interview by the author, Kenosha, WI, February 8, 2011. Traverzo, a member of the Lac Courte Oreilles Band of Ojibwe, was head of the TSA at the Milwaukee Public Airport at the time of his interview, after having served twenty-seven years in the United States military.
46. Until his death in 2012, the canoe shop remained active under Frese at 4019 N. Narragansett Avenue in Chicago.
47. "Local," *Chicago Tribune*, January 14, 1968, 3.
48. Louis Traverzo, interview by the author, Kenosha, WI, February 8, 2011.
49. Interview of Leroy Wesaw Sr., 8.
50. Claspy, *The Dowagiac–Sister Lakes Resort Area*, 128.
51. Ibid., 109–10, 128; Interview with Leroy Wesaw Sr., 10–12.
52. "Indian Center to Get Boy Scout Charter," *Chicago Tribune*, September 23, 1964, A6; "Indian Boy Scouts to Study City Lore," *Chicago Tribune*, October 18, 1964, N6.
53. Eli Suzukovich, interview by the author, Chicago, IL, February 16, 2011. Suzukovich, (Chippewa/Cree), holds a PhD in anthropology from the University of Montana. According to the Northwestern University website, "Currently a post-doctoral research fellow in psychology at Northwestern University, Suzukovich is the urban ecology coordinator for the American Indian Center of Chicago. He manages the center's on-site medicinal prairie garden, where medicinal, edible, and ceremonial plants are grown for use by Native community members." Http://www.wcas.northwestern.edu/epc/people/suzu.htm.
54. William Granger, "65 Canoeists Follow Route of Marquette," *Chicago Tribune*, April 14, 1968, 18.
55. "Big Pow-Wow Near Starved Rock," *Chicago Tribune*, April 7, 1968, H16.
56. David Sibbet, "Massive Canoe Trip, Conservationist Plans Fox River Flotilla," *Chicago Tribune*, June 23, 1968, S2.
57. Ibid.
58. Louis Traverzo, interview by the author, Kenosha, WI, February 8, 2011.
59. "Local," *Chicago Tribune*, January 14, 1968, 3.
60. Louis Traverzo, interview by the author, Kenosha, WI, February 8, 2011.
61. "Canoe Club Journeys down Chicago River," *Chicago Tribune*, January 9, 1967, G7.
62. No title, *Chicago Tribune*, August 29, 1968, N1.
63. No title, *Chicago Daily News*, January 26, 1971, 3.

64. "Indian Drums Beat a Salute to Service Men," *Chicago Tribune*, November 12, 1967, A11.
65. Kay Loring, "Tradition's Role in Indian Cooking," *Chicago Tribune*, February 16, 1971, A3.
66. "Indian Festival Set to Begin Tomorrow in Field Museum," *Chicago Tribune*, September 22, 1968, A4; "Indian Pow-Wow Offers Canoe Race in Lake," *Chicago Tribune*, September 22, 1968, N6.
67. American Indian Center Archives, photographs by Amalia Andujar, provided to the author by Cyndee Fox-Starr (Omaha/Odawa), special events coordinator for the Chicago American Indian Center.
68. "Indians Anticipate Annual Canoe Race on 'Big, Bad Water,'" *Chicago Tribune*, July 28, 1966, D3.
69. "Canoe Club Wins Trophy in Milwaukee Race," *Chicago Tribune*, June 30, 1966, H5.
70. "Indians Anticipate Annual Canoe Race on 'Big, Bad Water,'" *Chicago Tribune*, July 28, 1966, D3.
71. Ibid.
72. Ibid.
73. Ibid.
74. Ibid.
75. Ibid.
76. Ralph Frese, interview by the author, Chicago, IL, October 10, 2010.
77. Stephen A. O. Golden, "War Canoes Circle Manhattan Island," *New York Times*, April 30, 1967, 206.
78. No title, *Chicago Tribune*, September 14, 1969, N10.
79. Interview with Joe White, Chicago American Indian Oral History Project, February 14, 1984, Newberry Library and NAES (Native American Education Services) College Library, Chicago, IL, box 2, folder 16, pp. 2–3.
80. Ibid., 7–8.
81. Interview with Eli Suzukovich.
82. LaGrand, *Indian Metropolis*, 227.
83. Eric Hobsbawm and Terence Ranger, eds., *The Invention of Tradition* (Cambridge: Cambridge University Press, 1983).
84. Ralph Linton's "Nativistic Movements," *American Anthropologist* 45 (1943): 230–40. Other literature on the issue includes F. Allen Hanson, "The Making of the Maori: Cultural Invention and Its Logic," *American Anthropologist* 91, no. 4 (1989): 890–901; Roger M. Keesing and Robert Tonkinson, ed., "Reinventing Traditional Culture: The Politics of Kastom in Island Melanesia, *Mankind* 13, no. 4 (1982); James West Turner, "Continuity and Constraint: Reconstructing the Concept of Tradition from a Pacific Perspective,"

Contemporary Pacific 9, no. 2 (1997): 345–81; Robert Borofsky, *Making History: Pukapukan and Anthropological Constructions of Knowledge* (New York: Cambridge University Press, 1987); Roger M. Keesing and Robert Tonkinson, eds., "Creating the Past: Custom and Identity in the Contemporary Pacific," *Contemporary Pacific* 1, nos. 1/2 (1989): 19–42; and several articles by Jocelyn Linnekin, including "Defining Tradition: Variation on the Hawaiian Identity," *American Ethnologist* 10 (1983): 241–52; "Cultural Invention and the Dilemma of Authenticity," *American Anthropologist* 93, no. 2 (1990): 446–49; "The Politics of Culture in the Pacific," in *Cultural Identity and Ethnicity in the Pacific*, ed. Jocelyn Linnekin and Lin Poyer (Honolulu: University of Hawai'i Press, 1990), 149–73; and "On the Theory and Politics of Cultural Construction in the Pacific," *Oceania* 62 (1992): 249–63. For more on the "invented identity" debate and the use of "native," see also Teresia K. Teaiwa, "Militarism, Tourism, and the Native: Articulations in Oceania" (PhD diss., University of California, Santa Cruz, 2001). For a recent summary and discussion of the issue, see Vicente M. Diaz, *Repositioning the Missionary: Rewriting the History of Colonialism, Native Catholicism, and Indigeneity in Guam* (Honolulu: University of Hawai'i Press, 2010), 21–23.

85. Womack, *Red on Red: Native American Indian Separatism*, 42.
86. Leroy Wesaw, "Changing Values in the Indian Culture," Native American Educational Services, Student Field Projects, box 1, folder 2, Special Collections Research Center, University of Chicago Library, 1.
87. Ibid., 20.
88. *Pokégnek Yajdanawa*, Pokagon Potawatomi Tribal Newsletter (Dowagiac, MI, January 2011), 3. As a resident of Chicago and a tribal member, I was present at the event and introduced the guests.
89. Quote taken from notes by the author while attending the event.

Chapter 6. Monuments, Memorials, and the Continued Presence of the Potawatomi in Chicago

1. Philip J. Deloria, *Indians in Unexpected Places* (Lawrence: University of Kansas Press, 2004), 50.
2. Rodman Wanamaker proposed building a "National American Indian Memorial," which would have been larger than the Statue of Liberty. Ground was broken in 1913, but construction never advanced beyond the preliminaries. "Ends Peace Trip to the Indians," *New York Times*, December 14, 1913.
3. Marion E. Gridley, *America's Indian Statues* (Chicago: Amerindian/Towertown Press, 1966), introduction. Many such monuments are identified in Gridley's book, which

purports to be "A comprehensive compilation of facts and photos of statues honoring or memorializing the American Indian."

4. I use the term as defined by the Convention on the Prevention and Punishment of the Crime of Genocide, Adopted by Resolution 260 (III) A of the U.N. General Assembly on 9 December 1948, Entry into force: 12 January 1951. Http://www.preventgenocide.org/law/convention/text.htm.
5. The idea that a text can also be a monument has support. James E. Young has noted the intersections between memory devices, such as books, memorials, and monuments. Young argues that many narratives serve as memorials. James E. Young, *The Texture of Memory: Holocaust, Memorials, and Meaning* (New Haven, CT: Yale University Press, 1994), 6–7.
6. Ruth B. Phillips, *Trading Identities: The Souvenir in Native North American Art from the Northeast, 1700–1900* (Seattle: University of Washington Press). Phillips astutely captured the importance and the irony of Native peoples using natural materials and Indigenous skills and technologies to create items of interest to tourists. Curios, made by Indians for the general non-Native tourist trade, sold at such places as Niagara Falls, Wisconsin Dells, Cherokee, North Carolina, and Taos, New Mexico, and any other tourist site where Indians could be found, were different from Simon Pokagon's birch bark booklets or his *Queen of the Woods* novel in that his were not anonymous.
7. Elmore Barce, *The Land of the Potawatomi, (by a) Member of Indiana Historical Society* (Fowler, IN: Benton Review, 1919), 10.
8. Patty Loew, *Indian Nations of Wisconsin: Histories of Endurance and Renewal* (Madison: Wisconsin Historical Society Press, 2001), 84. See also R. David Edmunds, *The Potawatomis: Keepers of the Fire* (Norman: University of Oklahoma Press, 1978), 1–2; and William Duncan Strong, *The Indian Tribes of the Chicago Region: With Special Reference to the Illinois and the Potawatomi*, leaflet 24 (Chicago: Field Museum of Natural History, 1926), 17.
9. Frances Densmore, *Chippewa Customs* (St. Paul: Minnesota Historical Society Press, 1979; first publication 1929 by the Smithsonian Institution Bureau of American Ethnology as Bulletin 86), 40, 125, 149–54; plates 30, 46, 64, 162. In the 1960s amateur ethnologist Fred K. Blessing also documented and cataloged the many uses of birch bark by the Ojibwe of Minnesota and Wisconsin, including baby carriers, birdhouses, buckets for maple sap gathering, brimmed caps, cones for candy, drinking cups, curing rattles, torches, canoes, and housing. Fred K. Blessing Jr., *The Ojibway Indians Observed: Papers of Fred K. Blessing, Jr., on the Ojibway Indians from the* Minnesota Archaeologist (St. Paul: Minnesota Archaeological Society, 1977). See also Frances Densmore, "Uses of Plants by

the Chippewa Indians," in *Forty-fourth Annual Report of the Bureau of American Ethnology to the Secretary of the Smithsonian Institution, 1926–1927* (Washington, DC: Government Printing Office, 1928), 387–97.

10. B. O. Flowers, "An Interesting Representative of a Vanishing Race," *The Arena* 16 (1896): 244, reprinting the preface to *The Red Man's Greeting*. The preface is also reprinted in Simon Pokagon, *O-GÎ-MÄW-KWÈ MIT-Î-GWÄ-KÎ (Queen of the Woods), Also a Brief Sketch of the Algaic Language* (Hartford, MI: C.H. Engle, 1899, 1901), appendix, 253.
11. Pokagon, *O-GÎ-MÄW-KWÈ MIT-Î-GWÄ-KÎ (Queen of the Woods)*, 251.
12. Melea Powell, "Rhetorics of Survivance: How Americans Use Writing," *College Composition and Communication* 53, no. 3 (February 2002): 396–434.
13. Philip J. Deloria, *Playing Indian* (New Haven, CT: Yale University Press, 1999).
14. Therese O. Deming and Edwin W. Deming, *Indians of the Wigwams: A Story of Indian Life* (Chicago: Junior Press Books/Albert Whitman & Co., 1938).
15. Another example is Mary Catherine Judd, *Wigwam Stories* (Boston: Ginn & Co., 1917).
16. Captain O. W. Roland, *A History of Van Buren County Michigan: A Narrative Account of Its Historical Progress, Its People, and Its Principal Interests*, vol. 1 (Chicago: Lewis Publishing Company, 1912), 1–52, 12.
17. Edward B. Clark, "Indian Encampment at Lincoln Park, Chicago, Sept. 26 to Oct. 1 1903," in *In Honor of the City's Centennial Anniversary* (Chicago: Chicago Centennial Committee, 1903), 4.
18. Edward Livingston Taylor, "Monuments to Historical Indian Chiefs," *Ohio Archaeological and Historical Publications*, vol. 11 (Columbus: Ohio Archaeological and Historical Society/Fred J. Heer, 1903), 1–31; Pokagon, *Queen of the Woods*, 232.
19. Pokagon, *Queen of the Woods*, 233.
20. Taylor, "Monuments to Historical Indian Chiefs," 29.
21. Everett Claspy, *The Potawatomi Indians of Southwestern Michigan* (Ann Arbor, MI: Braun-Brumfield, Inc., 1966), 29.
22. Cecilia Bain Buechner, "The Pokagons," (*Indianapolis*) *Indiana Historical Society Publications* 10, no. 5 (1933): 327.
23. Cornelia Steketee Hulst, *Indian Sketches: Père Marquette and the Last of the Pottawatomie Chiefs* (New York: Longmans, Green and Co., 1912), 73, 76.
24. Gridley, *America's Indian Statues*, 23.
25. Ibid., 74.
26. Pokagon, *Queen of the Woods*, 13.
27. Daniel McDonald, *Removal of the Pottawattomie Indians from Northern Indiana* (Plymouth, IN, D. McDonald & Co., 1899).

28. A copy of the program is available at http://www.potawatomi-tda.org/indiana/chiefms.htm. McDonald, a representative in the Indiana legislature, delivered a speech promoting a bill to erect a monument to the Twin Lakes Potawatomi, on February 3, 1905. The monument was ultimately erected by the state and became the first monument to an Indian to be paid for by state funds. George S. Cottman, ed., "Address of the Pottawattomie Indians," (*Indianapolis*) *Indiana Quarterly Magazine of History* 1 (1905): 160–61.
29. "The Legacy of Daniel McDonald," *Culver through the Years*, http://www.culver.lib.in.us/daniel_mcdonald.htm#indians; "The First of Its Kind, Pottawattomie Monument at Twin Lakes Holds Unique Position in Country," *Culver Citizen*, September 9, 1909, 1.
30. Hulst, *Indian Sketches: Père Marquette and the Last of the Pottawatomie Chiefs*, 88. Some of the publicity surrounding the installation of the *tipi* in Ypsilanti from the local press includes the following: "Get the Spirit, Get a Tag and Help Buy Pokagon's Wigwam," *Normal News*, May 25, 1911, 5; "Indian Tepee to be Dedicated Next Week on Normal Campus," *Ypsilanti Daily Press*, June 10, 1911, 1; "Dedicate Birch Wigwam, Granddaughter of Pottawatomie Chief in Costume Will Officiate—Tepee to Remain on Campus as Permanent Feature," *Normal News*, June 15, 1911, 1; "Tepee Dedicated with Fitting Exercises on the Normal Campus Thursday," *Ypsilanti Daily Press*, June 16, 1911, 1.
31. Roland, *A History of Van Buren County Michigan*, 12. A slightly different version of the address that appears to be a copy of the original typed speech is available from the Special Collections, Eastern Michigan University Library, Simon Pokagon folder, Ypsilanti, Michigan.
32. John N. Low, Personal journal, entry for September 18, 2009.
33. *Program, Chief Shipshewana Day, Shipshewana Lake, Saturday, May 30, 1931* (Shipshewana, IN: Shipshewana Chamber of Commerce, 1931), 8–9.
34. Ibid., 3.
35. Potawatomi Indian Statue, http://www.idaillinois.org/cdm/fullbrowser/collection/stc/id/1148/rv/compoundobject/cpd/1202.
36. Dorothy DeWitte, "Ten Years Later, 'Ekwabet' Still Watches over St. Charles," *St. Charles Republican*, November 19, 1998, 7.
37. Richard E. (Mike) and Rachel (Rae) Daugherty were present at the dedication in 1988 and were consulted by the sculptor, according to their son, Kevin Daugherty. Kevin Daugherty, telephone interview by author, January 12, 2010.
38. Black Partridge was a Peoria Lake (Illinois) Potawatomi leader, also known as Mucketeypokee, Mucktypoke, Mka-da-puk-ke, Muccutay Penay, Makadebakii, and Mkadébk. Born around 1795, he died sometime around 1816. Edward Sylvester Ellis, *Black*

Partridge, Or, The Fall of Fort Dearborn (New York: E.P. Dutton, 1906).

39. Gridley, *America's Indian Statues*, 101.
40. "Marked by a Statue," *Chicago Daily Tribune*, December 18, 1892.
41. Juliette Augusta (Mrs. John H.) Kinzie, *Wau-bun: The Early Days in the North-West* (Chicago: Derby & Jackson, 1856); Juliette Augusta Kinzie, *Narrative of the Massacre at Chicago*, reprint (1844; New York: Garland Publishing, 1977), 16.
42. James A. Clifton, *The Pokagons, 1683–1983: Catholic Potawatomi Indians of the St. Joseph River Valley* (Lanham, MD: University Press of America, 1984), 38.
43. Jerry Crimmins, *Fort Dearborn* (Evanston: Northwestern University Press, 2006), 59.
44. The details surrounding the circumstances and nature of the so-called "Fort Dearborn Massacre," as it came to be known, appear to have been substantially supported by the literature and histories being written in the late nineteenth century, including Mrs. John Kinzie's *Narrative of the Massacre at Chicago, August 15, 1812 and of Preceding Events* (1844), and *Wau-Bun: The Early Days in the Northwest* (1873); Joseph Kirkland's *The Chicago Massacre of 1812* (1893); and *Heroes and Heroines of the Fort Dearborn Massacre: A Romantic and Tragic History of Corporal John Simmons and His Heroic Wife*, by Noah Simmons (1896).
45. Milo M. Quaife, *Chicago and the Old Northwest, 1673–1835* (Chicago: University of Chicago Press, 1913); Quaife, "The Fort Dearborn Massacre," *Mississippi Valley Historical Review* 1, no. 4 (March 1915): 566–70.
46. Simon Pokagon, "The Massacre of Fort Dearborn at Chicago: Gathered from the Traditions of the Indian Tribes Engaged in the Massacre, and from the Published Accounts," *Harpers New Monthly Magazine* 98, no. 586 (March 1899): 649–56. It should be noted that the title of the article and the reference to "massacre" may have been the doing of the editor of the magazine rather than the choice of Pokagon. See also Ann Durkin Keating, "Fort Dearborn," *Encyclopedia of Chicago*, http://www.encyclopedia.chicagohistory.org/pages/477.html.
47. Geoffrey Johnson, "The True Story of the Deadly Encounter at Fort Dearborn," *Chicago Magazine*, January 4, 2010, http://www.chicagomag.com/Chicago-Magazine/December-2009/The-True-Story-of-the-Deadly-Encounter-at-Fort-Dearborn.
48. "Fort Dearborn Massacre from an Indian's Point of View," *Chicago Daily Tribune*, Feb 7, 1897, 9.
49. "Fort Dearborn Massacre from an Indian's Point of View," *Chicago Daily Tribune*, Feb 7, 1897, 37. See also "The Massacre at Chicago," *Frank Leslie's Popular Monthly* (Frank Leslie's Publishing House, New York) vol. 10 (July–December 1880): 189–92.
50. Milo M. Quaife, *Checagou: From Indian Wigwam to Modern City, 1673–1835* (Chicago:

University of Chicago Press, 1933), 116–34. See also Lieutenant Linai T. Helm, *The Fort Dearborn Massacre with Letters and Narratives of Contemporary Interest*, ed. Nellie Kinzie Gordon (New York: Rand, McNally & Co., 1912).

51. Quaife, *Checagou, 1673–1835*, 112. Similar examples of the casting of the Potawatomi as savages and villains are in Noble Canby, "Chicago of To-Day," *The Chautauquan* (Meadville, PA: T. L. Flood Publishing, 1892), 324; *The Story of Old Fort Dearborn and Its Connection with A Century of Progress International Exposition* (Chicago: Committee on "History of a Century of Progress," 1933).
52. Flowers, "An Interesting Representative of a Vanishing Race," 240–50, 240.
53. Ibid., 242. The ostentatious and conspicuous consumption of the era is well documented by the satirist Thorstein Veblen, *The Theory of the Leisure Class* (1899; New York: Dover Publications, 1994).
54. Deanna Isaacs, "Blood on the Ground/Investing in the Future:, Neighbors Who Want the Fort Dearborn Massacre Monument Returned to Its Site Are Likely to Face a Battle." *Chicago Reader*, March 22, 2007, http://www.chicagoreader.com/chicago/blood-on-the-groundinvesting-in-the-future/Content?oid=924564.
55. "No 'Massacre' Fort Dearborn Historian Says," *Chicago Daily Tribune*, July 6, 1943, 24.
56. As a Potawatomi tribal member living in Chicago, the American Indian Center consulted me concerning my opinions on both issues.
57. Barce, *The Land of the Potawatomi*, 71.
58. Robert Loerzel, "Returning to Battle of Ft. Dearborn in the Name of a Park," July 31, 2009, broadcast, WBEZ 91.5, http://www.wbez.org/episode-segments/returning-battle-ft-dearborn-name-park.
59. Miriam Y. Cintrón, "One Final Battle Resolved at Fort Dearborn Park," (*Chicago*) *Gazette*, September 4, 2009, http://www.gazettechicago.com/index/2009/09/one-final-battle-resolved-at-fort-dearborn-park.
60. Remarks by Roger Williams to the author prior to the Battle of Fort Dearborn Park dedication.
61. "Fort Dearborn in Chicago History, part 2," http://examiner.com/historic-places-in-chicago/fort-dearborn-chicago-history-pt-2-the-murders-at-the-lee-farm-a-portent-to-the-massacre; Johnson, "The True Story of the Deadly Encounter at Fort Dearborn"; Loerzel, "Returning to Battle of Ft. Dearborn in the Name of a Park"; Ron Grossman, "Site of Chicago's Ft. Dearborn Massacre to Be Called 'Battle of Ft. Dearborn Park,' Chicago Park District Braved Skirmishes of Its Own over the Name," *Chicago Tribune*, August 14, 2009.
62. "Chicago Park Where Ft. Dearborn Massacre Occurred to Be Renamed 'Battle of Ft.

Dearborn Park,'" *Newsfornatives.com*, http://newsfornatives.com/blog/chicago-park-where-ft-dearborn-massacre-occurred-to-be-renamed-battle-of-ft-dearborn-park/.

63. Cintrón, "One Final Battle Resolved at Fort Dearborn Park."
64. Johnson, "The True Story of the Deadly Encounter at Fort Dearborn."
65. Grossman, "Site of Chicago's Ft. Dearborn Massacre to Be Called 'Battle of Ft. Dearborn Park.'"
66. In a recent manuscript about the battle, author Gillum Ferguson chooses to continue using "massacre."
67. A recent book also criticizes the "renaming" as an act of forgetting the truth in favor of multiculturalism. See Robert K. Engler, *Monarchs of August* (Des Plaines, IL: Alphabeta Press, 2011), 153–54: "By doubting the value of American civilization, they doubt American history. In short, for the sake of politics, they forget. . . . When a nation no longer agrees on its history, then we must agree it is less than a nation."
68. Lindsay Prossnitz, "Bicentennial of Battle of Fort Dearborn," *Chicago Tonight*, August 15, 2012, http://chicagotonight.wttw.com/2012/08/15/bicentennial-battle-fort-dearborn.
69. John Kass, "Statue—and Controversy—under Wraps, Mission to Bring Fort Dearborn Massacre Bronze out of Storage Means Taking on Political Correctness Brigade," *Chicago Tribune*, August 12, 2012, 2.
70. Ann Durkin Keating, *Rising up from Indian Country: The Battle of Fort Dearborn and the Birth of Chicago* (Chicago: University of Chicago Press, 2012), 238–44.
71. For an overview of the difficulty in writing exhibit labels that effectively communicate information to an audience, see Stephen Bitgood, "The Role of Attention in Designing Effective Interpretive Labels," *Journal of Interpretation Research* 5, no. 2 (2003): 31–45.
72. Heid Erdrich, *National Monuments* (East Lansing: Michigan State University Press, 2008).
73. Letter from museum director Jane Edwards to Basket Co-op member Rae Daugherty arranging a basket-making demonstration and sale, December 5, 1990; "Chicago Botanic Garden's Basketry Symposium," September 9–13, 1985, flyer, Michael B. Williams Papers, Dowagiac, MI. Jason S. Wesaw, also a Pokagon Potawatomi tribal member, exhibited at the Mitchell Museum in 2005, and his pottery has often been for sale in the museum's gift shop. Mitchell Museum of the American Indian archives, Evanston, IL.
74. Bernd Peyer, *The Thinking Indian: Native American Writers, 1850s–1920s* (Frankfurt: Peter Lang, 2007), 148. As the dean of the Chicago campus of Native American Education Service College (NAES) at the time and a tribal member, I had the opportunity to participate in the event.
75. Peyer, *The Thinking Indian*, 148.
76. Lauren Weinberg, "Lake Shore Thrives," *Time Out Chicago*, July 23–29, 2009, 42.

77. Clare Lane, "Vast Mural to Depict City's Indian Roots," *Chicago Tribune*, June 5, 2009, section 4, p. 2.
78. Chiraq Patel, "Native Americans Celebrated at Foster Underpass Mural," *Uptown Exchange*, November 2009, 10. As executive director of the Mitchell Museum in 2009, I was consulted on certain design aspects.
79. Lane, "Vast Mural to Depict City's Indian Roots," 2.
80. Weinberg, "Lake Shore Thrives," 42; Patel, "Native Americans Celebrated at Foster Underpass Mural," 10; Lane, "Vast Mural to Depict City's Indian Roots," 2.
81. Weinberg, "Lake Shore Thrives," 42.
82. Patel, "Native Americans Celebrated at Foster Underpass Mural," 10.
83. Discussed in greater depth in the next chapter.
84. Newberry Library, "Frontier to Heartland," curated by Tobias Higbie, Associate Professor of History, University of California Los Angeles, available at http://publications.newberry.org/frontiertoheartland/exhibits/show/perspectives/fourcenturies/introduction.
85. That relationship is akin to those peoples around the world who also believe in the spiritual and restorative properties of water, at such places as Lourdes, Mecca, and the Ganges River.

Appendix 4. Timeline of the 1812 Battle of Fort Dearborn

1. James A. Clifton, *The Pokagons, 1683–1983: Catholic Potawatomi Indians of the St. Joseph River Valley* (Lanham, MD: University Press of America, 1984), 38.
2. Jerry Crimmins, *Fort Dearborn* (Evanston, IL: Northwestern University Press, 2006), 59.
3. Randall Parrish, *When Wilderness Was King: A Tale of the Illinois Country* (Chicago: A.C. McClurg & Co., 1904), 186.
4. "The Massacre at Chicago," *Frank Leslie's Popular Monthly* (Frank Leslie's Publishing House, New York), vol. 10 (July–December 1880): 189–92.
5. Milo M. Quaife, *Checagou, 1673–1835* (Chicago: University of Chicago Press, 1933), 116–34; Lieutenant Linai T. Helm, *The Fort Dearborn Massacre with Letters and Narratives of Contemporary Interest*, ed. Nellie Kinzie Gordon (New York: Rand, McNally & Co., 1912).

Bibliography

Archives

Angola Public Library, Special Collections, Angola, Indiana.

Central Michigan University, Clarke Historical Library, Mt. Pleasant, Michigan.

Chicago History Museum, Research Center, Chicago, Illinois.

Harold Washington Library Center/Chicago Public Library, Special Collections and Preservation Division, Chicago, Illinois.

Michael B. Williams Papers, Dowagiac, Michigan.

National Archives and Records Administration (NARA), Great Lakes Branch, Chicago, Illinois.

Newberry Library, Edward E. Ayer Collection, Chicago, Illinois.

University of Chicago, The Joseph Regenstein Library, Special Collections and Research Center, Chicago, Illinois.

University of Michigan, Special Collections/Harlan Hatcher Graduate Library, Ann Arbor, Michigan.

Western Michigan University, Waldo Library, Special Collections and Rare Books, Kalamazoo, Michigan.

Publications

Achilles, Rolf. *Pride of Place: The Streeterville Story.* Chicago: SOAR, 2005.

Adam, S. K. *Extinction or Survival? The Remarkable Story of the Tigua, an Urban American Indian Tribe.* Boulder, CO: Paradigm Publishers, 2009.

Albers, Patricia, and Jeanne Kay. "Sharing the Land: A Study in American Indian Territoriality." In *A Cultural Geography of North American Indians*, ed. Thomas E. Ross and Tyrel G. Moore, 47–91. Boulder, CO: Westview Press, 1987.

Algren, Nelson. *Chicago: City on the Make.* Chicago: University of Chicago Press, 2001.

Andreas, A. T. *History of Chicago from the Earliest Period to the Present Time.* Chicago, 1884.

Anzaldúa, Gloria. *Borderlands/La Frontera: The New Mestiza.* San Francisco: Aunt Lute Books, 1987.

Armstrong, P. A. *Shabbona Memorial Association Appeal.* Chicago History Museum Archives, Shabbona Memorial Association Appeal Folder.

Aron, Stephen. "Pioneers and Profiteers: Land Speculation and the Homestead Ethic in Frontier Kentucky." *Western Historical Quarterly* 23, no. 2 (1992): 179–98.

Assmann, Jan. *Religion and Cultural Memory: Ten Studies.* Stanford, CA: Stanford University Press, 2005.

Bach, Ira J., and Mary Lackritz Gray. *A Guide to Chicago's Public Sculpture.* Chicago: University of Chicago Press, 1983.

Ballard, Everett Guy. *Captain Streeter, Pioneer.* Chicago: Emery Publishing Service, 1914.

Barce, Elmore. *The Land of the Potawatomi, (by a) Member of Indiana Historical Society.* Fowler, IN: Benton Review, 1919.

Barr, Juliana. "Geographies of Power: Mapping Indian Borders in the 'Borderlands' of the Early Southwest." *William and Mary Quarterly*, 3rd ser., 68, no. 1 (January 2011): 5–46.

Basso, Keith H. *Wisdom Sits in Places: Landscape and Language among the Western Apache.* Albuquerque: University of New Mexico Press, 1996.

Beck, David R. M. "The Chicago American Indian Community: An 'Invisible' Minority." In *Beyond Black and White: New Voices, New Faces in United States Schools*, ed. Maxine S. Seller and Lois Weis. Albany, NY: SUNY Press, 1997.

———. "Chronological Index of Community History—Chicago." In *Indians of the Chicago Area*, ed. Terry Straus. Chicago: NAES College Press, 1989.

———. "Developing a Voice: The Evolution of Self-Determination in an Urban Indian Community." *Wicazo Sa Review* 17, no. 2 (2002): 117–41.

———."Native American Education in Chicago: Teach Them the Truth." *Education and Urban Society* 32, no. 2, 237–55 (February 2000).

Beck, David R. M., and Rosalyn LaPier. "Crossroads for a Culture: American Indians in Progressive Era Chicago." *Chicago History* 38, no. 1 (Spring 2012): 22–43.

Becker, Michael, and George W. Wilson. "Tribal Leaders Seek to Maintain Traditional

Potawatomi Skills." *South Bend Tribune*, September 29, 1985, 3.

Bederman, Gail. *Manliness and Civilization*. Chicago: University of Chicago Press, 1995.

Behne, C. Ted. "The Birchbark Canoe: Back from the Brink." *Native Peoples Magazine* (July/August 2001): 53–54.

Benjamin, Walter. "Unpacking My Library." In *Illuminations, Essays and Reflections*, ed. Hannah Arendt. New York: Schocken Books, 1968.

Benton-Banai, Edward. *The Mishomis Book: The Voice of the Ojibway*. Haywood, WI: Indian Country Communications, Inc., 1988.

Bergstrom, Edward. "Cap Streeter: Squatter King." *Tradition* 4, no. 10 (1961): 23–31.

Berkhofer, Robert F. *The White Man's Indian: Images of the American Indian from Columbus to the Present.* New York: Random House, 1978.

Berlo, Janet C., and Ruth B. Phillips. "Our (Museum) World Turned Upside Down: Re-presenting Native American Arts." *Art Bulletin* 77, no. 1 (1995): 6–10.

Bielski, Ursula. *More Chicago Haunts: Scenes from Myth and Memory*. Chicago: Lake Claremont Press, 2000.

Bitgood, Stephen. "The Role of Attention in Designing Effective Interpretive Labels." *Journal of Interpretation Research* 5, no. 2 (2003): 31–45.

Blackbird, Andrew J. *History of the Ottawa and Chippewa Indians of Michigan: A Grammar of Their Language, and Personal and Family History*. Ypsilanti, MI: Ypsilanti Job Printing House, 1887.

Black Elk, Nicholas (author), John G. Neihardt (collaborator). *Black Elk Speaks: Being the Life Story of a Holy Man of the Oglala Sioux*. 3rd. ed. 1932; Lincoln: University of Nebraska Press, 2004.

Blessing, Fred K., Jr. *The Ojibway Indians Observed: Papers of Fred K. Blessing, Jr., on the Ojibway Indians from the Minnesota Archaeologist.* St. Paul: Minnesota Archaeological Society, 1977.

Blevins, Win. *The Dictionary of the American West.* College Station, TX: Texas A&M University Press, 2008.

Bollwerk, Elizabeth. "Controlling Acculturation: A Potawatomi Strategy for Avoiding Removal." *Midcontinental Journal of Archaeology* 31, no. 1 (Spring 2006): 117–41.

Borofsky, Robert. *Making History: Pukapukan and Anthropological Constructions of Knowledge.* New York: Cambridge University Press, 1987.

Bradley, Richard. *An Archaeology of Natural Places.* New York: Routledge, 2000.

Brodeur, Paul. *Restitution: The Land Claims of the Mashpee, Passamaquoddy, and Penobscot Indians of New England.* Boston: Northeastern University Press, 1985.

Bromley, Nicholas K. *Law, Space, and the Geographies of Power*. New York: Guilford Press, 1994.

Bronte, Patricia. *Vittles and Vice*. Chicago: Henry Regency Co., 1952.

Broomell, Kenneth F., and Harlow M. Church. "Streeterville Saga." *Journal of the Illinois State Historical Society* 33, no. 2 (June 1940): 153–65.

Brown, Robert Maxwell. "Backcountry Rebellions and the Homestead Ethic in America, 1740–1799." In *Tradition, Conflict, and Modernization: Perspectives on the American Revolution*, ed. Robert Maxwell Brown and Don E. Fehrenbacher, 73–98. New York: Academic Press, 1977.

Buchli, Victor, ed. *The Material Culture Reader*. Oxford: Berg, 2002.

Buechner, Cecilia Bain. "The Pokagons." (*Indianapolis*) *Indiana Historical Society Publications* 10, no. 5 (1933): 327.

Burbank, E. A. *Burbank among the Indians: As Told by Ernest Royce*. New York: Caxton Printers, 1944.

Callary, Edward. *Place Names of Illinois*. Urbana: University of Illinois Press, 2008.

Calloway, Colin G. *One Vast Winter Count: The Native American West before Lewis and Clark*. Lincoln: University of Nebraska Press, 2003.

Canadian Museum of Civilization. "Wave Eaters: Native Watercraft in Canada." Canadian Museum of Civilization, Gatineau, Quebec, Canada. Http://www. civilization.ca/aborig/watercraft/wainteng.html.

Canby, Noble. "Chicago of To-Day." *Chautauquan* 15 (April–September 1892): 323–29.

Capetillo-Ponce, Jorge. "Exploring Gloria Anzaldúa's Methodology in *Borderlands/La Frontera—The New Mestiza*." *Human Architecture: Journal of the Sociology of Self-Knowledge* 3, special issue (Summer 2006).

"Captain George Wellington Streeter." Editorial. *Journal of the Illinois Historical Society* 13, no. 4 (January 1922): 571–74.

"Captain George Wellington Streeter, Battling Hero of the 'Deestrick of Lake Michigan.'" *Journal of the Illinois State Historical Society* 13, no. 4 (January 1921): 571–74.

Carson, James Taylor. "Ethnogeography and the Native American Past." *Ethnohistory* 49 (Fall 2002): 769–88.

César's Bark Canoe. Directed by Bernard Gosselin. VHS. Montreal: National Film Board of Canada, 1971.

Chicago History Society. "Official Chicago-Day Program." Display ad. *Chicago Daily Tribune*, October 9, 1893, 1. Http://www.chicagohs.org/history/expo.html.

Chicago: Souvenir of Chicago in Colors. 1892; Chicago: V.O. Hammon Publishing Co., 1908.

Cintrón, Miriam Y. "One Final Battle Resolved at Fort Dearborn Park." (*Chicago*) *Gazette*, September 4, 2009. Http://www.gazettechicago.com/index/2009/09/one-final-battle-resolved-at-fort-dearborn-park.

Citizen Band of Potawatomi Indians v. United States, Docket 71, et al., 27 Ind. Cl. Comm. 187 (1972).

"Claims of J. B. Shipman and J. Critcher for Legal Services to the Pokagon Potawatomi." NARA microfilm roll 80, Office of Indian Affairs (OIA) Special Files. National Archives and Records Administration, Great Lakes Region, Chicago, IL.

Clark, Edward B. "The Amazing History of the Streeterville War." *Women's Home Companion* 29, no. 12 (1902).

———. *Indian Encampment at Lincoln Park, Chicago, Sept. 26 to Oct. 1 1903: In Honor of the City's Centennial Anniversary*. Chicago: Chicago Centennial Committee, 1903.

Claspy, Everett. *The Dowagiac–Sister Lakes Resort Area and More about Its Potawatomi Indians*. Dowagiac, MI: Self-published, 1970.

———. *The Potawatomi Indians of Southwestern Michigan*. Ann Arbor, MI: Braun-Brumfield, Inc., 1966.

Cleland, Charles E. *Rites of Conquest: The History and Culture of Michigan's Native Americans*. Ann Arbor: University of Michigan Press, 1992.

Clifton, James A. "Chicago, September 14, 1833: The Last Great Indian Treaty in the Old Northwest." *Chicago History* 9, no. 2 (Summer 1980): 86–97.

———. "Chicago Was Theirs." *Chicago History* 1, no. 1 (Spring 1970): 4–17.

———. "Leopold Pokagon: Transformative Leadership on the St. Joseph River Frontier." *Michigan History* 69, no. 5 (September/October 1985): 16–23.

———. *The Pokagons, 1683–1983: Catholic Potawatomi Indians of the St. Joseph River Valley*. Lanham, MD: University Press of America, 1984.

———. *The Potawatomi*. New York: Chelsea House Publishers, 1987.

———. *The Prairie People: Continuity and Change in Potawatomi Indian Culture, 1665–1965*. Iowa City: University of Iowa Press, 1998.

———. "Simon Pokagon's Sandbar: Potawatomi Claims to Chicago's Lakefront." *Michigan History* 71, no. 5 (September/October 1987): 12–17.

Clifton, James A., George L. Cornell, and James M. McClurken. *People of the Three Fires: The Ottawa, Potawatomi, and Ojibway of Michigan*. Grand Rapids: Michigan Indian Press, 1986.

Cohn, Scotti. "The Captain's War." In *It Happened in Chicago*, 66–70. Guilford, CT: Morris Book Publishing, 2009.

Colwell-Chanthaphonh, Chip, and J. Brett Hill. "Mapping History: Cartography and the Construction of the San Pedro Valley." *History and Anthropology* 15 (2004): 175–200.

Connerton, Paul. *How Societies Remember*. New York: Cambridge University Press, 2004.

Cook, James W. *The Arts of Deception: Playing with Fraud in the Age of Barnum*. Cambridge,

MA: Harvard University Press, 2001.

Coombes, Annie E. "Museums and the Formation of National and Cultural Identities." *Oxford Art Journal* 11, no. 2 (1988): 57–68.

Cottman, George S., ed. "Address of the Pottawattomie Indians." (*Indianapolis*) *Indiana Quarterly Magazine of History* 1 (1905): 160–61.

Covert, Ralph, and Griley Mills. *Streeterville: A Play*. March 18, 2001. Http://www.waterdogmusic.com/ralphcovert/streeterville.html.

Coward, John M. *The Newspaper Indian: Native American Identity in the Press, 1820–90.* Urbana: University of Illinois Press, 1999.

Cox, W. H., and W. E. Johnson. *The Greatest Conspiracy Ever Conceived, By any class of human beings in this Conspiracy, by a class of people who are devising by every way and means illegal and unjust to rob the legal owners of their Chicago Lake Front Lands and of their title and rights to quiet possession secured to them by treaty with the United States.* Chicago, December 1908.

Crane, Susan A. "Writing the Individual Back into Collective Memory." *American Historical Review* 102, no. 5 (December 1997): 1372–85.

Crimmins, Jerry. *Fort Dearborn*. Evanston, IL: Northwestern University Press, 2006.

Cronon, William. *Nature's Metropolis: Chicago and the Great West.* New York: W.W. Norton, 1992.

Cumming, John. "Pokagon's Birch Bark Books." *American Book Collector* (ed. William B. Thorsen) 18, no. 8 (1968): 14–17.

Cunningham, Lawrence J., Ward Kranz, and Manny Sikau. "Restoring Traditional Seafaring and Navigation in Guam." *Micronesian Journal of the Humanities and Social Sciences* 5, no. 1/2 (November 2006).

DA-MACK (John D. Williams). *The American Indian and His Origin*. Benton Harbor, MI: C.A. Spradling, Pub., 1933.

Dana-Sacco, Gail. "The Indigenous Researcher as Individual and Collective: Building a Research Practice Ethic within the Context of Indigenous Languages." *American Indian Quarterly* 34, no. 16 (Winter 2010): 61–82.

Danckers, Ulrich, Jane Meredith, and John F. Swenson. *A Compendium of the Early History of Chicago to the Year 1835 When the Indians Left.* River Forest, IL: Early Chicago, Inc., 1999.

Danzinger, Edmund. *Survival and Regeneration: Detroit's American Indian Community*. Detroit: Wayne State University Press, 1991.

de la Harpe, Bénard. "Account of the Journey of Bénard de la Harpe: Discovery Made by Him of Several Nations Situated in the West." Translated and edited by Ralph A. Smith. *Southwestern Historical Quarterly* 62 (October 1958).

Deloria, Philip J. "From Nation to Neighborhood: Land, Policy, Culture, Colonialism, and Empire in U.S.-Indian Relations." In *The Cultural Turn in U.S. History*, ed. James W. Cook, Lawrence B. Glickman, and Michael O'Malley. Chicago: University of Chicago Press, 2008.

———. *Indians in Unexpected Places.* Lawrence: University Press of Kansas, 2004.

———. *Playing Indian.* New Haven: Yale University Press, 1999.

Deloria, Vine, Jr. "The Indians." In *Buffalo Bill and the Wild West*, ed. David H. Katzive et al., 56–58. New York: Brooklyn Museum, 1981.

Deming, Therese O., and Edwin W. Deming. *Indians of the Wigwams: A Story of Indian Life.* Chicago: Junior Press Books/Albert Whitman & Co., 1938.

Densmore, Frances. *Chippewa Customs.* St. Paul: Minnesota Historical Society Press, 1979. First published 1929 by the Smithsonian Institution Bureau of American Ethnology as *Bulletin 86*, 149–54.

———. "Uses of Plants by the Chippewa Indians." *Forty-fourth Annual Report of the Bureau of American Ethnology to the Secretary of the Smithsonian Institution, 1926–1927.* Washington, DC: Government Printing Office, 1928.

Denzin, Norman K. *Handbook of Critical and Indigenous Methodologies.* Thousand Oaks, CA: Sage Publications, 2008.

De Vorsey, Louis Jr. "Silent Witnesses: Native American Maps." *Georgia Review* 56 (Winter 1992): 709–26.

DeWitte, Dorothy. "Ten Years Later, 'Ekwabet' Still Watches over St. Charles." *St. Charles Republican*, November 19, 1998, 7.

Diaz, Vicente M. *Repositioning the Missionary: Rewriting the Histories of Colonialism, Native Catholicism, and Indigeneity in Guam.* Honolulu: University of Hawai'i Press, 2010.

Dickason, David A. "Chief Simon Pokagon: The Indian Longfellow." *Indiana Magazine of History* 57 (June 1961): 127–40.

Domosh, Mona. "A 'Civilized' Commerce: Gender, 'Race,' and Empire at the 1893 Chicago Exposition." *Cultural Geographies* 9, no. 2 (2002): 181–201.

Dowd, Gregory E. *A Spirited Resistance: The North American Indian Struggle for Unity, 1745–1815.* Baltimore: Johns Hopkins University Press, 1993.

———. *War under Heaven: Pontiac, the Indian Nations, and the British Empire.* Baltimore: Johns Hopkins University Press, 2004.

Durham, Meenakshi Gigi, and Douglas M. Kellner, ed. *Media and Cultural Studies: KeyWorks.* Rev. ed. Malden, MA: Blackwell-Wiley, 2006.

Durkheim, Emile. "The Cultural Logic of Collective Representations." In *Social Theory: The Multicultural, Global, and Classic Readings*, ed. C. Lemert. Boulder, CO: Westview Press,

2010.

Dybwad, G. L., and Joy V. Bliss. *Chicago Day at the World's Columbian Exposition: Illustrated with Candid Photographs.* Albuquerque: The Book Stops Here, 1997.

Edgar, Blake. "The Polynesian Connection." *Archaeology* 58, no. 2 (March/April 2005): 42–45.

Edmunds, R. David. *Kinsmen through Time: An Annotated Bibliography of Potawatomi History.* Metuchen, NJ: Scarecrow Press, 1987.

———. *The Potawatomis: Keepers of the Fire.* Norman: University of Oklahoma Press, 1978.

Edwards, Mrs. L. *My Twenty Years Experience in Streeterville District of Lake Michigan.* Chicago?: N.p., ca. 1940.

Ellis, Edward Sylvester. *Black Partridge, Or, The Fall of Fort Dearborn.* New York: E.P. Dutton, 1906.

"Ends Peace Trip to the Indians." *New York Times*, December 14, 1913.

Engle, C. H. *Indian Drama . . . "Queen of the Woods."* Dramatized and published by C. H. Engle. Hartford, MI: Day Spring Power Presses, 1904.

Engler, Robert K. *Monarchs of August.* Des Plaines, IL: Alphabeta Press, 2011.

Erdrich, Heid. *National Monuments.* East Lansing: Michigan State University Press, 2008.

Ethridge, Robbie, and Sheri M. Shuck-Hal, eds. *Mapping the Mississippian Shatter Zone: The Colonial Indian Slave Trade and Regional Instability in the American South.* Lincoln: University of Nebraska Press, 2009.

Ewers, John C. "The Making and Uses of Maps by Plains Indian Warriors." In *Plains Indian History and Culture: Essays on Continuity and Change*, 180–90. Norman: University of Oklahoma Press, 1997.

Fernández-Armesto, Felipe. *The Americas: A Hemispheric History.* New York: Modern Library, 2003.

Finney, Ben R. *Sailing in the Wake of the Ancestors.* Honolulu: Bishop Museum Press, 2003.

Fixico, Donald L. "The Relocation Program and Urbanization." In *Indians of the Chicago Area*, ed. Terry Straus. Chicago: NAES College Press, 1989.

———. *Termination and Relocation: Federal Indian Policy, 1945–1960.* Albuquerque: University of New Mexico Press, 1990.

———. *The Urban Indian Experience in America.* Albuquerque: University of New Mexico Press, 2000.

———. *Urban Indians.* New York: Chelsea House, 1991.

Fleitz, David L. *Cap Anson: The Grand Old Man of Baseball.* Jefferson, NC: McFarland and Co., 2005.

Flowers, B. O. "An Interesting Representative of a Vanishing Race." *The Arena* 16 (1896): 240–50.

Fogelson, Raymond. "The Red Man in the White City." In *Columbian Consequences: The Spanish Borderlands in Pan-American Perspective*, ed. David Hurst Thomas, chap. 4. Washington, DC: Smithsonian Press 1991.

Fossett, Renée. "Mapping Inuktut: Inuit Views of the Real World." In *Reading beyond Words: Contexts for Native History*, ed. Jennifer S. H. Brown and Elizabeth Vibert, 74–94. Orchard Park, NY: Broadview Press, 1996.

Foucault, Michel. "Politics and the Study of Discourse." In *The Foucault Effect: Studies in Governmentality*, ed. Graham Burchell, Colin Gordon, and Peter Miller. Chicago: University of Chicago Press, 1991.

Fox, George R. "Place Names of Berrien County." *Michigan History Magazine* 8, no. 1 (January 1924): 6–35.

Gale, Edwin O. *Chicago and Vicinity*. Chicago: Fleming H. Revell, 1902.

Geary, Patrick. *Phantoms of Remembrance: Memory and Oblivion in the First Millennium*. Princeton, NJ: Princeton University Press, 1994.

Geertz, Clifford. *The Interpretation of Culture*. New York: Basic Books, 1973.

Gerwing, Anselm J. "The Chicago Treaty of 1833." *Journal of the Illinois State Historical Society* 57 (1964): 117–42.

Golden, Stephen A. O. "War Canoes Circle Manhattan Island." *New York Times*, April 30, 1967, 206.

Grande, Sandy. *Red Pedagogy: Native American Social and Political Thought*. Lanham, MD: Rowman and Littlefield, 2004.

Granger, William. "65 Canoeists Follow Route of Marquette." *Chicago Tribune*, April 14, 1968, 18.

Greenman, Emerson F. *The Indians of Michigan*. Lansing: Michigan Historical Commission, 1961.

Gridley, Marion E. *America's Indian Statues*. Chicago: Amerindian/Towertown Press, 1966.

Grossberg, Edmund Jess. *J.G.'s Legacy, with foreword by Walter Roth, President, Chicago Jewish Historical Society*. Glencoe, IL: Published by the author, 1994.

Grossman, James R., ed. *The Frontier in American Culture*. Berkeley: University of California Press, 1994.

Grossman, James R., Ann Durkin Keating, and Janice L. Reiff, eds. *The Encyclopedia of Chicago*. Chicago: University of Chicago Press, 2004.

Grossman, Ron. "Chicago's Seven Lost Wonders." *Chicago Tribune*, August 29, 2005. Http://www.chicagotribune.com/chi-0508290065aug29-story.html#page=1.

———. "Site of Chicago's Ft. Dearborn Massacre to Be Called 'Battle of Ft. Dearborn Park.'" *Chicago Tribune*, August 14, 2009.

Halbwachs, Maurice. *The Collective Memory*. Translated by Francis J. Ditter Jr. and Vida Yazdi

Ditter. New York: Harper Colophon, 1980.

———. *On Collective Memory*. Edited and translated by Lewis A. Coser. Chicago: University of Chicago Press, 1992.

Hall, Stuart, ed. *Representation: Cultural Representations and Signifying Practices*. London: Sage Publications, 1997.

Hallowell, A. I. "American Indians, White and Black: The Phenomenon of Transculturation." *Current Anthropology* 4 (1963): 519–31.

Hanson, F. Allen. "The Making of the Maori: Cultural Invention and Its Logic." *American Anthropologist* 91, no. 4 (1989): 890–901.

Harkin, Michael E., ed. *Reassessing Revitalization Movements: Perspectives from North America and the Pacific Islands.* Lincoln: University of Nebraska Press, 2004.

Harley, J. B. "Maps, Knowledge, and Power." In *The Iconography of Landscapes: Essays on the Symbolic Representation, Design, and Use of Past Environments*, ed. D. Cosgrove and S. Daniels, 277–312. New York: Cambridge University Press, 1989.

———. "Rereading the Maps of the Columbian Encounter." *Annals of the Association of American Geographers* 82 (1992): 522–42.

Hart, E. Richard, ed. *Zuni and the Courts: A Struggle for Sovereign Land Rights.* Lawrence: University of Kansas Press, 1995.

Harvey, David. *Justice, Nature and the Geography of Difference*. Oxford: Blackwell Publishing, 1996.

Hass, Kristen A. *Carried to the Wall: American Memory and the Vietnam Veterans Memorial.* Los Angeles: University of California Press, 1998.

Helm, Lieutenant Linai T. *The Fort Dearborn Massacre with Letters and Narratives of Contemporary Interest.* Edited by Nellie Kinzie Gordon. New York: Rand, McNally & Co., 1912.

Hendrix, Burke A. "Memory in Native American Land Claims." *Political Theory* 33, no. 6 (December 2005): 763–85.

———. *Ownership, Authority, and Self-Determination: Moral Principles and Indigenous Rights Claims.* University Park: Pennsylvania State University, 2008.

Hobshawn, Eric, and Terence Ranger, ed. *The Invention of Tradition.* Cambridge: Cambridge University Press, 1983.

Hochbruck, Wolfgang. "Between Victorian Tract and Native American Novel: Simon Pokagon's Ogi-mäw-kwe Mit-i-gwä-ki (1899)." In *Victorian Brand, Indian Brand: The White Shadow on the Native Image*, ed. Naila Clerici, 13–29. Turin: Il Segnalibro, 1993.

———. *Talking Back to Civilization: Indian Voices from the Progressive Era.* New York: Bedford-St. Martin's Press, 2001.

Howard, James H. "When They Worship the Underwater Panther: A Prairie Potawatomi Bundle Ceremony." *Southwestern Journal of Anthropology* 16, no. 2 (Summer 1960): 217–24.

Howe, Craig. "Keep Your Thoughts above the Trees: Ideas on Developing and Presenting Tribal Histories." In *Clearing a Path: Theorizing the Past in Native American Studies*, ed. Nancy Shoemaker, 161–80. New York: Routledge, 2002.

Howe, LeAnne. *Miko Kings: An Indian Baseball Story*. San Francisco: Aunt Lute Books, 2007.

———. "The Story of America: A Tribalography." In *Clearing a Path: Theorizing the Past in Native American Studies*, ed. Nancy Shoemaker, 29–50. New York: Routledge, 2002.

———. "Tribalography: The Power of Native Stories." *Journal of Dramatic Theory and Criticism* 14 (1999): 117–25.

Howey, Meghan C. L., and John M. O'Shea. "Bear's Journey and the Study of Ritual in Archaeology." *American Antiquity* 71, no. 2 (April 2006): 261–82.

Hoxie, Frederick E. *A Final Promise: The Campaign to Assimilate Indians, 1880–1920.* New York: Cambridge University Press, 1984.

———. *Talking Back to Civilization: Indian Voices from the Progressive Era.* Boston: Bedford/St. Martin's Press, 2001.

Hubbard, Bela. *Ancient Garden Beds of Michigan.* 1878. Reprinted in Susan Sleeper-Smith, *Indian Women and French Men: Rethinking Cultural Encounter in the Great Lakes.* Amherst: University of Massachusetts Press, 2001.

Huffman, T. "Plans to Live on a Reservation Following College among American Indian Students: An Examination of Transculturation Theory." *Journal of Research in Rural Education* 26, no. 3 (2001): 1–12.

———. "Resistance Theory and the Transculturation Hypothesis as Explanations of College Attrition and Persistence among Culturally Traditional American Indian Students." *Journal of American Indian Education* 40, no. 3 (2011): 1–23.

Hulst, Cornelia Steketee. *Indian Sketches: Père Marquette and the Last of the Pottawatomie Chiefs*. New York: Longmans, Green and Co., 1912.

Hurt, Douglas A. "Defining American Homelands: A Creek Nation Example, 1828–1907." *Journal of Cultural Geography* 21, no. 1 (2003): 19–21.

Hutchinson, Elizabeth. *The Indian Craze: Primitivism, Modernism, and Transculturation in American Art, 1890–1915.* Durham, NC: Duke University Press, 2009.

Incommce, L. "The Queen of the Woods, My Lida." *Grahams Magazine* vol. 36 (January–June 1850).

Indian Council Fire Records, 1920–1990. Papers, correspondence, scrapbooks, clippings, photographs, and publications of the Indian Council Fire, a Chicago-based organization supporting educational, legislative, and social services for urban and reservation Indians.

Newberry Library, Chicago.

Isaacs, Deanna. "Blood on the Ground/Investing in the Future: Neighbors Who Want the Fort Dearborn Massacre Monument Returned to Its Site Are Likely to Face a Battle." *Chicago Reader*, March 22, 2007. Http://www.chicagoreader.com/chicago/blood-on-the-groundinvesting-in-the-future/Content?oid=924564.

Iverson, Peter. *Carlos Montezuma and the Changing World of American Indians.* Albuquerque: University of New Mexico Press, 1982.

Johnson, Geoffrey. "The True Story of the Deadly Encounter at Fort Dearborn." *Chicago Magazine*, January 4, 2010. Http://www.chicagomag.com/Chicago-Magazine/December-2009/The-True-Story-of-the-Deadly-Encounter-at-Fort-Dearborn.

Johnston, Basil. *Ojibway Ceremonies*. Toronto: McClelland and Stewart, 1987.

———. *Ojibway Heritage*. Lincoln: University of Nebraska Press, 1976.

Jordan, Tracey Sue. "Braving New Worlds: Breed Fictions, Mixedblood Identities." PhD diss., Columbia University, 1999.

Judd, Mary Catherine. *Wigwam Stories*. Boston: Ginn & Company, 1917.

Kantowicz, Edward R. "Carter H. Harrison II: The Politics of Balance." In *The Mayors: The Chicago Political Tradition*, ed. Paul M. Green and Melvin G. Holli. Carbondale, IL: Southern Illinois University Press, 1995.

Kappler, Charles J. *Indian Affairs: Laws and Treaties.* Vols. 1–5. Washington, DC: Government Printing Office, 1904–1941.

Kass, John. "Statue—and Controversy—under Wraps: Mission to Bring Fort Dearborn Massacre Bronze out of Storage Means Taking on Political Correctness Brigade." *Chicago Tribune*, August 12, 2012.

Keating, Ann Durkin. *Rising Up from Indian Country: The Battle of Fort Dearborn and the Birth of Chicago.* Chicago: University of Chicago Press, 2012.

Keesing, Roger M., and Robert Tonkinson, eds. "Creating the Past: Custom and Identity in the Contemporary Pacific." *Contemporary Pacific* 1, no. 1–2 (1989): 19–42.

———. "Reinventing Traditional Culture: The Politics of Kastom in Island Melanesia." *Mankind* 13, no. 4 (1982). Special issue.

Keithahn, Edward L. *Monuments in Cedar: The Authentic Story of the Totem.* Ketchikan, AK: R. Anderson, 1945.

Kelly, Lawrence C. *Federal Indian Policy: Well-illustrated Survey of Federal Government Policy toward the Native American Population.* New York: Chelsea House, 1989.

Kinzie, Juliette Augusta. *Narrative of the Massacre at Chicago, August 15, 1812 and of Preceding Events.* Reprint. 1844; New York: Garland Publishing Inc., 1977.

———. *Wau-bun: The Early Days in the North-West.* Chicago: Derby & Jackson, 1856.

Kirkland, Joseph. *The Chicago Massacre of 1812: With Illustrations and Historical Documents.* Chicago: Dibble Publishing Co., 1893.

Kogan, Herman, and Lloyd Wendt. *Lords of the Levee: The Story of Bathhouse John and Hinky Dink*. Evanston, IL: Northwestern University Press, 2005.

Kohl, Johann Georg. *Kitchi-Gami: Life among the Lake Superior Ojibway.* Reprint. 1860; St. Paul: Minnesota Historical Society Press, 1985.

Labadie, Joseph. Papers. Special Collections Library, University of Michigan, Ann Arbor, MI.

LaGrand, James B. *Indian Metropolis: Native Americans in Chicago, 1945–1975*. Urbana: University of Illinois Press, 2002.

Landsberg, Alison. *Prosthetic Memory: The Transformation of American Remembrance in the Age of Mass Culture.* New York: Columbia University Press, 2004.

Lane, Clare. "Vast Mural to Depict City's Indian Roots." *Chicago Tribune*, Chicagoland Extra, June 5, 2009, sect. 4, p. 2.

Langdon, Frederick D. C. "The Wreck of the 'Reutan' and What Came of It." *Wide World Magazine* 7 (April–September 1901): 539–43.

Lantz, Raymond C. *The Potawatomi Indians of Michigan, 1843–1904: Including Some Ottawa and Chippewa, 1843–1866 and Potawatomi of Indiana, 1869 and 1885.* Westminster, MD: Heritage Books, 2007.

LaPier, Rosalyn R. "'We Are Not Savages, but a Civilized Race': American Indian Activism and the Development of Chicago's First American Indian Organizations, 1919–1934." Master's thesis, DePaul University, 2000.

Latrobe, Charles Joseph. "The Rambler in North America." Reprinted in *As Others See Chicago*, ed. Bessie Louise Pierce. Chicago: University of Chicago Press, 1933.

Lazarus, Edward. *Black Hills/White Justice: The Sioux Nation versus the United States, 1775 to the Present*. Lawrence: University of Nebraska Press, 1999.

Lears, Jackson. "Power, Culture, and Memory." *Journal of American History* 75, no. 1 (June 1988): 137–40.

Lester, Robert E., ed. *Native Americans and the New Deal: The Office Files of John Collier, 1933–1945*. Bethesda, MD: University Publications of America, 1994. Microfilm, reel 6.

Lewis, David. *We, the Navigators: The Ancient Art of Landfinding in the Pacific*. 2nd ed. Honolulu: University of Hawai'i Press, 1994.

Lewis, G. Malcolm. *Cartographic Encounters: Perspectives on Native American Mapmaking and Map Use.* Chicago: University of Chicago Press, 1998.

Limerick, Patricia Nelson. *The Legacy of Conquest: The Unbroken Past of the American West.* New York: W.W. Norton, 1987.

Linnekin, Jocelyn. "Cultural Invention and the Dilemma of Authenticity." *American*

Anthropologist 93, no. 2 (1990): 446–49.

———. "Defining Tradition: Variation on the Hawaiian Identity." *American Ethnologist* 10 (1983): 241–52.

———. "On the Theory and Politics of Cultural Construction in the Pacific." *Oceania* 62 (1992): 249–63.

———. "The Politics of Culture in the Pacific." In *Cultural Identity and Ethnicity in the Pacific*, ed. Jocelyn Linnekin and Lin Poyer. Honolulu: University of Hawai'i Press, 1990.

Linton, Ralph. "Nativistic Movements." *American Anthropologist* 45 (1943): 230–40.

Lipitz, George. *Time Passages: Collective Memory and American Popular Culture.* Minneapolis: University of Minnesota Press, 1990.

Loerzel, Robert. "Returning to Battle of Ft. Dearborn in the Name of a Park." *WBEZ 91.5*, July 31, 2009. Http://www.wbez.org/episode-segments/returning-battle-ft-dearborn-name-park.

Loew, Patty. "Hidden Transcripts in the Chippewa Treaty Rights Struggle: A Twice Told Story, Race, Resistance, and the Politics of Power." *American Indian Quarterly* 21, no. 4 (1997).

———. *Indian Nations of Wisconsin: Histories of Endurance and Renewal.* Madison: Wisconsin Historical Society Press, 2001.

Longfellow, Henry Wadsworth. *The Song of Hiawatha.* Reprint. 1885; North Clarendon, VT: Tuttle Publishing, 1993.

Loring, Kay. "Tradition's Role in Indian Cooking." *Chicago Tribune*, February 16, 1971, A3.

Maddox, Lucy. *Citizen Indians: Native American Intellectuals, Race, and Reform.* Ithaca, NY: Cornell University Press, 2005.

Mapp, Paul. "Atlantic History from Imperial, Continental, and Pacific Perspectives." *William and Mary Quarterly*, 3rd ser., 63 (October 1996): 713–24.

Marks, Nora. "Fading from the Earth: The Pottawatomies of the Michigan Hunting Ground, Dissipation and Their Inability to Live in Civilization Too Strong for the Remnant of the Once Mighty Tribe," *Chicago Daily Tribune*, February 15, 1890, 7.

Marsh, Dawn. "Creating Delaware Homelands in the Ohio Country." *Ohio History* 116 (2009): 26–40.

Martin, J. F. *Martin's World's Fair Album-Atlas and Family Souvenir.* Chicago: C. Ropp & Sons, 1892.

Martin, Lawrence T. "Simon Pokagon: Charlatan or Authentic Spokesman for the 19th-Century Anishinaabeg?" In *Papers of the 29th Algonquin Conference*, ed. David H. Pentland, 182–91. Winnipeg: University of Manitoba Press, 1998.

Mayer, Harold M., and Richard C. Wade. *Chicago: Growth of a Metropolis.* Chicago: University of Chicago Press, 1969.

McClurken, James M., comp. and ed. *Fish in the Lakes, Wild Rice, and Game in Abundance:*

Testimony on Behalf of Mille Lacs Ojibwe Hunting and Fishing Rights. East Lansing: Michigan State University Press, 2000.

McDonald, Daniel. *Removal of the Pottawattomie Indians from Northern Indiana*. Plymouth, IN: D. McDonald & Co., 1899.

McIlvaine, Mabel. "Chicago to Celebrate Indian Day." *Fort Dearborn Magazine*, September 1920, 3–4.

Megill, Allan. "History, Memory, Identity." *History of the Human Sciences* 11, no. 3 (1998): 37–62.

Michigan State Historical Society, Michigan Historical Commission. *Collections and Researches, Michigan Pioneer and Historical Society*, 14:260. Reprint. 1889; Lansing: Wynkoop, Hallenbeck, Crawford Co., 1908.

Millard, Joseph. "George Wellington Streeter—All This Out Here Is My Land." In *No Law But Their Own*, 111–58. Evanston, IL: Regency Books, 1963.

Miller, Francesca. *The Sands: The Story of Chicago's Front Yard*. Chicago: Valentine-Newman Publishers, 1948.

Miller, Jay. "Land and Lifeway in the Chicago Area: Chicago and the Illinois-Miami." In *Indians of the Chicago Area*, ed. Terry Straus. Chicago: NAES College Press, 1989.

Mitchell, Donald Craig. *Cultural Geography: A Critical Reader*. Malden, MA: Blackwell Publishing, 2000.

———. *Take My Land, Take My Life: The Story of Congress's Historic Settlement of Alaska Native Land Claims, 1960–1971*. Juneau: University of Alaska Press, 2001.

Moses, L. G. "Performative Traditions in American Indian History." In *A Companion to American Indian History*, ed. Philip J. Deloria and Neal Salisbury, 193–208. Malden, MA: Blackwell Publishing, 2004.

———. *Wild West Shows and the Images of American Indians, 1883–1933*. Albuquerque: University of New Mexico Press, 1996.

Mundy, Barbara E. *The Mapping of New Spain: Indigenous Cartography and the Maps of the Relaciones Geográficas*. Chicago: University of Chicago Press, 1996.

Nabokov, Peter. *Native American Testimony: A Chronicle of Indian-White Relations from Prophecy to the Present, 1497–2000*. New York: Penguin Books, 1999.

———. "Orientations from Their Side: Dimensions of Native American Cartographic Discourse." In *Cartographic Encounters: Perspectives on Native American Mapmaking and Map Use*, ed. G. Malcolm Lewis, 241–69. Chicago: University of Chicago Press, 1998.

Nesper, Larry. "Ogitchida at Waswagonning: Conflict in the Revitalization of Flambeau Anishinaabe Identity." In *Reassessing Revitalization Movements: Perspectives from North America and the Pacific Islands*, ed. Michael E. Harkin. Lincoln: University of Nebraska Press, 2007.

———. *The Walleye War: The Struggle for Ojibwe Spearfishing and Treaty Rights.* Lincoln: University of Nebraska Press, 2002.

Niles, W. H. *A Brief History and the Legal Standing of the District of Lake Michigan.* Chicago: Swanberg & Co., 1900.

———. *The Military Government of the District of Lake Michigan: Its legal standing as defined by Official letters and papers, by William H. Niles Military Governor–Captain George Streeter, the American Dreyfus, now in the States Prison at Joliet, Ill.* Chicago: Hufford & Co., 1903.

Nora, Pierre. "Between History and Memory: *Les Lieux de Mémoire.*" *Representations* 26 (Spring 1989): 7–25.

Norstrand, Richard L., and Lawrence E. Estaville, eds. *Homelands: A Geography of Culture and Place across America.* Baltimore: Johns Hopkins University Press, 2001.

O'Brien, Jean M. *Firsting and Lasting: Writing Indians out of Existence in New England.* Minneapolis: University of Minnesota Press, 2010.

O'Callaghan, E. B. *Documents Relative to the Colonial History of the State of New York.* Vol. 8. Albany, NY: Weed, Parsons, and Co., 1857.

Ortiz, Fernando. *Cuban Counterpoint: Tobacco and Sugar.* Durham, NC: Duke University Press, 1995.

Owens, Louis. *Mixedblood Messages: Literature, Film, Family, Place.* Norman: University of Oklahoma Press, 2001.

Parker, Robert Dale. *The Invention of Native American Literature.* Ithaca, NY: Cornell University Press, 2003.

Parrish, Randall. *When Wilderness Was King: A Tale of the Illinois Country.* Chicago: A.C. McClurg & Co., 1904.

Patel, Chiraq. "Native Americans Celebrated at Foster Underpass Mural." *Uptown Exchange,* November 2009, 10.

Penn, William S. *As We Are Now: Mixblood Essays on Race and Identity.* Berkeley: University of California Press, 1997.

Peyer, Bernd. *American Indian Nonfiction.* Norman: University of Oklahoma Press, 2007.

———. *The Thinking Indian: Native American Writers, 1850s–1920s.* Frankfurt: Peter Lang, 2007.

Phillips, Ruth B. *Trading Identities: The Souvenir in Native North American Art from the Northeast, 1700–1900.* Seattle: University of Washington Press, 1999.

Pierce, Bessie Louise. *A History of Chicago, 1673–1848.* New York: A.A. Knopf, 1937.

Pogorzelski, Daniel. "Olson Waterfall." *Forgotten Chicago,* September 7, 2009. Http://forgottenchicago.com/columns/northwest/olson-waterfall.

Poignant, Roslyn. *Professional Savages: Captive Lives and Western Spectacle.* New Haven, CT: Yale University Press, 2004.

Pokagon, Leopold. "Petition to President Andrew Jackson from Four Chiefs of the Pokagon Potawatomi along the St. Joseph River." In *Berichte der Leopoldinen-Stiftung im Kaiserthum Oesterreich* 9 (Vienna, 1836).

Pokagon, Simon. "The Chi-Kog-Ong of the Red Man." *New York Times, Sunday Magazine*, December 5, 1897, 7–10.

———. "The Future of the Red Man." *Forum* 23, no. 6 (August 1897): 708.

———. "Indian Superstitions and Legends." *Forum* 25 (1898): 618–29.

———. Letters. Great Lakes Branch of the National Archives, Chicago. Folder 81.

———. "The Massacre at Fort Dearborn at Chicago: Gathered from the Traditions of the Indian Tribes Engaged in the Massacre, and from the Published Accounts." *Harpers New Monthly Magazine* 98, no. 586 (March 1899): 649–56.

———. *O-GÎ-MÄW-KWÈ MIT-Î-GWÄ-KÎ (Queen of the Woods), Also a Brief Sketch of the Algaic Language.* Hartford, MI: C.H. Engle, 1899, 1901.

———. *Pottawattamie Book of Genesis: Legend of the Creation of Man.* Hartford, MI: C.H. Engle, 1900.

———. *The Red Man's Rebuke by Chief Pokagon (Pottawattamie Chief).* Reprinted with a new title that same year as *The Red Man's Greeting.* Hartford, MI: C.H. Engle Publisher, 1893.

Powell, Melea. "Rhetorics of Survivance: How Americans Use Writing." *College Composition and Communication* 53, no. 3 (February 2002): 396–434.

Pratt, Mary Louise. "Arts of the Contact Zone." *Profession* (1991): 3–40.

———. *Imperial Eyes: Travel Writing and Transculturation.* London: Routledge, 1992.

Pritchard, James. "New Buffalo Casino Boosts Tourism." *Detroit Free Press*, June 28, 2008. Http://archive.freep.com/article/20080629/FEATURES07/806290502/New-Buffalo-casino-boosts-tourism.

Program, 17th Annual Celebration, under the Auspices of the Indian Council Fire and the American Indian Day Committee . . . Olson Memorial Park. Author's personal collection. 1935.

Program, Chief Shipshewana Day, Shipshewana Lake, Saturday, May 30, 1931. Shipshewana, IN: Shipshewana Chamber of Commerce, 1931.

Prossnitz, Lindsay. "Bicentennial of Battle of Fort Dearborn." *Chicago Tonight*, August 15, 2012. Http://chicagotonight.wttw.com/2012/08/15/bicentennial-battle-fort-dearborn.

Quaife, Milo M. *Checagou: From Indian Wigwam to Modern City, 1673–1835.* Chicago: University of Chicago Press, 1933.

———. *Chicago and the Old Northwest, 1673–1835.* Chicago: University of Chicago Press, 1913.

———. *Chicago's Highways Old and New.* Chicago: D.F. Keller and Co., 1923.

———. "The Fort Dearborn Massacre." *Mississippi Valley Historical Review* 1, no. 4 (March 1915): 566–70.

———. "Garlic River Beginnings." In *Lake Michigan*, chap. 6. Indianapolis: Bobbs-Merrill Co., 1944.

Radstone, Susannah, and Bill Schwarz, eds. *Memory: Histories, Theories, Debates*. New York: Fordham University Press, 2010.

Rand McNally & Co. *Handbook of the World's Columbian Exposition: With Special Descriptive Articles.* Contributor Mrs. Potter Palmer. Chicago: Rand McNally & Co., 1893.

Ransbottom, Virginia. "Chief Menominee Still Stands Tall." *South Bend Tribune*, September 17, 2009, 1.

Redden, Paul. *Wild West Shows*. Urbana: University of Illinois Press, 1999.

Richter, Daniel. *Facing East from Indian Country: A Native History of Early America.* Cambridge, MA: Harvard University Press, 2003.

Ricoeur, Paul. *Memory, History, Forgetting.* Translated by Kathleen Blamey and David Pellauer. Chicago: University of Chicago Press, 2004.

Rigal-Cellard, Bernadette. "Simon Pokagon's *O-gî-mäw-kwe Mit-i-gwä-kî* (*Queen of the Woods*): A Deceptively Simple and Charming Romance of Love and Death in the Wild Woods." In *Before Yesterday: The Long History of Native American Writing*, ed. Simone Pellerin, 83–84. Pessac, France: Presses Universitaires de Bordeaux, 2009.

Rinehart, Melissa. "To Hell with the Wigs! Native American Representation and Resistance at the World's Columbian Exposition." *American Indian Quarterly* 36, no. 4 (2012): 403–42.

Riordan, Jim, and Arnd Kruger. *The International Politics of Sport in the 20th Century*. New York: Routledge, 1999.

Ritzenthaler, Robert E. "The Building of a Chippewa Indian Birch-Bark Canoe." *Bulletin of the Public Museum of Milwaukee* 19, no. 2 (1950): 1–33. Reprint. Milwaukee: Museum Board of Trustees, 1972.

Roediger, David A. *Wages of Whiteness: Race and the Making of the American Working Class.* Rev. ed. New York: Verso Books, 1999.

Roland, Captain O. W. *A History of Van Buren County Michigan: A Narrative Account of Its Historical Progress, Its People, and Its Principal Interests*. Vol. 1. Chicago: Lewis Publishing Co., 1912.

Rosenthal, Nicolas. *Reimagining Indian Country: Native American Migration and Identity in Twentieth-Century Los Angeles.* Chapel Hill: University of North Carolina Press, 2012.

Rothberg, Michael. *Multidirectional Memory: Remembering the Holocaust in the Age of Decolonization.* Cultural Memory in the Present. Stanford, CA: Stanford University Press,

2009.

Royce, Charles C. *Indian Land Cessions in the United States.* Compiled and presented as part 2 of the *Eighteenth Annual Report of the Bureau of American Ethnology to the Secretary of the Smithsonian Institution, 1896–97.* The report was printed by the Government Printing Office in 1899.

Ruoff, A. LaVonne Brown. "Simon Pokagon (1830–January 1899)." In *Dictionary of Native American Literature*, vol. 1815, ed. Andrew Wiget, 277–79. New York: Garland Publishing, Inc., 1994.

Rushton Indian Girl Canoes. Canton, NY: J.H. Rushton, Inc., 1910.

Rydell, Robert W. *All the World's a Fair: Visions of Empire at American International Expositions, 1876–1916.* Chicago: University of Chicago Press, 1984.

Sack, Robert. *A Geographical Guide to the Real and the Good.* New York: Routledge, 2003.

Sale Catalogues, Issues 1631–1654 (New York: American Art Association, Anderson Galleries, 1922), 104.

Salzman, Joshua. "The Chicago Lakefront's Last Frontier: The Turnerian Mythology of Streeterville, 1886–1961." *Journal of Illinois History* 9 (Autumn 2006): 201–14.

Sandburg, Carl. *The Complete Poems of Carl Sandburg.* 1911; New York: Harcourt, Inc., 2003.

Satz, Ronald N. *Chippewa Treaty Rights: The Reserved Rights of Wisconsin's Chippewa Indians in Historical Perspective.* Madison: Wisconsin Academy of Science, 1996.

Sauer, Carl. "The Morphology of Landscape." *University of California Publications in Geography* 2 (1925): 19–54.

Saunt, Claudio. "'Our Indians': European Empires and the History of the Native American South." In *The Atlantic in Global History, 1500–2000*, ed. Jorge Cañizares-Esguerra and Erik R. Seeman. Upper Saddle River, NJ: Pearson Prentice Hall, 2007.

Sawyers, June Skinner. *Chicago Portraits: Biographies of 250 Famous Chicagoans.* Chicago: Loyola University Press, 1991.

———. "The Eccentric Captain of Streeterville." In *Chicago Sketches: Urban Tales, Stories, and Legends from Chicago History.* Chicago: Loyola Press/Wild Onion Books, 1995.

Scharf, Albert F. *Indian Trails and Villages of Chicago.* Chicago: Chicago Historical Society, 1900, 1901.

Schmidt, John R. "Olson Rug Park, Former Chicago Landmark, Now Parking Lot." *WBEZ 91.5*, September 2, 2011. Http://www.wbez.org/blog/john-r-schmidt/2011-09-02/olson-rug-park-91037.

Schoolcraft, Henry Rowe. *Historical and statistical information, respecting the history, condition and prospects of the Indian tribes of the United States: Collected and prepared under the direction of the Bureau of Indian Affairs per act of Congress of March 3d, 1847.* Illustrated by S. Eastman. 6 vols. Philadelphia: Lippincott, Grambo & Co., 1851–60.

Schurr, Mark R. "Untangling Removal Period Archaeology: The Complexity of Potawatomi Sites." *Midcontinental Journal of Archaeology* 31, no. 1 (Spring 2006): 5–19.

Schurr, Mark R., Terrance J. Martin, and W. Ben Secunda. "How the Pokagon Band Avoided Removal: Archaeological Evidence from the Faunal Assemblage of the Pokagon Village Site (20BE13)." *Midcontinental Journal of Archaeology* 31, no. 1 (Spring 2006): 143–63.

Schwartz, Barry. "The Social Context of Commemoration: A Study in Collective Memory." *Social Forces* 61, no. 2 (December 1982): 374–402.

Secunda, W. Ben. "To Cede or Seed? Risk and Identity among the Woodland Potawatomi during the Removal Period." *Midcontinental Journal of Archaeology* 31, no. 1 (Spring 2006): 57–88.

Shackleton, Robert. "A Modern Corsair." In *The Book of Chicago*, chap. 13. Philadelphia: Penn Publishing Co., 1920.

Shafer, Harry J. "Art and Territoriality in the Lower Pecos Archaic." *Plains Anthropologist* 22, no. 75 (February 1977): 16–25.

Sheridan, Cecilia. "Social Control and Native Territoriality in Northeastern New Spain." In *Choice, Persuasion, and Coercion: Social Control on Spain's North American Frontiers*, ed. Jesús F. de la Teja and Ross Frank, trans. Ned F. Brierley. Albuquerque: University of New Mexico Press, 2005.

Shoemaker, Nancy. *A Strange Likeness: Becoming Red and White in Eighteenth-Century North America*. New York: Oxford University Press, 2004.

———. "Urban Indians and Ethnic Choices: American Indian Organizations in Minneapolis, 1920–1950." *Western Historical Quarterly* 19, no. 4 (November 1988): 431–47.

Sibbet, David. "Massive Canoe Trip, Conservationist Plans Fox River Flotilla." *Chicago Tribune*, June 23, 1968, S2.

Simmons, Noah. *Heroes and Heroines of the Fort Dearborn Massacre: A Romantic and Tragic History of Corporal John Simmons and His Heroic Wife*. Lawrence, KS: Journal Publishing Co., 1896.

Skinner, Alanson. "The Mascoutens or Prairie Potawatomi Indians: Part I, Social Life and Ceremonies." *Bulletin, Public Museum of the City of Milwaukee* 6, no. 1 (1923): 1–262.

Sleeper-Smith, Susan. *Indian Women and French Men: Rethinking Cultural Encounter in the Western Great Lakes*. Amherst: University of Massachusetts Press, 2001.

Slotkin, Richard. *Gunfighter Nation: The Myth of the Frontier in Twentieth-Century America*. New York: Athenaeum, 1992.

Smith, Linda Tuhiwai. *Decolonizing Methodologies: Research and Indigenous Peoples*. 2nd ed. London: Zed Books, 2012.

Sorkin, Alan L. *The Urban American Indian*. Lexington, MA: Lexington Books, 1978.

Squier, E. G., and Edwin Davis. *Ancient Monuments of the Mississippi Valley.* 1848; Washington, DC: Smithsonian Press, 1998.

Stamper, John W. "Shaping Chicago's Shoreline." *Chicago History* 14, no. 4 (1985–1986): 44–55.

Steedman, Carolyn. *The Archive and Cultural History*. New Brunswick, NJ: Rutgers University Press, 2001.

Stillman, Amy Ku'uleialoha. "Re-Membering the History of the Hawaiian Hula." In *Cultural Memory: Reconfiguring History and Identity in the Postcolonial Pacific*, ed. J. M. Mageo. Honolulu: University of Hawai'i Press, 2001.

The Story of Old Fort Dearborn and Its Connection with A Century of Progress International Exposition. Chicago: Committee on "History of a Century of Progress," 1933.

Straus, Terry, ed. *Indians of the Chicago Area*. Chicago: NAES College Press, 1989.

———, ed. *Native Chicago*. 2nd ed. Brooklyn: Albatross Press, 2002.

Straus, Terry, and Grant Arndt. *Native Chicago.* 2nd ed. Chicago: Albatross Press, 2002.

Strong, William Duncan. *The Indian Tribes of the Chicago Region: With Special Reference to the Illinois and the Potawatomi.* Leaflet 24. Chicago: Field Museum of Natural History, 1926.

Sturken, Marita. *Tangled Memories: The Vietnam War, the AIDS Epidemic, and the Politics of Remembering*. Berkeley: University of California Press, 1997.

Sutton, Imre. "Cartographic Review of Indian Land Tenure and Territoriality: A Schematic Approach." *American Indian Culture and Research Journal* 26 (2002): 69.

———. *Indian Land Tenure: Bibliographical Essays and a Guide to the Literature.* Orofino, ID: Clearwater Publishing Co., 1975.

Swenson, John F. "Chicagoua/Chicago: The Origin, Meaning, and Etymology of a Place Name." *Illinois Historical Journal* 84, no. 4 (Winter 1991): 235–48.

Taborsky, Edwina. "The Discursive Object." In *Objects of Knowledge*, ed. S. M. Pearce, 50–70. London: Athlone Press, 2002.

Tanner, Helen Hornbeck, ed. *Atlas of Great Lakes Indian History*. Norman: University of Oklahoma Press, 1987.

———. *The Ojibwa.* Philadelphia: Chelsea House Publishers, 1992.

Taylor, Alan. *American Colonies.* New York: Viking, 2001.

———. *Divided Ground: Indians, Settlers, and the Northern Borderland of the American Revolution*. New York: Alfred A. Knopf, 2006.

Taylor, Edward Livingston. "Monuments to Historical Indian Chiefs." *Ohio Archaeological and Historical Publications*, 11:1–29. Columbus: Ohio Archaeological and Historical Society/ Fred J. Heer, 1903.

Teaiwa, Teresia K. "Militarism, Tourism, and the Native: Articulations in Oceania." PhD diss.,

University of California, Santa Cruz, 2001.

Terkel, Studs. "Introduction." In *Chicago: City on the Make*, by Nelson Algren. Chicago: University of Chicago Press, 2001.

Tessendorf, K. C. "Captain Streeter's District of Lake Michigan." *Chicago History* 5, no. 3 (Fall 1976): 152–60.

Thomas, Cyrus. "Pokagon, Simon." Smithsonian Institution, Bureau of American Ethnology, Bulletin 30. *Handbook of American Indians North of Mexico*, 274–75. Washington, DC: Government Printing Office, 1910.

Thrush, Coll. *Native Seattle: Histories from the Crossing-Over Place.* Seattle: University of Washington Press, 2008.

Tilly, Christopher. "Metaphor, Materiality and Interpretation." In *The Material Culture Reader*, ed. Victor Buchli. Oxford: Berg, 2002.

Trachtenberg, Alan. *Brooklyn Bridge.* New York: Oxford University Press, 1965.

———. *Shades of Hiawatha: Staging Indians, Making Americans, 1880–1930.* New York: Hill & Wang, 2004.

Trennert, Robert A., Jr. "Selling Indian Education at World's Fairs and Expositions, 1893–1904." *American Indian Quarterly* 11, no. 3 (Summer 1987): 204.

Tuan, Yi-Fu. "Foreword." In *Landscape, Nature, and the Body Politic: From Britain's Renaissance to America's New World*, by Kenneth Robert Olwig. Madison: University of Wisconsin Press, 2002.

———. *Space and Place: The Perspective of Experience.* Minneapolis: University of Minnesota Press, 1977.

Turnbull, David. *Maps Are Territories: Science Is an Atlas.* Chicago: University of Chicago Press, 1989.

Turner, Frederick J. "The Significance of the Frontier in American History." In *Annual Report of the American Historical Association for the Year 1893.* Washington, DC: Government Printing Office and American Historical Association, 1894.

Turner, James West. "Continuity and Constraint: Reconstructing the Concept of Tradition from a Pacific Perspective." *Contemporary Pacific* 9, no. 2 (1997): 345–81.

Usher, Peter J., Frank J. Tough, and Robert M. Galois. "Reclaiming the Land: Aboriginal Title, Treaty Rights and Land Claims in Canada." *Applied Geography* 12 (1992): 112.

"The Vanishing White City: A Series of Beautiful and Artistic Views of the Great Columbian Exposition." *Columbian Art Series.* Vol. 1, no. 12. Chicago: Peacock Publishing Co., 1894.

Veblen, Thorstein. *The Theory of the Leisure Class.* 1899; New York: Dover Publications, 1994.

Vélez-Ibáñez, Carlos G. *Border Visions: Mexican Cultures of the Southwest United States.* Tucson: University of Arizona Press, 1996.

Vennum, Thomas, Jr. *American Indian Lacrosse: Little Brother of War*. Washington, DC: Smithsonian Institution Press, 1994.

———. *Earl's Canoe: A Traditional Ojibwe Craft*. Directed by Thomas Vennum Jr. and Charles Weber, with participation by Earl Nyholm. VHS. Watertown, MA: Documentary Educational Resources, 1999.

———. *Wild Rice and the Ojibway People*. St. Paul: Minnesota Historical Society, 1988.

Verdesio, Gustavo. "Forgotten Territorialities: The Materiality of Indigenous Pasts." *Nephantla: View from the South* 2 (2001): 85–114.

Vogel, Virgil J. "Indian Place Names in Illinois." *Journal of the Illinois State Historical Society* 55, no. 2 (Summer 1962): 157–89.

Waddell, Eric, Vijay Naidu, and Epeli Hau'ofa, eds. *A New Oceania: Rediscovering Our Sea of Islands.* Fiji: School of Social and Economic Development, University of the South Pacific in Association with Beake House, 1993.

Wagner, Philip L., and Marvin W. Mikesell. *Readings in Cultural Geography.* Chicago: University of Chicago Press, 1962.

Walker, Cheryl L. *Indian Nation: Native American Literature and Nineteenth-Century Nationalisms.* Durham, NC: Duke University Press, 1997.

Walker, Marietta. *Object-Lessons on Temperance, or, The Indian Maiden and Her White Deer.* Lamoni, IA: Herald Pub. House, 1912.

Warhus, Mark. *Another America: Native American Maps and the History of Our Land.* New York: St. Martin's Press, 1997.

Warren, Stephen. *The Worlds the Shawnee Made: Migration and Violence in Early America.* Chapel Hill: University of North Carolina Press, 2014.

Warren, William W. *History of the Ojibway People*. Reprint. 1885; St. Paul: Minnesota Historical Press, 1984.

Weinberg, Lauren. "Lake Shore Thrives: The Chicago Public Art Group Brightens the Foster Avenue Underpass." *Time Out Chicago*, July 23–29, 2009, 42.

Wesaw, Alex. "Mno-Bmadsen Featured in Business Publication." *Pokégnek Yajdanawa*, July 2013.

Wesaw, Leroy. "Changing Values in the Indian Culture." Native American Educational Services, Student Field Projects, box 1, folder 2, Special Collections Research Center, University of Chicago Library, 1.

White, Richard. *"It's Your Misfortune and None of My Own": A History of the American West.* Norman: University of Oklahoma Press, 1991.

———. *The Middle Ground: Indians, Empires, and Republics in the Great Lakes Region, 1650–1815*. New York: Cambridge University Press, 1991.

White, Richard, and Patricia Nelson Limerick. "Frederick Jackson Turner and Buffalo Bill." In *The Frontier in American Culture*, ed. James R. Grossman, 7–66. Berkeley: University of California Press, 1994.

Willard, Shirley, Susan Campbell, and Benjamin Marie Petit. *Potawatomi Trail of Death: 1838 Removal from Indiana to Kansas*. Rochester, IN: Fulton County Historical Society, 2003.

Willie, Lois. *Forever Open, Clear, and Free: The Struggle for Chicago's Lakefront*. Chicago: Henry Regency Co., 1972.

Wilson, Chris, and Paul Groth, ed. *Everyday America: Cultural Landscape Studies after J. B. Jackson*. Berkeley: University of California Press, 2003.

Wishart, David J. "The Dispossession of the Pawnee." *Annals of the Association of American Geographers* 69 (September 1979): 382–401.

Witgen, Michael. "The Rituals of Possession: Native Identity and the Invention of Empire in Seventeenth-Century Western North America." *Ethnohistory* 54, no. 4 (2007): 639–68.

Womack, Craig S. *Red on Red: Native American Literary Separatism*. Minneapolis: University of Minnesota Press, 1999.

Wood, Denis. *The Power of Maps*. New York: Guilford Press, 1992.

Young, James E. *The Texture of Memory: Holocaust, Memorials, and Meaning*. New Haven, CT: Yale University Press, 1994.

Yousef, Odette. "Do Descendants of Chicago's Native American Tribes Live in the City Today?" *WBEZ 91.5*, July 11, 2012. Http://www.wbez.org/series/curious-city/do-descendants-chicagos-native-american-tribes-live-city-today-100217.

Zerubavael, Eviatar. *Terra Cognita: The Mental Discovery of America*. New Brunswick, NJ: Rutgers University Press, 1992.

Index

C

D

E

F

M

N

Q

R

T

Y